John Franklin GOUCHER

CITIZEN OF THE WORLD

MARILYN SOUTHARD
WARSHAWSKY

Best wishes,

Marilyn Southard Warshawsky

Cover design: Jennifer Warshawsky Zigrino

Cover photos: Courtesy of Goucher College Library, Special Collections and Archives, Baltimore, Maryland, and Janet Miller Bernet

Table of Contents quotations: Diaries, speeches, and letters of John Franklin Goucher

For my husband, David Warshawsky,
who has shared my Goucher odyssey with me

Courtesy of Janet Miller Bernet

JOHN FRANKLIN GOUCHER: CITIZEN OF THE WORLD

Not what a man may do, but what he does; not what he gets but what he uses;
not what he gives, but what he shares with others, enriches him.
Diary of John Franklin Goucher, August 18, 1897

—————————◆◆—————————

CONTENTS

If a man's heart is right, he can always be happy.

When a person is busy trying to do good, life is a pleasure.

Home is given to us as a kind of Heaven.

For by ministry the soul thrives.

Nothing is accomplished without vision.

The object of a college education is not to make a living,
but to make a life.

Life is a treasure for investment. . . .
You cannot, in any adequate sense, keep it unless you invest it.

I have crossed the Atlantic 25 times, the Pacific 8, the Trans-Siberian
Railway twice, and the Suez Canal three times.

The glory of life is in its serviceableness.
Its gauge is personal efficiency to relieve human need.

I have only cared for the doing, to accomplish the task laid out for me
by my heavenly Father and if the work is done,
what matters it who did the work.

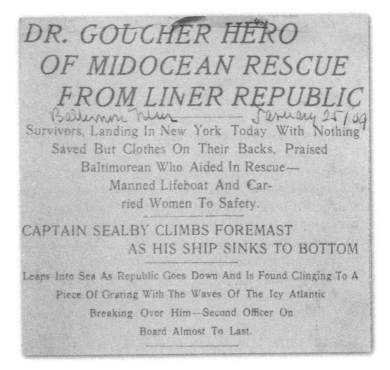

Baltimore News, January 25, 1909

Courtesy of the Baltimore-Washington Conference Archives,
Lovely Lane United Methodist Church, Baltimore, Maryland

THE LIFEBOAT

Introduction

—◆—

Every genuine effort to serve humanity, individually or collectively,
enriches the giver more than those
to whom he gives.[1]

John Franklin Goucher was as comfortable living out of a suitcase—
or more likely a trunk—as he was working in his study. His daughter
Janet recalled that while she was growing up, her father always
seemed to be just leaving on or returning from a trip. By the time
he retired as president of the Woman's College of Baltimore in 1908
(two years before it was renamed Goucher College), he had circled the
globe twice, crisscrossed the United States and crossed its northern
and southern borders, and vacationed from Florida to Alaska. Goucher
had explored London, Paris, and Rome; seen Shanghai, Peking, Seoul,
and Tokyo; and visited ancient sites at Pompeii, Athens, and Cairo.
He had made a dozen trans-Atlantic voyages by then, two across the
Pacific, and two passages through the Suez Canal. But one journey
in 1909 especially showcased his sense of adventure, his calmness in
adversity, his fortitude and faith in divine guidance.

On January 22 in New York, on a sunny and mild Friday
afternoon, Goucher and his friend S. Earl Taylor embarked as first-
class passengers on the *Republic*, a five-year-old, 570-foot steamship
of the White Star Line, bound for Alexandria, Egypt. By evening, as
the ship headed out toward the Atlantic, the weather changed, and a
fog "as thick as smoke" descended. At 5:30 the next morning, ship's
captain Inman Sealby was at the helm, peering into the darkness, when
he suddenly heard another ship's foghorn close by—too close. It was
the steamer *Florida*, about half the *Republic*'s size, inbound from
Naples and carrying more than 800 refugees from a recent earthquake
in Sicily and southern Italy, and thirty miles off course in the fog.[2]

Sealby gave two sharp blasts of his horn to warn the other vessel to turn to port, as the *Republic* did the same, hoping to avert a collision. But the *Florida*'s bow struck the larger ship in the side, ripping apart two cabins on the upper deck and breaking through the steel plates that protected the engine room. Then the *Florida* pulled away into the fog, part of her crumpled bow still stuck in the wreckage. The two ships were more than 200 miles from New York and nearly eighty miles from the nearest land.[3]

Goucher and Taylor were awakened by the blasts of the foghorns; then they felt several bumps and heard grinding sounds not far from their cabin. Taylor stuck his head out the porthole and saw a gaping hole in the hull less than fifty feet away. Soon the lights went out as the ship's engines were shut down. After dressing by the light of the electric torch Goucher always traveled with, Taylor went up on deck to investigate and returned to advise his companion to join him topside. Goucher declined, saying, "It is very comfortable here, and I'll see the damage in the morning." Even after stewards, carrying candles, came around and ordered all passengers to don life preservers and assemble on the saloon deck, Goucher calmly took his time. As he later recounted in his diary:

> I opened my trunk and took out my warmest and lightest
> clothing I had, so as to have the greatest warmth with the
> least bulk if we had to take to the water, and put my cardigan
> jacket under my [life] vest so I could do without an overcoat
> if needed. I placed in my pocket my letter of credit, air pillow,
> barometer, tea case, and several other things that might be
> of service to the passengers, locked my trunk and clasped it
> carefully and started for the upper deck.

On deck, Captain Sealby told the assembled throng that the ship's watertight compartments were holding and there was no immediate danger. But he warned them to be ready to take to the lifeboats if necessary.[4]

When Goucher looked around, he noted that "the passengers presented a strange sight, many of them being very inadequately dressed in whatever they had seized in the dark." Some were barefoot or wore mismatched shoes; women's previously carefully coiffed hair, let down for the night, was still in braids; and jewelry had been left behind. Despite the abrupt change in their status, there was no panic. There was confusion, however, as the passengers huddled in groups, trying to find safe spots on deck or attempting to put on life preservers under the feeble glow of a few candles held by stewards. Using his pocket electric torch, Goucher passed "from one knot to another," demonstrating to women and children how to correctly adjust their life belts.[5]

As dawn approached, he chose an out-of-the-way place to await further instructions—the skylight over the smoking room, drier than the deck and protected from the wind by the pilothouse and bridge. Some women who were traveling alone asked to join him, and he helped them climb up, but they still shivered in the biting cold. Before long he had made half a dozen trips below to retrieve clothing, shoes, and blankets for them, once over the captain's objection. He even took one woman to her cabin, providing some light for her until, he said, "She had completely dressed, even to her hat and veil."[6]

Goucher's assistance was only beginning. Five steamships and several other boats in the area had received the *Republic* Marconi operator's distress call and searched for the ship in the dense fog. The *Florida* had withdrawn to assess its own damage, and the *Republic* had drifted some miles from the collision site; the ships remained invisible to each other. Only the dying blasts of the *Republic*'s steam whistle allowed the *Florida* to find it again. Although the *Florida*'s prow was smashed almost to the bridge, it too had watertight compartments, and it seemed in less danger than the *Republic*, which was sinking a foot every hour.[7]

Early Saturday morning, not knowing when another vessel might reach them, Sealby contacted his counterpart on the *Florida* via megaphone, and they agreed to transfer the *Republic*'s passengers and most of its crew to the smaller ship, then a half-mile away. To handle the mass evacuation, the captain asked for male volunteers to help row the lifeboats. But even before these craft reached the water, there were hazards to face. The small boats had been lowered over the side of the *Republic* and hung ten or twelve feet below the high railing. Both rowers and passengers, wearing cumbersome life vests, had to climb down what was described as "a swinging sea ladder" before settling in for the ride.[8]

Despite his age (sixty-three), two recent hernia operations, and his slight frame, Goucher stepped forward to help, and as a news article would describe, he "rowed as well as the younger ones." Most people remained calm, even though their destination, the *Florida*, "could barely be made out under the search light [before it] faded away into the mist." Where a few men abandoned their oars as soon as they reached the ship, Goucher refused. For nearly two hours, with the temperature near freezing, he helped ferry several loads of passengers across what he described as "an oily, fog-shrouded sea." Once aboard the *Florida*, he and his fellow rescuees huddled together—tired, cold, and hungry. The supplies he had brought with him from his cabin came in handy: His tea case, he said, "helped a number of ladies who had sick headaches," and his air pillow "gave two others in turn comfortable rests."[9]

At first it was thought the smaller *Florida*, with her engines intact, could carry her load safely to New York. But in the end it was the *Baltic*, a sister ship of the White Star Line, that came to the rescue. Sailing at less than capacity, it had room to take on the 1,650 passengers and crew from the two damaged vessels, plus more than 3,000 sacks of mail retrieved from the *Republic*.[10]

Goucher recorded the *Baltic*'s arrival on January 23: "For nearly 10 hours she cruised within 1 or 2 miles of us till after dark, when she saw our rockets. Cir. 10 PM we heard her foghorn and soon saw her lights." As midnight approached, and using the twenty small lifeboats available between the two vessels, the ten-hour transfer began in the still foggy darkness, broken only by the *Baltic*'s searchlights. At first the larger ship was more than a mile from the *Florida*, as the sea grew increasingly rough. Goucher described his own ride:

> The sea was running high and it was very difficult to land and as we approached [the rope ladder of the Baltic], the officers ordered our boat to keep away as the ship was just starting to steam over, under the lee of the Florida to make the transfer of the passengers quicker and easier. Our small boat went back to the Florida and took on eight more passengers—not withstanding the protest of one of the women that we should

not let anyone else in. . . . [A]fter more than an hour and a half, beating around in the small boat, we reached the Baltic at 4:30 AM where some warm soup and a good cabin made us comfortable.[11]

By early Sunday morning, all from the *Republic* and the *Florida*, except for the captains and a few sailors who remained with their ships, had been safely transferred, and the *Baltic* began its journey to New York. Goucher slept for a short time in his new cabin, his first rest in more than twenty-four hours, and eventually he was able to send a wireless to his daughters, telling them he was safe. After breakfast, he slept again, waking in late afternoon to take part in "a very profitable service in the cabin" in thanksgiving for their safe deliverance.[12]

As the *Baltic* reached New York Monday afternoon, January 25, the bedraggled *Republic* passengers were greeted by what a newspaper called the "welcome music of thousands of voices raised in a chorus of cheers." They came down the gangplank, three days after they had departed, with no baggage and wearing the motley garments they had grabbed hastily in the dark two days before—"men in pajamas and blankets, children in almost nothing, women in all sorts of makeshifts in the way of garb." All were glad to be back on solid ground, and a tired but "smiling and calm" Goucher joined his friends waiting on shore.[13]

He did not tarry with them long. That same afternoon, Goucher caught a train to Baltimore for a hasty restocking trip, before quickly returning to New York. Forty-eight hours after arriving on the *Baltic*, he and Taylor were again at sea, bound for Liverpool. After a few days in London, they caught an express train to Brindisi, Italy, and from there sailed to Port Said. The two travelers finally reached Egypt in mid-February—a day ahead of their original schedule.[14]

When the *Baltic* had arrived in New York, reporters interviewed Goucher among other survivors. He did not speak of his own role in the rescue, but the papers in his home town of Baltimore celebrated his courage, with headlines proclaiming "Dr. Goucher Hero of Midocean Rescue From Liner *Republic*," "Dr. Goucher a Beacon," and "Dr. Goucher in Role of Hero." It was far from the only time during his life that Goucher's activities made the papers, although it was usually for acts less dramatic but ultimately of far greater consequence.

✳ ✳ ✳

Consider some hypothetical headlines you might see in a modern newspaper or an online news site that could have been written about John Franklin Goucher a century or more ago:

> *Benefactor, Facing Local Opposition, Opens Four Dozen Schools for Girls in Remote Villages in North India*

> *Leader of Historically Black College Seeks Equal Funding from the State*

> *American Caught in Battles Between Rival Parties in Western China*

> *College President Promotes Importance of a Liberal Arts Education in a Changing World*

> *Tourist Threatened on Trip to the Middle East*

Some of the issues and difficulties that Goucher faced in the last two decades of the nineteenth century and the first two of the twentieth are being encountered again in the twenty-first century.

It was an invitation I received from Japan in 2002 that first drew me to Goucher's multifaceted travels and projects. As chair of the Goucher College Board of Trustees and an alumna of the college in Baltimore, Maryland, I was asked to participate in the annual International Exchange Event at Aoyama Gakuin University in Tokyo. Like my alma mater, Aoyama Gakuin had been founded in the 1880s thanks to the vision and generosity of John Goucher (1845-1922) and his wife Mary (1850-1902). In 1907, during his second around-the-world trip, Goucher had written in his diary: "Spoke in the morning at the commencement of Aoyama Gakuin and in the afternoon attended the commencement of the Girls' Normal School. The former exercises were held in the new 'Goucher Hall' which though not completed was used for the first time for this service." The original building, also named in the couple's honor, had been damaged by an earthquake a dozen years before.[15]

Ninety-five years after Goucher described his own visit to the school, I was addressing an audience in another newly built Goucher Hall on the same campus; a devastating earthquake had claimed the second building as well, several years after it was built. My talk was about the mutual founder of the Baltimore and Tokyo schools, and standing on the stage that day, I felt I was following in his footsteps in some small way. I was struck by the fact that the lives of generations of students at that institution and my own had been influenced through the educational opportunities John Goucher had made possible. At that point I had only a basic knowledge of the scope of Goucher's life— although I had learned some about his shipwreck adventure. As there were no books about and few modern references to him, I left Tokyo determined to learn more about his work and beliefs and share them with a wider audience. My Goucher odyssey has since taken me to other East Asian as well as American cities for research, presentations, and travel over a dozen years. It also led to meeting Goucher family members—especially John and Mary's granddaughter, Janet Miller Bernet, who shared poignant childhood memories and stories about her grandfather, shortly before she died. Talking with her, looking at photos and memorabilia, I felt a direct link to John Goucher himself.[16]

What was it that made him stand out in his own time and even in our own? Some individuals have the vision to create projects that will change society. Others can execute plans and make that vision a reality. Still others have the resources to finance such projects. It is unusual to find one person who can do all three, but John Franklin Goucher was such a man. As a youth, he felt called to the ministry to spread the Christian gospel. That broad ministry in the Methodist Episcopal Church ultimately extended from pulpits in Baltimore to the pioneering and funding of mission projects around the globe. He studied and proposed ways to further evangelism in new arenas and in yet-unexplored places, from the American West to East Asia, opening educational opportunities at the same time. He offered counsel, oversight, and often hands-on management to those who brought his initiatives to fruition. In close consultation with his wife Mary, who was the love of his life and brought a fortune to the marriage, Goucher

8

was able to provide both initial and ongoing support for a wide variety of programs.

He was a founder and benefactor of Methodist missions and churches around the world, but I became especially interested in the scope and depth of his educational endeavors in the United States and Japan, and also in India, China, Korea, and elsewhere. As a Baltimore friend of Goucher once noted, "He had a passion for education and believed it was a panacea for many of the world's ills." Unlike many of his contemporaries at home or abroad, he championed schooling for everyone—female and male, all races and social classes, and all religions.[17]

Goucher was also willing to travel wherever the work of the Methodist Episcopal Church called him, or his curiosity and zest for life led him. He liked to see projects first-hand and didn't mind traveling to the center of the action, even over difficult or dangerous terrain. It was estimated that he logged more than one and a half million miles by land and sea (and once by air) in his lifetime. People in India who met him or knew his work called him "Goucher sahib jai"; in China, he was called "Ko Yok Hang"; in Japan, "Gaucha"; and in Korea, "Gawoocheo." He was well known to those working on the front lines of education and mission work, and as one Methodist publication wryly noted, missionaries looked forward to his visits "like the coming of a fairy godfather, and for much the same reason."[18]

How was Goucher able to do it all? He was a master organizer, who combined gentle persuasion with practicality, shrewdness, and business acumen. He brought people of varied viewpoints together to accomplish what needed to be done at home or abroad, and he fostered the creation of joint enterprises among those sharing common goals. Such arrangements, he believed, not only saved money but also enabled groups to achieve more together than acting separately. Often his motto seemed to be *carpe diem*—seize the day. While others might ponder an issue without acting, he was quick to grasp possibilities and take advantage of opportunities. As one acquaintance remarked, "He always had a program—a remedy—and it always spelled progress." Yet he also was patient. A fellow minister said that Goucher "laid broad and deep foundations" for the institutions he promoted. He understood that for many of them, he would not see "the full fruition of his labors in his lifetime."[19]

Many men like John Goucher who had the advantages of wealth and connections might have sought credit and the spotlight. But he was modest about his and Mary's philanthropy, which would total many million in today's dollars. His philosophy was, if the necessary work was done, it didn't matter who received the credit. Still, he was unable to decline some recognition: As noted, Aoyama Gakuin named more than one central academic building Goucher Hall. A town named for him in North India still bears the name Goucher. Toward the end of his life, the emperor of Japan and the president of the Republic of China each presented him with the highest decoration his country bestowed on a civilian. And in 1910, the Woman's College of Baltimore honored John and Mary's generosity and service by changing its name to Goucher College.

The story of John Franklin Goucher suggests what one person can accomplish—this man who started life in a small town and at his death was hailed as a "citizen of the world." One memorial tribute described a man who set an example that is relevant to today's interconnected but contentious, chaotic, and often xenophobic world: "To him there was no foreign land, to him no foreign man. He passed from one country to another without a sense of strangeness."[20]

COMMENCEMENT

OF THE

PITTSBURGH HIGH SCHOOL,

CONCERT HALL, JUNE 30, 1864.

PRAYER.   **MUSIC.**

1. ORATION—England and America............John F. Goucher.
2. ESSAY—Act well your Part......................Mary Hughes.

MUSIC.

3. ESSAY—Woman's Sphere.....................Annie M. Lange.
4. ORATION—The Future of Our Country,....Edward Demmler.

MUSIC.

5. ESSAY—Come up Higher...................Carrie M. Hartley.
6. ESSAY—Too Near.................................Kate Dain.

MUSIC.

7. ESSAY—The Germans in America, *with the Valedictory,*
                                        Julia M. Demmler.

MUSIC.

DISTRIBUTION OF DIPLOMAS.

MUSIC.

Courtesy of the Baltimore-Washington Conference Archives,
Lovely Lane United Methodist Church, Baltimore, Maryland

PREPARATION FOR LIFE

Chapter 1
(1845-1868)

———◆◆———

What a person is determines what he can do, as what he does, strengthens and develops what he is. Each person is the architect and builder of his own character.[1]

The warmth of summer was in the air when John and Eleanor Townsend Goucher welcomed their youngest child on June 7, 1845, in the southwestern Pennsylvania town of Waynesburg. The new baby was named John Franklin, but from childhood to early adulthood, he was known as Frank by family and associates, perhaps to distinguish him from his father. He joined nine-year-old Elijah, seven-year-old Ella, and four-year-old David in the close-knit family. Later in life, John Franklin wrote that his parents were among the most "outstanding and constructive" blessings to enrich his life. They gave him a loving, comfortable, and supportive home; instilled in him a love of learning; and raised him with examples of reverence for God and country that had been passed down through generations of the Goucher and Townsend families.[2]

John Franklin's interest in travel and adventure might have come from his relatives as well. On his father's side, family lore said that the earliest recorded ancestor, named Gaucher because he was left-handed, was a chief captain in the Second Crusade. Another ancestor was Gaucher de Chatillon, Count of Crecy, who was made constable of France, commander-in-chief of the army, in 1302. A contemporary relative of John F. Goucher said that a World War I map showed a "Fort Gaucher," named for an early family member, still standing on the outskirts of Paris.[3]

By the seventeenth century, descendants of the early Gauchers, then named Goucher, were living in Brittany, on the north coast of France.

They were Huguenots, members of the French Protestant Reformed Church—French Calvinists—who faced religious persecution and often death at the hands of their Catholic overlords and countrymen. Around 1647, Robert Goucher and his family left the country to settle in Wales. His three sons—Thomas, Robert, and Henry—enlisted with Oliver Cromwell, who was anti-Catholic and among those who had signed the execution order for England's Charles I. The Goucher brothers joined Cromwell's parliamentary-supported forces against the remaining royalists in Catholic Ireland, and each was awarded 100 acres of confiscated Crown lands as pay for his military service. By 1750, Thomas had settled in Ireland, and Robert and Henry had emigrated to America.

John F. Goucher's genealogical research revealed that Henry Goucher, his great-great grandfather, married and settled in what was then known as the "Connecticut Reserve," near Lowell, Ohio. His great-grandfather, also named Henry, made powder for the Continental Army during the American Revolution and received a land grant of 160 acres in western Pennsylvania as payment. Through his great-grandmother, Rhoda, John was a distant cousin of William F. McKinley, with whom he kept in contact through McKinley's years as governor of Ohio and president of the United States. Goucher's grandfather, John, was wounded in the War of 1812, and his father, another John, was born in 1812.[4]

On the Townsend side, Goucher learned, family tradition said "the earliest of their ancestors (of record) came to England with William the Conqueror, [in the year] 1066. Being of independent spirit he was unwilling to be under the restraint of camp life and located his quarters just beyond, hence he was called Townshend or Towns end." Goucher's maternal ancestors crossed the Atlantic in the mid-seventeenth century and settled around Egg Harbor, New Jersey. His great-grandfather, Daniel Townsend, was in the lumber business and served in the Revolutionary War, enabling John Franklin Goucher to become a member of the Sons of the American Revolution. When the war ended, Daniel moved to Peters Township near Pittsburgh, Pennsylvania, and bought 350 acres of land where generations of Townsends would eventually live. Goucher's grandfather, Elijah Townsend, was a prosperous farmer and became a first sergeant in the War of 1812. His mother, Eleanor, was born shortly after the war ended. Elijah later served as a justice of the peace, and it was said that "the poor always found in him a steadfast friend."[5]

After John Franklin Goucher's parents married in 1835, they moved several times with their children while his father studied, then practiced, homeopathic medicine. He began courses in Perryopolis, Pennsylvania, on the outskirts of Pittsburgh, and after the family's move to Waynesburg, he continued attending lectures while his youngest son was still an infant. He then moved on to North Georgetown, Ohio, for further homeopathic study. When young John was just two, his father moved the family yet again to set up practice in remote Lansing, Michigan.[6]

The Michigan Territory had become the twenty-sixth state in the Union in 1837, but when the Gouchers settled there ten years later, the area around Lansing was still largely wild and surrounded by dense forest. Shortly before their arrival, the state legislature decided to move the capital from Detroit to a more central location, and when legislators could not agree on another site, rustic Lansing Township was chosen. As the new seat of state government, the settlement soon grew around three villages—Lower, Upper, and Middle Towns. Dr. John Goucher built the first two-story house in Middle Town and set up his practice in his residence. In a short time, he owned several other properties in this section, the site of current downtown Lansing.

On a return visit as an adult, Goucher told the local newspaper that his father was a man who "took a great interest in church and educational work" during the family's five years in the rapidly growing town. As there were no organized religious services available, Dr. John Goucher "went around and got the church members in town to agree that whatever church had the most members, that should be the denomination of the organization." With no building in which to meet, the doctor then went before the first session of the Michigan state legislature in Lansing to ask for assistance. He secured permission to hold church services in the legislative hall of the newly built capitol for those wishing to gather for worship. He also was instrumental in organizing a school—a necessity with several school-age children in his own family. Before he left in 1852, he helped form a school district and became president of the town's first school board.[7]

Eleanor Goucher's ill health spurred her husband to move the family back east to Monongahela, Pennsylvania, near Pittsburgh and the Townsend family homestead. John Franklin, then seven, was sickly himself, likely suffering from the stomach ailments, headaches, and nosebleeds that afflicted him in adulthood. Goucher later recalled: "I was small for my age, having been frequently ill and compelled to spend much time in the house during my childhood and was then far from strong." He became especially close to his mother, who home-schooled him when needed, and his sister Ella, who created diversions, such as teaching him tatting (a handicraft using thread to form delicate lace) to help pass the time without playmates. These periods of homebound seclusion led him to mature quickly. During his boyhood solitude, he developed and nurtured the lifelong curiosity and broad interests that made a colleague once comment that Goucher knew more about more things than any other man he had ever met.[8]

Although he was often absent from school, he nevertheless excelled in his studies. His sixth-grade teacher said Goucher was able to "add figures at school faster than older boys," and she referred to him as "a gentlemanly boy" and "the brightest in the lot." One acquaintance of the period later said he was "a great favorite with schoolmates" when he did show up, and another recalled the twelve-year-old's appearance: "Your parents always dressed you like a little man, and you acted your part well along that line." The friend's description also hinted that girls were already taking notice of him: "[They] said you had ground squirrel cheeks and a dimple in your chin. You had a fine head of hair which you combed back of your ears." This combination of gravitas and good looks would endear Goucher to women young and old in years to come. [9]

By the time Goucher became a teenager, his brothers and sister had moved away from home: Elijah was following his father's footsteps and studying to become a homeopathic physician; David was starting a career in business; and Ella was attending school in Ohio. A September 1859 letter from Ella provided an example of her continued motherly interest in her younger sibling and gave a glimpse of his home and school life:

> When you write, I want you to tell me how good you are, if
> you do everything ma requires of you and obey pa, kind to your

associates, avoiding the company of bad boys. If you do, our parents will love you, others will sound your name with praise. You will have a happy heart and above all, God will love you.

I am inclined to think you proseic [sic] three [are doing] very well. Does pa ever send you to see his patients or how are you spending your time? What do you do for fun? Do you muster, are you captain and how many in your army? Tell me if you know anything about Europe. What book are you reading? When do you start to school and what will you study? When you write, do it in French as that is the language I use now [in school].[10]

The experience that set the course of Goucher's life came a few months later. Although the family was Presbyterian, in late November 1859, young John and his parents attended revival services at the Methodist Episcopal Church in Monongahela. Such gatherings, held over several evenings and sometimes led by a visiting preacher, offered an opportunity for spiritual renewal and reaffirmation of faith, as well as encouragement to repent and seek salvation. On the first night of services, Goucher and a young girl attending with him sat in a pew in front of his parents. He listened to the sermon and appeal and watched as penitents went up to the altar. The next evening they returned to church, and when the call came to go forward, John said to his friend, "Excuse me miss, I'll go to the altar." Thirty people were already crowding around the minister, and the only place for John was next to an "old backslider," a man who had returned to his sinful ways and was repenting yet again. The fourteen-year-old Goucher squeezed in next to him and fervently began to pray to God, "If you will forgive my sins, whatever you ask, I'll do with the greatest of pleasure." He felt the Holy Spirit urge him to preach the gospel, and he replied, "Anything you ask of me." Goucher related that his heart filled with joy at this exchange, and he was "delighted beyond measure."[11]

That Sunday, he shared this experience publicly with the congregation at the Methodist Church, and soon he was baptized and became a member. The minister, who lived in the parsonage behind the Goucher family garden, had always been friendly and often greeted his young neighbor by saying, "Well, John, what have you been doing for the Kingdom today?" After his conversion, Goucher asked himself that question on a daily basis, fulfilling the commitment he had made as a teenager.[12]

Shortly thereafter, young Goucher found himself living in a new environment when his father relocated his practice to a more urban setting in Pittsburgh. John Franklin's recent conversion and baptism led his parents to join Christ Methodist Episcopal Church, which many of Dr. Goucher's patients attended as well. In addition to finding spiritual sustenance through services and Sunday school, the young Goucher forged acquaintances there that proved valuable later. He soon became a favorite of its minister, Rev. Lyttleton F. Morgan, who encouraged his interest in the ministry and recommended the young man's membership in the Baltimore Conference of the Methodist Episcopal Church a decade later.

Because of his frequent absences from primary school, Goucher did not enter high school until the fall of 1860, when he was fifteen. He continued to excel in his studies, especially mathematics, but he also longed to take part in outdoor activities like other boys his age. He appreciated any time he spent on his uncle's farm, part of the Townsend family homestead, where he was able to roam freely and enjoy country life. These experiences led to what a relative called Goucher's lifelong "love of nature and living close to it." Perhaps to test his endurance and also to expand his knowledge, as a teenager he developed a desire to tackle the unknown—to be something of a daredevil. When he was older, he never hesitated to try new adventures, whether it was descending more than 300 feet by ladder into a Maryland copper mine, trekking through a Malaysian jungle, or flying in one of the first commercial "aeroplanes" from London to Paris.[13]

One of Goucher's defining experiences in Pittsburgh, which he recounted often later, was meeting Abraham Lincoln in February 1861. The president-elect was on a thirteen-day train trip from Springfield, Illinois, to Washington, D.C., bound for his first inauguration. He traveled on a succession of trains owned by various railroads along the route, and made stops at towns and cities in Ohio, Pennsylvania, and New York before passing through Maryland and Baltimore to reach his final destination. As the Republican Party candidate, Lincoln had won the presidency a few months earlier in a four-way race: The Democrats had split their ticket, nominating candidates representing northern and southern interests, and a new but short-lived Constitutional Union Party had nominated its own candidate. The long-simmering tensions of states' rights and slavery erupted in the secession of seven states between Lincoln's election and the beginning of his journey to Washington. This train trip provided an opportunity for people on the route to see their new leader and hear his views as the country teetered on the brink of a civil war.[14]

Lincoln stopped overnight in Pittsburgh, and the morning after his arrival, Elijah and David Goucher, who were home visiting, wanted to go catch a glimpse of him. Neither wanted to be responsible, however, for taking along young John. Thousands had gathered in teeming rain to greet Lincoln, and they feared their brother, who was slight of build and not physically strong, might get hurt in the crush. Dr. Goucher proposed accompanying his youngest son, but John asked to be trusted to care for himself, and his father finally allowed him to go off alone.

As it turned out, Goucher was able to gain access to the president-elect while his older brothers saw him only from the middle of a sea of umbrellas. John Franklin later related:

> Not being familiar with the ways of the world, I supposed it was proper if you wished to see a person, to go where he was. So I went to the Smithfield Street entrance of the Monongahela House and found several gentlemen going in to pay their respects to the President-elect. . . . The eagerness of my desire and my innocence of any sense of impropriety caused me to walk in with them without any hesitation.

The contingent included the mayor and city councilmen, each of whom assumed Goucher was the son of the other, so no one questioned his presence. As the men gathered near Lincoln's private parlor, the youthful Goucher stepped aside to watch each adult say a few words to the president-elect and shake his hand. John prepared to leave with the local dignitaries, but he noticed that after the public greetings, Lincoln's previously animated face became sad and weary. Struck by the change, he remained behind and came face-to-face with the soon-to-be-inaugurated sixteenth president. Goucher remembered "looking up into his deep, wonderful, kindly eyes," and as the others had done, he reached out his hand and said, "It is a great pleasure, Mr. President, to shake hands with you." As he later related, Lincoln "stooped and with the most gentle smile took it in both of his, covering my hand and arm almost to the elbow."

Lincoln then uttered a blessing that seemed to prophecy Goucher's future role in international affairs: "God bless you my son," he said. "Love God, obey your parents and serve your country, and you will give the world cause to remember and honor you." Goucher saw Lincoln one more time: Four years later, as a college freshman, he journeyed to Harrisburg, Pennsylvania, to see the slain president as he lay in state, en route by train back to Illinois for burial.[15]

A few weeks after his seventeenth birthday, Goucher faced his first major bereavement—the death of his beloved mother. This loss was traumatic enough that several years later, as a young minister, he still missed her. He wrote of his feelings in his 1869 diary:

> Seven years ago this afternoon, Christ called my mama home to himself and left me lonely. Though He has been with me ever since, I ofttimes feel very lonely and especially so have I been today. There was a little pic-nic [sic] given in the woods by some ladies and I had to appear pleasant—though I had much rather sat me down close-housed with memory and steadily viewed the almost—if not entirely—perfect life of mama which she lived in Christ Jesus.[16]

When his mother died, Goucher had two more years of high school to complete. As the only child remaining at home, he forged an even closer bond with his father. With his father's encouragement, he helped the doctor more in preparing and delivering the medicines that were part of his homeopathic practice, a routine Goucher continued on home visits during his college years. His report card for his senior year at Pittsburgh High School showed he was tardy a quarter of the time, most likely attending to medical business for his father before heading to classes, and he received nearly three dozen demerits for the year.[17]

Despite the separation it required, Goucher's father was willing to send John away after graduation to continue his education. Dickinson College, nearly 200 miles southeast of Pittsburgh in Carlisle, Pennsylvania, seemed a logical choice. Several of Goucher's Pittsburgh friends were students there already, and the college's connection with the Methodist Episcopal Church's Baltimore Conference, one of five surrounding conferences that provided annual support for Dickinson, would prove helpful to his desire to become a minister. He easily met the requirements for admission and was ready and eager to begin this new phase of his life.[18]

At the time of Goucher's enrollment in the fall of 1864, Carlisle and the surrounding area were feeling the effects of the Civil War. The year before, the town and college had had a direct brush with hostilities. On June 25, 1863, after days of worrisome news reports about approaching Confederate troops, a column of 10,000 rebels— Dickinson alumni or sons of alumni among them—arrived in town during commencement activities. The officers set up their headquarters and a hospital in two of the college buildings, and many soldiers camped on the college grounds, where they barbecued requisitioned cattle. There was fear that the town and college might be destroyed because of a United States cavalry school nearby. But newspapers reported that the southern troops, who remained in town several days, "took great pains to preserve the College and grounds from injury." When a regiment of Union soldiers arrived in Carlisle following the rebels' departure, however, the town was shelled unexpectedly by another passing Confederate unit. Both sides soon moved on to Gettysburg, just twenty-five miles away, and the horrendous conflict that began there on July 1.[19]

Dickinson College felt the war's impact in other ways. After hostilities broke out at Fort Sumter in April 1861, all but four southern students left. When the fall semester began that year, there were one-third fewer students than the year before. Wartime inflation kept some northern families from sending their sons to college, while other young men became soldiers. (At nineteen, Goucher was a year below draft age, but he might have been exempt from military service anyway because of his unpredictable health.) When he arrived by train on the Cumberland Valley Railroad in September 1864, there were only ninety college students on campus, with another forty-eight boys enrolled in the preparatory department. The six faculty members, who included the college president and the principal of the preparatory department, had multiple teaching and administrative duties but received only a portion of their salaries because of budget deficits.[20]

Twenty-six young men enrolled in the freshman class at Dickinson that fall, and Dr. John Goucher willingly paid the tuition and room and board expenses to count his son among them. The younger Goucher understood and appreciated the emotional and financial commitment his father was making and later acknowledged the advantages he had been given: "Father has been a wise, kind, and devoted parent, often sacrificing that I might have every need and facility to prepare for my life's work."[21]

College brought Goucher not only new academic challenges but also the experience of living on his own for the first time. As he was not a local resident, he was required to live on campus. Fortunately, he was able to room his first two years with a Pittsburgh friend, John Grier "Chum" Holmes, who was two years younger but had entered Dickinson the year before Goucher. Their room, lit by a gas fixture and heated in winter by a small stove, had few other amenities. But the pair made their bare quarters comfortable by buying new or second-hand furniture from local shops. Like any student, Goucher accommodated his spartan space to his needs. His granddaughter later related that his favorite way to study was to sit back and prop his feet up on a wall. To make the position both comfortable and efficient, he nailed a pair of slippers to the wall so he could slip his feet in easily.[22]

Being away from home meant Goucher also had to arrange for his own meals, as the college lacked dining facilities. Students either organized dining clubs which they managed themselves, or paid for board at private Carlisle homes approved by the faculty. Goucher found a homelike setting at the residence of Barbara Egolf. A mutual admiration grew between them, and he would stay with her when he returned to attend Dickinson events in the first years after graduation.[23]

Despite the small faculty and limited resources, the college offered a wide range of liberal arts courses, and Goucher took advantage of every academic opportunity during his four years of study. He remained interested in mathematics, and at the end of his first year, he won second prize in algebra and was awarded a book entitled *Female Prose Writers of America, with Portraits, Biographical Notices, and Specimens of Their Writings*. It seems an unusual prize for an all-male college, but in retrospect, it suited a young man who would become a champion of women's education. During his last two years, he was able to focus his coursework in Dickinson's newly instituted Biblical Department, which enabled him to earn a bachelor of arts degree and then enter the ministry without further theological study.[24]

Church attendance was an integral part of life at this Methodist-supported college. All students were required to attend chapel twice a day, except on Saturday and Sunday, when the evening service was omitted. On Sundays, the young men were obliged to attend two public worship services at a church designated by their parents or guardian. Goucher could have limited his attendance to Emory Chapel on campus, which was also open to local residents, but he craved a broader religious outreach and determined to put his beliefs into action. Perhaps because of his own early conversion, he understood the importance of reaching out and teaching young people about God. As he noted in a later speech on the world's evangelization, "When a child is converted it is a double work of grace, namely the salvation of a life and the salvation of a lifetime, with its untold opportunities and influence." He believed that the best time to influence youth was between the ages of twelve and twenty, when "the heart is like wax in its impressionableness, like bronze in its retentiveness."[25]

On his first Sunday in college, Goucher went into Carlisle and helped organize a Mission Sunday School Society in an underprivileged part of town known as "the barracks." Wearing a tailored suit and tie, he must have stood out among the more poorly dressed residents. Slender and barely five and a half feet tall, he began approaching boys he saw on the streets in the rough neighborhood to ask them to come to the Sunday school, which was designed to provide both spiritual and personal guidance for area youth. He persuaded two gang members he saw throwing sand at each other to attend, and their participation caused their friends to follow.[26]

During his junior year, Goucher became superintendent of this mission Sunday school, while carrying a full load of courses at Dickinson and teaching a young women's Bible class at Emory Chapel. In this new position, he was expected to oversee the school's administrative and religious organization. He learned that Rev. John Heyl Vincent, then secretary of the Methodist Sunday School Union and later co-founder of the first Chautauqua assembly, had developed a course of study named the Home Normal College. Goucher gathered a class of twenty-nine, including a dozen teachers from the Sunday school and members of his Bible class, to take the course. At the beginning of June 1867, Vincent held a Sunday school institute at Carlisle, and Goucher received the first diploma from the Home Normal College as organizer of this class.[27]

Several years later, this course of study evolved into a national correspondence course, the Chautauqua Literary and Scientific Circle (CLSC), which opened up learning opportunities to those who did not live near or have the money or time to attend a conventional college. Goucher would keep his own 1867 diploma, and when Vincent later saw it, he offered to replace it with a new one from the CLSC. Goucher replied that "the Klondyke [sic] gold mines couldn't buy it."[28]

Goucher did not spend all of his time in Carlisle studying or in religious outreach, however. He established his speaking prowess as a member of the Belles Lettres Society, one of two rival oratorical clubs on campus, and he won the silver medal of the Pierson Prize, one of two awards given to members of the junior class for excellence in both "declamation and composition." His prize-winning speech considered the question whether climate influenced the physical and intellectual development of individuals and nations. He noted that ancient civilizations that existed in colder or arid climates were often less developed because of the effort needed to survive; those in warmer climates, with fertile land, had more time for leisure and to develop intellectually and politically strong states. The United States, which Goucher claimed covered "over one-eighth of latitudinal extent of the world," was subject to "diverse climatic influences" that helped shape its progress:

> These [influences] of necessity produce men of diverse modification. We have neither a national style of thought, a national cast of features, nor any national peculiarities. Those characteristics for which we are noted abroad are confined to certain localities at home. Thus instead of our latitudinal extent contributing to our strength and assisting in the involution of our national individuality, it prevents our homogeneity of modification and to the same extent prevents our National development.[29]

Goucher's other interests ranged from the Shakespeare Club to the Chess Club. But he was not above taking part in one activity the college did not sanction. Dickinson College initially prohibited fraternities, so meetings of the four on campus were *sub rosa* until late in his college career, when they were reluctantly allowed. Goucher was a member of Sigma Chi, Omicron Chapter, and over the years, he maintained his Greek connections. In 1905, he was selected by the student members at Dickinson to be an "orator" at the dedication of their new fraternity house. Ten years later, while visiting schools and missions in East Asia, he was asked by the Sigma Chi fraternity brothers in Shanghai, China, to relate "some of the inspiring early stories of the fraternity, which you so largely helped to shape."[30]

Goucher was popular among his classmates, who affectionately called him "Goo-shay." But recurring bouts of illness, continuing from his younger years, caused him to leave college for two weeks in the fall and several weeks in the spring semester of his sophomore year. On his returns, his classmates received him back with "a hearty resolution of congratulations." In a history of the Class of 1868, a classmate credited Goucher with suggesting "a permanent class organization for convenience during our College course"—an innovation at Dickinson—that culminated in holding the first Class Day to celebrate commencement week. Of the twelve men who graduated in 1868, Goucher ranked third and was selected to give the coveted philosophical oration at graduation. In the nine minutes allotted him (one minute less than the valedictory address), he proposed to show "the Tendency of Thought to Gravitate Towards Truth."[31]

Three years later, Goucher received another diploma from his alma mater. At that time, Dickinson offered a master of arts degree to any graduate who had been out of college at least three years and had maintained a good moral character. An applicant only had to apply to the president and pay a five-dollar fee, which was returned if the degree were denied. Nine members of the Class of 1868 availed themselves of this opportunity. Goucher was asked to give a master's oration at the 1871 commencement ceremony, harking back to his graduation speech three years earlier. By then he was accustomed to addressing listeners from the pulpit.[32]

Goucher continued his relationship with Dickinson, and the school maintained close ties to its increasingly well-known alumnus. The college took notice of his rising stature in educational, church, and missionary work and conferred on him an honorary doctor of divinity degree at the 1885 commencement; a second honorary degree, doctor of laws, was awarded in 1899. The Carlisle press also promoted his name as a candidate for president of the college in 1888, noting, "Scarcely more than forty years old, he is healthy, robust, fond of work, sagacious in planning. His ideas are large, his ambition eager. . . . Under Dr. Goucher, the progress of the institution would be distinct, emphatic and impressive." But he was already involved with many other educational ventures and missions and not interested in the position. The paper chided the college for "bad management" that "allowed him to become committed to the erection of a woman's college in Baltimore, with the result of estranging that city from Dickinson, and diverting Goucher's beneficence from his alma mater." Indeed, while he continued to offer some financial support to Dickinson College during his lifetime, he would give the equivalent of several million in today's dollars to the college that would one day bear his name.[33]

Before Goucher could collect these later tributes from Dickinson, however, he had to fulfill his calling to the ministry. He ultimately chose the Bible verse Acts 20:24 as his lifelong inspiration: "But none of these things move me, neither count I my life dear unto myself, so that I might finish my course with joy, and the ministry, which I have received of the Lord Jesus, to testify the gospel of the grace of God." His first ministerial assignment as a member of the Baltimore Conference required him to carry out his mission on the back of a horse.

John Goucher's notes on his ministerial assignments,
1869-1882

A CALLING
TO THE MINISTRY–
FROM THE CIRCUIT
TO THE CITY

Chapter 2
(1869-1890)

———————◆◆———————

*The calling of a minister is indeed a delightful one though the work
is hard and the responsibility great.*[1]

The twenty-three-year-old Goucher faced important choices
following his graduation from college. Dr. John Goucher hoped
his son would become a partner in his medical practice and offered to
send him to medical school and then to Paris to study surgery. Although
he had majored in Biblical studies at Dickinson, at graduation he
received and was tempted by offers to join businesses where he could
use his mathematical skills. But the pull to the ministry was stronger,
and as Goucher told his father, "It was not from want of love for him,
nor from appreciation of his generous offer, but solely a matter of
conscience . . . and only because I felt '<u>woe is me</u>' if I preach not the
gospel."[2]

Years later, Goucher told friends he had received six distinct
"commissions" from God that shaped his life and work and often
overlapped in their execution: to become a Christian; to become
a minister; to minister to young people; to do missionary work; to
promote Christian education in all lands; and to work for the unification
of American Methodism, which had divided into the Methodist
Protestant Church, the Methodist Episcopal Church, and the Methodist
Episcopal Church, South, in the first half of the nineteenth century.
On two small note cards on which he recorded milestones in his life,
Goucher acknowledged the importance of the first two "commissions."

Although he had converted as a young teenager and attended church regularly, once he was at Dickinson, he began to face "a great wrestle" with what he called "rationalization." This struggle, he noted, required him "to relay the foundations of my belief," balancing his intellectual understanding and the tangible nature of the physical world, with the assurances of personal salvation and God's redemption and grace he found in the scriptures and in prayer. Ultimately, he said, "I was true to my doubts, and perfectly true to my beliefs. I saw no right to practice my doubts and every obligation to live my beliefs." Reaffirming the commitment to God he had made at fourteen, he chose the Biblical call, "Go ye into all the world, and preach the gospel to every creature."[3]

A few days after graduating in June 1868, J. Frank Goucher was examined by the Methodist Carlisle Quarterly Conference "concerning his gifts, grace, and usefulness." He was judged to be "a proper person to be licensed," and officially approved to preach. One of his Dickinson professors wrote to officials at Christ Methodist Episcopal Church in Pittsburgh, where Goucher had retained his membership, noting that he graduated "with very honorable distinction" and recommending him "as one whom we believe God has called to the work of the sacred ministry." His minister, Lyttleton F. Morgan, was planning to leave the Pittsburgh church in March 1869 to return to a pastorate in Baltimore, and Goucher wanted to follow him and receive his first full-time ministerial assignment from the Baltimore Conference.[4]

Goucher's first opportunity to stand in a pulpit as a minister came in the fall of 1868. During his third year in college, his father had moved his practice to Alliance, Ohio, and his sister Ella had married and lived with her husband on a farm nearby. The recent graduate spent the next few months reconnecting with his family as he awaited his move to Baltimore. To pass the time, Goucher again helped his father compound and deliver homeopathic remedies and made himself available to substitute for the local minister as needed. On a slip of paper, he recorded his first time leading a service: "Preached first sermon, October 18, 1868, on Malvern Circuit in Herrington's Stone Meeting House, cir. 7 miles north of Carrollton, Ohio." Although he had given many speeches at college, facing a congregation for the first time proved an unnerving experience. On that Sunday evening, "at early candle lighting," Goucher suffered a severe physical reaction in the middle of his trial sermon:

About 12 minutes after I commenced, or half through the sermon, everything became as black as midnight to me. I could not recall a point. I trembled. A heavy, cold perspiration burst forth all over me and I seemed in the grasp of the power of darkness. I stood and prayed so earnestly to Him who had called me to preach His message when deliverance came with great liberty. The struggle lasted but a few seconds, was not noticed by the congregation, but seemed several minutes to me.[5]

He considered the episode "no doubt a crisis in my life," a spiritual testing of his resolve to preach that he passed with divine help. A year later Goucher recalled that first sermon in his diary and noted that he had preached eighty-five times since then. He found his experience on this later date more rewarding: He preached "for 53 minutes to the fullest house I ever saw. Could hardly get to the pulpit. . . . The Lord was with me and we had a good meeting."[6]

After his inaugural sermon on the Malvern Circuit, he preached several times in the area. Goucher returned to Pittsburgh in late February 1869 to be examined by the local Quarterly Conference to join the Baltimore Conference. He was invited to speak at an evening service at Christ Church, presenting a different challenge: "The situation was not the most pleasant in the world as nearly all the congregation were my acquaintances and many of them my friends but I got through the service pretty well." He impressed his audience, passed the examination, and was unanimously recommended for membership in the Baltimore Conference, which was to hold its annual session soon after in Washington, D.C. Goucher was ready at last to begin his calling full time.[7]

At dinner time on March 1, Goucher, Morgan, and his college friend "Chum" Holmes caught the train for a fourteen-hour ride from Pittsburgh to Baltimore. Enjoying the luxury of a Pullman sleeping car, they arrived in time for breakfast. They made visits in town, then took another train to Washington and the Baltimore Conference meetings. There was much excitement and crowding in the city, as the session coincided with President Ulysses S. Grant's first inauguration. Goucher had an invitation to watch the hour-long procession from a comfortable window overlooking Pennsylvania Avenue, but he said he "much preferred a 'private box on the curb stone' with Holmes." Conference leaders also had arranged for attendees to be received by the new president at the Executive Mansion. Like any tourist in the capital, Goucher did some sightseeing, including a visit to Ford's Theater, where Lincoln had been shot.[8]

Goucher's first ministerial assignment was as junior preacher on the Baltimore Circuit, which was centered in Reisterstown, Maryland, in northern Baltimore County. His duties encompassed eight churches, with a total of more than 400 members and nearly 100 probationers, and he was to work under Rev. Tillotson Morgan, Lyttleton's brother. The two of them, plus a retired minister, traveled among the congregations, preaching at Sunday morning and afternoon services on a rotating basis. The junior preacher was also in charge of the circuit's seven Sunday schools, soon to be fourteen under Goucher's guidance. This was familiar work to him after his time at the Carlisle mission Sunday school, and it helped fulfill his third "commission," to minister to young people.[9]

Life on the circuit meant Goucher had no home of his own, as only the senior minister lived in a parsonage. The Baltimore Conference paid for his room and board with John L. Turner, a lay leader in one of his congregations, who lived near Pikesville, eight miles from downtown Baltimore and nine from Reisterstown. The Turner residence, Goucher noted, was "a very pretty place," with "a large stone house rough coated and sort of cream color, large orchards and pleasant grounds, a goodly number of flowers in the house and very pleasant people." The family consisted of Brother and Sister Turner, their son, two "maiden lady" sisters, and Turner's eighty-four-year-old mother. One of Goucher's first comments in his 1869 diary about his new position showed both some trepidation and optimism: "This is to be my home for a year if I live so long, and I think it will be a pleasant one."[10]

He and his hosts soon settled into a routine, and he appreciated the warmth of family life as he had in his youth. In the evenings, Goucher often read popular books or Shakespeare aloud to the Turners, and he helped them with the gardening during the day. The Turners made him welcome with simple touches such as putting fresh flowers in his room. They were pleased to listen as he practiced the Bible lesson he would present for his Sunday sermon; these gatherings, he said, turned into "one of the regular institutions of the week." He also became an "attending physician" for the Turners, using his knowledge of homeopathic remedies. When he first began treating them for such illnesses as colds, pneumonia, neuralgia, and stomach distress, Goucher said the family "had little faith in homeopathy." But with his successful treatments, he later added, "now they think it is very good indeed."[11]

At first, Goucher found meeting and visiting his parishioners in their homes or at work to be the hardest part of the job. He described himself as "naturally social at home," but he "disliked to go away." He remembered, however, a saying that "a house-going minister makes a church-going people," so he vowed to "try and cultivate a disposition of friendship and sociability." He began making calls around his circuit and was soon adept at visiting not only those already connected with his churches, but also potential members in the area. By June 1869, he had made more than 200 such calls.[12]

Goucher did not learn what he would be paid until several weeks into his duties, when his annual salary was set at $300. He was earning his own money for the first time, and while determined to regularly set aside a portion for savings and to support missions, he also had some immediate needs. He had been making his rounds with borrowed horses or buggies, sometimes traveling twenty or thirty miles a day for visits or church services. Using ten dollars from his first paycheck for a deposit, he paid $150 for a four-year-old bay mare he named Pet, promising to pay the balance in two installments before the end of the year. Careful of his finances, he likely purchased his livery from Civil War army surplus. By the time Goucher completed his first three months on the job, he and Pet had traveled more than 700 miles around the circuit in all weather; that total grew to nearly 2,500 miles by Thanksgiving.[13]

As Goucher traveled from church to church on his circuit, he often took tea or a meal with parishioners, as it was a special honor for a family to entertain a minister. If his travels and pastoral duties took him too far from home to return for the night, he stayed with a member of one of the congregations. These overnights could be very pleasant or most uncomfortable, and an itinerant preacher had to accept the latter without outward complaint. Goucher recounted the evening before and morning of his twenty-fourth birthday:

> I slept none last night owing to calves, chickens, Brother G starting to market so early, a boy crying with toothache, the chimney swallows. As a consequence in the morning was so complaining that I could eat no breakfast. Made several calls and was very used up. When dinner [lunch] came it was cold. Had pancakes, green onions, and very fat salt side meat and corn starch arrow root served with brown sugar and sour milk of which I could eat nothing.

Fortunately when he returned to the congenial Turner home that evening, he found "4 very nice bouquets, a large fruit cake and a set of chess and board for birthday presents."[14]

When Goucher started his job, he said he intended to divide his time "into three equal portions—eight hours for work and religious studies, eight hours for recreation, and eight for sleep." He soon learned that a preacher's life—especially on the circuit—did not allow for such tidy time slots. A sample of his daily schedule during his first year in the ministry showed how adept he became at juggling multiple tasks:

> The work passed off this morning as usual very pleasantly indeed and I enjoyed it much to be at my studies and more. . . . After dinner I had a ride of 22 miles to see Mr. Giles again. He is much worse than when I saw him last. He cannot certainly last long.

> Addressed Sunday school at Gill's School House at 7:45— talked 23 minutes, then rode 8 miles back to Reisterstown. Funeral awaited me at Odd Fellows Hall as we worship there while out of our church.

> Led [Sunday school] class AM at Stone Chapel before services. It was one of the best classes I ever saw. Dined at Dr. Fisher's. Talked to his Sunday school and opened it at 2 PM. Then went on to Pleasant Hill [Church] and talked to the school there another 25 minutes, then preached. The day being very warm and having 5 services, 3 of them extra, I am pretty well used up this evening.

Reisterstown—led class for Bro. Stone in the morning then went to service . . . Sermon was 34 minutes . . . Dined with Bro. Stone and then started to Mt. Pleasant. Addressed the Sunday school and preached over half an hour again. Took supper at Bro. Ward's where we had some singing. Then rode over to Bro. Fite's about 12 miles, making 20 miles ride today. I had to come here to be near Quarries [Church] for tomorrow.

Since Saturday [two days before] I have ridden 51 miles, made 16 calls, preached twice, led class and addressed one Sunday school.

Preached at revival [Mt. Pleasant], made 8 calls and rode 25 miles today.[15]

In addition to his ministerial duties, Goucher needed to pass several tests before becoming ordained as a deacon and elder in the Methodist Episcopal Church. He admitted his mind tended to wander while studying, but he gradually felt his "power of abstraction" was increasing: "practice makes perfect."[16]

When he did have his allotted time for work and study, Goucher often retreated to the woods to prepare his sermons, remembering the peace and freedom he had found in such spaces on his uncle's farm. In the summer months, he also began taking his congregations to the woods—much like the early itinerant Methodist ministers—instead of preaching indoors. But if it rained, it was the custom that nobody went to church, as travel to services was uncomfortable for parishioners and minister alike. When Goucher had a particularly hectic week, a rainy Sunday offered respite and a chance to rest. On one occasion, he had been so busy that when Saturday evening arrived, he had no sermon prepared for the next day. He nevertheless trusted that "the Lord God in whose service I am so worn down will provide for the morrow when it comes." He ended his diary entry for that day with, "So goodnight!" He awoke early the next morning, planning on preparing his sermon then, but it was raining hard. "I sang 'Praise God from whom all blessings flow' and went to sleep again."[17]

Goucher soon became comfortable making house calls, sometimes staying away from the Turners' for two or three days at a time in an effort to meet everyone living in a particular area. In addition to leading morning and evening services at churches on the circuit, he led mid-week prayer meetings and Sunday school classes. He often incorporated into his lessons items from nature with which his rural students were familiar, such as "an old straw stack" that could be seen outside the classroom window. His less weighty duties included attending church picnics and fairs. Such activities served a dual purpose. After attending a Strawberry Festival held by one congregation, he noted, "It seemed to please that they had the preacher with them." For him, it was "a good opportunity to talk with a good number of the members and get acquainted with them."[18]

The time on the road and all that preaching, teaching, and visiting often affected his never-robust health. His eyes sometimes bothered him, which he said was "a great privation," as he loved to read; he had nosebleeds; he suffered from "something like lumbago," painful for one who spent extended periods on horseback. The senior minister, Tillotson Morgan, was bedridden for a time, and Goucher assumed extra duties, aggravating his own ailments. He recorded on one occasion that he had a "headache, pain in my back, and strong fever." But he added, "I have no intention of getting sick as I have too much else to do just now." When he did feel ill, he often dosed himself with some of his father's homeopathic remedies.[19]

During the year, there also were protracted revival meetings at five of his eight churches. Every other night Goucher was "preaching and exhorting" attendees to profess their faith, much as the minister in Monongahela had done when Goucher himself was converted. This intense schedule went on for eleven weeks and he became exhausted. At one point he noted, "I am so worn down that I cannot sleep in a strange bed" while away from the Turners' house; another time he said, "I am nearly broke down. It is very hard to get around I am so fatigued." When he felt such stress, it helped to take a little break from work. During one busy period, he had a visit from his Dickinson College roommate. Goucher seemed rejuvenated when he happily wrote in his diary, "This AM I took 'Holmesy,' 'my old woman,' into Baltimore in the omnibus and staid [sic] all night in the city." Yet Goucher was willing to endure physical difficulties for the spiritual benefits, saying "Though the body is growing weak, the spirit is gaining strength quickly."[20]

Goucher's work was not tied to the eight churches alone. He also was responsible for helping organize the annual summer camp meeting, which offered visitors and families religious services, fellowship, and a vacation in the fresh air. Such camps began in the late eighteenth and early nineteenth centuries as part of the Second Great Awakening, a religious movement that focused on personal salvation and social reform in preparation for the second coming of Christ. These outdoor revivals were especially effective and popular in frontier areas that depended on itinerant ministers. As a late twentieth-century article about camp meetings notes, participants gathered from far and near for several days, living in tents or temporary huts, as a series of preachers "evangelized the faithful and not-so-faithful with fire and brimstone sermons." The Methodists organized many such meetings, which helped grow the number of adherents and led to an increase in the number of small churches in remote areas. The article adds that these meetings became especially popular after the Civil War with "a war-weary population mourning its dead and searching for spiritual meaning and solace."[21]

Among his other duties, the young minister spent his first months on the circuit traveling around with a member of the camp committee to find a location large enough for a crowd and with access to sufficient water, a job that required patience and negotiating skills. Finally a site in Reisterstown was chosen. In mid-August 1869, Goucher helped supervise the raising of 300 tents for living and meeting quarters and ensured everything was ready for both participants and preachers. He was looking forward to taking part in several days of spiritual immersion, as well as spending an extended period outdoors: "The life in the woods I know I shall like."[22]

During nine days of camp meeting, as many as 12,000 people came to listen to the various preachers and attend activities. Some arrived via streetcar or the Western Maryland Railroad; other visitors created "a jam of horses and carriages in the woods all around." Goucher said he enjoyed it all far beyond his expectations and was thankful for what he had been able to accomplish: "The Lord has blessed me peculiarly in my prayers for self and others, in talking to penitents and in bringing persons to the altar." When camp finally was over, Goucher spent a day catching up on his sleep. Three hundred people were converted during the revival period, and Goucher needed renewed strength to visit those new converts living in the area, to encourage them to attend one of the churches on his circuit.[23]

The Baltimore Quarterly Conference met during the camp meeting and gave Goucher a "unanimous vote of thanks" for the efficient way he had improved the circuit's Sunday schools and covered his other pastoral duties since he had begun in March. He was also lauded for making certain the camp meeting's nearly eighty visiting ministers were entertained. His early stage fright gave way to confidence, and he wrote in his diary, "The love of my work is increasing and I hope I am growing in ability to do it." He closed his diary on New Year's Eve 1869 with "a solem [sic] covenant for a more devoted life in His service for the future."[24]

Goucher's next two years on the circuit followed a similar pattern: preparing for services and Sunday schools, making pastoral visits, leading revivals, and organizing camp meetings. During this time he was ordained a deacon and accepted into full connection with the Baltimore Conference.

For his second ministerial assignment, in March 1872, he was put in charge of his own church at Catonsville, west of Baltimore, where the congregation was made up mainly of merchants, artisans, and clerical workers. In addition, he led a small church named "Thistle," attended by the nearby cotton-mill workers and their families, and he was responsible for Sunday school classes at both churches. But Goucher remembered—and was remembered by—his former parishioners. One leading member wrote, "I am obliged to you for your continued interest in the affairs of the circuit and especially for the disposition you still feel to encourage a camp meeting." Their former minister also continued to receive invitations to participate in church activities, such as a ladies missionary tea fundraiser or a Strawberry Festival, and there even were requests for him to send back some of his homeopathic remedies.[25]

Goucher's life and ministerial career were almost cut short, however, when he suffered sunstroke, and the local doctor thought he would be dead within days. The patient said he "did not care to be boxed up at Catonsville," so he asked to be taken home to Ohio. There, his father sat by his son's bed, and when the physical crisis passed, he smiled and said, "Well, my boy, you are going to get well." Goucher had not expected this outcome, and in his weakened condition, he felt like a physical and spiritual failure. He turned to the wall and began to cry quietly, saying, "Why don't I go now. I'm not fit to stay." He recounted that the Holy Spirit admonished him: "If you are not fit to stay, then you are not ready to die." He realized he was being challenged to do more in his life and replied, "Lord, I am willing to stay." Following a period of recuperation with his brother David, and a visit to his acquaintance Rev. Vincent, who had just staked out the Chautauqua grounds in southwestern New York State, Goucher returned to his ministry at Catonsville. After this experience, he said he was "never a quitter" of anything he undertook.[26]

At this time, the young minister was also studying to become a church elder. When asked in his examination to relate his view on the character of a Christian life, he wrote, "It is a life of purity, obedience, and faith." He also related his feelings about the duties of a minister: "To preach Christ in the pulpit and from house to house by word and deed, to administer the Sacraments and the [Methodist] discipline, instruct the children, and as far as may be, direct the activities and energies of his people in organized efforts for usefulness." These answers seemed to reflect his recommitment to his chosen field after his near-death experience.[27]

Goucher's work on the circuit and at Catonsville laid the foundation for increasing responsibilities and challenges in his assignments to four more churches between 1875 and 1890. Wherever he served, he understood the power of bringing Christians together to share and strengthen their faith. He knew such gatherings—whether in a church or tent meeting—drew in others as well and encouraged them to join the community of believers. But while communal worship was important to Goucher, he believed that Christianity was "not political, but personal, . . . not institutional, but inspirational." He thought the primary object of preaching was to secure a person's salvation, and he saw the pulpit not as an artificial barrier between himself and the congregation, but as a direct means of communicating spiritual truth through one individual to another.[28]

In one sermon, Goucher urged his parishioners to make God not "a Junior Partner in the concerns of life" but rather an integral part of one's daily routine at home, work, and play. He followed this path in his own life. He believed Christianity worked "directly upon the individual and through the individual upon society." As a mid-twentieth-century writer noted about Goucher, "He realized early the value of social principle that in bettering the conditions at the bottom of society, the improvement of the top would take care of itself." And so in his preaching, he encouraged his congregations to support church projects that benefited the unrecognized and underserved in their neighborhoods and in the larger world.[29]

Over the years, those who heard him speak, in or out of church, said he had "a fascinating way of being eloquent without appearing to know it." One of his daughters once observed that "he had the keenest interest in the fine shades of meaning and correct usage" of words, and a "respect for them in everyday conversation." She also remembered:

> There are two little words that will always be associated with him, the word 'love' and the word 'joy.' Love, he never used about a physical thing, but reserved it for those dearest to him, or for the causes and interests which commanded his deepest respect and loyalty. Joy expressed for him only the highest type of blessing, experiences of the spirit.

While Goucher was not considered a "fiery, magnetic speaker," he nevertheless held his audience "by reason and the profundity of his statements." His sermons sometimes lasted an hour or more, which was not unusual at the time. Even after he retired from active ministry, it was said that if Goucher were asked to offer a prayer at a church service, the audience heard two sermons that day.[30]

Prayer was an integral part of his public and private life, and his family said he spoke to God "as to his dear familiar Friend." In later life, he told one of his children, "I don't feel the necessity of getting down on my knees to say prayers for I believe I can truly say that I live in an attitude of prayer." As a boy, he said, he "used to wonder how God finds time to heed all the prayers that rise from earth, every day," but he came to know He was never too busy to listen. Goucher also knew that there were "no prayerless men." As he once told a congregation:

> Strike a man hard enough and unexpectedly enough, and
> unbeliever though he is, his first instinct will be a prayer. A
> poor sort of prayer, doubtless, but as genuine as a groan of
> anguish, and as certain of being heard in Heaven.

One of his favorite prayers was, "Save us from that exhaustion which comes when we starve ourselves of Thee." He himself kept daily devotions—three times a day during the week and five on Sunday—and marked the chapters in his Bible so he could complete reading it once a year.[31]

Goucher understood that a minister's personal life and habits were on daily display along with his religious beliefs. If he wanted his congregation to listen to and act on his message and to hold members' respect, a minister had to mind his behavior outside church as well. Goucher once gave a speech to the Baltimore Conference's Itinerants' Club on how pastors should act:

> In his social intercourse, as in the pulpit, [a minister] should
> be purposeful, true and unaffected, violating no propriety of
> language or deportment, neither stilted nor trifling, neither
> patronizing nor truculent, without an impertinent officialism or
> a pre-occupied indifference, but with an honest and affectionate
> interest in the things which interest the people to whom he
> would minister—approachable and commanding confidence.
> Without assumption or false humility, revealing a living, loving
> soul, fighting the same battles they are fighting and helping
> them win their battles. This will link him and his people with
> bonds of sympathy which will secure the highest appreciation
> and the fullest interpretation of his ministry.

Goucher noted it was equally important that a minister not appear in public with "his linen soiled, or his nails in mourning, or his hair tousled, or his shoes untidy." He also needed to "master his grammar, . . . be careful about his eating, . . . acquire ease in entering and exiting a room, . . . and never neglect to make courteous recognition of hospitality." He had seen seemingly qualified men lose pulpits by ignoring these considerations, and, more importantly, possibly lose "souls for [their] Master."[32]

As he progressed from pulpit to pulpit—usually every three years—Goucher also began to serve on or interact with many Baltimore Conference committees. As his friend Bishop Earl Cranston later noted about him, "A thoughtful boy, he became a thinking man." Increasingly he began to be known by the religious and lay leaders within the Baltimore Conference for thoroughness and a willingness to tackle any job. In the first years of his ministry, he assumed the mundane task of delivering mail to attendees during the annual meetings. Later he was called on to use his mathematical skills to gather statistics for reports, and served several times as treasurer of the Sunday School Union. He became involved with the local branch of the Freedman's Aid Society, which provided previously denied educational opportunities to African Americans, and with the Women's Foreign Missionary Society (WFMS), which began sponsoring projects for women and girls in India, China, and Japan. He also served on the Committee on Seminaries, whose members examined Methodist-sponsored schools within the conference. From each of these connections he gained knowledge about the many facets of the Methodist Episcopal Church's outreach, especially in the areas of education and missions. He began formulating his own ideas on how to address their needs.[33]

Goucher's career and accomplishments might have taken a different path, however, if he had not met the woman who shared his passion for God's work. With her love, support, and financial resources, he was able to fulfill his varied "commissions" in far-flung and long-lasting enterprises around the world.

Mary Cecilia Fisher
(c. 1870)

Courtesy of the Goucher College Library,
Special Collections and Archives, Baltimore, Maryland

THE PARTNER
OF HIS HEART

Chapter 3
(1869-1890)

————————◆◆◆————————

*The home life is the heart life and in the home the strength and
beauty of one's character find their unconventional expression.*[1]

Having grown up in a loving family, John Goucher naturally
wanted the joys of sharing a home with a wife and children of his
own. In college, his intelligence, good looks, and attentive manner had
made him popular with the young women of Carlisle and their parents.
When illness forced him to suspend his studies, his classmates noted
that his absences were "severely felt by the ladies," even though his
friends tried their best to replace him. When he revisited Dickinson
after graduation, he continued to field numerous invitations to teas,
dinners, and musical evenings. Joining the Baltimore Conference
and beginning his job on the circuit, he developed a new circle of
acquaintances and soon found "the partner of his heart."[2]

Within days of arriving at his new post, the young minister was
introduced to Mary Cecilia Fisher, who lived at Alto Dale, an estate not
far from the Turners' property. She was a member of his congregation
at Stone Chapel, a small neoclassical-style church built partially on
land her father had donated and accessible via a path from the Fishers'
home. Theirs was not a whirlwind courtship—it was eight years
before they married—but as one news article noted about the couple
many years later, "Surely so perfect a complement each of the other
with such responsibilities could not have had its roots in chance or
causeless coincidence. What seems like romance in human relations is
sometimes God making history and destiny."[3]

The couple's first meeting was not very romantic, however. A
few days before, Goucher had departed Baltimore on the Western

Maryland Railroad, traveling to Reisterstown to begin his ministerial duties. He arrived safely three hours later, but his trunk and valise had remained on the train and were left sitting on the platform at the next station. Minus fresh clothes and toiletries, the normally fastidious young preacher had to lead a prayer meeting that evening, where he met his first parishioners and spent the night with one of them. The next day, he found his trunk at the station, but someone had stolen the carpetbag containing $150 worth of clothes, his books and notes for sermons, and some photographs. Uncertain if it would be found, he borrowed a horse from another member of the congregation and rode to his new home at the Turners. He had to prepare to preach twice that Sunday using only the Bible in his room and paper and pencil borrowed from Sister Turner.[4]

Early on Monday, March 22, 1869, Goucher rode the nine miles from Pikesville back to Reisterstown after receiving word that a farmer had found a valise "broken open and lying in the road." It indeed was his and nothing was missing except some new socks, handkerchiefs, and underwear. The news of the lost case had traveled quickly through the church community over the weekend, and when he returned to the Turner home that evening, he found that the women attending a tea party in honor of Mary Fisher's birthday "had just agreed to meet and sew to refit me with linen and underwear." Picturing the members of his new congregation—including the attractive, nineteen-year-old Mary—working on such personal apparel must have made him uncomfortable, for he wrote in his diary, "Their kindness will not be tested so far." But this gathering made a great impression on him in another way, for he recorded on a small card he kept throughout his life: "Met Miss M. C. Fisher at Mr. J. L. Turner's. A birthday party."[5]

One of Goucher's first visits as a minister was to Alto Dale to meet Dr. John Fisher, Mary's father. He described the doctor "as fine a Christian character I think as I have ever met, wealthy but very pious and devout," noting that "he spends his time and money in the service of God." Fisher's family ties to the Methodist Episcopal Church went back to his grandfather, who had been a class leader of the Lovely Lane Society in Baltimore in the late eighteenth century as the church was organizing in America. Dr. Fisher himself had helped establish the first Methodist Sunday school in Cecil County, Maryland, where he had lived as a young man, and he was a leader at Stone Chapel.[6]

Descended from an Edinburgh-trained physician who had emigrated to Maryland in the late seventeenth century, John Fisher received a medical degree from the University of Maryland in 1824, and he practiced for many years in Cecil County. His older brother Alexander owned a successful mercantile business in Baltimore City, and when he died suddenly in 1853, he left his fortune and a recently purchased Baltimore County property to John and another brother, William. John bought out William's half of the site and named it Alto Dale. He tore down the existing frame dwelling and built a large stone and stucco-covered house for the family—his wife Sarah Elizabeth and son John, both of whom died soon after the move, and two daughters, Mary and Isabella, known as Belle. In this new location of nearly 300 acres, he gave up practicing medicine and became a "gentleman farmer." According to minutes of the Baltimore Annual Conference, both clergy and laymen acknowledged that Dr. Fisher's "clear judgment, gentle spirit, and unassuming manner rendered him a counselor often sought in neighborhood and [Methodist] conference perplexities."[7]

As the new man on the circuit, Goucher looked to Dr. Fisher for advice and assistance on matters critical to his success. He especially asked for help with those important introductions and visits with parishioners, so difficult for him at first. Soon the young minister became a frequent visitor to Alto Dale—for an early morning breakfast meeting, to plan for the upcoming camp meeting, to share tea or dinner, or even to spend the night after a late evening's church work. Dr. Fisher surely was helpful, but the appearance of Mary, who served as hostess for her widowed father, undoubtedly was an added incentive. Within six weeks of first meeting Dr. Fisher, Goucher recorded calling at Alto Dale three times in one day.[8]

It was not surprising that Mary Fisher stood out from other young women Goucher had known or courted. She was attractive, with auburn hair and a serene smile, and at barely five feet tall, was well matched to John's short stature. Despite her wealth, she preferred simple, modest dress, which later made even the poorest of her husband's parishioners comfortable around her. A slight limp from a childhood illness had not kept her from an active life, just as John had pushed himself to overcome his physical problems. Mary's mother died when she was nine, and friends said that she "was early called upon to preside over her father's house and to care for others who felt dependence on her," including sister Belle, two years younger. Like Goucher, Mary had developed a seriousness and sense of responsibility beyond her years. Along with physical beauty, she was known for her "grace, vivacity, brightness of intellect, and refinement," attributes that captured the attention of this eligible bachelor.[9]

While most girls and young women of the mid-nineteenth century were afforded only a rudimentary education, Mary had home tutors as a child and then graduated in 1867 from the fashionable Edgeworth School for Young Ladies, located in Mount Vernon Place near the Washington Monument in Baltimore. The curriculum included literature, history, fine arts, and scientific studies, which she continued to pursue in adulthood. While still a young girl, she traveled with her father to Rome, developing a life-long interest in travel, and it was said she spoke and read French as easily as English. She also relished playing anagrams and word games, which complemented Goucher's enjoyment of puns and his love of language and of finding just the right words for his talks and sermons. She was well suited to the young minister in intelligence and demeanor, curiosity and good humor.[10]

A spiritual connection also became central to Mary and John's relationship and eventual marriage. Mary had made a personal commitment of faith and joined the Methodist Episcopal Church the year after her graduation. She was known as "deeply and affectionately interested in everything that pertained to the life and activity of the church . . . and amid whose institutions she had been reared." Mary was already teaching Sunday school at Stone Chapel when she met John. Experienced with such teaching himself, he was impressed with her abilities and noted, "If there were more such teachers as Miss Fisher there would be more conversions." Lesson planning and visitations to Sunday school classes gave the couple a common purpose and extra reasons to meet. One of Goucher's diary entries suggests Mary's growing influence: A few months after meeting her he wrote, "For the past week I have had strong or rather peculiar thoughts and feelings as if there were about to be a change of some kind in my life."[11]

Dr. Fisher soon accepted that Goucher was more to Mary—and to him—than simply their local preacher. The itinerant Goucher made Alto Dale a second home, and he even took an interest in how the estate's farm was run. A Western visitor at this time recalled how John was included as part of the family: After being met at the train by Mary, the man and his wife were driven to "an old-time columned mansion, where we were welcomed by the venerable Doctor [Fisher] himself, and a beautiful, open-faced young preacher, the junior on the 'circuit.' This was 'brother Goucher.'"[12]

By the time John completed his tenure on the circuit and received his next assignment in 1872 to Catonsville, nine miles from Alto Dale, he and Mary had known each other three years. He was hesitant to ask her to give up the comforts of her longtime home for the uncertainties of being a preacher's wife and living on his annual salary. However, after his move to Baltimore's Huntingdon Avenue Church in 1875, and with $1000 per year in income, Goucher finally approached Dr. Fisher for permission to marry his daughter.

While he was fond of the young man and knew of his daughter's feelings for him, John Fisher was also a prudent and protective parent. Mary's considerable wealth, which she one day would inherit from her father and bachelor uncle, might attract frivolous suitors. When asked if he were after Mary's fortune, Goucher presciently replied, "I want her for her own sake. But I think I could do a great deal of good with the money too." Dr. Fisher gave his consent, and the couple became engaged as John was turning thirty and Mary was twenty-five. Another sign of Dr. Fisher's approval was that after the engagement, he designated his daughter's future husband as a beneficiary in his will, providing an annual annuity for him should Mary die after their marriage and before her father.[13]

The couple intended to marry in February 1878, just before Goucher's next ministerial assignment. But the wedding date was moved up owing to the sudden death of John Fisher three days before Christmas 1877. Amidst this sadness, but with family and friends close at hand, they decided to marry after the funeral and burial. On Christmas Eve, John and Mary said their vows in a simple ceremony at Alto Dale, performed by Goucher's friend, Rev. Lyttleton Morgan. Instead of exchanging rings, they had cut a twenty-dollar gold coin in half the night before the wedding, and each wore a piece on a neck chain throughout their marriage.[14]

A year later, Goucher wrote to his father with good news—the doctor was going to be a grandfather. The elder Goucher replied that he was very pleased with this "intelligence of most importance to my dear Mary, to my good boy, to myself, and to the world." John also told his father that Mary suffered from morning sickness and asked for a homeopathic cure. The doctor sent directions for two concoctions, which he knew John was capable of mixing and administering as needed. John and Mary's daughter, named Eleanor for Goucher's mother, was born in September 1879, and her grandfather was at Alto Dale with the parents to welcome her into the world. An acquaintance who visited the Goucher household after the baby arrived described John and Mary's joy:

> My visit [with you] had been such a refreshment to me, the sunshine of your home was so bright—and it was so easy to see, that to both father and mother the child was the very light of their eyes.

But deaths among infants were then far too common, and the baby lived barely more than five months. In a letter of sympathy, the same acquaintance wrote of the anguish that Eleanor's death brought her parents:

> I am writing to both of you upon whom so terrible a grief has suddenly come. I cannot tell you how sharp was the pang that went through my heart, when I read of the death of your little child. How hard is it to understand—you, to whom fatherhood and motherhood meant so much, who were so pre-eminently fitted to guide the slip of a little child—that you should sit with empty arms and aching hearts.[15]

Goucher wrote of his deep sadness to Charles Himes, a Dickinson friend, who also had a baby daughter: "No one knows how dear a new life can be but those to whom the treasure has been committed." But he also expressed the strength his faith gave him to go on: "The blow was sudden and severe but not without its ministry of love and blessing."[16]

Mary was already expecting their second child when Eleanor died. Another daughter, Janet, was born in October 1880, with her grandfather Goucher, "waiting the advent of an heir," again on hand. Since his other three children were childless, it's likely he hoped John might have a son to carry on the Goucher name. Nevertheless, all the family rejoiced with the arrival of another girl. In writing to a friend after Janet's birth, Mary admitted the ongoing pain of losing "our little one who is gone." But she proudly added, "Our baby is doing well — eating and sleeping being her whole life. . . . As these are all that is expected of a young lady three weeks old, we have voted her a good baby."[17]

A third daughter, whom they also named Eleanor, arrived a year and a half later. Elizabeth was born the following year, in the spring of 1883. Ella, Goucher's sister, wrote with congratulations, hoping Elizabeth was "as good as baby Eleanor was on her arrival and so let her dear parents rest comparatively undisturbed." She also wondered how they were managing sleeping arrangements with three children under the age of three. "Another crib?" she asked. "After a while you can have a row arranged on one side of your room." These close deliveries, occurring as the couple moved twice to John's new pastorates, took a toll on Mary's already fragile physical condition. After Elizabeth's birth, she had no appetite for food and her weakened leg was affected. Ella wrote to Mary, whom she called her "precious sister": "It is a great trial to be deprived of the use of your come-alongs," borrowing a term an acquaintance used for his legs, and she expressed hope that "yours will soon be strong and vigorous."[18]

Their last child, named for her mother, was born four years later. Goucher wrote the details of baby Mary's birth on another pocket-size card, a traditional place for recording important events in his life. He noted that she was born at the parsonage of First Church, where he was then minister, "in the room over the dining room, Saturday morning 6:45 o'clock, March 5, 1887." A friend sent congratulations and wrote, "To possess four such daughters is rare good fortune." Mary Goucher was again affected by the delivery, and a friend urged her "to have a long rest without a thought or care." Neither mother nor father, however, had such a respite. There must have been early problems with the child's health because within two weeks of her birth, Goucher added to his card, "[God] is trying me and He is giving me grace." Four months later, baby Mary was laid to rest beside her sister and Fisher grandparents in Baltimore's Greenmount Cemetery.[19]

In one of his sermons, Goucher said that "home is given to us as a kind of Heaven," and John and Mary, who doted on their daughters, created such a haven. Whatever their other responsibilities, the couple kept their family and their mutual deep faith in God at the center of their lives. Before breakfast each morning the family gathered to read scripture, knelt and held hands as they prayed together. The affectionate adults were often seen holding hands at other times. Goucher believed a wife was the heart and head of the household—"the determining factor in the moral, esthetic, and social atmosphere of the home." He fondly acknowledged that Mary was his "better two-thirds," and acquaintances praised her ability to charm "strangers into friends" and turn "friends to devotees."[20]

During the first dozen years of their marriage, while Goucher remained in the pastoral ministry, they made their home in whatever parsonage or rented house came with the position. But the family also spent a great deal of time at Alto Dale, which they had acquired on the death of Mary's father. This estate remained a comfortable and secure refuge as their lives grew increasingly busy. In 1883, thirty years after his father-in-law had acquired the property, Goucher remodeled the house, adding another floor and a four-story tower. It now had nineteen rooms, including his large paneled study, so there was ample space for family as well as frequent guests. Mary's unmarried sister Belle continued to live with them until her death in 1890, and at times, visitors might have been mistaken for permanent residents. A distant cousin of Mary's, an invalid and a "high church Episcopalian daughter of a priest," came to stay with them each summer. Enjoying the pleasant surroundings, she forgave the couple's Methodist beliefs and admitted that by some miracle, God would assure them a place in heaven.[21]

Despite their wealth and the size of the house, the Gouchers preferred living simply and employed only a few servants: a cook; a butler, whom Mary trained to serve meals; an upstairs maid to make beds and clean; and a driver, in charge of the carriages. A local woman stayed with the Gouchers to help care for Belle, and she also made clothes for the three little girls. Wherever the family lived, Elizabeth Goucher said, her father liked to consider his home as "'Liberty Hall' in distinction from houses where formality or ostentation lurked."[22]

When they were staying at Alto Dale in the 1880s, Goucher traveled by horse or buggy the nearly twenty-five miles to his work in the city and back. His purchase of his early mount Pet had worked out, so he did not hesitate to buy a carriage horse when needed. One that he bought, however, would stop at every bar as he drove to town. (Goucher later learned that the previous owner had been a drinker with a regular circuit of his own). Attempts to retrain the animal proved difficult, and it embarrassed this Methodist teetotaler to be seen stopping at such establishments, even if he never entered.[23]

Goucher had savored his boyhood experiences on his uncle's farm, and he encouraged his daughters, whom he affectionately nicknamed Bairn (Janet), Maidie (Eleanor), and Lassie (Elizabeth), to explore the barns, orchards, and streams at Alto Dale. Until they were five or six, the girls usually wore white, and their parents let them go barefoot to keep them hardy. Their mother said the trio lived outdoors as much as possible, where they "made the acquaintance of other inhabitants of the woods and fields."[24]

Next to the main house, their father built them a one-and-a-half-story playhouse. Named "Cricket," the twenty-square-foot building had four rooms filled with miniature furniture, many pieces of which had been in the Fisher family for generations. The girls gathered a host of dolls to take up residence, watched over by a "cook" named Aunt Polly. A favorite pastime was to invite their parents and even house guests to join them for a meal they prepared on the little household's small black stove. A visitor's fond description of the girls gave an inkling of the carefree life John and Mary provided their daughters at Alto Dale: "I see those dear little children now, hopping along or stepping softly with their little bare feet through the wide airy hall." Another family friend always affectionately called them "the three fairies" for their ethereal demeanor.[25]

John and Mary enjoyed life at Alto Dale as much as their daughters did. Goucher loved the land and was a good steward of his farm, which he was credited with managing "in a most businesslike and systematic manner." He liked to spend time walking around the property and was a familiar sight to his tenant farmers. Carrying a long wooden staff and dressed in a suit—white in summer and darker shades in other seasons—he regularly checked on the bounteous crops and orchards and the state of his animals, including milk cows and pigs that provided sausage and spare ribs for his table.[26]

Always eager to learn new things, Goucher studied ways to improve agricultural yields. An article in *Hoard's Dairyman*, a national dairy publication, made mention of his plan to increase the output of his ten cows. In the previous year, each had produced enough milk to make 300 pounds of butter; for the following year, his goal was to increase that total to 360. The story, mentioned in *Zion's Herald*, found a minister running a successful small farm to be something of a curiosity: "Evidently the reverend gentleman is a good dairyman as well as a good shepherd of souls." Goucher must have been considered an expert in dealing with horses as well, as a missionary wrote asking him for "kind hints on 'how to break a pony'" so as not to spoil its gait for the saddle.[27]

The couple took care to make the grounds at Alto Dale as attractive and welcoming as the house. Mary grew flowers, especially her favorite roses, and her husband ordered persimmon, peach, and other trees from a contact in Japan. A later Japanese purchase included maple trees, chrysanthemum roots, a rare hydrangea bush, and morning glory seeds. Paths were lined with boxwood hedges and decorated with statuary. In time, the greenery at Alto Dale became infused with historic connections. On one visit to England, Goucher obtained ivy cuttings from the grave of Methodist founder John Wesley, and planted them under a shade tree where they quickly spread.[28]

Alto Dale was an idyllic setting for celebrations, and the Fourth of July was a highlight of the summer for the family. As a great-grandson of Revolutionary War participants, Goucher made certain the American flag flew from the house's tower. Mary, who depended on a cook for meals, always baked a special lemon-flavored sponge cake for the Fourth, as well as for John's birthday in June. He enjoyed the camaraderie and noisy excitement of the festivities, as the tenant farmers and their families joined the Gouchers and their house guests in setting off fireworks. Elizabeth Goucher recalled one such occasion: "As the enthusiasm of the day waxed more and more daring in exploits with the then new heavier fire crackers, a large galvanized corrugated ash tin was blown into the air to land flat as a pancake." One guest, a Methodist bishop, found an empty apple barrel, and after lighting a trail of fuses attached to fire crackers underneath, he sat on top. Both he and the barrel were blown several inches into the air. Her father and the family, Elizabeth said, always considered that particular holiday "the triumph of Fourths of July."[29]

One visitor noted, "So genuine is [the Gouchers'] welcome that you feel a sort of joint ownership in the surroundings." A missionary's wife wistfully summarized the appeal that Alto Dale held for family and guests alike. On her return to hot and dusty North India after a furlough, she wrote to Mary:

> I do not forget an item connected with our sweet visit. The barn, the old spring house in the pasture, where we went to drink milk, the church on the hill [Stone Chapel], the rolling fields and meadows, the lively house with its stars and stripes floating from the tower, the flowers, the green house with its beautiful plants, the strawberries. Oh! The strawberries. Is it not a lovely place to live?[30]

Goucher enjoyed such a pleasant lifestyle, some people thought he might abandon his vocation after marriage. As one Baltimorean commented: "When a considerable fortune came under his control I supposed he would get preacher's sore throat or some other convenient ailment and retire from the itinerancy and spend the rest of his days in dignified leisure. But instead he bowed his shoulders to the burden and worked on harder than before." Mary was in complete sympathy with her husband's plans to undertake a wide range of local, national, and international projects to promote the ministry, missions, and education. She and John became active partners in deciding how her inherited wealth—said to be over one million dollars (approximately $25 million)—could do the most good. *[Note: Monetary values, here and in future chapters, have been converted to 2014 dollars, and appear in parentheses after the original figures.]*[31]

Goucher's philosophy of philanthropy was: "The only way to get anything *out* of money is by using it; and the way to get the *most* out of money is by dedicating it to God." When each new year began, the couple sat down together to determine where to direct their largess over the coming months, and how much to donate to various causes. As a friend later observed, they "planned in faith, they planted in continents." Their generosity included Goucher's own home ministry. After his marriage, Goucher declined to take a salary from any of his posts, and through both fundraising and personal financial support, he built three major Methodist churches in Baltimore in less than ten years. This trio of buildings—along with scores of new churches constructed on the American frontier and in other countries through the Gouchers' donations—garnered for him the title "builder of churches."[32]

1773.   1887.

DEDICATION

OF THE NEW

First Methodist Episcopal Church,

Baltimore City Station,

St. Paul and Third Streets,

Sunday, November Sixth, 1887.

JOHN F. GOUCHER,   -   -   Preacher in Charge.

EDWARD L. WATSON,
CHAS. D. SMITH,   Junior Preachers.
JOHN M. SLARROW,

Courtesy of the Baltimore-Washington Conference Archives,
Lovely Lane United Methodist Church, Baltimore, Maryland

CHURCH BUILDER IN BALTIMORE

Chapter 4
(1869-1890)

───────◆◆───────

Methodism is rich in ministries, both personal and organized.[1]

Goucher first became familiar with building churches during his years as a junior preacher. While helping oversee construction at several locations on the Baltimore Circuit, he absorbed critical lessons. He became adept at working with varied personalities within a congregation and assisting with necessary fundraising. He learned how to keep a congregation interested and intact as it met at an alternate site during construction. Perhaps most importantly, he learned that a minister's strong leadership and organization were needed to keep a project on track and moving forward. The young minister saw the difficulties caused by delays at one of the churches and in his diary expressed his impatience at the slow progress: "There has been talk and trouble enough about the church so far to build two or three churches, growing, in great part, out of the extreme cautiousness of some members." Goucher determined early in his career there would be no such delays in any construction projects he led as minister.[2]

After serving three-year appointments at Catonsville and Baltimore's Huntington Avenue Methodist Episcopal Church, just north of the city line, Goucher had his first chance to test this resolve. In March 1878, a few months after his marriage, he received his fourth assignment from the Baltimore Conference, this time to the Gilmor Street Church, located downtown on the city's west side. He described the church, of which he was only the second pastor, as "a frame house with an L on the north rear. On piers, open below and <u>cold</u>. High bank in front and colored people all around." During this period, it was not unusual for working class whites and blacks in Baltimore to live near each other, with whites living on the main streets and blacks living in housing on the alleys in between. Goucher was comfortable working and living in this racially mixed neighborhood.[3]

In the same description he recorded the difficulties he had to address at the church:

> When I went, the house was uncomfortable, there was debt on it. They owed some ground rent—on ground for which they could not get a title. And had a note of $400 out on previous pastor's salary. The people were not organized nor was there any homogeneity among them. They had been brought together by a tent meeting and much of the material was light.

Goucher set out to change the situation. Membership increased so much during his first year as minister, the frame house became even more inadequate as a place of worship. He sold the building to a local African-American congregation and led a small group of members to buy a lot further north on Gilmor Street, facing Harlem Park. This city-owned, two-block square included walkways and a pagoda, springhouse, and fountain, and the park sparked construction of dozens of new houses in the neighborhood. Goucher knew this boom would lead to an increased demand for services such as schools and churches within walking distance of these houses, and he purchased some property nearby as a personal investment.[4]

Goucher quickly organized a Building Committee and made plans to erect a substantial stone chapel on the new site. With Mary's help, he involved the women of the congregation in raising funds for its furnishings. Their projects included "personal entertainments," a "junk shop," and a "Potato Supper and Parlor Sociable—Light Eaters 25 cents, Hearty Feeders 50 cents." This last event, held at the parsonage a few blocks from the church, took place just days before the Gouchers' baby Eleanor died. Despite his grief, Goucher pushed on to complete the building in June 1880. When the chapel was dedicated, some debt remained, but during Sunday morning and evening services, Goucher urged the congregation to open the renamed Harlem Park Methodist Episcopal Church with a clean financial slate. Gifts ranging from a few dollars to $200 were pledged, and by the end of the day, the debt was covered. By the time Goucher left his appointment the following

March, three years after his arrival, church membership had nearly doubled.[5]

Goucher was similarly motivated at his next assignment to the Strawbridge Methodist Episcopal Church, then part of the larger Howard Street Station. When he became minister of this 300-member congregation in Spring 1881, Goucher recognized that maintaining the status quo would mean the eventual demise of the church, for the area was becoming increasingly commercial as the city grew northward. A more promising location was needed. He tackled the issue directly in his first sermon, entitled "Rise Up and Build," even though he knew there was a risk some parishioners living near the church might not travel to its new location.[6]

Goucher was not one to look backward or waver once he had developed a plan. He proposed building a new church further north on donated land, and to spur the project on, he and Mary offered the congregation $18,000 ($430,000) to begin construction. Like the Gilmor Street Church, the old one was sold to an African-American congregation; while the new church was being built, Goucher held services in a tent on an adjacent lot. By New Year's Eve, nine months after he was assigned to Strawbridge, he and his congregation welcomed the year 1882 with a Watch Night service in the finished chapel. The granite church itself, called "an ornament to the quarter of the city where it stands," was dedicated six months later, free of debt, and its name amended to Strawbridge Station in the City of Baltimore. As Goucher surmised, a third of the congregation did not follow him to the new location, but his long-term thinking proved justified: The church served generations of parishioners until closing for services in 2009.[7]

Goucher's greatest challenge in church building still stands as testimony to his personal faith, diplomacy, energy, and creativity: Lovely Lane United Methodist Church. His association with the congregation began in March 1883, when after only two years at Strawbridge, he became pastor of the First Methodist Episcopal Church, then at the corner of Charles and Fayette Streets in the heart of downtown Baltimore. He faced a congregation divided on both its future and his selection as minister.

First Church had the distinction of being considered the direct descendant of the Lovely Lane Meeting House, where the Methodist Episcopal Church was first organized in America at the 1784 Christmas Conference in Baltimore. The rapid growth of Methodist adherents in the city caused the church to move to larger quarters two years later, when it was renamed Light Street Church to reflect its new location. After a fire a decade later, it reopened across the street and became known as "a center not merely of the mother church of Baltimore," but also "provided a central rallying place for Methodists of the country." Also called Baltimore City Station, the Light Street Church prompted the creation of other Methodist congregations in the city, including a group that established the Charles Street Methodist Episcopal Church.[8]

The Light Street Church occupied the same location for more than seventy years, until the city condemned the site to make way for downtown's rapid commercial development following the Civil War. The Charles Street Church was also increasingly surrounded by businesses, and parishioners began moving north to more fashionable areas. The needs of both congregations were met when the Charles Street members sold their church to Light Street's in 1869, and the former built a large Gothic Revival stone church on Mount Vernon Place, facing Baltimore's Washington Monument. With the razing of the Light Street Church and its congregation's move to the vacated Charles Street structure, its name was no longer appropriate. Since it traced its roots to the original chapel on Lovely Lane, its members chose to call it First Methodist Episcopal Church.[9]

It was not long, however, before membership at First Church began to decline as the area's demographics changed. Sunday school classes were suspended because of poor attendance. The congregation was also deeply in debt. By the time the city wanted to buy the church property in order to widen Fayette Street, the once-thriving congregation was facing severe losses of both human and financial capital.

Yet there were severe divisions among those with the power to decide what course of action to follow. While the church building was to be razed, the congregation still retained the neighboring Sunday school property. Some members felt they could make a new start by building on that site, using funds from the sale of the church; others suggested merging with another Methodist congregation, possibly one in Baltimore County. Those who wanted to remain near the current location raised the legal argument that the church was incorporated "in the city or precincts of Baltimore" and could not move beyond the city limits.[10]

In the midst of this turmoil, the Board of Trustees of First Church asked Bishop Henry W. Warren not to renew the annual appointment of the serving minister, and to bring in someone who could provide new leadership, act decisively, and resolve the conflicts. Five candidates were considered, and Goucher received the majority of trustee votes. Nevertheless, those opposed to moving circulated a petition to block his appointment. Knowing his reputation for moving the Gilmor and Strawbridge congregations to new locations, they feared he would favor selling the property and building a new church elsewhere—a fear that proved justified.[11]

Lewis H. Cole, secretary of the board, wrote Goucher at the beginning of March 1883, urging him to cut short his assignment at Strawbridge and become pastor at First Church, despite the petition. Speaking for the majority, he listed both the personal and professional characteristics that trustees felt made the thirty-seven-year-old minister "just suited for this work":

> 1. Because you are calm, patient, and courteous to a degree far beyond that of the average Christian man in your intercourse and discussions with those who differ from you.
>
> 2. Because you have considerable experience in directing the location and building of churches, which would be worth thousands of dollars to us in our new enterprise.
>
> 3. Because of your well-known interest in all that pertains to our common Methodism in Baltimore, and your skill in giving direction and shape to realize the advancement of these interests.

Cole appealed to Goucher's commitment to expand the kingdom of God wherever and however possible and added: "What I have said here of a personal character is no flattery, nor is it written to influence you, as I am sure you could not be influenced by mere personal consideration. The cause is what you want to serve, and for the sake of the cause, we want you."[12]

When Bishop Warren appointed Goucher to First Church, he accepted. He was already involved with the Baltimore Conference's plans for the centennial of American Methodism in 1884, and he knew that Methodists around the country were beginning to look to Baltimore and First Church, with its historic connection to the Lovely Lane Meeting House. What better time to begin a new "Monumental Methodist Episcopal Church"?

As an attempt to calm divisions, the Board of Trustees accepted a recommendation to postpone any decision on moving and building for three months. Before the time was up, however, Goucher had met with several leading members and solicited not only their opinions of a proposed move but also the first donations toward a new building. By July 1883, he called a meeting of the congregation's male members to vote on resolutions to allow the trustees to sell the downtown property and purchase a new site for a church, Sunday school, and parsonage. He also received approval for a six-member Building Committee to contract and build, as appropriate, to serve the needs of the congregation.

Another resolution, a supposed olive branch to those who feared a move to the county, directed the Building Committee to select a site that would accommodate a majority of the congregation and observe the perceived charter mandate to remain in the city or its precincts. But even as this last recommendation was being voted on, Goucher and other trustees were considering a plot of land in Baltimore County known as "the Belt," three blocks north of Boundary (now North) Avenue, then the city line. After a bridge had been built over the Jones Falls waterway in 1875, the land beyond became ripe for development. When Goucher was pastor at nearby Huntingdon Avenue Church in the years before his marriage, there were only a few dozen buildings in the area, but he had seen the potential in this largely open land and had kept it in mind.[13]

The lot Goucher was considering was on the corner of St. Paul Street Extended and Brown Street (now 22nd Street). In August, he negotiated a long-term lease for the property, which was purchased seven years later. The following month, he bought the first of several adjoining lots for his personal portfolio, much as he had done in the Harlem Park neighborhood. The proposed church site brought renewed legal challenges and petitions from some members, but the church's lawyer interpreted the word "precincts" to include "environs" or "suburbs" of Baltimore, and the Building Committee moved ahead with the project, despite the opposition calling it "Goucher's Folly." Even a Goucher friend, who did not share the minister's vision, asked him why he planned to build "a cathedral in a cornfield."[14]

A late twentieth-century note on the area's designation in the National Register of Historic Places confirms Goucher's foresight in locating First Church in this location:

> This was an important period of explosive urban expansion
> of Baltimore City northward. During the last two decades of
> the nineteenth century, the district was transformed from open
> country land to a densely built urban area containing elegant
> residences of architectural merit constructed for the new
> upper, middle classes, wealthy from Baltimore's prosperous
> nineteenth-century commerce.

The area's population doubled from 1880 to 1890 as the church was being built, and those living in this new district wanted to attend services nearby. Goucher and First Church were able to answer that growing demand.[15]

Along with his pastoral duties and trying to rebuild the Sunday school, Goucher chaired the Building Committee, leading more than forty-six meetings from his arrival in 1883 until 1887. That position had its advantages: He often formulated plans and made decisions on his own before meetings and then sought agreement later. The committee held its first meeting in early August 1883 to discuss what features and materials they wanted in the church, but Goucher had already been in contact with architect Stanford White, of the New York firm McKim, Mead and White, about fees. That four-year-old partnership had never designed a church, but the minister knew the firm's work on several prominent Baltimore homes. Goucher was not intimidated by the design process, having interacted with architects on previous church-building projects. Architect David Wright, who in the late 1970s wrote a historical study of Lovely Lane United Methodist

Church and its construction in preparation for its future restoration, notes: "What Goucher may have seen in the New York firm was a degree of cosmopolitan and firsthand understanding of European architectural precedent unavailable locally." Indeed, Goucher had absorbed ideas for features for the new church during a continental tour with a friend in the summer of 1877. He was ready and eager to share his thoughts with White, who had traveled to Europe the following year.[16]

The Building Committee approved the firm's making preliminary drawings, and White, not yet thirty, became the lead architect. As Wright notes, Goucher and White both "loved life and people," but had very different personalities. The minister was urbane, educated, and reserved, while the architect was animated and had a "spark." Yet he adds, "The contrasting personalities must have complimented and reinforced one another."[17]

A letter from White to Goucher illustrates how each played to his strengths during the building process. Goucher had asked White to prepare a paper describing the project's overall design philosophy to the public. The architect did so, but made it clear to Goucher he preferred a different division of labor:

> I do not think writing descriptions of anything—much less of our work—is my forte. I send you the unhappy result of my attempt with a stenographer. . . . You, of course, are the proper one to write this [piece]. . . . I am at your service in anything I can do, but for Heaven's sake, don't ask me to endeavor to further evolve any more literature.[18]

Goucher was not as averse to stepping into the architectural realm as White was to writing about the edifice that also became known as "White's Baby." When the early drawings were in hand, Goucher came back to the Building Committee with his preferred floor plans for the chapel and Sunday school rooms. On motion of the members, "Bro. Goucher's plan was substituted for that part of the plan proposed by the architects." Over the next few months, McKim, Mead and White submitted more detailed drawings, and while the Building Committee continued to examine them, meeting minutes noted that "various suggestions made by the pastor were approved" to be incorporated as well. At the committee's request, Goucher traveled to the architects' New York office several times so he could "acquaint them with the desired changes" in person. The minister later became as involved with furnishings and finishes as he had with the structural design— from examining samples of bentwood chairs for the Sunday school rooms to helping select the company to build the organ.[19]

Even before final drawings were complete, Goucher made certain the project remained visible to his congregation, still attending services downtown, by organizing a groundbreaking ceremony in November 1883. But resistance to the move continued, and a fellow Building Committee member later complained to the minister about opposition "sometimes coming from those who should have given words of cheer instead of impeding your onward march." At the ceremony, however, the slightly built but determined Goucher struck the ground with twelve strokes of a pick ax and shoveled the dirt into a nearby cart. No one doubted his resolve to move forward.[20]

Excavation was underway by the following March, just a year after Goucher became minister at First Church. Construction difficulties arose, but he continued to display a take-charge attitude. When he found out that the ground in the area of the nearly 200-foot tower appeared to be "spongy" when dry and "soft and slushy" when wet, making it inadequate to support the heavy structure, he called in a civil engineer to address the problem. At the next Building Committee meeting, Goucher notified members of the difficulty and then presented the engineer's plan for approval and implementation.[21]

After the groundbreaking, Goucher and the Building Committee marked other milestones. The cornerstone, inscribed with the date 1884 to mark the centennial of Methodism, was laid that fall. By December 1885, the small congregation finally moved from downtown and dedicated the completed chapel. Members of Goucher's former Huntingdon Avenue Church decided to merge with First Church, swelling attendance. Lewis Cole, who had encouraged Goucher to accept the position as minister, wrote praising his dual role: "You are greatly beloved by your people and they request you to be not only their leader in completion of the church building, but they believe you to be above all others known to them better suited for the spiritual upbuilding of this great enterprise."[22]

Work progressed on the auditorium, as the main sanctuary was called, and on the attached parsonage where John and Mary and their daughters were to live. While awaiting its completion, Goucher made a trip Italy in early 1886, with Mary accompanying him, to examine Methodist missions there on behalf of the Missionary Society in New York. As if building churches in Baltimore were not enough, he pledged funds to the resident missionary in Rome to build a much-needed Methodist chapel in a country dominated by Catholicism. While in the city, Goucher had seen an antique altar he considered adding to the couple's collection, but he related that he and Mary had decided "rather than take away an altar with us, to leave one in Italy." As in his home town, he became involved with the purchase of land and the architectural plans for a church, this one to be built in Pontedera, near Pisa.[23]

While White was acknowledged as First Church's architect, a Baltimore newspaper credited Goucher's influence on the final design: "The many interesting features of detail are due to the thought and observation of Dr. Goucher, who . . . gleaned many ideas and suggestions from the celebrated cathedrals of the Old World." He especially influenced two important features in the auditorium that remain attractions to the church. For the main floor, he proposed installing stained glass windows around the room on which to engrave the names of all past and future ministers assigned to First Church and Baltimore City Station, beginning with Francis Asbury in 1773. He envisioned the windows as a way both to honor his predecessors during the centennial of Methodism and to extend this historic link into the future.[24]

The decoration of the vaulted, 25,000-square-foot dome over the auditorium received equal consideration. Goucher came up with the idea of painting it to represent the heavens as they would appear over Baltimore at 3:00 A.M. on November 6, 1887, the morning of the church's dedication. To ensure accuracy, he contacted a member of the United States Astronomical Department in Washington to prepare a chart, and asked an astronomy professor at the Johns Hopkins University to supervise the artists' installation of the Milky Way and more than 700 individual planets and stars.[25]

Such a large, complex building was costly. By the time the church was finished, its value, including the grounds, was estimated at nearly $250,000 ($6.4 million). The Board of Trustees, which Goucher chaired, had directed the Building Committee not to incur any debt for the project. Only a little more than $100,000 (approximately $2.5 million) was available from selling the old church and parsonage, however, and the minister took the lead in finding the remaining funds. Over the four-year construction period, John and Mary donated nearly a quarter of the needed amount, and he persuaded other wealthy and generous Baltimore Methodists to make additional contributions. He found new ways to inspire and cajole others to step forward with funds as well.[26]

Before the 1885 chapel dedication, the treasurer of the Building Committee estimated that $20,000 ($508,000) was required to pay existing bills and continue work. At the morning dedication service, Goucher explained the shortfall to the audience and said he expected to raise the money before everyone left the chapel. *The Baltimore Sun* reported, "This announcement caused a smile to spread through the congregation as everybody seemed to think it impossible to gather in so much in so short a time." But the article added, "Mr. Goucher meant business." He proposed dividing the amount into 200 shares of $100 each ($2,540), payable in ten equal monthly installments. An individual could pledge to take one or more shares or even a partial share. Goucher sent six collectors into the congregation, and while Bishop E. G. Andrews and a visiting minister from New York, Rev. James A. King, spoke to the congregation about God's loving a cheerful giver, Goucher mingled with his parishioners and friends to encourage pledges.

The newspaper story continued:

> In a few minutes, [Goucher's] voice was heard in one corner of the chapel saying, 'I'll be responsible for the last forty shares but cannot give the names of the subscribers.' This started the movement and each solicitor began calling out the number of shares he was disposing of.

While serious about the purpose, Goucher nonetheless liked to inject a little levity to keep the participants engaged. When, from the pulpit,

Rev. King said, "I was about to say—," Goucher interjected from the audience, "—five more shares," which made everyone laugh. Within half an hour, more than $17,000 ($432,000) was raised, including an additional $800 ($20,300) from Goucher himself. The remaining shares were spoken for during the evening service.[27]

At the dedication of the completed church nearly two years later, $52,000 ($1.34 million) in final expenses remained to be paid. Three services were held that day, and overflow crowds of 3,000 in the morning and 2,000 at night filled the auditorium and chapel. Goucher again asked for pledges on the spot. By the time the evening service ended at 11:00 P.M., enough funds had been pledged to cover the debt. (He had another reason to rejoice: Two days earlier and five thousand miles away, the 200-seat Goucher Chapel he and Mary had sponsored in Italy was dedicated.)[28]

Planning and building this "Monumental Church" required a great deal of Goucher's time, but he still remained focused on his primary work as a minister. He had arrived at the Charles Street location to find a congregation in turmoil, with only 100 parishioners. By the time of the dedication at St. Paul Street in 1887, he was preacher-in-charge of First Church, again known as Baltimore City Station, and also oversaw three assistant ministers serving at nearby "mission" churches he helped build to reach "the less favored sections of the contiguous territory." A Methodist publication highlighted the programs available to parishioners at these sites: "mothers' meetings, sewing schools, and other evangelical agencies, all planned and carried on through [Goucher's] counsel, energy and management." As an out-of-town newspaper noted, through the relationship among the four churches, he "established the modified form of the old circuit system . . . and practically answered the question what shall the large churches do in the great cities."[29]

By 1890, after twenty-one years in the active congregational ministry, Goucher left Baltimore City Station with more than 1,200 church members and probationers and 1,700 students in four Sunday schools. When the area north of Boundary Avenue was annexed in 1888, First Church was again located in Baltimore City.

One of John and Mary Goucher's early donations

CHURCH EXTENSION IN THE AMERICAN WEST

Chapter 5
(1879-1919)

———————◆◆———————

The special mission of Methodism is that we shall go from hamlet to hamlet and proclaim Christ to the world.[1]

In an 1876 article in *Zion's Herald*, a minister in an Iowa town described the chaos he had found when he arrived three years earlier: "[T]here had never been a sermon preached in the place, and they had fourteen liquor shops, with a population in the village of less than two hundred." He had gathered together nearly a third of the town as a congregation, but there was no church in which to meet. He needed a small loan in order to build one.[2]

Such stories about settlers and westward expansion were repeated frequently in Methodist publications of the decade, along with urgent requests for building churches in cities and towns throughout the growing number of states and territories. Goucher was already familiar with the work of the Church Extension Society, which had been established in 1864 to raise money to erect new churches or rescue those in distress. As part of their duties, he and other Methodist ministers were expected to collect money annually from their congregations to send to the society for allocation to needy areas such as Iowa. Responding to calls for public support, John and Mary offered the society a major gift in 1879 as he was preparing to move his own Gilmor Street Church to its new home on Harlem Park.[3]

The demand for Church Extension Society funds had always outpaced the amount raised. To supplement annual collections, the society established a loan fund to make money available to more locations. Some loans went to aid existing churches, especially those impacted by the Civil War. As the population embraced the notion of

"Manifest Destiny"—the idea that the United States had an almost divinely inspired mission to expand across the continent to the Pacific Ocean—more money was requested for church building than church repair.

Goucher read these compelling stories of western migration and studied the figures. An article in the *Christian Advocate* estimated that in the two years before 1879, "more than one million of our American people have sought homes beyond the Mississippi." In addition there was "a heavy influx from Europe, while the 'exodus' of our colored people from the South contributed to the swell all over those vast plains and up into the valleys and mining regions of the Rocky Mountains. Everywhere, from the Rio Grande in the south to the Red River of the north, the people are making new homes." Federal legislation such as the 1854 Kansas–Nebraska Act and the 1862 Homestead Act, as well as various state homestead-exemption laws that provided free land, had encouraged this migration. The surge westward also was spurred by the spread of railroads, economic depression at home and abroad, and the discovery of gold and silver.[4]

The Methodist Episcopal Church moved west with the settlers. From its beginning in America, Methodism grew rapidly, an article about early missions claimed, because it did not hesitate to exchange "the arm-chair of the parson for the saddle of the itinerant," reaching people wherever they lived. According to David Hempton, a social historian of religion, the Methodists "generally followed, but sometimes anticipated, population migrations"; they were "constantly aware that the religious spoils went to those who were in first." By the mid-1870s, the Missionary Society, overseeing both foreign and domestic work, supported more than 3,000 Methodist missionaries in states and territories beyond the established conferences. An 1879 Church Extension Society report spoke of the importance of taking the lead in new areas: "The first Church in a place to move in building secures all the outside aid of the towns. All kinds of sinners, and nearly all kinds of saints, aid that first Church."[5]

Goucher believed that Christianity underpinned the discovery and settlement of America and was a dominant influence on its early government and development. Thus it was important to him that Christians continue to play a leadership role—especially through

Methodism—in shaping the expanding nation. While one friend considered him to be patriotic "in every fiber of his being," Goucher also agreed with C. C. McCabe, assistant corresponding secretary for church extension, that the Church was "more the symbol of our civilization than the flag itself." Goucher remembered how his father organized the first religious services in Lansing, Michigan, and how they contributed to the town's prosperity. But he also knew that many new settlers, unlike the majority of his Baltimore parishioners, had barely enough resources to survive from day to day. As a *Christian Advocate* article reported about a district in Kansas, "The people are poor. They live in huts and dugouts, and fare poorly. They have no money with which to build either fine houses or cheap churches."[6]

McCabe traveled extensively in the West and saw countless examples like this one. He wanted to build 400 new churches annually, but existing loan funds could not keep up with requests. In response, he came up with the idea of creating a specific Frontier Fund within the society's broader loan fund. He put out the call for the 10,000 active Methodist ministers to raise, or individuals to give, an additional ten dollars a year to provide $100,000 ($2.45 million) annually. Congregations or individuals also could provide $250 (approximately $6,000) for a loan to help build a single church.[7]

Goucher learned from various reports that a small loan to buy lumber, nails, and glass could be enough for a missionary or minister to coax his congregation into providing the labor and additional monies needed to complete a church. Considering the effectiveness of such loans, and responding to what McCabe called "the demands of the hour," John and Mary offered the Church Extension Society not ten or 250 dollars, but $10,000 ($245,000) to create their own Frontier Loan Fund. The gift was to remain anonymous, with recipients believing the loans came from the society's own funds. This plan resonated with Goucher's practical nature. He preferred giving seed money to start a project and believed the beneficiaries should take ownership by raising additional funds themselves.[8]

Goucher was interested in the spiritual benefits of the couple's gift, but he was also a prudent businessman. He did not make donations without first considering how the money would be administered. He placed several conditions on their Frontier Loan Fund gift, asking about interest rates on the investment and limiting the full cost of any church receiving a loan, so the Church Extension Society could maximize the number of churches and congregants affected. A. J. Kynett, corresponding secretary of the society, wrote Goucher to praise the wisdom of his plan, and the two men met in February 1880 and agreed on terms. Apparently Goucher was not yet well known in Methodist circles outside Baltimore, because Kynett ended his initial letter by saying, "Excuse me for addressing you as 'Esq.' It is so seldom that a Methodist preacher can enjoy the luxury of such generous giving that I failed to identify you."[9]

Goucher wanted his and Mary's fund to "contribute to enterprises which are strictly on the frontiers, small in their beginning, but which may have all the brighter prospects for the future because they start in and may grow with communities which have not as yet attained to considerable proportions . . ." As part of the agreement, he expected regular statements from the Church Extension Society, and a handwritten account detailed loans made to fourteen churches both in 1880 and in 1881. Eight years after the Frontier Loan Fund's inception, fifty-four churches had been built, with the majority of loans ranging from $200 to $300. By the beginning of the twentieth century, locations earmarked for new churches dotted every western state and territory. Over twenty years, the Gouchers' initial $10,000 gift helped build more than 100 churches.[10]

In addition to reviewing written reports, Goucher had occasion to visit some of these churches as he traveled on personal or church business—as in December 1891, when he and Mary passed through Las Vegas, New Mexico. Old Town had been settled in 1835 through a Mexican land grant, and it became a stop on the Santa Fe Trail. New Town was established and prospered with the arrival of the Atchison, Topeka and Santa Fe Railway in 1879. The *Western Christian Advocate* reported that "a beautiful [Methodist] church, built in modern style, thirty by forty-five feet, with tower and belfry, and plastered, painted, and seated" opened the following year—thanks in part to a $400 loan given anonymously through the Gouchers' fund. By the time the couple arrived in town more than a decade later, church membership had grown from twenty-four to nearly 120.[11]

Goucher also received information about the diverse and expanding western population through personal exchanges with those on the front lines. In the summer of 1892, B. C. Swarts, superintendent of the Indian Mission Conference (reorganized as the Oklahoma Annual Conference a few months later), wrote Goucher about the challenges he was facing. The Oklahoma Land Run of April 1889 opened two million acres of unassigned lands to settlers. On the first anniversary of the opening, Swarts reported there were "probably 60,000 people here (some estimate 90,000) where one year ago today there was not an inhabitant." The Organic Act of 1890 created the Oklahoma Territory, and three land runs in September 1891 opened nearly a million acres of Indian lands, purchased by the government, to approximately 20,000 additional homesteaders. The so-called Cherokee Outlet, what the superintendent described as "6,000,000 acres of the very cream of the Indian Territory," also was due for settlement. In a letter to *Zion's Herald*, he claimed the Indian Mission Conference was "the most promising, as it the most rapidly growing, of all our home missions.[12]

Swarts told Goucher about the pressing need for more ministers to cover the burgeoning conference, and he also pleaded for increased funding to support those already working in the territory. There was an ongoing call for more churches to welcome the rapidly growing population, and pastors urged settlers in their charges "to go forward and build." As Swarts told Goucher, "The heroism of our preachers is marvelous, as much of the <u>money</u>, which goes into these church buildings, is really taken from what they would receive but for such churches being built." Local congregations were expected to supplement the small salaries the ministers received from the Missionary Society, but the region's struggling farm families—living in dugouts, sod houses, or shacks—had little extra to give. Many ministers in the conference were living in straitened circumstances as well.[13]

Swarts's own finances were precarious. Knowing Goucher's reputation as a man who took an interest in individuals as well as organizations, Swarts felt comfortable writing a personal letter seeking aid for his family. Three of his daughters had died in a two-year span; his wife and young son were almost invalids; the health of another daughter, who had cared for her mother and siblings, was fragile. Their doctor recommended the surviving family drink milk and cream to aid their recovery, but with his meager salary, Swarts could ill afford it. He wanted to buy a cow, but he told Goucher, "I have not one dollar with which to buy [one]." He then hinted, "I hope the Lord will put into the heart of some dear servant of his to help me to get a cow." Goucher often provided assistance to friends in difficulty, so while there is no recorded reply to this missive, it's likely the Swartses were soon drinking fresh milk.[14]

While some donors might eventually lose interest in such an extensive project, over the years Goucher continued to insist on receiving regular information about the use and administration of his and Mary's loan fund, requesting "the name, location, cost and loan to each Church assisted . . . with, if possible, its seating capacity and an indication as to the development each Church has made." He was pleased to learn that in some communities, the church they aided had "swarmed into two or three churches or become the leading church in its area." When the Methodist Episcopal Church later wanted to raise $80,000,000 (more than $1 billion) to mark the centennial of the Missionary Society's founding, Goucher recommended producing what might be called a campaign case statement, using the structure and results of their anonymous fund as a model for other church extension campaigns.[15]

Four decades after it was established, the Gouchers' loan fund had helped build more than 175 churches across the West. Goucher wrote in 1919, "I have deep gratitude in knowing that many of these Churches, encouraged in their early struggles by the 'Frontier Loan Fund,' have developed with the communities to whose prosperity they have contributed . . . and are foremost in aiding in National and World Movements for extending the Kingdom of God." Many Methodist congregations that once were beneficiaries of the Gouchers' support continue to carry out that mission to this day.[16]

International connections,
Tokyo, Japan (1907)

Courtesy of the Baltimore-Washington Conference Archives,
Lovely Lane United Methodist Church, Baltimore, Maryland

OPENING DOORS IN
FOREIGN LANDS

Chapter 6
(1879-1889)

━━━━━━━━━━━━━━━◆◆━━━━━━━━━━━━━━━

*Grace is not to be gaged by the size of the gift, but by the spirit and
purpose to relieve need at personal cost.*[1]

Goucher acquired a reputation as a church builder, responsible for
more than 250 churches at home and abroad over his lifetime.
But a plaque in the sanctuary of Lovely Lane United Methodist
Church, dedicated in honor of his seventy-fifth birthday, reminds us
that he also became known as a "father of colleges and universities,"
a "missionary pioneer," and a "brother to all peoples" as he sought
to answer his varied "commissions." Many poignant and powerful
stories were told of his international influence. A native of North
India once walked more than twenty miles to catch a glimpse of John
Goucher, who had offered him years of free schooling, despite his low
caste. A young girl in Korea, whose only name might be One, Two, or
Three in a family of unwanted daughters, was able to attend classes in
Seoul because John and Mary sponsored the opening of the Methodist
mission in that country. They offered needed funds and hospitality to
several young Japanese men studying in the United States, who later
led universities back home. And poor Chinese women, who otherwise
might have died unattended, received medical treatment in a hospital
the couple built in a city outside Peking (Beijing).[2]

These are only a few examples of the Gouchers' international
impact from the early years of their marriage. As a young man, John
had been drawn to the work of missions, whose aim, he believed, was to
"inaugurate the kingdom of mutual love and fellowship between God
and man" in all parts of the world. A friend said that early in Goucher's
ministry, he prayed daily for missions and began to focus his prayers

on one particular country for each day of the week. He even offered to serve as a missionary himself, but the Missionary Society turned him down for one position because of his record of poor health. Even so, he began setting aside a portion of his small salary for missionary work, and from his Baltimore pulpits urged congregants to contribute as well. He also read and studied missionary literature and figures, listened to missionary speakers, and corresponded with missionaries in the field.[3]

With Mary's encouragement and financial resources, Goucher began to propose his own solutions to promote missions. Starting in the fall of 1879, the Methodist Missionary Society and its General Missionary Committee in New York began getting letters from a young minister "with a strange name," who was always suggesting "new doors that he found to be ajar, or new methods of approach which he thought might be tested to advantage," and offering funding to back up his recommendations. After investigating Goucher's ideas, the society soon recognized that "the attractive character of the proposals, and the sanity of the suggestions, showed the correspondent was no idle dreamer."[4]

The Missionary Society of the Methodist Episcopal Church in America was founded in 1819, and the General Missionary Committee supervised all its missionary endeavors. As Dana L. Robert, an authority on mission history and theology, notes, "The mission policy of 19th century Methodism, whether in the United States or beyond, was that of expansion. As soon as Methodism had established itself in one location, it moved on. . . . Despite thin ranks and shoestring budgets, Methodist missions pushed onward, driven by evangelistic zeal." By the last quarter of the century, there were missions in Africa, Latin America, Europe, South and East Asia, as well as in western states and territories in the United States.[5]

The General Missionary Committee met annually to determine where and how missions were to be established, how many missionaries and native workers were employed in each station, and how much money was needed to support a mission for the following year. The bulk of the committee's annual funds, Goucher once wrote, came not from large contributions but countless small ones representing "organized poverty" or "real blood money." Many gifts were donated through the personal sacrifices of Methodist parishioners around the country.[6]

Funds had to be distributed over a wide area, and individual committee members often favored one mission area over another. Questions arose about disbursements: Which missions showed the most progress or had the best prospects for evangelization? Should missions in non-Christian countries such as China or India be allocated more funds than those in Christian countries such as Germany or Italy? There were always more requests than the committee could fulfill.

The General Missionary Committee also debated what proportion of funds should be given to domestic versus foreign missions. Goucher himself thought it unfair to consider the two types as separate and distinct, and cautioned against choosing whether to be identified with "the salvation of those of our own land or of foreign lands." To Goucher, "Missionary work of both branches is alike dear to God." Nevertheless, he understood the importance of supporting Methodist missions in Christian nations in Europe and Latin America where Catholicism held sway, and he sought to weaken the hold of state-supported churches in Germany, Switzerland, and the Scandinavian countries. He especially believed, however, that work in non-Christian countries tended to be more "soul wearing and discouraging" for missionaries, demanding more time to plant and reap the rewards of evangelization. Thus he saw their needs as more pressing and deserving of a larger share of funding.[7]

One can see Goucher's enthusiasm for the world's conversion when, while only in his mid-thirties, he was chosen over more senior ministers in the Baltimore Conference to deliver its annual Missionary Sermon in both 1881 and 1882. In the latter address, he spoke about the role of the United States, with its historic Christian base, in furthering missionary endeavors:

> America seems destined to be the key to the world. . . .Through this land the lines of travel and commerce must ever flow. Here the greatest intellectual forces and social influences will find their battle ground. . . . Our mission is from this center to radiate truth, exhibit living illustrations of virtue, and proclaim righteousness to all nations.

Goucher used facts and figures in his talk, as he often did in sermons, to show that Christianity already possessed "the strategic points of the earth from which to advance" through missions. He had studied their status and the need to spread the gospel in "heathen lands," where, he said, "All the false systems [of idolatry] that have clouded men's minds and held their souls in bondage are giving way, while Christianity, with undimmed luster is advancing."[8]

Beyond Methodism, in the mid-to-late nineteenth century, two other factors influenced American Protestant churches' responses to missionary work and its financing: the Third Great Awakening and the "three-self theory." The former was marked by spiritual revival and social activism; it encouraged the spread of evangelism around the world and gave rise to increasing missionary outreach. The latter was promoted by Rufus Anderson of the Congregational American Board of Commissioners for Foreign Missions. Religious historian William R. Hutchison calls Anderson, who began his work in the 1830s, "the outstanding organizer and theorist of foreign missions in the nineteenth century." Anderson's tenets stated that the role of a missionary was to be "a planter only," developing self-supporting, self-governing, and self-propagating indigenous churches among converts in new lands. It was "not the missionary's business to export or advocate" his home civilization or the doctrine or organization of his own church, but to train native ministers. He believed the missionary should be "an itinerant," leaving or moving on once new preachers were ordained and churches established.[9]

Hutchison points out that, for Anderson, the missionary movement had to distinguish between secular activities that were "urgently required," such as medical missions, and others that were "intrusive or simply not important to the work of evangelization." Dana Robert writes that under the three-self theory, education was considered "an adjunct to evangelism, important insofar as it supported the raising up of a native ministry and Christian wives as helpmeets." To be useful, courses should be taught in the local language or dialect rather than in English. Robert points to early Methodist activity in Foochow (Fuzhou), China, where missionaries followed Anderson's guidelines and refused "to teach English or secular subjects on the theory that such teaching pulled converts out of the church and into secular pursuits and alienated them from their own people." Hutchison adds, "Anderson thought the missionary movement's substantial and central commitment to education, in India and elsewhere, was a vast mistake."[10]

Goucher's views on education differed from Anderson's: "Always and everywhere Christian education is the fundamental condition for world evangelization. It is the most constructive, far-reaching, effective, and economical form of evangelization possible, for no nation can be evangelized from the outside." While he hoped Christianity would spread through exposure to missionary preaching, Goucher also realized that making education available could open a population's heart to a missionary's message and lead to conversions. He later commented that "enervation, want of aggressiveness, and sterility characterize all missions which ignore educational work and limit themselves to evangelical activities." The ministry had to be a teaching ministry and its disciples, wherever they lived, had to be learners. If not, "Evangelism, without education, faces fanaticism and reaction."[11]

As a practical matter, Goucher agreed that native churches ultimately should become self-governing and self-supporting rather than missionary-led and -sponsored, but he felt this was more likely to occur among broadly educated congregations. He believed that education provided training for good citizenship and the development of character, and he understood that an educated population could help influence a country's future. As he once told a conference on missions, "When the seed [of education] has been planted, development is inevitable."[12]

Goucher's daughter Janet offered a reason why her father was such a strong proponent of schools: "He looked out upon the greed, the suspicion, the fear, the hate of the world and saw in Christian education the 'healing of the nations.'" He believed that education should be available to everyone, regardless of gender, race, creed, or class, and he encouraged the teaching of the 3-Rs in schools he supported, as well as training in ethics and spiritual matters. Together, Goucher felt, these disciplines prepared individuals for useful and productive lives in the church and society. He spoke of the importance of Christian-based schools at that same conference:

They break down prejudice, eradicate superstitions, destroy
fanaticism, nullify the force of heathen traditions, awaken a
better appreciation of the dignity of man, bring students to
realize the common relationship of all men and of their vital
relationship to the Creator of us all, secure and beget an earnest
desire for His personal favor.[13]

Goucher also believed that the progress of educational institutions
"should be an evolution, with standards suited to the needs of the
particular mission, changing from time to time as these change,
and not based upon the ideals of some other land or different field."
Whenever possible, students should receive their education as close
to home as possible. Otherwise, he said, when children were sent to
another region or country for schooling at an impressionable age, they
often became "more or less denationalized," and less sympathetic to
the customs and needs of home on their return.[14]

Goucher saw the value of teaching both in the vernacular—the
local language or dialect—and in English. He knew that teaching in the
native tongue was useful at primary levels, where classes were fairly
homogeneous, but he thought mission schools should stress a mastery
of English at the upper levels, where students from varied backgrounds
and locations came together. The key role of mission colleges was to
"educate the student in the use of his faculties, ground him in the first
principles of knowledge, in the various departments of thought and
effort, and in the ethics and central truths of the gospel"—a job best
accomplished in English. Goucher also understood the practicality
and cost efficiency of teaching a diverse group in English rather than
trying to accommodate a variety of dialects.[15]

Christian institutions were for Goucher more effective than public
schools in reaching a broad spectrum of students, especially those who
had been ignored or disenfranchised because of their race, gender,
class, or caste. Students of all religions were welcomed to the schools
he sponsored if they were willing to take part in daily prayers, hymns,
and Bible readings alongside studying academic subjects. Making
educational opportunities available to both boys and girls and men
and women was especially important to him, as he saw the sexes as
essential to and supplementing each other rather than one dominating
the other. Of course, he was not above considering the matchmaking

possibilities schools afforded, and the educated Christian families that might result. In North India alone, Goucher once estimated, there were about 200 weddings between former students annually, when the schools he and Mary founded had been in operation a few years.[16]

From his earliest support of international missions, Goucher became a mentor and friend to many natives and missionaries. He nurtured these personal relationships, serving at times as a banker, advisor, or confidante. He and Mary often welcomed these individuals to Alto Dale while they were studying in the United States or on furlough. When John loaned money to young people to further their education, he expected repayment, but he was generous with terms and extensions. He believed they would value their education more if they had to help pay for it, though he usually gave the repaid funds to a student's home mission or to support another student. As one recipient noted, "You solved the difficult problem of aiding me without robbing me of my self respect."[17]

Goucher's missionary speech at the 1882 Baltimore Conference was considered worthy of publication, and a Methodist paper hailed him as "a wide reader of missionary literature and a careful observer of all matters on the subject," adding, "probably no member of the Baltimore Conference is as conversant with our and other missionary fields." Goucher's combination of thoughtful plans and financial backing was tantalizing to the cash-strapped Missionary Society as new areas for exploration continued to open. The society not only accepted his proposals for expanding missionary activities, but made him a member of its Board of Managers in 1884.[18]

In the same period, an editorial in the *Christian Advocate* introduced Goucher to the broader Methodist audience as "a young man, scarcely upon the plateau of middle life that lies between youth and old age," whose method was "to inquire minutely, weigh deliberately, decide firmly, execute steadily." It continued: "His is a character that finds reward in the acts he performs—a reward which would be rather soured than sweetened by adulation." Indeed, he preferred that his and Mary's gifts received little, if any, publicity. But once their donations began to become known, a leader in the Missionary Society told him, "You cannot escape your fame—your marvelous generosity is too inspiring to the Church to be kept secret. . . . It will do you no harm and do the Church great good."[19]

John and Mary's early donations in this regard were varied. Sometimes they were relatively modest one-time gifts: $100 (approximately $2,400) to publish a Methodist hymnbook in Spanish for missions in Mexico, or a donation for a church piano and communion set in Japan. He might also help a missionary project avoid financial embarrassment, as when he and Mary gave $5,000 ($119,000) to clear the debt of the Methodist Book Concern in Bremen, Germany, that printed Christian tracts for that country and Switzerland. The couple responded to requests for aid in more remote areas as well, providing a stipend for a missionary teacher in northwestern Brazil. Missions in Africa also received periodic support. One Methodist bishop called Goucher the "honest though unofficial mother" of the East African mission because of his valued support when it was founded.[20]

Sharing his thoughts on philanthropy, Goucher once told a missionary conference that he believed God wanted "the possessions He has entrusted to men so invested that they will realize the largest return." In considering what projects he and Mary would fund each year, Goucher looked for investments in "much fruit" places, following the Biblical charge, "Ye have not chosen me, but I have chosen you, and ordained you, that ye should go and bring forth fruit, and that your fruit should remain . . ." He considered his options with the heart and soul of a minister and the head of a businessman. He chose those locations that would bring the greatest return for the money in both lives helped and souls saved, and where funding had the potential for lasting influence. Thus the major thrust of the couple's international donations from 1879 to 1889 was focused on four countries he believed met that criteria—Japan, India, China, and Korea. Each presented its own set of challenges both for missionaries and for Goucher. At the same time he was carrying out his ministry and building churches in Baltimore, his attention and finances were also drawn to the other side of the world.[21]

Goucher Hall
Anglo-Japanese College of Tokyo
(1893)

Courtesy of the Archives of Aoyama Gakuin,
Tokyo, Japan

THE JAPAN MISSION AND THE ANGLO-JAPANESE COLLEGE OF TOKYO

Chapter 7
(1879-1889)

————————◆◆————————

Education determines the development and efficiency of one's life and is as essential as life itself.[1]

Goucher read and studied a variety of missionary literature, but it was through his personal connection to two men—Robert S. Maclay and Julius Soper—that he learned firsthand about the Japan Mission and its needs. Maclay graduated from Dickinson College the year Goucher was born and then spent twenty-three years as a leader of the Methodist mission in Foochow, China. He maintained his membership in the Baltimore Conference and attended meetings when he was home on furlough. Soper was also a conference member and was ordained an elder along with Goucher at the annual meeting in 1873. Maclay had been encouraging the Missionary Society to establish a new Methodist mission in Japan, and that same year, he and Soper were sent to open a station there—the former to Yokohama as the mission's superintendent and the latter to Tokyo.

Through the "gunboat diplomacy" of Commodore Matthew Perry, Japan had signed a treaty with the United States in 1854, opening it to western trade and influences. The country began to change from a feudalistic political order under the shogun to a centralized government, headed by the emperor but overseen by an oligarchy that controlled several ministries. The new leaders understood that Japan needed to unify and modernize to counter western influences, but they resisted any efforts to promote Christianity. Wooden signboards placed along roadsides read: "The Prohibition of the Christian Religion should be strictly observed," or "Heretical Religions are strictly prohibited."

Those who disobeyed such orders were punished. But in a report to the Baltimore Conference in 1876, Soper related that the public signs were being taken down just as the Japan Mission was getting started, although the laws still stood for now. The Japanese government was trying to stay neutral, offering the missionaries support or condemnation depending on the winds of public opinion.[2]

The missionaries had to work around this ambiguity. Extra-territoriality clauses in treaties between Japan and other countries allowed foreigners to live in settlements or concessions set apart in several large cities in the empire. While this arrangement exempted foreigners from Japanese jurisdiction, it also restricted their movements. They could not buy, rent, or live on property outside those areas, constraining missionaries from preaching and teaching among the native population. Soper was optimistic about the future of their work but added: "Yet, on account of the circumscribed limits of aggressive work, the uncertain attitude of the Government, and the long and deep seated prejudice against Christianity, the progress of the Truth must necessarily be slow, the first few years."[3]

Goucher took an active interest in such reports, and in September 1879, he wrote the superintendent offering $20,000 for the Japan Mission ($490,000). The missionaries greeted such news as "an answer to prayer." Earlier in the year, Maclay had opened an academy and seminary, the Mikai Theological Institute, in Yokohama with Missionary Society funds. Half of the Gouchers' donation would reimburse the society for that outlay, freeing up those funds for other needs. Maclay reported his personal appreciation, telling Goucher, "It is gratifying to me to think the old Baltimore Conference is to have through the beneficence of one of its members the distinguished honor of initiating a movement."[4]

Asked by Goucher to suggest uses for the other half of the money, the missionaries requested that the donation be devoted to a publication fund for building a headquarters and printing religious materials to "help banish superstition and error" among the Japanese. But in the end, Goucher decided it more prudent to offer educational assistance to young people instead. He placed the remaining money with the Missionary Society as an endowment, and stipulated that three-quarters of the interest be used for annual scholarships to the institute to train Japanese pastors, and the remaining quarter to buy books for its library.[5]

Maclay wrote their benefactor, "While the decision at which you finally arrived in regard to the matter is not exactly in the line of our suggestion, we nevertheless accept with hearty approval and sincere thanks for your decision." When the Missionary Society wrote officially to accept the donation, it offered "to affix the name of the Patron to the institution," but Goucher declined any recognition for his and Mary's gift.[6]

In the fall of 1881, Goucher offered other educational assistance in Japan, this time to high schools in the cities of Nagoya, Matsushiro, and Hirosaki. Because of an economic depression, authorities in these cities were no longer able to pay Japanese residents to teach English classes. Instead, they asked the Methodist General Missionary Committee to send Americans to teach English a few hours a day in the schools, allowing them to pursue missionary work as well. Each city's population agreed to supply housing and pay part of the missionaries' salaries.[7]

Goucher approved of this proposal, saying that "such an arrangement would give our missionaries access to hundreds of those who must become the leading minds of new Japan a few years hence, and be an official, or at least public endorsement of our workers." As an incentive, he offered to support a married missionary at each school for five years. However, Martin Vail, principal of the Mikai Theological Institute and member of the Japan Mission, wrote Goucher soon after that because of the depression, the three cities were unable to meet the promised housing and salary expectations. Without that local support, the plan could not be implemented, even with Goucher's offer. But Honda Yoitsu, head of the Hirosaki school and later the first bishop of the Methodist Church of Japan, asked if Goucher might consider paying the salary of a Japanese instructor to teach English at Hirosaki. At Vail's request, Goucher agreed to establish a native professorship there for five years.[8]

For health reasons, Maclay was sent home on furlough, and in January 1882, he met with Goucher in his friend's "cozy study" at 2313 to discuss prospects for the Japan Mission. The missionary brought Goucher up to date about work at the institute and at a boys' boarding and day school known as "Tokyo Eigakko" (Tokyo English School) that Soper had started within the foreign concession there. Although the Japanese frowned on direct proselytizing, they were more eager than ever to learn English in order to interact and compete with western nations.[9]

Goucher saw an opportunity for the Japan Mission to strengthen its educational efforts and proposed combining the Yokohama and Tokyo schools to establish an Anglo-Japanese University in the capital. The proposed university was to be open to students of all religions, but Goucher wanted to educate these young men (and prospective future leaders) under Christian auspices. He also wanted to train more Japanese preachers to take charge of self-supporting churches. Toward these ends, he and Mary offered $5,000 in gold ($119,000) to purchase land in Tokyo for the campus. Maclay immediately informed the Missionary Society in New York, and Goucher's merger plan was accepted.[10]

The Japan Mission had to overcome land-ownership restrictions before the new institution could launch. Later stories about Goucher's accomplishments would state that he was the first foreigner granted permission by the Japanese government to buy property outside the foreign concession. He did initiate and finance the ultimate purchase from Baltimore, but the process required intricate negotiations on several fronts in Japan. In Maclay's absence, Vail appealed to John A. Bingham, the United States minister to Japan, for assistance in navigating the bureaucracy. It was Bingham's opinion that the only way the mission could secure property so it couldn't be confiscated or used for other purposes, was to form a Japanese company to buy and own land on behalf of the Missionary Society in New York. A committee of Japanese Christians—two preachers and three laymen—was appointed for this purpose.[11]

Maclay returned to Japan by the end of 1882, and he wrote Goucher about Bingham's meeting with the Japanese minister of education and his appeals to the government on behalf of their cause. Some factions remained hostile to foreigners, but according to Maclay, the American minister stressed "the importance of education as a factor in national progress." Bingham had likened Goucher's plan to the well-known bequests of James Smithson and George Peabody to promote education in the United States. Knowing Goucher's aversion to public recognition, Maclay told their benefactor, "I trust your modesty will not be too severely shocked by the tone of [Bingham's] commendation."[12]

The mission also had an ally in Tsuda Sen, one of the first Japanese baptized by Soper and a strong supporter of westernization and Christianity. He operated the Gakunosha School of Agriculture in Tokyo and was interested in its becoming a branch of the new university. He became one of the members of the Japan Committee, organized to find a location for the proposed university and buy the land on receiving government approval. The group considered three plots in Tokyo, but their preferred choice was a twenty-five-acre parcel near the emperor's residence, Aoyama Palace. It had once been the site of the daimyo of Kishu's home, and more recently had served as a government farm, promoting modern agricultural methods. (Soper was familiar with the location from purchasing fresh, American-style fruits and vegetables.) The committee praised the site for "the large size of the lot, the low price of the land, the eligibility and healthfulness of the situation and its celebrity in Japan as the site of the Model Farm." Even the name of the area—Aoyama or Green Mount—sounded providential.[13]

In January 1883, acting on behalf of the Missionary Society (and Goucher), the Japan Committee was able to purchase and take possession of the Aoyama land—the first time the Japanese government allowed such a transaction. By August, the committee received full authority from the Japanese government to set up the school and employ foreign teachers. Members of the mission were granted permits to reside and teach at the Aoyama site, another critical concession. Maclay told Goucher they were not yet ready to open at the university level, but the government had given permission to name the institution Tokyo Eiwa Gakuin—the Anglo-Japanese College of Tokyo. (That name would be changed to Aoyama Gakuin before the end of the century.)[14]

As its first president, Maclay opened the college that October, with classes held in one building, a dormitory that had been moved from Yokohama to the new campus. The following month, he wrote Goucher with the good news that the school "receives attention and excites interest in Japanese circles from which Christianity has long been excluded." The curriculum was divided into two areas—theology and academic studies, all taught in English. To ensure adequate faculty, Goucher made a new five-year pledge, offering not only to support two Japanese teachers, but also to cover the salary of John O. Spencer, a young teacher and principal from Pennsylvania. Spencer became head of the English section and taught a course in Tsuda's agricultural school. After taking up his duties, Spencer wrote Goucher, "I have never had the pleasure of your immediate acquaintance but I know you by the good that you have done. In a large sense I am your man here in Japan . . ."[15]

The new Anglo-Japanese College quickly prospered. Within six months of opening, the student population grew from fifty to nearly 100, and the need for additional space became critical. A donor from the American Midwest paid for the theology school building, which included a library, partly filled with books bought through John and Mary's earlier endowment. The Gouchers again stepped forward to pledge $3,000 toward the academic building, with the expectation that the Missionary Society would find the remaining funding. After this new donation, Maclay told his friend, "You may leave behind you many memorials of your beneficence, but no one I am sure will shed more luster on your name or afford you higher satisfaction in the ages to come, than the movement you are building in the highest thought and purest instincts of the people of the beautiful empire."[16]

This offer was just the start. When no additional funds became available, Goucher pledged another $12,000 to pay for this main, multi-purpose building, housing classrooms, a chapel, library, laboratory, faculty room, and office. (The combined $15,000 building pledge would be worth approximately $380,000 in 2014.) Shortly after its dedication in June 1887, Maclay wrote again to their benefactor, "It must be gratifying to you to bear in mind that years ago your mind was directed to this field and that some of the funds entrusted to your care have been invested in this work." While Goucher was pleased with the progress of the college, he objected to any personal recognition for its success. Even so, Tokyo Eiwa Gakuin named that academic building—the centerpiece of the new campus—Goucher Hall. Owing to future earthquakes in Tokyo, it would be the first of three such buildings named in honor of the man whom the Japanese considered the institution's founder.[17]

Mile marker - Kumaon, North India (2008)

Courtesy of Kaushik Bagchi

GOUCHER SCHOOLS
IN INDIA

Chapter 8
(1882-1889)

———————◆◆———————

The problems of childhood are the problems of the centuries. They are continually changing but ever present. . . . A nation's words today are the trustees of its tomorrows. The rising generation are acquiring the ideals, discipline and attainments which interpret their environment and they will transmit to their posterity.[1]

Goucher's sights were set on not only the small East Asian island of Japan, but also the large South Asian country of India. The reports that he received in the late 1870s from Methodist missionaries in North India's Rohilkhand District were compelling. Located in the United Provinces (today's states of Uttar Pradesh and Uttarakhand), the district covered, according to one missionary, 2,900 square miles, stretching from the Ganges River in the south to Nepal and the Himalayas in the north. This area, a little larger than Delaware, contained nearly 1,200,000 people scattered over 2,500 small villages and towns. Trails connecting them were, according to another missionary who traveled them regularly, "deep in dust" for nine months of the year and "rivers of mud" for the other three. Most people were illiterate and extremely poor, earning only one to two dollars per month, and were among the lowest castes in Indian society. Children were expected to work if they wanted to eat. The customs of idolatry, child marriage, polygamy and polyandry—both men and women having multiple spouses—held many in bondage.[2]

Beyond that, the isolation of and distances between villages meant there were not enough government or missionary schools available for the district's children, the girls especially. To survive, missionary schools depended on appropriations from the home society in the United

States, as well as grants-in-aid from the colonial government. Cycles of famine and plague in the country sometimes caused government aid to be diverted to other areas, and when such disasters struck North India, the missionaries opted to open orphanages rather than schools. Christian converts needed extra support, as they often were shunned by their Hindu and Muslim neighbors. As one missionary told Goucher, "We must help these poor people; and the very best assistance we can give them is to provide educational advantages for the children." John and Mary answered this call.[3]

Methodist missionaries had arrived in India in 1856, and the India Mission Conference, the first conference in Asia, was established in 1864, just as Goucher was entering his freshman year at college. Later, when he offered his daily prayers for different missions worldwide, Thursdays were devoted to India. As a young circuit minister in Baltimore County, he helped direct his congregations' annual missionary collections to that country. One year, the churches designated their money "to educate a girl in India, to be named Nannie Turner," her surname likely being that of Goucher's host family. At another time, they supported two girls, plus an Indian woman Bible reader who visited homes where women led traditionally secluded and restricted lives. In addition to their 1879 donation to support missionary and educational work in Japan, John and Mary proposed giving $5,000 that year ($122,000) to educate more girls in North India, which by then had a Methodist conference of its own. When Rev. Edwin W. Parker, the presiding elder of the district and later a bishop, learned of the gift, he welcomed this offer of stable funding, but then asked the couple to give an equal amount for boys' education.[4]

At Parker's recommendation, Goucher wrote to Methodist boards in the United States that oversaw missions and education, officially offering the money as an endowment. He expected it to pay a specific rate of interest and asked about security for the funds. They were unable to agree on terms, however, and Goucher withdrew the offer.

Still, the need for schools in North India continued to grow. By the early 1880s, there were nearly 4,500 Indian Christians scattered among more than 300 villages and towns in the Rohilkhand District, supported by only 200 schools. Parker wanted to add primary schools in unserved and underserved areas and wrote to the home Missionary

Society appealing for funds, but the General Missionary Committee was overextended. Money for schools already in operation was threatened, and Parker feared the foothold the missionaries had established in North India might be lost.

After withdrawing his 1879 proposal, Goucher began to ponder a different way to donate to the region, one in which he would have more direct say and influence. As Bishop Cyrus Foss later explained, Goucher "became convinced that the greatest need of our work there was vernacular schools in the humblest villages, where the low-caste boys and girls should be taught." This belief coincided with Parker's needs, and even as the missionary was writing to New York for aid, the minister was writing to him from Baltimore. Goucher agreed to establish fifty new primary boys' schools within the North India Conference and support them for five years—a proposal unprecedented in its sweep. He had seen that piecemeal projects with uncertain funding were not working, and he wanted to be able to measure how a concentrated number of schools in one region might, over an extended period of time, affect Indian students, families, and society, as well as the spread of Christianity. These schools were to be open to Hindus and Muslims as well as Christians, and he wanted "the benefit of this fund to extend to both sexes alike" when the time was right.[5]

Goucher also recognized that there could be no far-reaching influence without talented students being able to continue on to higher education. He added to his proposal 100 scholarships to Parker's Central School in Moradabad, which had been in operation for seven years. Goucher stated that these funds "entitled the boys of the lower schools of greatest ability, application and acquirements to free tuition, board and clothing while making satisfactory progress towards the Government Exams which is usually 9 or 10 years." Success in these exams provided young men with educational and job opportunities not otherwise available to them. When Parker presented this Goucher proposal to the General Missionary Committee in the fall of 1882, it unanimously accepted the "generous proposition" for immediate implementation.[6]

As a businessman, Goucher established criteria for use of the couple's funds—a pledge of $5,000 per year for five years ($119,000 to $130,000 over that period). To safeguard the existing mission schools and increase their number, he stipulated that the Missionary Society must not reduce its funding for North India's primary schools in light of his infusion of capital for new ones. Rather than have the funds administered from New York, he appointed a five-member Committee of Supervision from among experienced area missionaries to put the plan into effect and oversee its operation. Members were allowed to choose the villages in which to open schools and develop the general curriculum, but Goucher expected each school to begin the day with Bible reading, hymns, and prayer.[7]

All activities were to be conducted in the local dialect, as Goucher understood that the majority of students would remain in their own area and needed education in the vernacular, rather than English, to overcome caste limitations and enjoy better employment opportunities. He also hoped some of the students' secular and religious lessons might filter back into their homes and aid their uneducated parents. Perhaps most importantly, he wanted to increase conversions in the district over the long term. He believed this goal might best be achieved through Indian Christians, educated in their own dialect, reaching out to others in their villages and environs. In a later speech about missions and education, Goucher spoke of this important way to gain converts: "Hearts must be reached by heart power [and] the mother tongue is the language of the heart."[8]

Goucher also wanted Indian teachers in the classrooms. He expected them to be Christians (and Methodists), and they had to pass three proficiency exams within four years of employment in order to continue teaching and get a raise in salary. This stipulation enabled them to broaden their own education and opened opportunities for future advancement.[9]

Goucher wrote Parker that he would send quarterly payments to cover rent, books, and salaries for each village school, and to ensure they were being administered according to his specifications, he requested that each school's quarterly report be sent to him at home. He kept detailed records: the location of each primary school; the name of the teacher and any assistant and the salary paid; the number of students attending each month and the average attendance; the cost of rent, books, and repairs; and the total cost for each school. He also wanted to know the number and names of scholarship students at

Parker's boarding school. He reviewed these reports carefully and felt free to contact committee members with his questions or concerns.[10]

By the beginning of 1883, the committee had opened village schools in ten missionary circuits, each comprising a main town surrounded by numerous small villages. Three to seven schools opened in each circuit, each overseen by an Indian superintendent. Classes were held in the open air, with students sitting on the ground around the teacher; during the rainy season, they continued in huts. At the end of August, the first report from the committee's treasurer, D. W. Thomas, showed forty-six of the fifty schools were already open, with forty-nine teachers and assistants and nearly 800 students. Three months later, that number grew to 940 "scholars," as Goucher always called them. Goucher's example inspired others: James H. Frey, a wholesale druggist in Baltimore, offered to support thirty new schools in the neighboring Oudh District, as well as several scholarships to the Bareilly Theological Seminary.[11]

The number of village schools in the Rohilkhand District grew to sixty, as Goucher stepped up to sponsor ten more. Thomas told Goucher that some of the original schools had been relocated from one village to another, since "owing to caste and other prejudices, we cannot always know whether parents will continue to allow their boys to attend." There was a concern about a government proposal to withdraw aid from schools offering religious instruction. Thomas reported that "the several missionary bodies in India opposed the proposition so strongly that the government did not think it wise to adopt it." He reported other good news as well: "Several boys and young men belonging to the Goucher Schools have been converted this year and others are hopeful inquirers."[12]

There were no primary students prepared to receive scholarships for the Moradabad boarding school during the first year aid was available, so the Committee of Supervision asked Goucher's permission to use that money to enlarge the current building there; two wings were added with his approval. Then Thomas asked, "Can you do anything for us towards the creation of the dorms . . . instead of scholarships?" He mailed architectural and space plans for the proposed compound—coinciding with Goucher's early immersion in architectural plans for Baltimore's First Church—and awaited his benefactor's response.[13]

Goucher wrote back that his money was intended for schools and scholarships—not for grounds, enclosures, or a principal's house. But he understood that the 100 new students expected would need housing, and that the mission lacked discretionary funds for that purpose. After meeting with Parker, then in the United States on furlough, Goucher agreed to build five "barracks" for his scholars, plus a cookhouse and godown, or storehouse. By the spring of 1884, thirty-four students became eligible for scholarships, and in his quarterly payment, Goucher included an additional $1,000 (approximately $25,000) to expand the grounds to three acres. The remaining scholarship funds were diverted toward building the barracks. After these improvements, the school was able to raise its level from Middle Anglo Vernacular to become the Goucher High School—the only Christian-sponsored high school among five million people. For the first time, Christian students in the province could receive the education needed to attend college.[14]

Parker visited as many village schools as he could in the sprawling 200-mile-long district, and told Goucher that in some places a few girls were reading alongside the boys. The missionary wrote: "I am more and more convinced that gradually we can make a success of the 50-60 girls' schools also. Kindly allow us to start them as we can find openings . . . Perhaps 25 one year and the balance the next."[15]

The Gouchers had intended to provide support for girls' primary schools, and he sent sufficient funds to open them. The men in the villages resisted, but Goucher insisted that if they wanted to keep the boys' schools, they had to accept girls' schools as well. The Committee of Supervision's fourth-quarter report for 1885 indicated that twelve girls' schools had opened, teaching nearly 150 students; by the second-quarter report for 1886, there were twenty-nine girls' schools and 450 scholars. Parker asked Goucher to gradually add forty scholarships to send the most talented of these girls to his wife's boarding school in Moradabad, and the first recipient was given the name "Annie Goucher."[16]

Between 1885 and 1886, total attendance for the boys' and girls' schools grew from over 1,100 to nearly 1,800. Among both Indians and missionaries, these village institutions became known as "Goucher Schools." Not everyone realized the word "Goucher" was actually a man's name, however. Rev. N. L. Rockey, who would spend many years as a missionary in India, recounted his first encounter with the name:

> My first Conference was Bareilly, 1885. There I first heard the word "Goucher.". . . But I had no idea what it meant. I naturally enough thought it a Hindustani word defining some kind of school. I concluded that it meant village or primary or something of that nature. Two weeks later, when we had joined our first appointment, which was at Bijnor, . . . I learned that we had half a dozen "Goucher" schools and concluded that the term "Goucher" was the name of a fund, an income that was separate and distinct from the mission appropriations. Several weeks later, Dr. E. W. Parker, our presiding elder, made his first visit to us to start us on our work, and he told us the history of the word, the schools, the fund, and of the man back of them. From that day to this, Dr. Goucher, whom later I came to know very well, was to me one of God's heroes.[17]

As the number of boys' primary schools grew, so did the number of students eligible to attend the high school in Moradabad. The necessary barracks at the high school were completed, but Parker appealed to Goucher again for additional funds for improvements. The compound was in the shape of a parallelogram, with the dormitories, cookhouse, and dining area enclosed within a wall. The plans called for the latrine to be within the wall as well, but given the hot climate and blowing winds, Parker thought the arrangement detrimental to "neatness and health." His usual benefactor readily covered the cost of buying a corner lot outside the wall to move the latrine.[18]

Indeed, Goucher became accustomed to pleas for additional funds from missionaries in every country where he offered support, especially when annual appropriations were reduced. They had few other resources to call upon and relied on his interest and concern. Although grateful for John and Mary's generosity, many did not hesitate to ask for more, and often for considerable sums. Missionaries in India were no exception. One requested an additional $20,000 to $25,000 ($488,000 to $610,000) to endow a professorship or the position of principal at the Bareilly Theological Seminary, the next stop for some older boarding students. The principal of the Centennial School in Lucknow asked for funds to upgrade his high school to a college, pleading, "Will not you and Mrs. Goucher kindly put us on our feet with $50,000 ($1.28 million) and let us call it 'The Goucher Mission College'?" The couple declined both offers.[19]

At times, Goucher turned down a monetary request from a missionary only to fund another of his or her projects. One missionary, who had enjoyed a "most comfortable and pleasant" rest at Alto Dale while on furlough in 1884, approached his host for a gift or loan to pay off land on which he was building a church. Goucher instead offered him six scholarships for a newly opened institute to train native missionaries—a contribution more consistent with the Gouchers' interest in education. Occasionally he delayed or ignored answering a missionary's request. A principal of a boys' school in Calcutta (Kolkata) wrote soliciting funds to buy a lot on which to build a new school. When he received no reply, he wrote Goucher again, tactfully declaring, "It would be a pleasure to hear from you."[20]

Goucher's friend Parker understood the demands on John and Mary's resources, saying, "I shall always tell you my wishes but shall not complain if you are not able to do all I wish done." Others, however, expected the couple to cover whatever was needed. After they had paid for additional land and built the barracks at the Moradabad compound, school treasurer Thomas suggested they then pay for the wall surrounding it. Another missionary advised Goucher, if he had any more money to give, the man knew just how to spend it.[21]

In addition to money, Goucher gave missionaries a sympathetic ear. Many in North India wrote candidly to him about issues they faced overseeing his schools. They wrote of having to break down the attitude of "Why learn to read at all—our fathers did not." Village leaders, who owned the surrounding land and extracted usage fees from village farmers, often tried to break up the schools, fearing an educated population might rebel against this feudal system. One correspondent also reported, "Sometimes the [Hindu] priests frighten [the Indians] and sometimes they think they must have their boys to work to help obtain food." Missionaries found that attendance was better in winter than summer, as many boys went to the cooler hill stations to work in the hot season. Nevertheless, Indians highly valued the opportunities Goucher Schools offered. Parker wrote that if an established school closed in a village, "the people will plead for it again before a month is gone." The Brahmins, the highest caste

Hindus, wanted separate Goucher Schools for their sons after seeing lower caste boys get ahead. But Goucher insisted the castes be taught together to break down social barriers.[22]

Goucher also knew of the missionaries' concern for girls and boys who had been married at ages six or eight before entering the Goucher Schools. They related that the children's parents considered it "a great disgrace for a child to grow up unmarried," and even though the young couple did not live together, they were bound by law to honor the contract when they were older. While single boys were given preference for scholarships to board at Moradabad, Parker noted that sometimes a particularly bright but married student was "just the boy we want." But how to deal with the fact that the boy "has a wife in her home, he knows nothing of her or she of him, only that they were married sometime and that sometime she will be his wife"? Parker asked Goucher to fund additional scholarships for the young brides to attend his wife's boarding school, so they might be educated at the same time and location as their husbands.[23]

Whether students were single or already married, one of Goucher's goals in offering schooling to both sexes was to create educated (and preferably Christian) homes and families to help shape India's future. Although boys and girls attended separate schools, he encouraged the missionaries' efforts to gather boarding school students together on Friday and Sunday evenings for songs, prayer, and Bible readings, thus providing an acceptable place for them to meet and learn together. Later, Goucher met and described one couple who exemplified what he wanted to accomplish with this coeducational mingling and breakdown of caste segregation:

> The second head master of the boys' high school [in Moradabad], Jacobs and his wife, also show the possibilities of the sweeper class. He was an outcaste, the son of a sweeper, and has passed along to his MA [master of arts degree]. Two years all the boys he sent up for the [government] exams passed. He was attacked, setting forth his low birth and vigorous efforts made to keep high caste and Muhamedan [sic] boys away from his school. They only advertised his success and increased the attendance. People thought it strange he did not marry as they did also of a young woman in our school for girls. She passed on to the Medical College at Agra and

when she returned was placed in an emergency in one of Lady Dufferin Hospitals and did so well has been promoted there till now she receives 125 rupees per month and treats Brahmins and Europeans. When she had completed her medical course she and Jacobs married as they had promised each other long before to do when they were equipped for life. Both are very capable and highly respected.[24]

Goucher was pleased with the measurable success of the schools and scholarships. After the couple's initial five-year pledge ended, he continued to make annual contributions, even though Parker wanted him to endow the projects. The number of Goucher village schools in the Rohilkhand District varied from year to year, but by 1889, there were over 100 in operation, educating more than 2,200 boys and girls. As Parker told their benefactor, "We could not get on without your schools." At that time, all 100 scholarships for boys and twenty for girls were being employed at the Moradabad high schools. Parker noted that since the Goucher boys began boarding in 1884, the school had prepared five students to attend college, sent two into government service, and one to medical school. Thirty-eight had become teachers and seven were attending theological school. Other graduates went back to their villages and were working independently rather than at menial tasks. In addition, both boys and girls were winning prizes in written and oral competitions against students from government schools and the schools of other denominations.[25]

Consequently, the number of Christians in the district had doubled, and they now were spread over more than 450 villages. Parker praised Goucher's original plan: "The scheme exactly as you have it is the best work ever offered in India as a separate work. And no other work has ever paid such results." It was so beneficial that he made one more request of his friend: "I wish you could find for us more men—or even one more—who will support just such a system of schools as you have. . . . I am sure that the 'much fruit' will come." In the 1890s, Goucher found that second donor—his longtime friend John Grier Holmes—and he finally made a trip to the subcontinent to visit his North India schools and scholars.[26]

China's Third Class Chia-ho Decoration,
conferred on John Goucher in February 1921

*Courtesy of the Baltimore-Washington Conference Archives,
Lovely Lane United Methodist Church, Baltimore, Maryland*

THE CHINESE DRAGON

Chapter 9
(1879-1889)

━━━━━━━━━━◆◆━━━━━━━━━━

The most populous nation of Asia is China. . . . Its position, history, national characteristics and possibilities mark it the most important factor in the evangelization of Asia.[1]

John Goucher had noticed China's need for missionaries as well, and to many Chinese, he was soon known as Ko Yok Hang. A native minister from Fukien (Fujian) Province, son of China's second Methodist convert, had translated Goucher's name when he and Mary made one of their first donations to that country. These words not only became associated with that particular gift, but also became a symbol of support to Chinese Christians in Methodist circles throughout the country. Before the end of the 1880s, Ko Yok Hang's influence extended from the seaboard city of Foochow and its surroundings to the area around the capital of Peking, and also to remote regions along the Yangtze River in western China.[2]

While the mission in Japan offered Goucher numerous possibilities to expand Methodist influence there, the sheer size of China and its population attracted the Baltimore minister to the country he once referred to as "the Chinese Dragon." He learned from his friend Robert Maclay, who had spent more than two decades in China, and from other missionaries in the field, about the many opportunities for Christian expansion in this diverse land. From Goucher's congregational work with members of the Baltimore chapter of the Methodist Women's Foreign Missionary Society (WFMS), he also was familiar with its work on behalf of women and children in China. The question for John and Mary was, how and where to direct their funds to make the most impact in that country.[3]

Maclay and other early Christian arrivals had laid the foundation for Goucher's involvement. In the early nineteenth century, American

Protestant missionaries were barred from China, and those who came in the 1830s hid their purpose for being there by working for foreign merchants. Even these men were restricted to trade in the port of Canton only, and they had to deal solely with the Cohong, a small group of officially licensed Chinese merchants, to carry on their business. The 1842 Nanking Treaty that ended the First Opium War between Great Britain and the Qing dynasty extended the number of open ports to five and enabled British merchants to do business with whomever they pleased. American businessmen and missionaries wanted the same access and pushed President John Tyler to negotiate the first treaty between the United States and China. The 1844 Treaty of Wanghia (also known as Wangxia) gave the United States most-favored nation status alongside Great Britain, and fixed tariffs in treaty ports. More importantly for the missionaries and their sponsors, it allowed Americans to buy land in these ports and build churches and hospitals.[4]

Within three years of the treaty, the Methodist Episcopal Church opened its first Chinese mission in Foochow, in the southeastern Fukien Province. In 1858, the Treaties of Tientsin (Tianjin) between China and western nations increased the number of ports open to foreigners; legalized the importation of opium; allowed foreign legations in the formerly closed city of Peking; and permitted travel, trade, and missionary activity to spread to the interior of the country. This expansion led to the opening of new stations in Kiukiang (Jiujiang) in central China and Peking in the north.[5]

When John and Mary decided to make a donation to China in late 1879 (the first of several they would offer over the next few years), he asked the superintendent of the North China Mission, Hiram H. Lowry, and representatives of the WFMS to recommend an investment that promised the best results for long-term evangelism. Opening an orphanage was one suggestion, but the Chinese were often suspicious of foreigners taking control of and "kidnapping" their children. Another suggestion was to provide more medical services; as a history of Methodist foreign missions notes, such work was a means of opening doors otherwise still closed to foreigners. Lowry himself told Goucher that such relief would "do greater and more permanent good than an orphanage and reach more directly into the homes of the people."[6]

Outreach was critical in Chinese mission work, where women, who lived under a male-dominated class system, were denied an education and often pressed to become concubines or slaves. Upper-class women lived in seclusion, and young girls underwent foot binding as a marker of beauty and to attract a rich husband. In times of economic distress, unwanted baby girls were killed. Although most foreign missions included a male doctor on their staff, the customs of East Asian countries (and South Asian as well) generally discouraged any contact between men and women, making medical diagnoses difficult or inaccurate. John and Mary understood and believed in the importance of nurturing the body as well as the mind and soul, and they were drawn to improve the physical condition of these isolated and neglected women and children.

The Gouchers' interest in helping women coincided with an unexpected opportunity that needed funding. Dr. Leonora Howard, whose training had been supported by the WFMS, arrived in Peking in 1877 to assist Lucinda Coombs, the first western woman doctor in China and the first to open a hospital for women of all social classes. When Coombs left the WFMS the following year to marry, Howard took over her work in Peking. She also had an itinerant practice, bringing care to remote villages outside the city. In 1879, the viceroy of Chihli (Zhili) Province, Li Hung-chang (Li Hongzhang), summoned her to Tientsin, about seventy miles southeast of Peking, to treat his wife. The doctor stayed a month, taking care of not only Lady Li but also other well-born women. In appreciation, the viceroy turned a memorial temple into a dispensary and offered to let Howard open a small ward for women.

John and Mary stepped in to offer $5,000 ($122,000) to the WFMS to fund a full-fledged hospital in Tientsin—the Isabella Fisher Hospital for Women, named in honor of Mary's sister. Missionary Mary Porter Gamewell, who ran a school in Peking, wrote Lowry that such a hospital "entirely under mission control could be more concentration of effort, less waste of Miss Howard's energies, and more satisfactory to evangelical work." Clara Cushman, treasurer of the WFMS in North China, wrote Goucher to thank him for the money to purchase land and erect a building: "I fully expect the investment of your money is going to do much good for the women of north China, in relieving the poor suffering bodies and above and beyond that, in leading them to seek the Physician of Souls."[7]

Goucher was interested in all of the details, and Leonora Howard wrote him in the spring of 1881 to give a preview of the nearly completed hospital. After working with architectural plans for church sanctuaries and steeples in Baltimore, Goucher must have been intrigued to study the layout and amenities of this new building on the other side of the world. It included a main section, plus general and private wards. The hospital incorporated modern medical features, such as a skylight over the operating table, along with traditional Chinese ones, such as kangs—platforms heated from below and topped with multiple beds—that kept patients warm in the cold North China winters.[8]

The Fisher Hospital opened to fanfare that October. In attendance were the governor-general and other prominent officials from Tientsin, along with the United States minister to the court at Peking and consuls from other countries. Howard now centered her medical work in Tientsin rather than the capital, and the WFMS expanded services for women by building a training school adjacent to the hospital property. After the hospital had operated successfully for several years, Gamewell again wrote Goucher to praise his "vision that could see so clearly at such a long distance."[9]

Meanwhile, the Foochow Mission was becoming the center of a growing Methodist Christian community in the south. During its first ten years, conversions were slow, but by 1870, seven Chinese had been ordained as ministers, and there were more than 900 church members and an equal number of probationers. The missionaries had also established several boys' and girls' schools in the area. The first Methodist annual conference in China was established in Foochow seven years later, with five American missionaries and fifteen Chinese members; the Methodist system of church governance gave Chinese preachers voting rights and leadership roles within the conference. As Dana L. Robert, a historian of missions and mission theology, notes about the work in Foochow, "Remarkably quickly given the difficulty of the field, American Methodism had succeeded in planting a 'native church' with a 'native ministry.'"[10]

By 1880, there were six districts in the conference, expanding out from Foochow, and the number of Chinese pastors grew to fifty-two. With strength in numbers, they pushed for more emphasis on education, including higher standards in Methodist schools and teaching classes in English to both boys and girls. The native pastors' call fostered dissension between the Chinese and some of the missionaries, and even among some missionaries themselves. Robert explains:

> Their success in evangelism and church-planting gave the
> Chinese pastors the moral authority to press the mission
> for services that would help the Chinese converts improve
> their lot in life. The Chinese saw Methodism not only as a
> means of salvation, but of social improvement as well. In this
> holistic vision they were supported by a few missionaries
> who presented their case before the Board of Missions. They
> were opposed by other missionaries who believed that higher
> education in English would undercut the evangelistic witness.[11]

Amidst this turmoil, Maclay visited his former colleagues in Foochow in 1880. He told of the growing influence of Christian education in Japan in training future leaders, and urged them to expand their own educational offerings. Missionary Franklin Ohlinger, another acquaintance of Goucher, agreed and wanted to establish a college in that city. At the end of the year, a Chinese merchant hastened the project by offering a substantial donation to acquire a site and a building for the new institution. In January 1881, a temporary Board of Trustees was elected for what became the Anglo-Chinese College, the first Methodist college in Asia; Ohlinger was appointed as principal. They planned to model the school on the standards of American and European colleges, and as a history of the college noted, the school was founded "along broad lines using English as a means to obtain liberal collegiate and professional education."[12]

Ohlinger and the trustees spent the next several months trying to raise the additional funds needed to open. Writing in Methodist publications, these advocates sometimes made reference to Goucher's support for education in Japan and asked others follow his example. Ohlinger also contacted Goucher directly, suggesting a donation to start one of the professional schools. The trustees still needed to ask the General Missionary Committee for formal authorization to open, and a few weeks before the November 1881 meeting, Ohlinger told Goucher, "A donation just now would do a two-fold service—it would accomplish grand results for the Master's Kingdom and second, inspire the Committee with the desired enthusiasm."[13]

Goucher did not need this second reminder. As Robert points out, the founding of the college "marked a significant shift in mission theory toward the inclusion of higher education as an appropriate form of mission activity"—a move that Goucher approved and helped advance through his personal financial support. He advised the General Missionary Committee:

> I desire to donate, say not less than $7,000 ($167,000) to secure or assist in securing a suitable lot of ground and building for a Theological Department of the Anglo-Chinese College at Foochow provided 1) The General Missionary Committee give the enterprise endorsement and support; 2) They send an ordained man to take charge of the Theological Institute.

The committee assented, and Charles H. Fowler, corresponding secretary of the Missionary Society, wrote Goucher to thank him for his latest contribution: "You are continually putting us under renewed obligations for your vigorous help."[14]

Although Goucher was ready to donate the money, problems developed at the Foochow end. Within a few months of the offer, Ohlinger wrote that he was still waiting for the Board of Trustees to iron out the relationship between the college and the Theological Department: "Some of the more worldly-wise among us have an aversion to the term 'theology' and expressed a wish that the donation had been made to the Medical Department." But he added, "Most of us, I think, are still of the opinion that it was highly fitting to mention the Theological Department first in the constitution and that it should have the prominence your timely donation gives it."[15]

Finally in January 1883, more than a year after Goucher's pledge, Ohlinger sent him a proposal to buy a site and plans for a departmental building that included student and lecture rooms, a dining hall, library, and chapel. The missionary requested that his benefactor send the promised funds, and also asked if the general college population could use some of the space until the full complement of theology students was filled. Goucher was not satisfied that his gift was being directed correctly. Bishop I. W. Wiley wrote apologizing for the delay in launching the Theological Department, as well as for Ohlinger's overstep in wanting to use Goucher's donation for other than its intended purpose.[16]

A deep division also remained among the American Methodist missionaries at Foochow over teaching English at the college, one that Robert calls "a virtual war." She explains the root of the problem: "To introduce English in defiance of three-self tradition was a tacit admission that evangelism, narrowly defined, was no longer the aim of missions." Wiley gave Goucher his view of the situation:

> We have difficulty of course in inaugurating this new education movement in China as we do in all new and important things. There are conservatives who are never ready to move forward and there are progressionists who are in too big a hurry. Fogyism and over-zeal have here as elsewhere done us in. But the movement is important, needed, timely and only needs to be wisely guided.

He asked Goucher not to withdraw his support for the Theological Department and pledged that they would not touch the money unless its use was satisfactory to the donor. Goucher agreed to extend his 1881 offer through the missionary year 1884, "with the hope that the conditions may be complied with before the expiration date of that time."[17]

It was not to be. The new department was supposed to open at the beginning of 1885, but Bishop Wiley died without addressing what missionary Nathan Sites called "any irregularities in mission and educational work in Foochow." He credited Goucher with persuading the General Missionary Committee to approve the Anglo-Chinese College in the first place through his original pledge. But Sites admitted to him that after years of delay, the mission at Foochow had proven "unworthy of your gifts." Goucher withdrew his offer for the Theological Department.[18]

While Goucher was frustrated on the educational front in Foochow, during the early 1880s he was able to help provide much needed spaces for worship in the conference. As the growing Chinese ministry fanned out to the surrounding countryside, there came more requests for new churches. Goucher had seen the pattern before and stood ready to help. He knew through experience with the Frontier Loan Fund that a small amount of seed money could spur larger fundraising efforts within a community. But instead of loaning money to build churches in the Foochow area, he offered a cash donation toward constructing several buildings, challenging Chinese Christians and members of the Foochow Conference to come up with the rest of the money.

The congregations sent Goucher letters of gratitude, along with drawings of the new churches with their granite foundations, earthen walls, and traditional tiled roofs. Sites translated one letter from the Chinese trustees of the Sing Tong Chapel, in a district outside Foochow. It related that after a dozen years together, church members had lacked a suitable place to worship until now. "[T]hanks to you, beloved minister, . . . for sending us sixty dollars to aid us in building a church." The trustees also noted the timeline for construction, which began "on the 12th day of the seventh moon of last year [1882] and completed on the 3rd day of the fifth moon of this year and dedicated on the 3rd day of the fifth month." Sites told their supporter that all the Goucher-sponsored churches were "most highly prized by the little membership that worship in them." Goucher was glad to learn that his aid had spurred the beneficiaries to raise more than three times the amount he had donated for the churches.[19]

But even before Goucher pledged funds for a college and churches in Foochow, he was contemplating support for another venture in China. The Methodists had carried on mission work in the Foochow area since the late 1840s and the northern and central regions since the 1860s, but there was no mission station in western China, reachable only by an often perilous and weeks-long trip up the Yangtze River. Foreign merchants were pushing trade in that direction, the British government had stationed a consul in the Szechuan (Sichuan) Province, and Roman Catholic missionaries were already preaching there. Ohlinger and Sites in Foochow believed the time was right to make a move. Sites posed the question to missionary secretary Fowler in New York: "Shall not our American Methodist Episcopal Church be among the first to enter this promising field of over 20 million souls . . . ?" Even as Ohlinger was considering opening the new college in Foochow, he was writing Goucher in August 1880, promoting West

China as especially ripe for missionary work because it was "a natural approach to the eight provinces as yet unoccupied by Protestant missionaries and also to Tibet."[20]

At the November meeting of the General Missionary Committee, Bishop Wiley presented a proposal to fund a West China station. But members were wary of assuming even more mission debt, and the motion was tabled without action. Goucher, however, had been thinking about the unusual opportunity the new mission offered, and he was unwilling to let it fail without offering the committee an incentive. As the 1880 session was ready to close, he sent a letter, read by Wiley, in which he and Mary pledged $5,000 a year for two years ($119,000 a year) to send experienced missionaries to set up a mission in western China. The committee accepted, and a project that might have been delayed indefinitely became viable.[21]

Goucher recommended Ohlinger to lead the new station because of his demonstrated interest, but Wiley named Spencer Lewis and Lucius Wheeler, a former missionary to North China, to the post. They (and their families) left for China in the fall of 1881. Wheeler took the arduous journey up the Yangtze to scout a location for their base, and the following year they established the mission in Chungking (Chongqing). Wheeler painted Goucher an encouraging picture of the opportunities there: It was a prosperous, commercial city, with well-to-do citizens; there was a friendly disposition toward foreigners; parents were interested in new schools; and he was already holding religious services on a small scale. These prospects confirmed Goucher's optimism in expanding into this region.[22]

Goucher gave an unexpected gift of $3,000 ($71,700) for the new mission in October 1882, and reconfirmed his second-year pledge of $5,000 at the General Missionary Committee meeting the following month. This offer spurred the committee to raise its appropriation for West China. It promised to give "rigorous prosecution to this mission," and sent a medical missionary to join the two men and their families already in place; the WFMS also assigned Wheeler's daughter to open a school for girls.[23]

Just before the committee's 1883 meeting in New York, Fowler acknowledged that the mission in West China was beginning to grow rapidly, and he expressed the need for another station in Chengtu

(Chengdu), the capital of Szechuan Province. He wrote Goucher, "Your past liberality to this field exceeding your original promise encourages me to ask your attention to the question whether you will be able to give us another advance for next year." Committed as Goucher was to the long-range progress of the West China Mission, he did not expect to sponsor its operation indefinitely. At the moment he was more interested in helping to open another East Asian territory he had been hearing and reading about—Korea.[24]

Pai Chai Hakdang,
Seoul, Korea (1887)

Courtesy of the Appenzeller/Noble Memorial Museum,
Seoul, Korea

ENTERING KOREA, THE "HERMIT KINGDOM"

Chapter 10
(1883-1889)

━━━━━━━━━◆◆━━━━━━━━━

The Church, individually and collectively,
is required to go and teach . . .[1]

A serendipitous meeting—Goucher might have attributed it to God's guiding hand— finally led him to undertake a plan for Korea similar to the West China mission. Returning to Baltimore after a trip in September 1883, Goucher happened to share a train car with special envoys from Korea's King Kojong as they traveled to Washington, D.C. Korea had recently signed a treaty establishing friendship and trade with the United States, and was trying to shed its perennial image in the West as the "Hermit Kingdom." The envoys had come to meet President Chester A. Arthur, travel to New York and Boston, and learn about American customs and government agencies. Dressed in their native attire, they attracted Goucher's curiosity and interest. Through their interpreters, the young minister questioned them about conditions in their country, and before leaving the train he extended and they accepted an invitation to visit him at Alto Dale. Combining this firsthand knowledge from the envoys with other information he had acquired about Korea (also known as Corea), he was ready to act quickly to give the Methodists "the honor of pioneering missionary efforts" in that country.[2]

Over many centuries, Korea had faced internal upheavals and external encroachments that ultimately spurred the country's isolationism and aversion to Christianity. Before the establishment in the late fourteenth century of the Yi or Choson (Joseon) dynasty, of which King Kojong was one of the last rulers, Korea had been invaded by the Mongols, who ruled China and maintained influence in Korea for more than a century. The early Choson kings retained ties to the Chinese, and Confucianism became the official religion. They also instituted a number of reforms, including the creation of a native Korean alphabet, Hangul, for use by commoners instead of the Chinese characters used by the elite.

An entrenched, hierarchical, and hereditary class structure hindered the country's progress, however, and the rigid, unwieldy system was rife with court intrigues and political conflicts. Adding to the instability were two unsuccessful Japanese invasions in the late sixteenth century. In the mid-seventeenth, the Manchus made two incursions into the country, after which Korea became a vassal state of China's Qing dynasty. Over the next two centuries, Choson rulers closed their country's borders, limiting its contact with nations other than China.[3]

By the mid-nineteenth century, Korea regarded the opening of both China and Japan to western influences with unease. The country was determined to maintain its isolation, despite sometimes hostile attempts by the English, French, Russians, and Americans to open relations; this continued seclusion earned Korea the western nickname the "Hermit Kingdom." Internally, various clans struggled for power and to exert influence on the line of royal succession. In 1863, King Kojong was selected as ruler at age eleven. His father acted as the Taewongun or prince regent until the boy reached majority, and the elder retained ties to China and enforced the isolationist policy. He also renewed bloody persecutions of Catholic priests, who had entered the country from China in the late eighteenth century. For Korea's rulers, Christianity was tied to western attempts to enter the country, and converts were considered threats to the Confucian-based society.

King Kojong and his wife Queen Min formally began their independent reign in 1873, a few years after a new, equally young emperor assumed the throne of Japan. Through earlier treaties, that country had begun to open its borders to western influence and had recently established a legation in the Chinese capital, moves that made Korea appear even more isolated. Elite opinion was divided on how to proceed. Queen Min's clan was conservative and pro-Chinese, while others in government felt that trade relations with Japan and the West would benefit the country.

King Kojong's foreign policy was more progressive than his father's, and he finally signed treaties of friendship with Japan in 1876, and with the United States, Great Britain, and Germany in 1882. The emergence of the "Hermit Kingdom" not only set the stage for future rivalry between China and Japan for dominance over Korean affairs, but also prepared the way for American missionaries to enter the country, although teaching religion was still prohibited.[4]

Even before meeting the envoys on the train, Goucher had been hearing about Korea, later called the Land of the Morning Calm. After the Korean-Japanese treaty was signed, Methodist missionaries in Japan came into contact with a growing number of Korean students, including three studying English with Robert Maclay's wife. Martin Vail, representing the Japan Mission, wrote Goucher shortly after the United States and Korea signed their treaty, asking him to take a year's leave of absence from his Baltimore ministry to visit the "Island Enterprise" and China. Of Korea, Vail said: "That country is no longer a closed land, and in a few months we shall begin to learn more and more about it. It might be interesting for you to visit that land." Editorials and articles in the *Christian Advocate* appealed to readers for funds to open a mission there.[5]

The General Missionary Committee held its annual meeting in November 1883, and Goucher offered funds toward the main academic building at the Anglo-Japanese College in Tokyo and renewed his ongoing pledge for the Theological Department at the Anglo-Chinese College in Foochow. He also indicated that he and Mary would donate $2,000 ($48,800) to help open a new station in Korea if a married missionary were assigned to oversee it. Bishop I. W. Wiley told Goucher that he held this particular proposal until the close of the meeting "so as not to interfere with other appropriations and also that it might stand out as a special appropriation." This tactic proved successful, as the committee accepted the gift and approved an additional $3,000 ($73,100) for the Japan Mission to open work in Korea.[6]

Since Robert Maclay was superintendent of the Japan Mission, Wiley asked him to visit the country to determine the best way to begin. Goucher offered to pay his travel expenses, but Maclay reported in March 1884 that United States ministers to Japan and Korea strongly advised delaying a new mission because of political unrest in Korea. Undeterred, the superintendent wrote his friend three months later that he was boarding a steamer for a two-week voyage from Tokyo to Seoul. Looking ahead, he speculated that he might scout a new missionary site around Gensan (Wonsan), in Korea's northeast, perhaps as early as the following year. He asked John and Mary to think about that contingency as they went about "forecasting the future and arranging plans for helping the work of the Lord during the year 1885."[7]

After traveling more than 1,400 miles by sea, stopping briefly in Fusan (Busan) and finally landing in Chemulpo (Incheon), about twenty-five miles west of Seoul, Maclay contacted Goucher on July 2, 1884, with a triumphant message: "It affords me very sincere pleasure to write you from the capital of Corea." He met with the resident United States minister, Lucius H. Foote, and talked with Kim Ok Kyun, a highly placed official in the foreign office, who presented the missionary's appeal to King Kojong. Maclay followed up with Goucher at the end of July, saying the king was favorable to a mission that would open schools and take on hospital work in Seoul, despite what Maclay characterized as "the prejudices of many Coreans and opposition of a powerful body of [the King's] officers." He also notified the Methodist General Missionary Committee: "As far as I know, our Church is the first to be recognized by the Corean government, as a helper in the career of reform and progress on which it has entered."[8]

Maclay sounded a note of caution, however, warning of events that would soon hamper the mission's progress. In Seoul, fifteen hundred Chinese troops were stationed in a fortified camp, and there was also a small Japanese garrison in place. As Maclay related to Goucher, "Formerly the struggle was conducted at long range. Now they face each other in the capital of the Kingdom." Maclay also advised, "China and Japan are profoundly interested in Corean matters and their interests are sufficiently antagonistic to make them thoroughly watchful of each other's movements."[9]

At the same time Maclay was writing with good news from Seoul in early July 1884, Wiley was corresponding with Goucher from New York. The bishop promised to "watch the opening and enter as soon as it is safe and wise to do so." Goucher pressed that educational and medical work should begin in Korea "at the earliest moment competent agents could be secured." As an added incentive, he renewed his so-far untapped $2,000 pledge from the previous November's General Missionary Committee meeting, and offered an additional $3,000 ($74,700) to purchase a site for the mission in Seoul, provided that an experienced, ordained missionary preacher and a missionary doctor (both married) be sent to the field some time in the following year.[10]

Finding the right men to send into uncharted territory was the next step. Writing from Seoul, Maclay told Goucher that the chief challenge for the first arrivals would be loneliness in a land whose people were "scarcely prepared to appreciate the benefits to result from intercourse with Western nations." Wiley chose Dr. William B. Scranton for the medical position and had a minister in mind to fill the other. When that candidate declined, Henry Gerhard Appenzeller was suggested. Appenzeller was just completing his studies at Drew Theological Seminary in New Jersey and was interested in Japanese mission work. But when Wiley died suddenly in Foochow, the appointment was left to a new bishop, Charles H. Fowler.[11]

Goucher's sizeable donations, the careful thinking behind them, and his broad contacts with young ministers and missionaries in the field gave him a reputation as a knowledgeable source, and by the mid-1880s, church leaders began looking to him for recommendations to fill particular assignments. For example, in the summer of 1884, Bishop William Taylor asked him to "select a few, even half a dozen" men to go to India and also to find several men—white or black—for African missions. Naturally Goucher was also consulted about who would lead the new station he and Mary were funding in Seoul.[12]

Fowler leaned toward Appenzeller, whom Goucher had met two years before during an event at the Gouchers' home. But as J. M. Reid, corresponding secretary of the Missionary Society, wrote to the aspiring missionary, "Brother Goucher feels that we ought to have someone with experience in the mission field or at least considerable experience in the work of the Church—building, diplomacy, etc." However, after the bishop, secretary, and donor met in Baltimore before Christmas that year to consult on the matter, Reid gave Appenzeller the good news that "Bishop Fowler and Bro. Goucher have decided to appoint you missionary to Korea."[13]

Events in Korea in December 1884 threatened to derail the Methodists' plan to enter the country right away. The rivalry between government factions—one backed by Queen Min and her pro-Chinese officials versus one led by members of the Japanese-backed Progressive Party—flared into a bloody coup. The insurgents favoring Japan were defeated, and the conservative pro-Chinese side remained in charge for the time being, but there was a residual breakdown in order and an increase in crime. Reid told Appenzeller after his appointment, "I fear the anti-foreign party is in the ascendant."[14]

Even so, the Appenzellers and the Scrantons—and Scranton's mother Mary, going to Korea under the auspices of the Women's Foreign Missionary Society—sailed from San Francisco at the beginning of February 1885. They reached Maclay in Tokyo three weeks later, when Appenzeller immediately notified Goucher of their arrival. He advised that two Korean officials were in the city to arrange matters for the new mission, and reassured Goucher that the Korean government was "very open for missionaries to go forward."[15]

Bishop Fowler named Maclay superintendent of the Korea Mission and Appenzeller as his assistant. The new missionary spent his time studying mission procedures and acquiring equipment for the new station, and at the end of March, he and his wife sailed for Chemulpo. They arrived on Easter Sunday 1885, a seemingly auspicious date on which to enter into a new Christian enterprise. But on their arrival, authorities warned Appenzeller about continued unrest and told him that neither the United States legation nor any other power could provide protection. He and his wife returned to Tokyo.[16]

Scranton, traveling solo, arrived in Seoul about a month later, in early May. He was met by Horace N. Allen, a Presbyterian medical missionary, who had been sent from his post in China the previous fall and was the first Protestant missionary to begin work in Korea. Since direct evangelizing was prohibited, Allen was assigned to the United States legation in Seoul as its physician. He had gained favor with the Korean royal family by successfully treating the king's injured nephew during the December coup, and the king supported Allen's opening a hospital, named Gwanghyewon (House of Extended Grace). He was joined in April 1885 by another Presbyterian missionary, Horace G. Underwood, who was restricted to working at the hospital.

The overworked Allen welcomed Scranton as a fellow physician and asked him to help at the hospital until the Methodist mission was set up. This connection earned Scranton official recognition from the government.[17]

By early June, nearly a year after Maclay had visited Seoul to explore the possibility of opening a mission, Scranton was ready to send for his family and the Appenzellers. Preaching Christian doctrine was still prohibited, but the king and others were receptive to the benefits of education and medical treatment the newcomers offered. With the Gouchers' money, Scranton bought property for the Methodist mission compound on high ground in the Chungdong neighborhood, near the Deoksugung Palace, the American legation, and the Presbyterian mission. Appenzeller later described it as "four acres in the King's own city and that in a part sure to become the home of foreigners. . . . We have been happy in the thought of our pleasant location and the bright prospects before us."[18]

Goucher finally had what he had argued for: an ordained minister and medical doctor and their families in Seoul, laying the foundation for Methodist mission work at an advantageous site. But these steps were only the beginning of what the Goucher donation—the first of many—ultimately brought to Korea in the areas of education, health, and religion. Appenzeller did not delay in starting his own school once he arrived in Seoul, introducing western-style education to the Confucian-oriented society. As yet unfamiliar with the language and forbidden to preach publicly, he began offering classes to two male students in his home during the summer of 1885. The following June, he formally opened the country's first modern school for boys. The first students were a handful of young adult men, some already married. They wanted to learn English, which was considered a path to advancement, as the government was urgently looking for translators to deal with its increasing interactions with the West.

An outbreak of cholera that summer brought public panic and killed hundreds. But in November 1886, Appenzeller wrote in his journal that the more than thirty students then enrolled made the school the largest in Korea. He acknowledged that there was "no pretense of teaching religion but one hour daily—only English," because "the law against Christianity is evidently known and feared by some at least."

He once handed a religious tract to a student, who quickly returned it, "fearing he would lose his head if discovered." But an early twentieth-century biographer of Appenzeller spoke of the impact of the new learning style, in contrast to a Confucian education, which relied on rote learning and memorization: "It taught the pupil to think."[19]

The biographer added that the school became increasingly popular among Korean parents who hoped such an education would carry their sons on to "fortune and royal favor." In February 1887, King Kojong acknowledged the school's reputation by giving it an official name—Pai Chai Hakdang, the Hall for Rearing Useful Men. The head of the Foreign Office delivered a painted sign board with the name calligraphed in large blue letters, for display over the entrance. Appenzeller appreciated the honor, for it brought, he noted in his journal, "recognition by the government and standing before the Koreans not held before." Although under mission auspices, it was now perceived as a public rather than a private institution, attracting still more students.[20]

By the end of the 1887 school year, several dozen young men were enrolled, and that August, Appenzeller laid the cornerstone for the College Hall at Pai Chai Hakdang. He wrote a memorandum for the occasion that would have pleased Goucher by affirming his aims. The hall, Appenzeller said, was "built for the dissemination of liberal Christian education throughout this land," giving the Missionary Society of the Methodist Episcopal Church "the honor of erecting the first building of this kind in Korea." Despite the ban on teaching Christianity, a few students did convert. The Hall for Rearing Useful Men continued to grow, and ten years after the first classes held in Appenzeller's home in 1885, Pai Chai Hakdang began to offer college-level courses.[21]

On a parallel track, in May 1886, Mary Scranton founded the first school in Korea for girls and young women at her son's house on the mission compound. Before then, public education for girls did not exist. They might be taught at home to read and write Hangul, the Korean script, and daughters of the yangban, or noble class, received some training in the Confucian classics. But after the age of eight or nine, girls were secluded with the women. Appenzeller wrote in an article that "a Korean woman, regardless of her station, is expected to do two things well—cooking and sewing." As his biographer commented, "In old Korea, a female was only one man's daughter, wife, or mother, without a personality of her own." They often were not even granted names. When there were numerous daughters in a family, they were simply numbered, and a man might not know his wife's name when they married.[22]

Given Koreans' general suspicion of Westerners and Christians and their motives, missionaries had to overcome many handicaps in recruiting students. As a history of Mary Scranton's school explains, there were "macabre rumors that Westerners sucked the blood of children and plucked out their eyes, or kidnapped them to be sold in a faraway country." Scranton began her school with one short-term student, Lady Kim, a concubine of a high-ranking official who wanted to become an interpreter for Queen Min. The first long-term student, a ten-year-old girl, enrolled only after Scranton signed an agreement never to take her out of the country without permission.[23]

After this modest start, the school grew to seven students and moved early in 1887 from the Scranton home to new quarters on WFMS property nearby. Soon after he had bestowed the name Pai Chai Hakdang, King Kojong designated its sister school Ewha Hakdang— the Pear Blossom School—perhaps because, as tradition notes, there was a pear orchard on the Chungdong hills where Ewha first began. As with Pai Chai's official designation, this name "acknowledged the institution as a public school, expressing trust in the missionaries who ran it." In the early years, Ewha students often were orphans or children whose parents couldn't support them, so the school took the form of a boarding school, providing food and shelter as well as learning. Mary Scranton was soon well-known in the capital and respectfully referred to as "*the* old woman."[24]

While both schools introduced western educational practices, William Scranton pointed out in an article for the *Christian Advocate* that the missionaries did not proselytize for western dress or customs. Instead, he related, "We take pleasure in making Koreans better Koreans only. We want Korea to be proud of Korean things. . . . In the short time we have been at work here, we see that we are slowly doing what is in our hearts to do and are showing Korea Korean possibilities." Pai Chai Hakdang and Ewha Hakdang also differed from government-sponsored schools in the students they accepted. Just as Goucher promoted gender and class equality in his schools in India, Appenzeller and Mary Scranton educated students regardless of their heritage or status in society.[25]

As Appenzeller was launching his educational campaign in 1885, Scranton, his medical colleague, opened a small dispensary in his home on the mission compound that fall. The following June, Appenzeller wrote in his journal of the Korean mission's three-fold success: His boys' school formally opened; Mary Scranton started her educational work with girls and women; and "Dr. Scranton went into his new hospital yesterday." In Seoul's Chungdong district, the doctor had bought and remodeled two adjacent houses, one with a waiting room, operating room, and five wards for men, and one with three wards for women. During his first year there, he saw more than 2,000 patients, most of them poor, and many of whom came from outside the city to see the physician. Needing additional help, William and Mary Scranton appealed to the WFMS to send a woman doctor, and a women's health clinic was opened in 1887 on the Ewha Hakdang grounds. As in China, the allures of such medical care—and education—quietly opened ears and hearts to the missionaries' message.[26]

King Kojong gave William Scranton's institution an official name—Si Pyung Won, or Universal Relief Hospital, and his mother's clinic became known as Boguyeogwan—the Center for the Care and Treatment of Women. The king appreciated the benefits of western-style medicine, fearing (as Goucher once told a friend) assassination attempts. (A favorite method, Goucher maintained, was to grind glass very fine and put it in food.) The king felt more secure with the Methodist Dr. Scranton as well as the Presbyterian Dr. Allen available to treat him or the royal family.[27]

The missionaries had not forgotten their underlying task to publicly introduce Christianity to Korea. As Appenzeller told J. M. Reid at the Missionary Society in New York, "The moment I know enough of the language and the doors are opened, we want to enter before the Devil can shut them again." During the first months in the country, Appenzeller and the Presbyterian Horace Underwood had held religious services in the home of one or the other, on respective compounds. The services were attended by staff from the American legation and families of both denominations, plus a few Japanese Christians attached to their legation in the city. Shortly after formally opening his school, Appenzeller led a union service at the American legation, declaring himself "honored to be the first to preach" in this more public setting in Seoul.[28]

Despite Koreans' apparent distrust of foreign religions, the number of Methodist followers grew. In early Fall 1887, Appenzeller purchased a small house—eight feet by eight and six feet high inside—near the mission compound. There he opened the Bethel Chapel, the place he called—and is still considered—"the cradle of Methodism" in Korea. That October, he recorded holding the first formal Methodist service in a church in the "Hermit Kingdom," with four Koreans present. Two weeks later, he and Scranton led the first communion service in Korea, with five converts. A second house was soon purchased next door, expanding the space for services and meetings as the congregation grew. On Christmas Day that year, Appenzeller was pleased to note that, after two and a half years in the country, he was able to preach in Korean for the first time.[29]

John Goucher keenly appreciated these achievements he and Mary had helped sponsor. One eulogist would later note, "It was characteristic of Dr. Goucher to realize intuitively the broader relations of movements of the times. . . . He was ever interested in the laying of foundations whose greater values might appear only after many years." While this statement could apply to many projects he supported around the world, the Korea Mission was a particular success. The Korean Methodist Church, celebrating its 130th anniversary in 2015, has more than 10,000 ministers and 1,500,000 members, worshipping in more than 6,300 churches in the Republic of Korea. Now Korean missionaries are spreading the gospel abroad: more than 1,100 of them are scattered in several dozen countries around the globe, including the United States. On the educational front, both Pai Chai and Ewha have grown to encompass high school and university campuses, and they remember and honor John and Mary Goucher's role in their founding.[30]

Spanning the years 1879 to 1889, Goucher devoted much thought and many resources to establishing and supporting missions, churches, a hospital, and schools abroad. In India, China, Japan, and Korea alone, he and Mary contributed approximately $120,000 over that period (nearly $3 million). But they did not neglect the educational needs of two underserved and overlooked populations in their home city—African Americans and young women.

Home of the Centenary Biblical Institute/Morgan College
1881-1917
(*The Promethean,* 1955)

Courtesy of the Beulah M. Davis Special Collections Department,
Earl S. Richardson Library, Morgan State University,
Baltimore, Maryland

THE CENTENARY
BIBLICAL INSTITUTE

Chapter 11
(1879-1889)

━━━━━━━━━━◆◆━━━━━━━━━━

*The protection accorded children and the provision for their
education mirror accurately a nation's
civic condition and perspective.*[1]

In 1879, as John and Mary Goucher began donating to Japan and
China, they also made a gift that helped open a new door for African
Americans in Baltimore. Goucher strongly believed they should
have the same educational opportunities as others, so they could be
independent and make a better life for themselves, their families, and
their communities. To put this belief into practice, the couple made a
major contribution to the Centenary Biblical Institute, founded in 1867
to educate "pious young men, especially colored, for the ministry in
the Methodist Episcopal Church."[2]

Bishop Levi Scott, a white man who had converted early in
life at a Methodist meeting held in a black couple's home, was an
early champion of the school. In 1866, he had secured $5,000 from
the Missionary Society in New York to establish the institute, which
received ongoing support from the Methodist Freedman's Aid Society,
started the same year to help educate newly freed slaves. As the
Board of Bishops declared at the society's founding, "The time may
come when the states in the South will make some provision for the
education of the colored children now growing up in utter ignorance in
their midst. But thus far they have made none, nor perhaps can it soon
be expected of them. . . . The emergency is upon us, and we must begin
to work now." As a minister, Goucher was familiar with the society's
charge and with the Centenary Biblical Institute. Each Methodist
congregation in a conference was assigned an annual amount to raise

for Freedman's Aid, and the Baltimore Conference used its collections to support this local black institution.[3]

At one of the institute's first board meetings, Bishop Scott had given its trustees a charge that would resonate for Goucher, who would be involved with this enterprise for more than forty years: "May God prosper the work of our hands and enable us to tell favorably and powerfully on the improvement and elevation of a people long neglected and oppressed." After Goucher's 1879 gift, he continued to work with black and white ministers and lay leaders in broadening African Americans' educational opportunities. He became a central force in developing the Centenary Biblical Institute into Morgan College, today the historically black Morgan State University.[4]

By the time Goucher joined the ministry and the Baltimore Conference in 1869, there had already been a long association between African Americans and Methodism in Maryland. Historian Christopher Phillips states that Methodism, with "its simplicity and informality . . . as well as its general warmth and evangelical fervor, led many black people into its fold." He adds that perhaps its greatest appeal to African Americans was the Church's early opposition to slavery. From the mid eighteenth century into the early nineteenth, class meetings—small gatherings in private homes—brought blacks and whites and men and women together for religious discussions and prayer. Baltimore's black and white Methodists also joined forces to build chapels at Lovely Lane and Strawberry Alley, where free blacks, slaves, and whites intermingled in the pews. White clergy also performed marriages, baptisms, and funeral services for black parishioners. African Americans comprised over thirty-five percent of Baltimore Methodists by 1800, and nearly half by 1815.[5]

Nevertheless, African Americans grew to feel increasingly marginalized in mixed congregations. As Phillips notes, in early nineteenth-century Baltimore and the upper South, "White members of mixed churches suffered increased tensions from the conflict between Christian fellowship and the southern racial system." Seating became racially segregated, and services favored "white decorum" over the animated spontaneity of black worship. There also were no black leaders within the church. African-American Methodists, Phillips concludes, "now found their status in the church circumscribed as sorely as in society itself."[6]

In response, some black parishioners started their own Methodist churches, although the preachers could not be ordained and were not accepted as members of the Baltimore Conference. (They were considered helpers to white ministers assigned to black churches.) One early site for black fellowship was a meetinghouse opened on Sharp Street in 1802 as the African Academy, later known as the Sharp Street Methodist Episcopal Church. It served as "a multipurpose agency" during the antebellum years: a meeting place for blacks "to discuss and to plan strategy; to raise money to purchase the freedom of slaves; to serve as a school where deprived and exploited people could learn to read and write; to aid in the Liberian (African) colonization; to discuss the effectiveness of the slavery abolitionist movement and to hear its advocates speak." It also would play an important role in the early life of the Centenary Biblical Institute.[7]

By 1844, the issue of slaveholding finally produced a schism, leading to the formation of the Methodist Episcopal Church, South. At the time, the Baltimore Conference included churches, circuits, and stations in much of Maryland, Washington, and northern Virginia, and congregations voted on which branch they wanted to join. Most in the Baltimore Conference decided to remain in the established Methodist Episcopal Church. Representatives of black churches at the 1848 and 1856 northern General Conferences petitioned to establish conferences of their own, but the motions were denied. At the 1864 conference, the ministers of sixteen black Methodist congregations, mainly from Maryland, asked friends in the Baltimore Conference to present the motion on their behalf, and several white Baltimore delegates successfully sponsored the establishment of a new Washington Conference including nearly 8,000 black parishioners. At last, these congregations gained autonomy from white churches, reporting only to the General Conference.[8]

One issue of particular concern for the Washington Conference was expanding educational opportunities for African Americans within its boundaries. On the eve of the Civil War, Baltimore had the largest free black, as well as total black population of any American city. But few attended school regularly; resources were scarce, and there were too few qualified teachers. Many whites viewed educating African Americans as unwise or unnecessary. Free black children in Maryland were in effect still enslaved; if not in service or working at home, they could be indentured or apprenticed to a white master, without pay, by the courts.[9]

In 1826, a law was enacted to create public primary schools in Baltimore, supported by a tax on white and black property owners, but only white children were allowed to attend. Later, black citizens and white supporters petitioned to remedy this imbalance, but they were rejected by the mayor and City Council. An article about pre-Civil War education for African Americans states, "The majority of whites were opposed to educating the black population for fear that they would begin to challenge their position." Consequently African-American schools in Baltimore were found mainly in black and white churches (Methodist among them), whose Sabbath schools offered instruction in reading and some writing. By 1859, there were fifteen church-affiliated or privately operated schools in the city for free and enslaved African Americans. No matter how valued and eagerly sought, such educational opportunities remained all too rare.[10]

Following the ratification of the new Maryland constitution of 1864, more than 87,000 slaves in Maryland were emancipated on November 1, 1864, just as the new Washington Conference concluded its organizing session, with Bishop Scott in attendance. Members knew that without advances in education, there would be scant progress for the state's 80,000 free blacks and the many thousands about to become free. Although the new constitution required the General Assembly to provide free public schools in every school district, supported by an education tax levied on property owners, it still did not designate any schools for the children of black taxpayers. That document's framers worried the constitution would be defeated if such schools had been mentioned. Many white Marylanders still "either feared or considered impossible the proposal to elevate Negroes through education to a higher social or economic level."[11]

The state distributed the tax monies intended for public education to Baltimore City and the counties according to their entire school-age populations. But it was left to each jurisdiction to administer the funds. For two years, school boards allocated no money to build black schools. It was not until 1867 that the Baltimore City Council finally assumed control over black schools, and agreed to allocate African Americans' property taxes toward their own primary schools. As Phillips indicates, "Not until after the Civil War were black Baltimoreans allowed to attend the city's public schools, which they had been financially supporting since 1826."[12]

Although education laws were gradually being enacted in the mid-1860s under the new state constitution, private and religious organizations, aligned with some public initiatives, first advocated and raised funds for a more organized system of black schools in Maryland. One such group was the Baltimore Association for the Moral and Educational Improvement of the Colored People, familiarly known as the Baltimore Association. Founded in November 1864, it included more than thirty local businessmen, lawyers, and ministers, and became a conduit for support from interested groups in the North. It also received a boost from the Baltimore City Council, led by members sympathetic to black education; it allocated $10,000 ($155,000) to the Baltimore Association. After just one year, that organization had established seven schools in Baltimore City, most teaching 200 or more students, and eighteen smaller schools in neighboring counties. By 1867, there were more than 100 black schools in Maryland, enrolling over 2,500 students in Baltimore and about 5,000 elsewhere, mostly on the Eastern Shore. This growth did not come without friction, especially in rural areas. Teachers were verbally threatened and sometimes physically assaulted; classes were disrupted by drunken intruders; and arsonists set fire to buildings that housed black schools, burning at least a dozen by 1867. An article about the Baltimore Association reports, "It seemed that every church with a school [for blacks] was in danger."[13]

The Methodist Episcopal Church also set up black primary schools in the city following the Civil War, and its Freedmen's Aid Society contributed funds to start a Colored Normal School for teacher training. Blacks donated money and labor to build their own schools, such as the African Institute and the Wayman Academy, named for a bishop of the African Methodist Episcopal Church. In 1865, forty African-American men formed an association and purchased a building to open the Douglass Institute, named for Frederick Douglass, a former Maryland slave. Speaking at the school's dedication, he called the event an indication of "the rise of a people long oppressed, enslaved and bound in the chains of ignorance, to a freer plane of life, manhood, usefulness and civilization." But even with private and public initiatives, there remained an acute need for schools of all levels.[14]

In this context, thirteen white ministers and lay members of the Baltimore Conference became founders and trustees of the Centenary Biblical Institute of the Methodist Episcopal Church, using funds Bishop Scott had obtained from the Missionary Society. Among those trustees were William Harden, a minister and delegate to the General Conference that had approved the organization of the Washington Conference; Thomas Kelso, a businessman and the first president of the institute's Board of Trustees; and Francis A. Crook, another businessman who would work with John Goucher a few years later in establishing and supporting a local women's college. When the institute opened in April 1867, it offered an informal series of lectures to those who were already preaching or wanted to become preachers, and students were taught by three trustees who were ministers. Classes met in the basement of the Sharp Street Methodist Episcopal Church, which provided a home for nearly five years.[15]

By 1872, the institute's Board of Trustees, which now included four black members, recognized the need for a more permanent home. They purchased and furnished a house on Saratoga Street in downtown Baltimore for new headquarters, and with the support of the Freedmen's Aid Society, hired the Centenary Biblical Institute's first full-time president. Two years later the critical need for black teachers prompted the addition of a Normal Department to train both men and women. Within five years, the institute had grown so much—with nearly eighty students—it had outgrown the house on Saratoga. The board decided to sell the property and purchase another for classes, renting a separate house for the president, who had been living with his family in the institute's cramped quarters.[16]

During this expansion, Goucher stepped in to set the Centenary Biblical Institute on a new path toward longer-range opportunities for African-American students. In September 1879, he was appointed to a Baltimore Conference committee to advise the trustees on the acquisition of more space. They had found property downtown they were prepared to buy, but Goucher, seeing this was a crucial moment for the school, suggested an alternative. First, he offered a plot of land he owned in West Baltimore, not far from Gilmor Street and Harlem Park, where he was building a new church. A newspaper article described the donated site as commanding "the finest view of the city and harbor to be obtained anywhere, except from the top of the Washington monument."[17]

Goucher also promised to help fund a new building. The minutes of the Baltimore Annual Conference recorded the importance of this gift to the institute's future:

> Rev. John F. Goucher has been the instrument to set on foot and render possible, a plan that promises to place this enterprise upon an ample and secure foundation. Profoundly impressed with the vast possibilities of good to this neglected people in adequate educational facilities for training especially of secular and religious teachers, and having it in his power to aid materially in their realization, he purchased a site admirable in character and location, on which to erect a building adapted to the uses of the Institute. The presentation of this ample and wisely chosen site, valued at about ten thousand dollars ($245,000), he accompanied with a donation of money of five thousand dollars ($119,000), conditioned upon the contribution by others of a sum sufficient to complete a building in size and construction comporting with the locality, and the needs of the school.[18]

While he and Mary could have paid for the entire enterprise, Goucher preferred to offer enough seed money to make it viable and encourage stakeholders to raise the remaining funds—the same plan he had followed with the frontier and Foochow churches. He wanted even small donors to feel they had played an essential role.

The institute's trustees immediately began making personal donations, and members of the Washington Conference also pledged toward the "Goucher Challenge," as it became known. Before the end of 1879, the board had formed a five-member Building Committee, to which the young minister was appointed. Plans for a three-story stone structure were put out to bid the following spring. Perhaps remembering the delays in church building during his years on the circuit, Goucher offered another $500 ($11,900) as an added incentive, if the construction contract were awarded according to the agreed-upon specifications.[19]

Over the following year—while continuing his pastoral work and becoming increasingly involved with foreign missions and schools—Goucher tracked the new building's progress. When it was dedicated in May 1881, some debt remained. A portion was raised at the dedication ceremony, but Goucher pledged an additional $1,000 ($23,900) if the rest of the shortfall were raised by September. When the new building at Edmondson and Fulton Avenues opened that fall, 116 students were enrolled. White area residents were initially unhappy, but a team of conference visitors, representatives from several neighboring conferences who reviewed and assessed Methodist schools, later reported that those who were "inimical to the project of planting an institution in their midst" soon began not only "to regard the building as an ornament, but complimented the students by attesting that no instance of unbecoming conduct [had come] under their observation."[20]

Not surprisingly, Goucher was nominated to the Centenary Biblical Institute's Board of Trustees and was elected in January 1880. Within three months, he became its vice-president. He had known its president, Rev. Lyttleton F. Morgan, since his teenage years in Pittsburgh and considered him "as kind as a father." At Morgan's retirement in 1883, Goucher became president of the board at age thirty-eight. Conference visitors, examining the progress of the institute that year, proclaimed, "The election of the Rev. J. F. Goucher to fill the vacancy is a guarantee of even more vigorous efforts to promote the work of the institution."[21]

Once the institute had moved into new quarters, the Board of Trustees addressed issues relating to faculty, finances, and curriculum. At the first meeting after Goucher became president in 1883, the trustees heard a detailed committee report that warned the school was shifting from its original mission of training ministers to training teachers. Although the charter had been amended in 1879 to admit students of "good moral character" to prepare for other professions, as well as teaching—courses considered "anomalies" for a Biblical institute—it was expected that the Normal Department would close when the school met the desired standards for theological training. But in the sixteen years since the institute's founding, no students had graduated from its theological program, and no students were then pursuing the full theological course. Instead, conference visitors noted, "the Normal or Academic Department of the Institute is at present the predominant one."[22]

In response, Goucher led the trustees in approving a committee's recommendations to strengthen the curriculum and raise admission standards. The preparatory course was to be eliminated, and the Theological Department was to have a detailed program of religious study, with students admitted only after passing core courses in English, math, and science. The number of students enrolled in the Normal Department had increased substantially since its inception, and by the mid-1880s, teachers trained there were serving in nearly sixty public schools. But there remained an enormous need for black educators. The 1880 census indicated there were more than 600,000 African Americans ten years of age or older in the territory of the institute's supporting Methodist conferences, which included Maryland, Delaware, Virginia, West Virginia, and Washington, D.C. While many could read, about sixty percent could not write. As W. Maslin Frysinger, the institute's president, noted, "The difficulty is to obtain teachers." Under the new board recommendations, teacher training continued. The trustees decided, "For the time then present and not yet passed away, . . . the Institute could do more effective service for the colored race by this modification of its original ideal."[23]

Funding for this expanded curriculum was not easy to find. The Freedmen's Aid collections from the various conferences had never provided more than half of the institute's annual budget, and revenues from tuition were meager. The treasurer's report at the June 1884 trustees' meeting tallied the slim margin under which the institution was operating: The balance for the year was $1.75 after expenses. Yearly shortfalls were usually made up through private donations, and it was well known that the Gouchers' were among them.[24]

As one of its projects for the 1884 Methodist centennial, the Baltimore Conference considered creating an endowment to alleviate the institute's ongoing financial crisis. Goucher came forth with a donation to start the campaign. President Frysinger proclaimed, "The Rev. John F. Goucher contributes $5,000 ($124,000) of the $50,000 ($1.24 million) we have asked toward endowing the Centenary

Biblical Institute. Ten such friends would make us feel as though we were walking in 'golden slippers.'"[25]

The Washington Conference and the black Delaware Conference, also established at the 1864 General Conference, both pledged funds, but three years after Goucher made his original endowment gift, only a little more than half of the goal had been raised from all the conferences involved. The president of the board then issued another challenge. Goucher agreed to give yet another $5,000, provided Frysinger could secure the remaining money from other sources over the 1887-1888 academic year. Balancing the institute's annual and long-term fiscal needs became a continual concern for Goucher during his tenure on the board, and his philanthropy often came to the rescue.[26]

In the midst of addressing financial issues, Goucher and his fellow trustees were called on to help the Delaware Conference open a Methodist-affiliated school in a mostly rural area with a large black population. White residents "were either reluctant or indifferent to providing public secondary schools" for African Americans, and black ministers in the Delaware Conference knew whites would feel "no little indignation over the establishment of a 'colored institution' immediately on their suburbs." Without the approval and backing of the institute's board, they realized the institution they wanted— offering basic preparatory courses and some agricultural and vocational training—would never come to be.[27]

In August 1886, Goucher and Frysinger visited Somerset County, Maryland, to survey potential sites that might be appropriate and affordable. They had found none by the end of a long and frustrating trip and were set to return to Baltimore by boat. By chance—or perhaps divine design, to Goucher's mind—they learned of the Olney property, near Princess Anne, the night before they departed. Its several acres, a deserted mansion, and outbuildings were being sold for $2,000 (approximately $52,000) as part of an estate settlement, although it was valued at several thousand dollars more. Wasting no time, in the middle of the night, the two men traveled a half-mile to visit the property and toured the house "from garrett to cellar," according to Frysinger, by the light of a coal-oil lamp. They quickly realized that the location was perfect.[28]

After looking it over again at daybreak, before anyone realized their interest, Goucher made a $500 ($13,000) down payment on the property. To obscure their purpose, the sympathetic white Methodist minister who had hosted the visitors overnight, purchased it "for a church purpose" and then deeded the estate to the Centenary Biblical Institute. Considered a branch of the institute, the new school was named the Delaware Conference Academy, "a school of industry and learning for the children of [the area's] former slaves." It opened in September 1886 with fewer than a dozen students, but at the close of the academic year, there were nearly forty. By the end of 1887, Frysinger asserted in the *Christian Advocate* that after the school opened, formerly disaffected but practical white neighbors saw that improvements to the property had actually increased local real estate values: "The common sense for which they are proverbial asserted itself, and the whole community now favors our enterprise." As the academy settled in, however, a late twentieth-century statement by two historians is likely more accurate: "[I]n the early years of the school, social practice dictated that [it] be treated as an alien and potentially troublesome institution in the community."[29]

Following the establishment of this branch in Princess Anne, the Centenary Biblical Institute began a transformation of its own under Goucher's leadership. The institute was ready to move up from "academic to collegiate grade," as the June 1889 trustee minutes recorded, by offering the state's first bachelor's degrees to black students. Such a step would enable "young men and women to continue their studies into the higher grades who would cease student life at this point when it now terminates with us because they cannot go to more expensive schools." To recognize the institution's elevated status and expanded scope, the board recommended a rebranding. Goucher and other trustees suggested the name Morgan College, in honor of Rev. Lyttleton F. Morgan's years of dedication and support.[30]

As the last decade of the nineteenth century approached, Goucher had helped build and sustain two African-American institutions— Baltimore's soon-to-be-chartered Morgan College and the affiliated preparatory and industrial school in Princess Anne. As important as these achievements were to him, however, he had a competing commitment to establish and nurture another school—the Woman's College of Baltimore City.

Goucher Hall
The Woman's College of Baltimore (c.1900)

Courtesy of the Goucher College Library,
Special Collections and Archives, Baltimore, Maryland

THE WOMAN'S COLLEGE
OF BALTIMORE CITY

Chapter 12
(1881-1889)

———————◆◆———————

No race has ever risen higher than the standard of its womanhood.
Elevate that and you elevate the race.[1]

Unlike many men of his era, John Goucher believed there were "three normal relations of woman to society" in the United States—as a wife and mother, as a wage earner, and as a volunteer helping improve her community. While he saw her role in the home as the most important for extending Christian civilization, he also recognized that every woman might be called upon "to occupy any one of these [positions] or all of them in turn, and possibly all of them at once." Men could choose a vocation and train for it, he said, but for women it was "impossible to determine beforehand in which of three relations she will find her chief opportunity." She needed the intellectual, physical, and spiritual training offered by a college education to qualify her "for efficiency in them all."[2]

The idea that women could have multiple roles in society and were worthy of sufficient education to handle them was not fashionable during much of the nineteenth century. It was not considered beneficial to provide women with more than the ability to read and write, run a household, and perhaps paint and play a musical instrument. Many men thought women did not have the mental or physical strength to handle more; others felt that higher education would take them out of their proper "sphere" as wives and mothers and ruin their lives.[3]

The centennial of the organization of the Methodist Episcopal Church in America provided the occasion on which Goucher and other Baltimore Methodist leaders set out to change these prejudices. The bishops and delegates to the 1880 General Conference discussed ways to celebrate the upcoming 1884 milestone, and "the cause of education" was declared to be the most appropriate focus. Each Methodist conference was to determine what projects would be supported by its congregations' collections. For several years, the Baltimore Conference had been discussing "the need of a Conference Seminary for the higher education of our youth, male and female," since there was no such institution within its bounds and strictly under its jurisdiction. Spurred by the centennial edict, at the annual meeting in March 1881, members appointed a special committee of five ministers and five laymen to consider the matter.[4]

Goucher was on that special committee, and also chaired the conference's standing Committee on Seminaries, which examined schools already under conference patronage. Goucher exerted his influence on the latter to help move the new seminary forward, when the special committee was unable to create a plan after two years of deliberations. As a colleague noted, Goucher was "wide awake to his obligations and his opportunities as chair of the standing committee, and doubtless at his suggestion, it espoused the cause of the long-talked-of and much debated Conference Seminary." This cause was outside the standing committee's purview, but that was "a trifling matter" to Goucher: "The door was open; he and his committee entered."[5]

At the March 1883 Baltimore Annual Conference, Goucher's Committee on Seminaries reported, "We believe the time has come when this demand [for a seminary] must be speedily met. Longer delay would be costly and perilous beyond measure." His committee recommended, however, that the seminary be for women only, rather than coeducational: "Already we have suffered irreparable loss for the want of such an institution. Many young women of our Church are educated in other denominational schools or in schools without denominational character, and in numbers lamentably large, are lost to Methodism." Goucher's hand was seen in the formation of yet another special committee—named "in an unusual way to his own mind," according to a colleague—to devise a plan to establish such an institution.[6]

Goucher shaped its leadership by nominating John Blackford Van Meter to chair the new ten-member Committee on Seminary (as distinct from the Committee on Seminaries). A former chaplain in the United States Navy who became minister at the Huntington Avenue Church following Goucher, Van Meter also was editor of *The Baltimore Methodist*, where he had been writing articles promoting the seminary idea for some time. While not on the new committee himself, Goucher kept in close contact with its members in the months that followed and, from behind the scenes, helped create policies and work out details for the proposed school. The committee shifted away from the idea of establishing a seminary, with its lower academic level, and "the purpose to create a college was born." As Van Meter noted, there were "many the midnight hours which found [him and Goucher] conspiring in deliberation over these points."[7]

There were obstacles to overcome from within the Baltimore Conference, however. At the 1883 annual meeting, a Centenary Committee, reviewing suitable centennial projects, approved opening a school for young women but also recommended providing a "generous and thorough endowment" of Dickinson College and an endowment for the Centenary Biblical Institute. The many champions of Dickinson in the Baltimore Conference saw a new school for women as a rival for financial support. Goucher himself supported both his alma mater Dickinson and the institute, but he also understood the critical need for educational parity for women. As he noted when the Woman's College of Baltimore City finally opened, "The object of the ages has been to broaden man, but woman has been deprived of the facilities to prepare herself to go hand in hand with him. . . . The marvel is, how with her few opportunities, she has done so well."[8]

There was also pushback from outside Methodist circles. Goucher recalled later, "When the project of founding in Baltimore a college for women to be equal to the best found anywhere was first broached it met with both passive and active resistance—the inertia of indifference and the opposition of disfavor." Opponents said it would be impossible to find enough qualified students because no schools in Maryland or the District of Columbia prepared girls to enter college. Others said southern social customs would discourage young women over seventeen or eighteen from wanting to spend four years in rigorous college work. Without enough interested and qualified students, the college would be unable to recruit good faculty or attract funding. In sum, "Such a comprehensive and necessarily expensive institution must miserably fail if attempted in Baltimore, because it would be impossible to secure sufficient financial co-operation in the South."[9]

During Christmas week 1883, a time perhaps chosen as a symbol of the nearly century-past Christmas Conference, Goucher provided a rallying point to push the project forward. He attended a Committee on Seminary meeting and asked Van Meter to read a letter in which he offered the Baltimore Conference a plot of land he owned on St. Paul Street, next to the proposed location of the new First Church, that might serve as the site for the first college building. If that site were rejected, he would donate $25,000 ($610,000), the value of the land, to seed the college project. After deliberations, the committee voted to accept the property. Either offer was provisional; for its part, the Baltimore Conference would have to raise $175,000 (approximately $4.4 million) for buildings and the "nucleus of an endowment" between March 1884 and March 1885. In his letter, Goucher also wrote that while he desired the new institution to be "positively Christian in its influence," he recognized that if it were to be "vigorous, consistent and efficient," it must be "non-Christian or denominational" in its management and in accepting students.[10]

A report noted that Goucher's challenge "was intended to rouse the many rather than secure the imitation of a few," and it inspired quick response. More than 1,000 Methodist women in and around Baltimore met in January 1884 to consider forming "an association of ladies in the Baltimore Conference on aid of the enterprise started by Mr. Goucher." The minister presided at the meeting, and Bishop Matthew Simpson, who also attended, was astounded at the number, noting that it was usually difficult to "call together large audiences where the subject of education was the particular theme." But Goucher's address on the "necessity and practicability" of founding and endowing "an institution, thoroughly first-class in every particular, for the higher education of our daughters," was of deep concern to the women present.[11]

Goucher was familiar with all of the usual objections, but he preferred to emphasize positive factors. Baltimore was, he noted, the center of Methodist traditions, and population figures confirmed the strength of the Church's influence in the area. While the city's population had grown more than twenty-four percent over the past decade, membership in the Methodist Episcopal Church had increased almost twice as much in that time; more than one-third of Marylanders were Methodists. Baltimore Conference members had already shown strong support for church projects, and he believed they could raise adequate funds once more.[12]

Goucher also believed it was particularly appropriate that women help inaugurate plans for the institution, as they had played important roles in Christian service and in the growth of Methodism locally and nationally. He urged them to action: "Today, if the women of this conference join hearts and hands in this noble work in gratitude for what God hath done for them and as an earnest purpose that their daughters shall be better qualified for work in the future, nothing shall be impossible to them." In response the group formed the Women's Educational Association, whose members pledged to "enlist in active co-operation every man, woman, and child" among the 35,000 Methodist church members and 40,000 Sunday school students in the Baltimore Conference. Volunteers were ready to spread the word and raise the funds to meet Goucher's challenge.[13]

When the Baltimore Conference held its annual meeting in March 1884, Van Meter, as chair of the Committee on Seminary, recommended that members at last "take definite action towards the foundation of a FEMALE COLLEGE within its bounds." He recognized that Dickinson and the Centenary Biblical Institute were worthy of support, but urged that preachers and congregations now focus their fundraising on the foundation and endowment of a women's college—not a seminary. Otherwise, he said, "to divide our effort will be to defeat it from the start." Van Meter said Goucher's gift and challenge had "transformed a fancy, with which the conference was dallying, into a potentiality which must either be accepted and worked out, or rejected and abandoned." After discussion and some dissent, conference members ultimately approved the recommendation; the project was feasible and should become the special focus of centennial fundraising. They also expressed their "high appreciation of Mr. Goucher's generous proposition," and many began making personal pledges toward the $175,000 goal.[14]

As a step forward, Bishop Edward G. Andrews appointed a new Committee on Female College, comprised of twelve ministers and twelve laymen. It was empowered to incorporate during the year as a Board of Corporators for the new institution, and to control all money and property donated for its use. Goucher was elected one of the vice presidents and made a member of a Committee on Charter. With the campaign underway, *The Baltimore Methodist* began publishing a monthly supplement, paid for by Goucher, to highlight its needs and progress. He also defrayed the cost of all printing, mailings, hall rentals, travel expenses, and fees during the campaign, so every dollar raised went to the cause.[15]

The Women's Educational Association quickly organized another mass rally in May 1884 to secure subscriptions. Enthusiasm for the project was demonstrated by the large turnout, with more than 1,000 people turned away. Even so, those who did get in were slow in responding with pledges. Goucher and two other members of the new committee each pledged $5,000 ($124,000) for the Female College; by the end of the meeting, according to a news report, $32,000 (approximately $800,000) was raised, "no mean evening's work."[16]

In *The Baltimore Methodist—Supplement*, the women acknowledged a "feeling of vexation" that Goucher had to step forward to help yet again:

> We think Mr. Goucher has done his part towards the founding of this College. He may not thank us for saying what we do about it. He knows nothing more about the contents of this supplement than does any other of its readers, and he had no control over what goes into it, or this allusion would be stricken out by him. His subscriptions have already run up to $30,000 ($734,000). It ought to be remembered, too, that this is only one of many objects of his beneficence to all of which he has given and is giving largely. When it is remembered how wealthy men usually employ their means, his wide and carefully considered liberality deserves the admiration of his brethren. . . . It deserves the emulation of those who, like him, are able to do great things for the church. Is there no one to follow his example and by LARGE GIFTS added to his promote this great interest?[17]

The following months brought more such meetings, where Goucher and Van Meter were often the motivational speakers. Letters and brochures extolled the merits of the project; ministers preached its benefits from pulpits; and women went door-to-door canvassing for funds. But those Van Meter called "conference 'hostiles'" spread "ugly insinuations" trying to dissuade potential donors, especially the wealthy. They spread the rumor, started when Goucher donated the site, that he and a few other prominent area landowners were "ambitious men who were seeking notoriety" and who "were charged with floating a land improvement scheme under cloak of religious education." Some of these rumor-mongers were Dickinson partisans who opposed the rival school; others were landowners or affiliated with churches in different areas of the city who wanted the new school to serve their interests or convenience. It was logical that property values increased in any neighborhood where a school opened, and as Van Meter reasoned, it was not difficult for detractors "to persuade those willing to believe that the economic effect of the enterprise constituted the genuine reason for the undertaking."[18]

Such attacks did not bother Goucher. He already had been dealing with members of his congregation who objected to buying land and moving First Church from downtown to a northern location. To him it was a practical matter to have the new college tied physically and spiritually to First Church. Contrary to detractors' assertions, the *Christian Advocate* suggested that the new church and college "together would contribute a monument worthy to be erected in the centennial year" of Methodism. Nevertheless, some proponents were discouraged when only about half of the needed funds were pledged by Fall 1884. It was noted, however, that "only one voice never for a moment lost its confident ring—that of John F. Goucher."[19]

As 1885 began, with the Baltimore Conference's annual meeting and Goucher's deadline for fundraising less than three months away, $115,000 toward the $175,000 challenge had been subscribed. The Committee on Female College decided it was "expedient" to incorporate at that time, and on January 26, 1885, after Goucher had the necessary papers drawn up, the charter for the Woman's College of Baltimore City was signed and executed. (The charter was changed in 1890 to delete the word "City" from the title, and thereafter the institution was known as the Woman's College of Baltimore.) The "corporators," or "incorporators" as they were sometimes called, held their first meeting ten days later. As a member of the Committee on Charter, Goucher suggested bylaws for the college, which were adopted.[20]

Several years later, Goucher detailed the significance of the words chosen for the name of the new institution:

> Woman's: It was in the first place to break down all prejudice against the word woman in a part of the country where all females above childhood age were called ladies or females. . . . Furthermore, this was to be, not a college for women parading in men's attire, but a college for women as women.

> College: It was, moreover, not to be an academy or lyceum or finishing school, not strut about under the pretentious title of university . . . but it was to be a college in the true sense.

> Baltimore: It was first of all a college for women of *Baltimore*, the educational key position for the whole south and a region where higher education for women was taboo. . . . This was then to be a college to break down prejudice against higher education for women among women of Baltimore.[21]

Although now a legal entity, the college's physical existence still depended on having sufficient pledges and cash on hand to meet Goucher's original challenge. The Baltimore Conference thus began its annual meeting on March 5, 1885, with a sense of both trepidation and hope. At a rally the first evening, Goucher took the floor to try to coax the remaining $60,000 ($1.5 million) from the audience. He pledged one-third of that amount himself, and several other corporators and leading laymen increased their contributions; smaller gifts trickled in from individuals and ministers on behalf of their congregations. Goucher then offered an additional $20,000 ($508,000), spurring other donors over the goal line. A newspaper article noted that the gathering then burst into applause, and "the doxology was sung with a will."[22]

At that stage, John and Mary's contributions to establish the college totaled $70,000 in land and cash ($1.75 million). Before the conference was over, members adopted a resolution thanking Goucher for their "munificent donation" to the college, "ensuring its successful foundation and making memorable the centennial year of Methodism." It was suggested that the corporators consider "recognizing this great liberality in the name of the institution," but Goucher firmly refused to have their name attached, as he had a few years earlier with the Mikai Theological Institute in Yokohama. Mary's maiden name, Fisher, was also proposed, but he respectfully declined that as well. Members also expressed "high appreciation" for Van Meter's role. The two men had formed a partnership that shaped not only the founding of the college but also its development in years to come.[23]

At one of their first meetings, the corporators discussed opening the college for classes in Fall 1885, if possible. But the facilities and faculty were not yet in place, no students had been recruited, and there was no president to lead the institution. Van Meter nominated Goucher for the position, but he "earnestly and positively declined." He was already busy with his ministerial work, overseeing the construction project at First Church, and working and traveling as a member of the Board of Managers of the Missionary Society. It was almost a year before William Hersey Hopkins, acting president of St. John's College in Annapolis, accepted the position. In his new role, he went to Europe for a year to study higher education for women at the best institutions and to scout for faculty.[24]

Goucher's declining the presidency did not signal the end of his commitment, however. The new institution still lacked a main building in which to begin its academic life. As a member of the board's Building Committee, Goucher became as involved with that project as he was in completing First Church next door. From the time he began working with Stanford White on the church's design in 1883, he likely talked with the architect about plans for the college as well, since the materials for the new buildings—granite walls and red tile roofs— matched those of the church. The college would honor its Methodist roots and use the church's chapel as an auditorium for services and events. The pointed connection between church and college can be seen in an early perspective drawing of First Church, done by a local architect working from White's plans. Although the establishment of the college for women was not yet certain, the drawing shows a large, solid building situated next door.[25]

The corporators authorized the start of the college's first building in January 1886, and that October, more than 1,000 people attended a ceremony to lay its cornerstone. There was standing room only in the newly completed chapel at First Church as Goucher led the opening service. The party on the platform included Bishop Andrews, Bishop A. W. Wayman of the African Methodist Episcopal Church, and Daniel Coit Gilman, president of the decade-old Johns Hopkins University. After the service, the crowd moved to the college site next door. Into a granite block inscribed with the date 1886, Goucher deposited a copper box which contained a Bible; the charter of the college and a list of donors; a register of the Johns Hopkins University; a directory of Baltimore school teachers; and city, state, and Methodist newspapers. After masons set the stone in place, Goucher tapped it three times with the handle of a trowel, as if blessing the institution's future. He gave a brief closing prayer, dedicating "the cornerstone of this building for the higher education of woman, under auspices of the Methodist Episcopal Church."[26]

There were still some roadblocks to quick completion, however. Labor problems slowed construction, and there were financial complications. The corporators required that $100,000 of the $175,000 subscribed for the new college be "preserved inviolate as an endowment fund." Less than $150,000 had been received, with many donations in the form of land rather than cash. There would not be enough money to complete the planned structure without dipping into the endowment. Goucher again stepped in. He directed that the $45,000 ($1.1 million) in cash he and Mary had already given be used for the building, and he offered to advance the remaining funds needed for materials and labor.[27]

As was his custom with their donations, Goucher offered this pledge with a condition designed to spur others to action. The college was to give him promissory notes for this additional sum, payable on June 1, 1890, but he would waive repayment if the college had $100,000 or more in cash or investments in hand by the deadline—a requirement that was met. In all, the Gouchers contributed $130,000 (approximately $3.3 million) for the three-story, forty-room building. Part of the money had been set aside as a dowry for their first daughter, Eleanor; the building, in the shape of the letter E, became for them a memorial to her brief life.[28]

The Woman's College of Baltimore City finally held its first classes in September 1888 in the nearly completed Goucher Hall, named for Mary and John "against his earnest protest." Soon after, Baltimore

Mayor Ferdinand C. Latrobe, noting the city's recent annexation of the area north of Boundary Avenue, praised this important new and unexpected educational institution—a women's college to complement the already famous Johns Hopkins University for men. Now there were two colleges and two Goucher Halls on opposite sides of the world that owed their existence to the foresight and generosity of John and Mary Goucher.[29]

As the last decade of the nineteenth century arrived, the Gouchers' philanthropy in Baltimore totaled nearly $225,000 ($5.7 million) to assist First Church, the Centenary Biblical Institute, and the Woman's College of Baltimore City. Added to their donations for the Frontier Loan Fund and their four "much fruit countries," John and Mary contributed more than $360,000 (appproximately $9 million) to support major projects for missions, schools, and churches at home and abroad between 1879 and 1889.[30]

REV. JOHN F. GOUCHER, D.D.,
President Woman's College of Baltimore.

Epworth Herald, December 3, 1892

*Courtesy of the Baltimore-Washington Conference Archives,
Lovely Lane United Methodist Church, Baltimore, Maryland*

THE BALANCING ACT

Chapter 13
(1890-1897)

———————◆◆———————

The only way to meet one's responsibilities and discharge one's obligations is by living a life of helpfulness.[1]

Goucher's active life became even more busy and complicated during the 1890s and beyond. He sometimes stayed up late to do research and to study reports, treatises, letters, and appeals he received from around the globe. His days often were spent in consultations with the many people requesting meetings. When a friend asked why he did not designate certain hours for uninterrupted work, he replied, "As I look at it, the man who wants to see me is the man I want to see." (He met with women too.) Some might say he had poor time-management skills, but this quip speaks to Goucher's openness to involvement with diverse people, and his ability to juggle whatever projects he might undertake.[2]

Bishop Cyrus D. Foss, with whom Goucher later traveled around the world, described the forty-five-year-old minister's work early in 1890: "Happy is the man who can command the means, and, (what is far more rare) who has the brains, heart and persistent will to make such a contribution to his own and of this coming generation." He took on an even wider and more varied portfolio during the last decade of the nineteenth century. His expanded activities addressed his continuing commitment to his personal "commissions," but he always made time for family and home life. These competing demands required a great deal of mental and physical energy and often compromised his health. A history of Goucher College notes, "It seems remarkable that a man not particularly robust or strong should have been able to do so many things."[3]

The continued growth of the Woman's College of Baltimore was central to Goucher's work during the decade. In May 1890, William Hersey Hopkins resigned as president; the position, he said later, was "very near crushing me." Hopkins knew the president needed to be a fundraiser, but he had no aptitude or appetite for that. The Board of Corporators, known as the Board of Trustees after April 1891, again turned to Goucher, unanimously electing him to succeed Hopkins. He was officially notified by letter. Trustee Francis A. Crook urged him to accept: "We know your preference for the Pastorate and the sense of duty in given circumstances, which governs you. And while we feel the occasion is one of great importance to you and your future, it is not less so to the college, over whose inception and equipment you have watched and toiled so faithfully and unselfishly."[4]

Despite his varied projects at home and abroad, Goucher gave the idea careful consideration, reflecting his deep belief in the enterprise's mission. He asked when he would be required to begin and what his responsibilities might be. Not wanting him to slip away a second time, the board passed a resolution leaving "the duties of the Presidency to the discretion of the President, and also the time for his entering upon said duties." After prayer and careful thought, Goucher accepted the position, later acknowledging, "Had not my call from the Lord to the work of College President come as clearly as the call to the Pastorate I would not have consented to this charge." The trustees of First Church lightened his pastoral load so he could begin his new job part-time in September 1890. He chaired his first faculty meeting that month and led his first college chapel service as presiding officer a few weeks later. The Baltimore Conference released him as a congregational minister during its annual meeting the following March.[5]

In 1907, the *Pittsburgh Christian Advocate* recorded Goucher's early expectations for the institution. He knew it could "not afford to be little and low, and then grow into a first-class college; it must take first rank at the beginning and make its way on this plane." Even before he became president, he and other corporators had pushed for facilities and equipment that would move the college to a premier position in higher education. During Hopkins' brief tenure, the college built next to Goucher Hall what was considered the best-equipped gymnasium at any women's college in the country. For Goucher, it was as important as classroom space; he believed "a disciplined body is as essential to a thoroughly educated woman as a cultured mind or loyal spirit." Students also needed a welcoming place to live. Initially the corporators had not planned a residence hall, believing out-of-town students would live in private homes or boarding houses. It quickly became clear, however, that parents expected the college to protect and supervise their daughters. Home A, as it was first known, opened in January 1890.[6]

One concern had become apparent as soon as the Woman's College opened for classes—a shortage of qualified students. During the opening year of 1888-1889, there were more than 125 young women enrolled, but only ten were considered ready for college-level courses. The other students, ranging in age from sixteen to thirty, had varying educational credentials, or were taking non-degree courses in music, art, or elocution. Inquiries about the college were pouring in from around the country, attesting to the demand for women's education. By the start of the third academic year in September 1890, there were more than 300 students from twenty states, but only forty were of collegiate grade. Goucher had to tackle the enrollment issue soon after he became president; it would require more building and more funds.[7]

At the local level, Goucher had an ongoing series of meetings with Mayor Ferdinand C. Latrobe and his superintendent of education, explaining that Baltimore's public high schools were "of much inferior grade to high schools of other cities and towns throughout the country and inadequate to the work they propose." One early member of the Woman's College faculty said she often heard Goucher say that when the college opened, "The only girls from Baltimore public schools who could have passed the entrance examinations were those graduated from the colored high school." He said that was because African-American voters demanded that their sons have an education equal to what white boys received at the prominent high school City College. Since black public schools were coeducational, girls benefited too. (The Woman's College, it should be noted, did not admit African-American students.)[8]

The Baltimore *Afro-American* later wrote that Goucher caused a stir in the city by asserting that white girls attending Western and Eastern Female High Schools "were not receiving as good a training as the children of the cooks of their parents at the Colored High

School." When he asked the mayor and superintendent to raise the standards at these two schools to match the best high schools in the country, his request was treated "first with indifference and afterward peremptorily declined." Goucher reported that the Woman's College thus was "compelled to do one of three things—to make provision for the preparation of those who might desire to enter its freshman class, seriously to lower its entrance requirements, or go without students."[9]

Goucher and the board were not willing to compromise on the standard they had set when they called the institution a college. The answer to the dilemma was to establish a preparatory department, the Girls' Latin School, the first of its kind in the city and state and one of few such schools south of the Mason-Dixon line. Its structure was guided by the recently established Association of Colleges and Secondary Schools of the Middle States and Maryland, which was beginning to set college admission criteria and formulate the characteristics of a proper college. To meet association requirements, in Fall 1890, the board set up the preparatory department as a separate entity, with its own principal and faculty, though overseen by the college president. Because of space limitations, these students were to use classrooms on the second floor of Goucher Hall only, and had to enter and leave the building by a single stairway.

The separation between collegiate and sub-collegiate students became physical as well as academic when Catherine Hooper Hall, designed by Stanford White, opened for preparatory students at the beginning of the 1893 school year. A Baltimore newspaper praised the thirty-room structure's interior; a reader noted Goucher's attention even to décor:

> Walls [are] tinted in a soft French gray, the color being mixed in the third coat of plaster. President Goucher got the idea of this wall treatment from a fragment of plaster picked up at Pompeii, and the method of thus mixing the coloring with the final coat of plaster has been used in all of the Woman's College buildings.[10]

To accommodate the growing number of students at all levels, Home A was assigned to the preparatory students, and three new residence halls were built. As at First Church, Goucher often took a hands-on role at groundbreaking ceremonies, including one on a cold November day. A news article described a man who was familiar with agrarian life at Alto Dale as well as an executive's office:

> President John F. Goucher, of the Woman's College of Baltimore, yesterday assumed the role of a farmer. With coat collar turned up, he grasped the rough handles of a plow and turned a beautiful furrow at the southwest corner of Maryland Avenue and 24th Street. He was soon convinced that such an innocent-looking thing as a plow was not as easily handled as the reins of the Woman's College, for it can be said that in steering the plow of education he was seldom jarred and shaken up as he was when holding on to the handles of a furrow-turner.[11]

※※※

The students weren't the only ones in need of different accommodations. Goucher's new position called for a change in the family's living arrangements, since he and Mary and their three daughters had to vacate the parsonage at First Church when he left the ministry. While Alto Dale remained their country home, the new president needed a residence in the city that would enable him—and Mary—to become an integral part of the college. As he became more and more involved with local, national, and international church, education, and mission work, he also wanted a convenient and comfortable place to welcome what his oldest daughter identified as visitors of "all kinds and conditions of men, races and creeds."[12]

To address these needs, John and Mary built a new brick home at 2313 St. Paul Street diagonally across from Goucher Hall, where he had his office. This mansion, too, was designed by Stanford White, based on a palace Goucher had seen during an earlier visit to Florence, Italy. It was completed in the fall of 1892 at a cost of more than $100,000 (nearly $2.7 million). But its style was said to be "simple and strong, rather than ornate"; the first-floor rooms were "especially designed for entertaining," accommodating up to 200 at a reception. The interior was finished in various woods, the downstairs fireplaces made of Italian marble and Mexican onyx. Despite the elegant décor, there were homey touches, such as portraits of the three Goucher children in the drawing room. In the hallway stood a clothes rack that a newspaper once said "would be identified in any part of the globe by the most casual acquaintance of Dr. Goucher by a single hat which always finds its place there." They also kept the same servants, who traveled between Alto Dale and 2313—as the in-town house was familiarly known then (and referred to in this book)—when the family moved to the city in the fall and back to the country in the spring.[13]

On the second floor were five bedrooms and two baths, plus a small sewing room that became a repository for mysterious packages Goucher sent back from his various journeys. Often oddly shaped and stuffed with straw, these boxes and containers prompted no end of speculation from those left behind. One family member called it "Christmas three times over" when the traveler returned to open them. On the top floor were two additional bedrooms and bathrooms, along with John's large study and library, which ran the length of the house. The room's windows, with seats beneath, overlooked both First Church and the college campus, and numerous shelves and alcoves held his books and sundry artifacts brought back from around the world. If he wanted to work there at odd hours, he could do so without disturbing the household by way of a spiral staircase built into the closet of the second-floor master bedroom. He also installed an elevator so Mary, plagued by leg problems, could more easily move between floors. The three Goucher daughters attended primary school in the neighborhood, and then Girls' Latin School, almost next door to their home.[14]

The Gouchers' in-town house was built for hospitality; as a friend once noted, "Its guests were of all nations, but the menu distinctly American and its service simple and democratic." It also was a haven for students from the Woman's College. If a young woman became ill, Mary might bring her to 2313 to provide care; if another were homesick, she was asked to tea in a homey atmosphere. Although reserved herself, Mary was said to know how to "help the timid and retiring to self-expression and self-esteem but she invariably inspired to higher standards and achievements the purposeful, aggressive girl." When a father of a student was asked what part of the curriculum prompted him to send his daughter to the college, he said he hadn't heard much about the academic program, but he had met Mary Goucher and wanted his daughter to be just like her.[15]

Many students remembered "pleasant autumn evenings in the town house" with the Gouchers, and their daughter Janet noted that during her childhood, nearly every Sunday there were college guests at their table. Sometimes thirteen people gathered for a meal. Free from any superstitions but understanding some visitors might not be, her father "was careful to seat himself last, lest undue anxiety should overtake any of his guests in discovering this dilemma."[16]

Janet also recalled that foreign students at the Woman's College or Girls' Latin often spent holidays with the family. Many missionaries who knew Goucher, especially those stationed in India, China, and Japan, entrusted their daughters' education to him, and students native to those countries also came to attend school. Students from closer to home enjoyed the Gouchers' hospitality as well. One Thanksgiving, several New Englanders who were unable to go home celebrated the day with them. One professor remembered that Goucher "could carve a turkey better than anybody I ever saw." He must have been well-known for this skill, as a missionary once wrote asking for turkey-carving tips.[17]

The couple hosted many other gatherings during their months in town. Each fall they held an evening reception for college seniors, faculty, trustees, and local alumnae. A newspaper account of one party stated the "parlors and halls of the house were decorated with potted palms and ferns," and Mary gave each woman guest a bouquet of white roses and violets as a memento of the evening. At Christmas, the Gouchers invited the seniors to help trim the family's tree and sing carols. Even Methodist men attending nearby Johns Hopkins University were treated to a party, which was said to be a way for John and Mary to screen potential suitors for their students.[18]

The couple often opened their doors to members of the Baltimore Conference and to visiting missionaries and bishops of the Methodist Episcopal Church. They would also host the Eclectic Club, an ecumenical group of sixteen Baltimore clergy that met eight times a year to hear papers presented by members. At any gathering, Goucher offered a quiet wit, often telling jokes at his own expense, and he was esteemed as a good conversationalist, ready (said one acquaintance) with "an infinite fund of anecdote." Whether in a crowd or meeting one-on-one, speaking to a student or to a bishop, friends attested he had "the rare ability of giving his entire attention to anyone who talked with him." Another acquaintance judged that he "lived *with* people, not *off* them, in his social life."[19]

In the summer, the Gouchers hosted gatherings at Alto Dale, and one guest echoed the feelings of many others who visited there: "The day was lovely, and the occasion one long to be remembered by those who had the good fortune to be among the participants." The most eagerly anticipated event of the college year was Alto Dale Day, held in early June for seniors, faculty, and "hall" students. That tradition began with the first graduating class in 1892 and continued until 1914.[20]

Early on, Goucher arranged for a special North Central Railroad train to take visitors from downtown to a stop near the couple's home in the Greenspring Valley. A guest described how John met them, with a "broad brimmed hat on his head, a tall English walking cane in his hand, and a courteous winning smile, and a kind word for some, witty remarks for each and all." Goucher led them through the woods, past Cricket—his daughters' playhouse—to the wide porch where they found Mary, who like her husband knew all the students' names. In later years, he arranged for the party to come via special cars on the Baltimore and Northern Electric Line. Guests were deposited at the estate entrance on Reisterstown Road, known to trolley conductors as Goucher's Gate. As ever, their host was there to greet them, and carriages stood ready to carry those unable to walk the quarter-mile to the house.[21]

Guests spent the afternoon relaxing in swings and hammocks, walking in the woods or among the gardens, while the more energetic staged foot races or enjoyed a hayride. It was said Goucher "moved with a natural ease among his guests, going from group to group, from individual to individual," giving tours or showing his varied collections. Mary also wandered among the guests, and one alumna testified, "Our memories picture her in many places, at many times, but we cannot think of her with more pleasure than as our hostess at Alto Dale."[22]

Sunset brought a picnic supper, illuminated by Japanese lanterns that were strung over the lawn and in the trees. Once, guests were offered Turkish Delight candy that Goucher had brought back from a recent trip to the Middle East. As darkness grew, everyone sang old college songs and improvised new ones. Then came the highlight of the evening. At the far end of the lawn, torches were arranged to form the shapes of four numerals, indicating the graduation year, and more torches glowed, one for each departing senior. One graduate recalled: "Dr. Goucher and a small group of us walked beside the torches and called the class roll. . . . For us the moment was full of meaning, the president, friendly and understanding as we talked together of the past and of the days to come."[23]

While Alto Dale and 2313 were their main residences, the family would also spend time at the "cottage" Goucher had built for the family at Mountain Lake Park in Western Maryland, near Oakland. Begun in 1881 as a summer retreat by a group of Methodist ministers, and easily reached by the Baltimore & Ohio Railroad, the resort offered vacationers a respite from city heat and humidity. Covenants prohibited gambling, card playing, dancing, and alcohol — all "sins" the Goucher family already shunned as good Methodists. To ensure Mary Goucher enjoyed a thorough rest, the cottage had no kitchen; its owners and their guests would walk through the woods to take meals at a nearby hotel or boarding house. Yearly camp meetings and Chautauqua-style educational programs brought speakers such as Billy Sunday, William Jennings Bryan, and President Grover Cleveland. Never completely off duty, Goucher took an active role in community governance, and served as president of the Mountain Lake Park Association Board of Directors for several years.[24]

※※※

The first commencement at the Woman's College on June 9, 1892, along with the Alto Dale event, baccalaureate service, and Class Day, marked an important milestone for Goucher, Van Meter, and others who had been champions of the new college. The day began with rain, but auspiciously the weather cleared in time for the ceremony. The auditorium of First Church was filled with music, and the altar area was decorated with palms, masses of white lilies, and pink and white roses. Wearing caps and gowns delivered just before the service began, five young women, who had completed four rigorous years of college classes, led the academic procession. Goucher proudly told the commencement audience, "This occasion marks for the Woman's College the beginning of years. Hitherto it has promised to be. Today it is."[25]

For this event, Goucher had taken it upon himself to design the first college seal to affix to the five parchment diplomas. (It was used until 1910.) The president related he had worked on the seal while traveling by train to New York to attend a meeting of the Board of Managers of the Missionary Society. A history of the college explains:

> As [Goucher] was fond of thinking of the triple powers to be
> trained by education—body, mind, and soul—he selected the
> triangle to embody them; as he was a firm believer in passing
> on to others any blessings that were received, he placed rays of
> light emanating from the three sides of the triangle as indicative
> of service rendered through education.[26]

The college's high admission requirements induced many secondary schools to raise their own standards, in hopes of placing students at the Woman's College. When Goucher gave the second commencement address in 1893, he noted that forty-two schools in sixteen states had asked that their graduates be admitted. But he pointed out that Baltimore public schools—especially the all-white Eastern and Western Female High Schools—were still slow to adjust their curricula to prepare students for college. He made a subtle dig at these segregated schools:

> But there is hope ahead. The experiment is being tried on
> colored girls of Baltimore, and the High School to which
> they are admitted offers Latin and other opportunities as good
> in a general way as are provided for white boys. If it works
> well with them, no doubt the less favored white girls will be
> accorded similar privileges.

By the end of the 1890s, more high schools in Baltimore and around the country were graduating qualified students, and over 300 were enrolled at the Woman's College.[27]

Goucher's and the trustees' insistence on aiming high was quickly vindicated. In the college's third year of operation, the United States commissioner of education placed it in the highest category, Division

A, alongside fourteen other women's colleges. In 1893, Daniel Coit Gilman, president of the Johns Hopkins University, announced that since courses at the Woman's College closely corresponded to those offered at Hopkins, Woman's College graduates who completed the academic requirements for the newly opened Johns Hopkins Medical School were certain to be admitted. As Goucher reported to the Baltimore Annual Conference that year, "The College is no longer an experiment. Those who honestly doubted the need for such an institution can doubt no longer."[28]

Credit for this academic achievement goes not only to the facilities and equipment Goucher helped fund, but also to the faculty he helped hire and the working atmosphere he cultivated. One early member of the biology department wrote, Goucher "was without experience in academic work, but was not handicapped by that fact. He relied upon the teacher's knowledge of his own problem and brought out to the full the teacher's best." Everyone understood the president "was back of us to give us every possible aid, and we went to him continually." They regarded him as a "wise and tactful" leader.[29]

In 1894, Goucher hired physician Lilian Welsh to head the then-uncommon department of physiology and hygiene and physical training. She was the first—and for several years the only—woman professor on staff. Welsh said that in the beginning, it was not Goucher's policy to appoint women as full professors. But she spoke positively of his interactions with faculty:

> It was [his] open mindedness and fairness of judgment that enabled Dr. Goucher to make what, in my opinion, was his most valuable contribution to the educational policy of the College. Having chosen his faculty and tried them out, he charged them with the duty of making the College, in his own words, 'second to none in efficiency.' He saw to it that they were not restricted in their teaching. Academic freedom they had. Academic license they never desired.[30]

In some instances, Goucher upheld a faculty member's prerogative to apply the latest pedagogical theory, but then he might have to "parry the onslaughts," as Welsh put it, from members of the Baltimore Conference or others who felt a course was not proper for a Methodist institution. He took a supportive stand when John Van Meter introduced scholarly criticism of the Bible into his religion courses. Detractors called for Van Meter to be fired, but as Janet Goucher later testified, on that front her father "waged a real warfare and won." Van Meter stayed.[31]

Even the names of the residence halls were criticized. At first they were simply called Homes A, B, C, and D, but students wanted more elegant names. Goucher asked for recommendations from students, but none were adopted by the Board of Trustees. Finally, Joseph Shefloe, professor of Romance languages and literature, whose ancestors had come from Norway, suggested at an 1898 alumnae dinner that the halls be named for the Norse gods—Alfheim, Glitner, Fensal, and Vingolf for starters, leaving room for naming future residences and offering unique names among Baltimore institutions. Shefloe reported there were complaints about giving pagan names to buildings on a Christian campus. Goucher "assured the objectors that there was enough genuine Christianity in the college to nullify any connotations of paganism."[32]

✳ ✳ ✳

While a newspaper reporter might feel that "the plow of education" was easier for Goucher to control than the "handles of a furrow-turner," a college president's work, like a farmer's, was never-ending. One of his biggest challenges and greatest burdens from the 1890s on was managing the college's financial needs, as debt increased in tandem with its academic reputation. Some later commentators fault Goucher for a lack of long-range financial planning, as the college's debt grew from $25,000 in 1890 to approximately $400,000 a decade later ($671,000 to $11.6 million). David Wright, the architect who prepared a study for the restoration of Lovely Lane United Methodist Church, observes: "Goucher's greatest fault may have been his inability to recognize that his own incredible spirit of giving was the exception rather than the rule in charitable activity." One of Goucher's twentieth-century detractors concedes the point, "Himself enthusiastic, he was convinced that the college would never lack the necessary funds."[33]

Despite his seeming lack of fiscal prudence, Goucher was well aware of the financial challenges. He urged the Baltimore Conference and its congregations to continue their support for an "enterprise so well begun," but his appeal was not met with enthusiasm. Goucher believed the trustees were ultimately responsible for expenses, and he suggested addressing shortfalls by asking them to pledge their own money and urge others to give. He set the example. When he first became president and was homebound with a bout of rheumatism, he wrote the board's Executive Committee to report he had personally borrowed $4,200 ($113,000) to cover salaries in arrears. Repayment of the loan—one of many the college would take out in the years to come—was due in a month, and Goucher worried that if the obligation were not met, the college's credit would suffer. He suggested the members of the Executive Committee should personally cover the amount to show devotion to their work, and he was willing to contribute a fair portion.[34]

Fiscally imprudent though it was, Goucher and the trustees thought it necessary to let the institution expand beyond available funding. In a November 1893 report to the board, the president noted, "A plant less comprehensive and an institution of lower grade and less complete would have failed." With limited resources, he argued, "We are living, but do not enjoy the fullness of life." A member of the Finance Committee insisted that the college "cannot retreat, it cannot even pause, it must advance," and Goucher led that charge. To meet obligations for the coming year, he recommended the college raise $200,000 ($5.4 million) from trustees and friends and he would add $50,000 ($1.4 million). The total, he said, would "double the capacity of the college and broaden its influence."[35]

That money proved difficult to raise, but Goucher and the trustees pushed ahead with their expansion plans. As the *The Baltimore American* noted, "Sometimes it seems as if President Goucher has the ability to wave a wand and create a building. The manner in which the Woman's College is growing is almost marvelous." To help fund this growth, he made personal loans so the college could purchase nearby land before the burgeoning area was consumed by housing. Several other parties also lent money toward building expenses and interest payments. The trustees tried to balance the annual budget by raising tuition, room, and board fees, but that money covered only about two-thirds of faculty salaries; other sources of income rarely met remaining expenses. Only in 1895 could Goucher report that receipts exceeded annual expenses. The surplus was $396 ($11,500) and made possible because each year Goucher either declined his salary or returned it. When asked why, he explained that the money saved could pay the tuition of "worthy but needy students who would otherwise have been unable to continue their work."[36]

Goucher never missed a chance to publicize the college's needs. While he often appealed to the Baltimore Conference to increase its financial support, he even engaged in fundraising at commencement. At the second he presided over, he told the audience it was better to have one great, strong, idealistic institution than forty smaller and less perfect ones. He urged his listeners to help liquidate the college's debt and increase the endowment. But four years later, in 1897, the debt was still rising and private contributions falling due to a long-sluggish economy that left the usual donors with stagnant businesses or devalued securities. While Goucher sometimes made emotional appeals to parents about the importance of the college to their daughters, at commencement that year he argued that support made good business sense. The Woman's College was "an advertising medium and financial agency bringing money to Baltimore—more than $250,000 annually or more than $800 for every business day of the year" (more than $7.4 million per year or $23,600 per day). He pointed out that the revenue the college brought to the city every year was large compared to what its citizens contributed, Methodists or not.[37]

The college's donors were mainly from the Baltimore area and the Baltimore Conference, but Goucher realized he needed to widen the base. He enjoyed seeing new places and meeting new people and was already used to traveling on personal or church business. As an article about him once noted, "The railways and routes of travel of his own land were familiar footpaths." The trustees gave him great latitude in that regard; the Executive Committee "authorized the president to call on and delegate John Van Meter to perform any work appertaining to his office during his absence or otherwise." Goucher recommended Van Meter be named dean of the college, allowing the president to spend more time away, knowing the college was in capable hands. While later critics attributed the college's financial difficulties to Goucher's absences, he promoted the college and made valuable contacts during his varied travels.[38]

While not an academic, Goucher was considered an expert on education issues. He was a delegate to an 1891 commission, appointed by Methodist bishops, to discuss reorganizing and unifying the educational work of the Methodist Episcopal Church, and the setting of criteria for establishing and classifying colleges and universities under its auspices. Pursuant to the commission's work, the General Conference created a University Senate, charged with formulating minimum requirements for a bachelor's degree and reporting to the Methodist Board of Education. The senate was comprised of fifteen experienced educators, including Goucher and the presidents of Boston, Syracuse, Northwestern, DePauw, Ohio Wesleyan, and Denver Universities. Between quadrennial meetings, its work was overseen by an Executive Committee that included Goucher. He also was a member and vice president of the College Presidents' Association, representing nearly five dozen Methodist colleges and universities. Through such high-profile positions and frequent speaking engagements at institutions and conferences around the country, he was able to spread the word about the Woman's College of Baltimore and the kind of education it offered. Once, after Goucher returned from stops in several large western cities, a Methodist publication noted that the college received a surge of applications. This response convinced the administration to set up agencies in different locations such as Kansas City to examine prospective students' credentials.[39]

By the end of the college's first decade of classes, Goucher could report that the United States commissioner of education had placed the Woman's College of Baltimore among the top fourteen of all colleges and universities in the country—a select list that included Harvard, Yale, and Princeton. Despite its shaky financial underpinnings, the college met the standards for institutions "having the most ample furnishings, the most efficient faculties, and doing the most thorough work." President Goucher was also proud of the accomplishments of the college's first graduates: They "go back to their homes to enter society or to take up some line of professional work, and their influence on the life of the communities to which they go is immeasurable."[40]

✳ ✳ ✳

The Woman's College was not the only Baltimore school that required Goucher's attention. He continued as president of the Board of Trustees of Morgan College (formerly the Centenary Biblical Institute), whose new name had been approved by the Maryland legislature in the spring of 1890, and he oversaw the charter changes the state required to allow it to offer college-level courses. Goucher was also involved with other state and federal issues related to Morgan. Overcoming obstacles to women's education was challenging enough, but responding to government obstruction and delays to advancing higher education for African Americans required both perseverance and diplomacy. During his long association with Morgan College, Goucher was unfazed by critics who questioned his involvement. His daughter Janet reported that many "resorted to contemptible statements, one of which was that Father's interest in the Negro might be traced when one saw the kink or curl in his hair." That innuendo did not faze him at all. "He again continued in the course he believed was just and right."[41]

As the 1890s began, Goucher reported to the Morgan trustees that the public state university—the Maryland Agricultural College at College Park in Prince George's County—not only refused to admit African Americans to its law department but declared it "inexpedient to admit such [individuals] to any of the departments in the above named institution." When black students appealed to Morgan College to establish a law school, trustees agreed to consider the matter but soon recognized that it was not financially feasible. Even so, with the state university denying admittance to African Americans, Morgan became even more important as a regional center for black higher education and teacher training at a time when one-third of black Baltimoreans over the age of twelve were illiterate. Meanwhile, Morgan's Princess Anne branch provided, as a *Maryland Historical Magazine* article reports, "instructional services to blacks that the county school systems in Maryland either could or would not."[42]

In light of such restrictions, Goucher and two other Morgan College trustees conferred with Gov. Elihu Jackson to negotiate for an African-American institution in Maryland to receive federal funds. The Morrill Act of 1862 had allotted federal land to be used for or sold to support a public college in each state (that hadn't seceded from the Union) for agricultural, mechanical arts, and military training. A Morrill grant had funded the Maryland Agricultural College—now the University of Maryland, College Park. A second Morrill Act in 1890 provided $15,000 ($403,000) in federal funds for each state or territory, with annual increases thereafter, but with a stipulation: A state either had to show that race was not a factor in admission to a land-grant college, or had to establish a separate institution for persons of color. Maryland's whites-only public college would have to work with a black institution "to conform with the spirit and letter of the law for like facilities." As one historian notes, "The major concern of state officials was to meet the legal requirement to divide federal appropriations with a school for blacks in order not to jeopardize federal funding of white schools."[43]

The Delaware Conference Academy in Princess Anne seemed a logical partner for the Maryland Agricultural College, owing to its location and its background in vocational training. On the last day of December 1890, Goucher signed an agreement between Morgan College and the Agricultural College, designating the academy as the eastern branch of the state land-grant institution. The agreement between the private black and public white schools stipulated that "a sum of money not exceeding $3,000" of the state's federal appropriation for the year 1891 be allotted to the rural black school, renamed the Princess Anne Academy. The money would go toward hiring a superintendent and two special instructors in agriculture and mechanical arts, and providing free tuition and use of tools to enrolled students. The appropriation was renewable, and with prospects bright, Goucher offered to buy 105 acres of land adjoining the original Olney estate for the agricultural program. He advanced $1,500 ($40,300) to secure the mortgage until the trustees raised funds, but he forgave the loan when the price proved higher than expected.[44]

As the Princess Anne Academy received its first federal funds, the Morgan College board appointed Goucher, college president Francis J. Wagner, and another trustee to a standing committee overseeing the academy's progress. Goucher chaired another trustee committee that applied to the state legislature for funds to erect academy buildings. They soon realized that black land-grant colleges were "separate but unequal," in the words of educators John and Ruth Ellen Wennersten: "Although there may have been hopes among the Methodist leadership that the economic and educational fortunes of the institution would improve with the conferring of land-grant status on the school, the actual practice dictated otherwise. Like other black land-grant schools, Princess Anne Academy was sorely neglected by state and federal agencies."[45]

The 1890 Morrill Act called for "a just and equitable division" of available funds, not an equal division. Several Morgan trustees had protested this imbalance when the agreement between schools had been signed, and the Wennerstens note that throughout the 1890s, "Funding for the Maryland Agricultural College increased significantly while that of Princess Anne Academy remained static." By 1900, the academy continued to receive the lesser share of state and federal aid—seldom more than thirty-nine percent of what Morrill regulations allowed. This discrepancy was rationalized because "funding was based on the number of black farmers in Maryland," about one-sixth of the white agricultural population. By 1916, Princess Anne Academy received only twenty percent of the money authorized by the second Morrill Act. Federal money "kept the school alive" but didn't fund the school sufficiently to truly fulfill its land-grant mission.[46]

While Goucher and the Morgan trustees oversaw the Princess Anne project in the early 1890s, they also approved another branch school in Lynchburg, Virginia. The Washington Conference had secured ten acres of land and offered $5,000 ($134,000) in cash to establish a school there; members of Morgan's board visited the site and selected the location for a central building. Once home, Goucher gave speeches to black Baltimore congregations to raise funds and secured a bequest toward the new building; he and two other donors each pledged $3,000 ($80,500) if two more people would do the same. The money came in, and by the fall of 1893, the Virginia Collegiate and Industrial Institute was open to students, its central structure a replica of the Morgan College building.[47]

The Lynchburg and Princess Anne schools directed capable students to Morgan College for further education and provided industrial training not available at the Baltimore institution. Securing adequate funding to grow and maintain the college and its affiliates was an ongoing challenge for Goucher, Wagner, and the trustees, however. The four conferences that supported Morgan didn't fully cover expenses, and a largely impoverished student population precluded a rise in tuition revenues. Beyond that, as Wagner reported to the board in 1894, in the Maryland legislature they were often "defrauded by small politicians" who short-changed black institutions. To help balance Morgan's budget, Goucher continued to assume all or part of any deficits at the end of an academic year. (As at the Woman's College, he also looked to wealthy Methodists to make special donations as needed.) He used one of his favorite and most effective fundraising tactics as well: setting out a challenge. For example, during Morgan's first year as a college, he offered to relieve a $5,000 debt ($134,000) if friends of the institution added the same amount to the endowment before the end of the academic year. As a newspaper article of the mid-1890s noted, Goucher both encouraged the black population to "develop their [own] resources" for the institution and "stimulated the liberality of others" in the white community.[48]

✳ ✳ ✳

Throughout the 1890s, Goucher was called upon to assist other educational institutions as well. He was consulted early in the creation of the American University in Washington, D.C. George Washington had first proposed the idea of a national university a century before, but only recently had Bishop John Fletcher Hurst purchased ninety acres of farmland at the edge of the city to build such an institution, under the auspices of the Methodist Episcopal Church. Goucher described a February 1890 meeting with Hurst at his Washington home:

> He laid before me in detail the plan for a great Methodist University as far as it had any plan—rather talked over with me the project—& had me lunch with him. Called a buggy (and a white horse) & drove me out to the proposed site.[49]

Goucher believed the project was feasible but would require at least $10 million ($268 million) "to place it on a proper footing." Two years later, Hurst, who had become the university's chancellor, asked Goucher's permission to nominate him to the Board of Trustees. Hurst said he would take it as a personal favor, telling Goucher, "You are one of the men who see the importance of our cause and were one of the first to give it a word of cheer and a strong helping hand." Though he appreciated the honor and felt the association and work would be congenial, Goucher declined. His time, he wrote, was "so mortgaged by other duties already assumed that it will be impossible for me to meet the requirements of the position."[50]

It was not long, however, before the two men were vying for funds for their respective institutions. According to an agreement reached at the 1892 Methodist General Conference, American University was to teach only graduate courses; its organizers were not to "interfere with the support of other institutions by undue efforts to secure contributions from their constituency"; and the university was not to open before raising $5 million beyond the value of its grounds. Goucher soon discovered, however, that Hurst and associates were violating the agreement. As Goucher told the Woman's College trustees, the new university's advocates were "so active in presenting its claims to the patrons and friends of [our] College, to those who had promised to give us funds, as well as to others to whom we were looking for material assistance and who constitute our natural constituencies, as to seriously interfere with our development."[51]

Perhaps even more galling to Goucher was that several newly elected trustees of the Woman's College were asked almost immediately to serve on American University's board and "urged to give their preference to the latter office." He must have wondered if Hurst's earlier request for him to become a trustee of American University was an attempt to get him to shift his allegiance—and funds—to the new enterprise. Goucher finally protested to the General Conference that American was encroaching on the territory of other educational institutions, including the Woman's College and likely Morgan as well. [52]

Despite this contentious situation near home, Goucher became a frequent and favorite speaker at educational institutions across the country. His interests in the American frontier extended to education as well as church building, and he lent his support and fundraising expertise to some newly created Methodist colleges in the West. One news article hailed Goucher's "splendid management," adding that he knew how "to take a collection, as well as grace the presidency of a college." He was asked to speak at an 1895 fundraising rally at Montana Wesleyan College, founded in 1889, the year Montana became a state. As he did in promoting the Woman's College of

Baltimore, he offered a businessman's perspective, highlighting the financial benefits of the university to the town of Helena, along with the school's importance to Montana's youth. As at First Church, he proposed reducing the institution's debt by dividing it into shares of $100 each. At the end of the evening's rally, nearly half the amount needed to sustain operations was pledged.[53]

In 1896, Goucher delivered the baccalaureate address at Puget Sound University in Tacoma, Washington (now the University of Puget Sound). Another young institution, Puget Sound had an opportunity to acquire a branch location at a low price but lacked necessary funds. The chancellor told the audience he had mentioned this dilemma to "a prince of the church," who, without hesitation, gave him a check for the purchase as an anonymous present. In the midst of loud applause, someone in the crowd cried out, "Three cheers for Dr. Goucher," a cry taken up by others—although the chancellor never named him.[54]

At the same time, Goucher maintained his ties to Bishop John H. Vincent, co-founder of the Chautauqua Assembly and the distance-learning Chautauqua Literary and Scientific Circle. In 1897, Goucher was asked to address more than 1,000 CLSC graduates on the Assembly grounds in western New York. Following a colorful parade to the amphitheater, he spoke on "Individualism," voicing some of the beliefs he had put into practice at home and abroad:

> The progress of humanity is gauged by the progress of individualism. Slavery has given way to citizenship, and men plead not for special privileges, but demand their common rights. . . . Man and woman are recognized as having natures diverse in functions, incapable for being substituted the one for the other, but supplemental and of equal worth. . . .
>
> When we are confronted by misery which needs relief, suffering which requires sympathy, folly which should be reproved, or ignorance waiting for counsel, it is not an impertinent intrusion upon the serenity of our souls, but a high privilege offered to realize larger life, giving opportunity for ministries which strengthen and enrich the giver more than they can the recipient.

He also chastised "those slaves of frivolity" in any community who "work so hard to enjoy doing nothing."[55]

✳✳✳

No one could accuse Goucher of squandering his time. An 1893 newspaper article, "The Important Men of Baltimore," said that his multifaceted work demonstrated his confidence in "the certainty and the permanence of Baltimore's development," and called him "an earnest and helpful friend of the Greater Baltimore." A Methodist publication later stated he was "closely identified with all the philanthropic movements of the Monumental City and ready for every good word and deed" to improve the education, health, and well being of all its residents, white and black. Another newspaper article, simply entitled "G," noted that the names of the three most prominent late-nineteenth-century Marylanders in their fields began with the letter G: Arthur Pue Gorman, in politics; Daniel Coit Gilman, in education; and James Cardinal Gibbons, in religion. Acknowledging Goucher's leadership within the state, the reporter promoted that if one wanted "to transform a trio of important Gs into a quartet," the name Goucher, the benefactor and champion of the Woman's College, should be added.[56]

As a churchman and an educator, Goucher became involved in the 1890s in many issues of the Progressive Era, a response to the ills of urbanization and industrialization. Maryland historian Robert Brugger has written that Baltimore Progressives needed to look "no farther than their backyards for heavy work. Their cause brought together religious caring, social awareness, and scientific findings" to tackle such problems as illiteracy, overcrowded tenements, and a lack of health care for the poor. Goucher took an active role in the Charity Organization Society of Baltimore (COS), founded by Gilman and other community leaders in the early 1880s. At a time before public social service agencies, the COS "developed a system of investigating and regulating charitable cases in the city." It kept watch on institutions providing services and created a central exchange to coordinate the work of churches and charities aiding poor families and neglected children. Goucher served on its board for many years and became a vice president. His varied connections enabled him to bring in funds and volunteers to sustain COS services such as tutoring, field trips to the country, providing shoes and clothing to needy students, and helping them obtain medical care.[57]

Closer to campus, he and Professor Lilian Welsh encouraged Woman's College students to engage in community outreach. North Baltimore charity workers wrote him in appreciation of a Girls' Club that students had started, "to which working girls—and those who ought to work—can go for a helpful evening once a week." On the other end of the educational spectrum, Goucher was elected to the Board of Managers of the new Kindergarten Association. That starter grade did not yet exist in the Baltimore school system, and the association set out to raise funds for and awareness of "the establishment of kindergartens in those parts of Baltimore where they are most needed." Goucher understood that in Baltimore as in India, educating the poorest and youngest residents produced long-term benefits.[58]

With his love of the outdoors, Goucher also worked to increase his and the public's knowledge of nature and natural history. In 1893, he was elected a lifetime member of the Maryland Academy of Sciences, forerunner of the Maryland Science Center. Academy president Arthur Bibbins later stated that during Goucher's nearly twenty-year membership, he had "probably done as much to make possible the proper study of the ancient animal and plant life of Maryland as any other one person." For proof, he suggested consulting various state and United States Geological Survey Official Reports where Goucher's name appeared. Bibbins recalled many regional excursions with the enthusiastic Goucher, who dealt "very saucy blows with his geological hammer in his effort to liberate perfect crystals from their stony prisons." The hammers, he said, sometimes came home "very decidedly disabled." The amateur geologist often took tools along on remote travels, in case he came across any interesting rock formations. (He lost one set in his luggage when the *Republic* sank.)[59]

✳ ✳ ✳

If anyone were ever "bitten by the travel bug" it was Goucher, and he sometimes came up with his best ideas on a trip. He said the idea for the Woman's College came to him "like a flash" on a train between Brooklyn and Baltimore, and as noted earlier, a chance meeting with

Korean envoys on a train led to his interest in opening a mission in their country. In the early to mid-1890s, he took several extended trips, often with Mary along, that combined church or educational work with much-needed rest and recreation. Back home, he enjoyed sharing his travel experiences, especially with Woman's College and Johns Hopkins students. Giving talks and showing pictures and artifacts he had brought home exposed these young people to the cultures and issues of the broader world.[60]

At the end of 1891, several months after Goucher assumed the presidency of the Woman's College full time, the board's Executive Committee recommended he take "a necessary rest of a month during the present winter," at the same time the Missionary Society was asking him to inspect Methodist missions in Mexico. Those duties were scheduled for early in the new year, but he and Mary left Baltimore in early December to include a trip to Las Vegas Hot Springs in New Mexico. John was suffering from bouts of rheumatism and recurring work-related headaches; Mary had never fully recovered after the birth and death of their last daughter, and had a lingering cough and persistent weakness in one leg. For ten days they rested at the rustic yet elegant Montezuma Hotel, enjoying the warm restorative waters and crisp mountain air. That year Janet, Eleanor, and Elizabeth celebrated Christmas at home without their parents, but William Shelley, principal of the Girls' Latin School, looked in and reported to the girls' parents that he was greeted by "bright eyes and glad hearts," adding that the "dear girls passed as happy a Christmas as possible without your loving presence and tender ministries."[61]

At the end of December, John and Mary crossed the border into Mexico. On reaching Mexico City, Goucher had an interview with President Porfirio Dias to discuss education, and he and Mary enjoyed the sights and attended a bullfight. Then they traveled further into the country to visit several Methodist missions. At one, Goucher saw a Sunday school that fueled his hopes for Christianity breaking down barriers worldwide: The class consisted of "five little fellows," he reported: "an Aztec, a Spaniard, a negro and a half breed and the teacher was Japanese." (The teacher also doubled as the Japanese government's minister to Mexico.) Near the end of January, the Gouchers reached the Yucatan Peninsula and from there sailed to

Havana. Returning to Baltimore, John learned his beloved father had died in Missouri in their absence.[62]

On another occasion, John and Mary took a steamship to Alaska after he had spoken at educational institutions in Portland, Oregon, and Tacoma, Seattle, and Vancouver, Washington. Even as he enjoyed the scenery from deck, Goucher could not help calculating the economic potential of this remote territory. In a newspaper article recounting their trip, John opined that the United States's purchase of Alaska from Russia in 1867 was "the greatest real estate deal in history." He figured the cost at about one-half cent per acre, and estimated that there were nearly nineteen square miles of land per resident.[63]

In Alaska, Goucher met several old Russian families and inspected Methodist- and Presbyterian-sponsored missions schools. He was fascinated by native customs, some of which reminded him of the Japanese. He also studied totem poles, comparing the way each told of a family's ancestry to an English or French coat of arms. The couple brought back more treasures for their collection, including a 200-year-old Russian painting, a native fishhook, and a totem (emblem of ancestry) that had been worn by an Alaskan healer.[64]

As part of their 11,000-mile round trip, they passed through Yellowstone on their way back to Baltimore. Nearly a decade earlier, Goucher had visited the country's first national park with a friend. Mary, at home at Alto Dale at the time, wrote to an acquaintance that the men were traveling in "primitive style," seeing the sites from horseback and sleeping in tents. Goucher picked up samples of lichen, which he tucked away in his desk on returning home. A few years later, those samples had turned the drawer into a miniature garden, which he liked to show to guests. Mary said he had "struck 'Wonderland' indeed" on that first trip, and now he could share some of those wonders with her.[65]

Early in 1895, Mary and John finally took what might be considered a very belated honeymoon—a trip to Egypt. For once, both of them were in good health, and John had no speeches to give or missions to inspect. On the trip, Mary kept a diary, whose first shipboard entry hinted at her excitement: "Good accommodations, excellent service, and the presence of [God] Our Father combine to ensure a good time to John and myself in our anticipated Nile Trip." Via the Azores, Genoa, and Alexandria, they reached Cairo, where John purchased some unusually large souvenirs—two mummies that he sent back to display at the college museum in Goucher Hall. (On his return home, he tried to unwrap one before a rapt audience, but according to a news article, the mummy withheld her secrets.) At another stop, Mary rested on the piazza of the Mena House while John and a fellow traveler climbed "old Cheops" in sixteen minutes. During a return visit eleven years later, Goucher recorded in his diary that this time it took him twenty minutes—but only because a woman in the party slowed him down.[66]

John and Mary also took a cruise up the Nile; at the Valley of the Kings, they saw the temples of Karnak and Luxor, and porters carried them in chairs to view the tombs. On their return to Baltimore, John proudly and often told one story about his wife. Mary had entered one of the gloomy tombs with a guide, who inquired if she were afraid. No, she said, and was looking around when suddenly an Arab elder came in, sat at her feet, and began crassly chewing tobacco. She wanted the guide to ask him to leave, but he shook his head, "No, no—he sheik." Mary tried to ignore the interloper, but finally she had had enough. She drew up her five-foot frame, pointed directly at him, and commanded in a tone that needed no translation, "Go away." He looked at her and sullenly left. Mary's guide, awed by her boldness, turned to other visitors and said, "She sheik herself!"[67]

Mary and John did not always leave their three young daughters at home. Like other families escaping winter weather, one year they trekked south to visit several resorts along the Florida coast. On a side trip from St. Augustine to Anastasia Island, they saw what locals called a deep-sea monster, apparently a huge octopus that had been washed ashore; its partial remains weighed seven tons and took six horses to pull out of the surf. Goucher the naturalist likely calculated its original size and shape, its diet, and the distance it had traveled.[68]

As much as Mary enjoyed traveling with her husband, she understood she could not always accompany him on his many trips. But in extending an invitation to a woman whose own husband often traveled, she revealed how much she missed John during his absences:

> I planned something that I should enjoy and I hope you will think kindly of it. That is for you to come here sometime in

August and comfort me in my <u>widow</u>hood. . . . Depending upon you to solace me (I'll try not to be <u>too</u> blue).

As her acquaintances knew well, Mary never let "her private wishes and yearnings come between her husband and his work."[69]

✳ ✳ ✳

That work included not only his responsibilities in Baltimore, but also his growing involvement in the national affairs of the Methodist Episcopal Church. Besides serving on the Board of Managers of the Missionary Society since 1884, he was elected—in 1888 and in eight successive elections—to be a delegate to the quadrennial General Conference, the Church's supreme court and legislative body. When a senior agent of the Methodist Book Concern died in 1889, Goucher was considered for a lead management position at the Church's publishing arm. Bishop E. G. Andrews wrote a confidential letter to sound him out about the job, assuring Goucher he had the backing of the Board of Bishops, with no one competitor holding "any clear track." Goucher thanked Andrews and other "brethren" for the offer, but felt they greatly overestimated his abilities. He declined the position:

> I am ready to undertake any work to which the Lord, through the Church and my conscience may call me, but though the Church might be unanimous in its choice, my conscience would not approve of my acceptance of the Book Agency or of any position which is so largely secular in its character.[70]

His feelings about and connections to missions and missionary work remained strong, however. One Methodist publication noted: "[He is] a sympathetic, critical and specially intelligent traveler, and our missions are always encouraged and helped by his presence and the church is instructed and strengthened by the information he secures." Missionaries turned directly to him for advice and support. As one once told him, "[Y]ou can and do appreciate more than any of the ministers or laymen I meet at home the difficulties of our work, its need, and the manner now best calculated to lend us real assistance." Even bishops sought his counsel. An 1896 article in *The Baltimore*

Sun noted that Joseph C. Hartzell, the newly appointed bishop to Africa, purposely stopped in the city for several hours en route to his assignment so he could "consult with President Goucher of the Woman's College, who has a wide knowledge of the foreign missions of the Methodist Episcopal Church."[71]

Considering all he had accomplished for the Church, there was talk of making Goucher himself a bishop. When he was proposed for it in 1892, there were sixteen bishops, elected by the General Conference, with jurisdiction over more than 100 domestic and foreign annual conferences and various areas of special interest. At the time, a bishop held lifetime tenure and was based in a city convenient to his assigned conferences, but he spent considerable time traveling to conference meetings and events. He was also responsible for making pastoral assignments to churches within his territory and often had additional educational or ecclesiastical duties. Elections of new bishops might resemble old-fashioned political conventions, with delegates casting multiple ballots before any candidate received sufficient votes.[72]

The 1892 General Conference considered appointing four to six additional bishops, with likely candidates including already-prominent figures, such as the secretaries of the Missionary Society and the Church Extension Society, or agents of the Book Concern. *The Baltimore American* noted that the Baltimore Conference rarely produced "bishop timber," but this year was an exception. The article glowingly described John Goucher's qualifications:

> He does not owe anything to any combines, having absolutely refused to have any deal with anybody for any office. He is yet a young man, but his name has been almost a household word in his denomination because of his superior intellectual gifts and for the princely liberality of his benevolent gifts. . . . He has been the inspiring genius of the Woman's College from its beginning in 1888, and without his management and generosity its splendid buildings and equipment could not have existed. As its president, Dr. Goucher is the right man in the right place, pre-eminently. In the previous general conference . . . his name was prominent as a missionary secretary. Now, if he does not refuse it outright, he will be in the ideas and ballots of many for the highest position in the gift of the church.

But Goucher had no interest in—and did not feel called to—this prestigious but ultimately confining position. The article ended: "This is a clear case of the office seeking the man, not the man the office."[73]

Goucher's name was again proposed as a possible bishop at the 1896 General Conference, and he was assured that three-quarters of the delegates were pledged to vote for him on the final ballot. A local news article boosted the hometown candidate: "The Methodist Church would go a long way and fare much worse to find a man who would fill that exalted office. Dr. Goucher is one of us. We know him, and know of his work, and any honor the Methodist General Conference confers upon him, he will wear worthily." Goucher insisted God had called him to educational work, and told a friend that even "if elected unanimously, he would be compelled to rise to his feet and decline the offer."[74]

As we have seen, this educational work included not only the institutions in Baltimore, but also the schools in the "much fruit" countries of South and East Asia in which he and Mary had taken such an interest in the previous decade. In the 1890s, he deepened those ties to India, China, Japan, and Korea, and made his first around-the-world journey to see firsthand the fruits of his efforts.

John Goucher (rear) with Bishops Isaac W. Joyce,
Cyrus D. Foss, and James M. Thoburn, Allahabad, India,
January 1898

*Courtesy of the Baltimore-Washington Conference Archives,
Lovely Lane United Methodist Church, Baltimore, Maryland*

EXPANDING CONNECTIONS ABROAD

Chapter 14
(Fall 1897-1900)

—◆◆—

*To accept from one's self less than the best one can give
or be is spiritual tragedy.*[1]

In 1893, it looked as if Goucher would get that firsthand view of what he had accomplished abroad, when the Missionary Society asked him to accompany Bishop Cyrus Foss on a visit to missions in South and East Asia. But the trip was postponed after Foss was injured in an accident. Out of sight did not mean out of mind for Goucher, however; until the trip was rescheduled for 1897, he kept current with affairs in each of the countries where he was involved. Through reading and research, correspondence with or home visits from missionaries, and his work on the Board of Managers of the Missionary Society, he continued to offer support and advice from Baltimore, closely following the progress of every project he and Mary had initiated.

For example, the couple continued to renew their annual commitment for primary schools in North India's Rohilkhand District, and by the early 1890s, there were nearly seventy schools for boys and fifty for girls, surpassing the original plan for 100 total. More than 3,000 students attended daily. The allotment of Goucher scholarships for boarding schools in Moradabad was filled, and on state exams, many of these students' scores matched or exceeded those of students from government-sponsored schools.

At the time, Goucher considered relinquishing direct involvement with the boarding schools, letting the Missionary Society distribute the annual allotment as needed. This idea alarmed missionary Edwin W. Parker, who had been working with the primary and secondary school plans since their inception. He told their benefactors: "Your scheme is *just* right as it is. . . . Nothing in our work would hurt me more than to have this scheme disturbed." To press his point, Parker mentioned a recent Baltimore Conference meeting he had attended, where some spoke out against supporting the Woman's College at the expense of other conference-supported schools. Parker feared that, without Goucher's direct guiding hand, his boarding school would be similarly placed "in competition with so many other things and at risk every time of so many votes [on the Board of Managers] in the contest for the division of funds." As a final appeal, he urged, "Don't, dear Brother and Sister Goucher, give up your boys and girls. I do wish I could persuade you to make the scholarship aid one of your permanent endowment schemes."[2]

Goucher had no interest in creating such an endowment, preferring to keep working to maintain and even increase the number of primary schools. While Parker appreciated the work being done at the elementary level, he thought the boarding schools, which provided an education for the brightest students, were a better way to train young men and women for service to the Church and to India. But Goucher believed that more students (and their families) could be reached through village schools. As another missionary wrote of these schools' influence on a community: "I have a number of instances in mind now in which the people were so prejudiced against us that they would not permit us to enter their houses but as soon as we established schools in their midst their attitude toward us was immediately changed." In some Goucher Schools, students came from as many as seven castes, a small breakthrough in India's rigid class system.[3]

One way Goucher helped the cause was to convince "Chum"— his friend John Grier Holmes from Dickinson College days—to follow his example and fund twenty new schools in the neighboring Hardoi district. Opening in 1895, they were modeled on the Goucher Schools, and Goucher recommended they be located near enough to the boarding school in Moradabad—a five-hour, sixty-cent train ride away—to enable the best students to continue their education beside his own scholars.[4]

There were other concerns Goucher had to address from afar. Fluctuating currency exchange rates often made his school payments come out short, and missionaries wrote to say the money he sent didn't always cover expenses. They also felt the pinch in their own pay as the Missionary Society decreased its appropriations. Many reduced their own salaries to continue paying Indian preachers and lay workers, and looked to Goucher to be their voice on the Board of Managers. One correspondent appealed to Goucher that his "Indian heart will be stirred to do all for us you possibly can." Edwin Parker wrote him about one successful intervention: "I wish to thank you on behalf of the missionaries of North India for your faithful efforts on our behalf in securing us the Gold payments of salaries. . . . I cannot possibly tell you what a relief this will be to us in India."[5]

Severe famine, causing eight to ten million deaths, hit India in the second half of the 1890s, as did bubonic plague, which killed more than 100,000 people in the Bombay area in an eighteen-month period. The missionaries responded, often at a cost to mission programs. Several wrote Goucher, asking for either his own financial help or his assistance in soliciting it from others. They described the suffering they saw: a mother trying to sell her two children for two rupees to buy bread, the "living skeletons," and the "cries of the starving for food." The missionaries helped distribute donated food to hundreds of people daily, and Methodist orphanages and schools were overwhelmed with 2,000 to 3,000 abandoned children, many of whom died before they could be helped. Goucher made his own donation to a girls' orphanage in Madras, and urged members of the Women's Foreign Missionary Society to do likewise, especially those he knew in Baltimore.[6]

Goucher also helped another women's college grow during this period—this one in Lucknow, India. He was already familiar with the work of Isabella Thoburn, one of the first two women sent to India in 1870 by the WFMS. She had joined her brother James, a missionary who later became a bishop, and started a small school open to girls of all castes and religions in the town bazaar. In time, it grew into a boarding school and high school, and by 1886, it was offering a few college classes. Those who wanted to complete a degree, however, had to go to the government-sponsored secular universities in Calcutta.

Thoburn, like Goucher, knew the importance of educated women to families and society, especially in India, where many girls and women spent their lives in seclusion. She wanted to raise her school to college level under Christian auspices, and to raise funds, she wrote articles aimed at the American public and gave speeches while on furloughs to the United States. Goucher shared her aims, and in 1891, offered to pay a teacher's salary at the college, later named for Thoburn. She hired Lilavati Singh, a graduate of Thoburn's high school and Calcutta University, who wrote Goucher to note his good timing: "About the time that I must have been writing to [Thoburn], a gentleman who was himself the president of a woman's college, and who was much interested in missions, had offered to give seventy-five rupees a month for a year to a native teacher. And then she asked me if I would work with her next year."[7]

Thoburn wrote as well, thanking Goucher for helping make ends meet "where I feared they would come short." This donation began a long association between the Lucknow and Baltimore women's colleges. Thoburn also asked "if the young ladies of your college could not help us" with books and equipment. This request led to annual contributions from the Woman's College (later Goucher College) for more than forty years; the two institutions also exchanged students and faculty for several decades into the twentieth century.[8]

※ ※ ※

Even as Goucher spent considerable time and resources on his projects in India, he was increasingly drawn to challenges presented in Japan, China, and Korea. In an 1894 speech, he said, "By the consensus of missionary activity and investment, Asia is the great mission field of the world. There are more [Church] Societies and more laborers at work, larger annual investments, more people needing Christianizing, more varied opportunism, greater obstacles to be overcome, and more encouraging results than in any other part of the world." Part of recognizing religious and educational opportunities was staying current about the region's political developments. The uneasy and often hostile relations within and among the three countries sometimes spilled over to affect mission and school affairs. Russia, England, France, Germany, and the United States also sought to gain trade advantages and exert their influence where they could.[9]

In Japan, the emperor had granted a new constitution in 1889, and a bi-cameral Diet was established the following year. Three hundred members were elected to the lower house in the first national election, although the emperor retained ultimate power, and a group of elder statesmen made all the important decisions. Missionary Martin Vail told Goucher that these changes brought "a general revolution along many lines," noting, "Young Japan, ambitious, proud, but always seeking the highest material advantages, is about to be tried in the balance. Will she be found lacking?"[10]

After years of accepting unequal treaties with Western powers, Japan was eager to show its strength on the global stage. Motoro Yuzero, whom Goucher had supported while he studied in the United States and who then taught at the Anglo-Japanese College, wrote that while his countrymen were grateful for foreign aid, they did not like to give up their "national character" to receive it. Jennie Vail, Martin's sister who also taught at the college, told Goucher that Japanese students were "beginning to feel their oats" and becoming restive; Martin Vail reported several anti-foreign incidents in Tokyo. On the mission front, Julius Soper, Goucher's friend from the Baltimore Conference, told him the populace wanted "equal rights, privileges and power in all management of our work in Japan." The people felt they were in an inferior position, which they found "galling and humiliating."[11]

In the midst of this turmoil, late in 1893 Goucher received a letter from a committee representing the Board of Managers of Tokyo EiWa Gakko, the Anglo-Japanese College in Tokyo. It suggested changing the institution's name. The committee said the term EiWa (Anglo-Japanese) "grates harshly on the Japanese ear when spoken and when written is unsightly and induces unfavorable criticism." The name made it sound like a language school that taught only English and Japanese, rather than an institution embracing collegiate, theological, and preparatory departments. Its Japanese administrators wanted a name that would "express the proper character of the college" and attract students in a competitive academic market. In a time of national unrest, the whole name gave "the impression of a foreign institution which in these days does not too highly recommend it to parents of students."[12]

The committee suggested the name Aoyama Gakuin—Aoyama Institution of Learning—the nearest equivalent to calling it Aoyama College. The new name also identified the school with its desirable location in Tokyo. The committee sought Goucher's "permission to effect [sic] such change," adding, "We all feel under unexpressible [sic] obligation to you . . . and wish to do nothing in the matter which is not perfectly agreeable and intelligible to you." If Goucher approved, members requested he notify the Board of Managers in New York at his earliest convenience. The name was officially changed within the year, but Aoyama Gakuin faced another kind of upheaval—an earthquake that struck Tokyo, Yokohama, and Kawasaki in June 1894. Goucher Hall was partially destroyed and needed repairs, slowing the college's growth.[13]

In addition to Japan's internal tensions early in the 1890s, the country was also concerned with its external security, seeing Korea as "a dagger pointed at the heart of Japan." As Henry G. Appenzeller (the first missionary the Gouchers funded in Seoul) pointed out, "Korea derives her importance in the Far East from her position on the map." China's Qing dynasty had long claimed Korea as a subordinate state, and the Russians sought an opening to gain a year-round seaport. The Japanese, with their own business interests in Korea, wanted to end China's influence there and to annex the weaker nation.[14]

Clashes between Chinese and Japanese troops in Seoul in the mid-1880s had delayed the opening of the Methodist mission, and while Appenzeller and other missionaries gained favor with King Kojong for their educational and medical endeavors, they often were at the mercy of a tug-of-war between foreign influences within the Korean government. When the Tong Haks, devoted to Eastern learning, rose up against corrupt magistrates around the country in 1894, King Kojong and Queen Min requested help from China, and 2,000 soldiers quickly arrived to help quell the rebellion. To Japan, this violated a treaty with China not to send troops into Korea without notifying the other nation; Japan in turn sent 6,000 troops to Seoul to assist its neighbor. As Appenzeller wrote in an article about the escalating conflict, "Korea relies on China. . . . The king is helpless," and, "Japan has seized the capital." Koreans and missionaries alike feared that an "insignificant uprising in the southern part of Korea" would escalate into war.[15]

At the end of July, Japanese troops raided the palace and forced King Kojong to declare Korean independence from Chinese domination, while authorizing a pro-Japanese council to establish governmental and social reforms. Chinese troops were to be expelled. As feared, by August, Japan and China were at war. The combatants were of unequal size, but in battle after battle, the well-equipped and western-trained Japanese army and navy overcame China's ill-prepared and regionally organized army and badly maintained navy. A few months after the Sino-Japanese War ended in April 1895, Japan prevented Queen Min and her pro-Chinese ministers from reasserting their influence; a small band infiltrated the palace and assassinated her.

Although not directly involved in the war, Russia remained interested in Korea and its resources. In the winter of 1896, fleeing Japanese pressure, King Kojong retreated with his son to the Russian legation in Seoul, near the American legation and the Methodist mission. He soon gave an unusual audience to Appenzeller and his Presbyterian colleague Horace Underwood, which the pair saw as acknowledging their work in Korea and their missions' sympathy for the besieged royal family. When the king left the Russian legation the following February, he responded to the growing movement for Korea's independence by proclaiming himself emperor of the Taehan Cheguk, the Great Han Empire, and supporting some domestic reforms. An Independence Club, founded while the king was under Russian protection, stirred up the people's desire for increased rights, but the government favored absolute monarchy; the organization was disbanded and its leaders arrested by the end of 1898.[16]

In this period, Emperor Kojong also attempted to assert Korea's commercial and logistical position with foreign powers, but he remained a weak leader, tugged and pulled by both Russia and Japan. Nevertheless, Korean schools under Methodist sponsorship continued to grow. As Japan assumed more control over Korea (and its educational policies) later in the 1890s, Goucher's good reputation with the Japanese leadership helped the Church move forward with its work in Korea.

✳✳✳

Following the Sino-Japanese War, power in East Asia shifted from China's weakened Qing dynasty to an increasingly modern Japan.

China faced additional inroads by foreign powers that had forced it to accept unequal treaties earlier in the century. As Goucher summed up the situation in his 1894 speech, "For more than a century, the effort of the nations has been to pry open a door of entrance. It has been done and China is flowing out where others seek admission." Indeed, as these nations vied for commercial and territorial spheres of influence, the country was said to be "carved up like a melon." Yet Goucher saw this "Boneless Giant," as he alleged China was called, "waking up and giving suggestions of her importance." He assessed the situation for his listeners:

> If England and Russia lock jaws upon Asiatic soil, China will dictate the terms of peace. Because of her relation to these powers, she is a factor, and an increasing factor, in European politics. The British Lion and the Russian Bear are alike unwilling to come within the coils of the Chinese Dragon. If I mistake not, the Anglo-Saxon and the Chinaman will be the potential forces determining the outcome of human development.

Goucher also painted a vivid picture of the Chinese people at that time:

> [They] combine the endurance of the German with the energy of the Yankee. Their cues point back into the forgotten past, but through their almond eyes they are looking beyond the present. They are the monied men of Penang. They own two-thirds of all the property in Singapore, outside of the government buildings. They are the accountants, bankers, importers and exporters of the Indian Archipelago. They have established themselves in Australia and New Zealand, the Sandwich Islands, and the West Indies, Europe and Mexico, and have gained a foothold in the U.S.[17]

Their foothold in America was tenuous, however. The 1882 Chinese Exclusion Act placed a ten-year moratorium on Chinese immigration for both skilled and unskilled workers; the 1892 Geary Act extended the moratorium, limited the rights of Chinese already in the United States, and required them to carry residency permits. These restrictive laws stemmed from fears about the economy and jobs, mainly in the western states following the rise of Chinese immigration, especially during the mid-century gold rush and the construction of the first transcontinental railroad in the 1860s. These acts made it difficult for any Chinese resident of the United States to go home for a visit and then return; Chinese families often were permanently separated by immigration restrictions. In a later diary entry, Goucher wrote about the far-reaching consequences of such policies:

> About the middle of the [1800s], China was sending her strongest, most alert, aggressive and promising young men to the US, in steadily increasing numbers, to be educated in our colleges and universities. These men, by ability and purpose, were divinely appointed and self chosen to be the leaders and determining factors in the development of the New China, giving to it ideals, trend and organized form. Had we been true to the opportunities thrust upon us, we could have staid [sic] at home and simply through common civility secured the alignment of the Celestial Empire to the Kingdom of God.

> We legislated for the exclusion of the Chinese contract labor, which, grant for the sake of argument, was prudential, or even wise, yet we permitted the politicians, in servile obedience to the dictates of a godless socialism and tyrannical labor organizations, which were alike un-American in their spirit and self seeking in their purpose, to enforce the exclusion acts with such arduous cruelties as to make it impossible for a self-respecting Chinaman, whether student, merchant or tourist to seek entrance to any of our ports. The rising tide of Chinese students was turned back or deflected to Europe and the Chinese leaders today, except those educated in America previous to 1882 are largely atheistical, when had we been even moderately humane, they would have been evangelical.[18]

When the Exclusion Act came up for renewal in 1892, Goucher spoke against it at that year's Baltimore Annual Conference, offering a protest resolution, which was unanimously adopted. He noted that if this resolution and similar ones from other conferences did not sway the federal government, at least they would show the Chinese that the Methodists and their missionaries recognized their worth.[19]

Goucher credited the strength of the Chinese people. But the Qing dynasty, based in Peking, could not prevent Western powers from extending their influence deep into the country, nor could it adequately govern or feed a population of 450 million. Its bureaucracy was overwhelmed, and local leaders increasingly took over governing their regions. Rebellions or riots undermined the imperial authority, as foreign intrusions disrupted various locales around the country. Goucher was particularly interested in developments in West China's Szechuan Province, specifically in Chungking, which he called the "Chicago of China," and the provincial capital of Chengtu, 1,100 miles southwest of Peking in "one of the most fertile and populous portions of the globe."[20]

The Methodist missions in the Szechuan region had twice come under attack. In the mid-1880s, a few years after the Gouchers had funded the first Methodist mission in Chungking, it and other Protestant and Catholic missions were destroyed in an anti-Western frenzy, instigated by an unruly mass of students in the city to take civil and military exams. The Chinese government funded their rebuilding, and the missionaries resumed work among the scattered church membership; in 1889, the Methodists expanded their operation, opening a new station in Chengtu. Six years later, that mission also found itself under siege. Rumors had been spreading for weeks that missionaries were killing children, baking their bodies, and harvesting their eyes and bones for medicinal purposes. When the riots began, civilian and military authorities did little to quell them. The Protestant and Catholic missions—houses, chapels, hospitals, and schools—were destroyed or their contents carted off.

Goucher received a firsthand account from missionary H. Olin Cady. He and his wife had barely escaped the mission and were hidden by a Chinese neighbor, who was repeatedly asked by authorities if there were any foreigners in his house. Cady told Goucher of covertly watching everything they had built being destroyed or looted, "even the paving stones and the tiny shrubs and trees." The Cadys escaped after dark to the yamen, the office and residence of a local Chinese magistrate, where they found the other Protestant missionaries—eighteen adults and eleven children—squeezed into tight quarters. They remained there eleven days until they could board boats to Chungking, where they waited until it was safe to return. The British and American governments demanded additional recompense from China for this destruction. Despite the violence, Goucher held firm to his belief that Szechuan Province was "the strategic point of all Asia" for extending evangelism, and he renewed his own support.[21]

✳✳✳

On hearing about these events unfolding half-way around the world, Goucher was eager to undertake his delayed fact-finding trip for the Missionary Society. In late 1897, Bishop Foss was sent to administrate upcoming church conferences in India (which then included today's Pakistan and Bangladesh), Burma (Myanmar), and Malaysia. Goucher was asked to inspect and report on the work and financial administration of the Methodist missions and schools, totaling more than 1,200 day schools and 32,000 students across South Asia. The six-month trip, for which Goucher paid all his own expenses, eventually took him and Foss around the world, and included visits to various mission and educational projects in Southeast Asia and Japan.

This assignment came at a convenient time for Goucher. He told a reporter that although he was not ill, his doctors told him his "present stress of duties, without relaxation, would mean a complete breakdown later on." An extended journey now would let him combine work with what he considered to be relaxation. If he put it off much longer, "someone might have to go with me to take care of me." The board of the Woman's College, knowing the pressures he was under, encouraged him "to consult his own convenience and pleasure as to the time and length of his vacation."[22]

On an early October day, Goucher made final preparations at the college to leave for several months. He finished correspondence with his secretary, then held his office hours. A reporter for a Baltimore newspaper, seeking an audience, said "the hall in the vicinity of his door presented much the appearance of the waiting room of a popular physician," with his visitors' needs being "almost as varied as those of political applicants." Goucher led the customary chapel service at First Church and returned to Goucher Hall, where the students awaited him. According to another local paper, "The students gathered around him, giving three times, with much spirit, the college yell. . . .This was followed by a ringing cheer, 'Goucher, Goucher, Goucher!'" He, in turn, "acknowledged the compliment by many smiles and bows and shook hands with each of the seniors."[23]

That evening, after saying goodbye to his wife and daughters, he drove into the city from Alto Dale to catch the train north. The next morning, with friends such as "Chum" Holmes there to see them off, Goucher and Foss set sail from Hoboken, New Jersey, on the *SS Kaiser Wilhelm II*, bound for Naples. Goucher carried a letter from President William McKinley, a distant cousin, requesting any assistance the travelers might need en route. After a side trip to Rome, where Goucher again examined mission accounts, the pair headed to Brindisi to meet a steamer to Bombay. Among the more than 500 passengers were several Indian princes and princesses and a maharajah; five British lords, including Lord Kinnaird, whom Foss called a "special friend of missions"; and thirty-six missionaries heading to posts in India. The voyage took them via the Suez Canal into the Red Sea, where the intense heat, according to Goucher, disturbed the passengers' "peace, rest, comfort and patience." Wearing the lightest clothing and sleeping on deck brought some relief until the ship reached the Arabian Sea. Not wanting to miss an opportunity for educational and spiritual engagement with the missionaries on board, Goucher organized a series of group "conversations," assisted by Lord Kinnaird.[24]

Nearly a month after leaving home, the bishop and college president arrived in India. They began a 10,000-mile odyssey that took them to conferences and meetings from Bombay (Mumbai) on the west coast, to towns farther north along the Ganges and in the Himalayan foothills, and then on to Delhi and back to Bombay. They continued southeast to Madras (Chennai) on the Bay of Bengal, then north by steamer to Calcutta (Kolkata) for Christmas. From there they traveled back along the Ganges to Moradabad, headquarters of the Goucher Schools and boarding high schools, and then to Lucknow and Isabella Thoburn's college. Finally they returned to Calcutta to catch a steamer to Rangoon (Yangon) and made their way to a church conference in Singapore.[25]

Goucher told the Methodist publication *The Indian Witness* that he was pleased to see first-hand the work with which he had "only been familiar at a distance." He said he had "come as a learner, to get helpful light on many problems which are of special interest to

the Church at home and of importance to our work in this empire."
He added that while he wanted to see the architecture and investigate
India's social problems—especially those concerning caste and gender
separation—he was most interested in "the great moral and spiritual
problem."[26]

He and Foss spent nearly three months in India, and in their
travels, Goucher encountered things he had only read about or heard
from others. They reinforced his belief that Christianity and Methodist
institutions could have a beneficial impact. On Christmas Day 1897,
he wrote he was "disgusted with the cruelty, cunning and cupidity
of heathenism." In his diary, he catalogued disturbing scenes he
witnessed, such as a wedding parade with two brides, ages six and
nine, being led along on horseback. He visited the Towers of Silence,
where the corpses of Parsis, followers of the Persian prophet Zoroaster,
were eaten by vultures. He passed the ghats, a series of steps leading
down to the water, where Hindus cremated their dead so that the ashes
might wash away. (Along the Ganges, he also saw lepers bathing in
one area and upper-caste Brahmins in another.) He was saddened by
the thousands of Bengali widows, rejected by their families and denied
food, who had come to a temple to die. He also observed the antics of
"so-called holy men": Some had kept their arms stretched out straight
or upright for more than five years until their joints were stiff; another,
standing on one foot, had kept his other leg drawn up and had not
lain or sat down in eleven years; and several had heads and shoulders
covered in dust or had hair longer than their bodies.[27]

Other men were standing, sitting, or reclining on blocks or beds
of spikes. Foss related an interaction between his companion and one
such precariously perched man:

> Dr. Goucher, to whom everything seems by a strange
> magnetism to come, wanted one of those spikes, and he said
> to the man as he was working away at one of them, "Let me
> have one of those spikes." The man said, "O, no! It would
> be sacrilege; and it could not be taken out, it has grown to be
> part of the wood." At last the doctor said, "It would not be a
> sacrilege for me to have it for I am a foreigner from another
> country, and I think it will come out easily for me; let me see";
> and [Dr. Goucher] reached down to the spike he had been
> working at and lifted it slightly, and it came right out before the
> man's eyes, to his great amazement.

Goucher then asked for a second spike to give to Foss. Although the man again objected, he gladly accepted a silver coin when Goucher pulled another spike from his platform.[28]

Goucher was heartened, however, by the various Methodist gatherings, camp meetings, and conferences he and Foss attended. They gave Goucher a chance to meet many missionaries he had been corresponding with and to see their work, and to visit some of the schools and scholars he and Mary had been supporting since the mid-1880s. He spent time at the boys' and girls' high schools in Moradabad where their scholarship students boarded, and noted that some older buildings in the Goucher compound now needed improvements. While on site, he ordered cost estimates and took steps to fix problems. At some stops he made, Goucher School primary students came to visit him. He quizzed them on their theological training and baptized the ones he found qualified, declining to baptize others he considered "not well enough instructed." Students and teachers would also come out to meet him at rail stations, where he would talk with them while his train was stopped. They usually carried banners and flowers and gave him salaams—making low bows as they gestured with hand to forehead.[29]

Bishop Foss recorded another, quieter welcome he saw Goucher receive at dawn one morning when their train stopped to change engines. Unable to sleep in the hot stuffy compartment, Goucher dressed and climbed down to take a little walk and get some fresh air. The lone person on the station platform, a young Indian man, came over and knelt before him, saying "I am your servant, and you are my savior." Goucher, puzzled and discomfited, told him to rise and asked what he meant. The man explained he was a Goucher School graduate: "All that I am and have I owe to you. Hearing that you are traveling through on this train, I walked more than twenty miles just to see your train pass. Now God has let me look into your face."[30]

Goucher had been supporting schools and scholarships for more than a dozen years, enough time for him to assess their long-term influence on individuals and on the spread of Christianity. At the Bareilly Theological School, more than half of the students studying to become ministers had graduated from Goucher Schools. At one local meeting, he discovered that forty-six of the preachers and teachers attending and six of the Bible women (who talked with women secluded at home) had been trained in Goucher Schools; at another gathering, sixty-seven had been Goucher scholars. Goucher noted that in one district, four schools started in 1885 were "the foundation of all that has been done" in the area. Thanks to the schools, about 2,000 Indians in the area had become Christians, and 100 preachers, teachers, and "exhorters" had received training. Goucher recorded in his travel diary that the primary and boarding schools had furnished "400 of the active and efficient workers of our church all over India." Even more important, "Through these schools, and the preachers and evangelists converted and trained in them, there have been 30,000+ converted to God." Overall he gave his educational experiment good grades: "I am much pleased with the success of our schools." But as a businessman who received annual reports and kept records on how his money was spent, he concluded, "The administration can be much improved."[31]

Nevertheless, Goucher still wanted to follow up on previous discussions with Parker about increasing the number of primary schools where lessons were taught in the native language. While still traveling, he pledged that he and Mary would support new schools in new locations for five years: ten among the Gujarati people in western India; ten in the Trans-Godavari district of the South India Conference; two in Nepal; and two in or at least near Tibet. Then, he said, "When Tibet is opened we will have workers ready to enter the land." He required that the schools be established only where there were no other missionary schools. Still committed to easing class and gender distinctions, he stipulated that students be drawn from the lowest castes, and that both boys and girls were to receive instruction, together or separately.[32]

Along with his own schools, Goucher visited many others in his travels—more than 150 during his stay in South Asia—including other Methodist primary schools, some of the village schools recently sponsored by "Chum" Holmes, and Isabella Thoburn's women's college in Lucknow, where he was her guest. He stopped at the Bareilly Theological School and its accompanying Woman's Theological School, the Agra Medical School, and India's five major universities (in Bombay, Madras, Punjab, Calcutta, and Allahabad), all modeled after the University of London. They struck him as good schools, but he cautioned that India's educational problems remained formidable. Most adults were so poor or poorly paid that their children had to work instead of attending school. Only about twelve percent of the school-age population received any education. But he saw "almost boundless opportunities for Christian conquest" if the Methodist Episcopal Church and its missions could further address the region's needs.[33]

✳✳✳

Wherever Goucher and Foss went in India, they were greeted with crowds of well-wishers who had been anticipating their arrival. In Hardoi, students, Christians, and workers lined the road to the mission compound. Bedecked with garlands, the visitors traveled by elephant, as monkeys chattered in the trees. When Goucher spoke at a mass meeting the next day, the audience shouted "Goucher Sahib Jai" and also offered thanks to Memsahib Mary Goucher. According to *The Indian Witness*, at the Hathras mela, a religious gathering of the Agra and Kasganj Districts, more than 1,000 singing natives lined up to greet the visitors as they walked from the train to the tent homes where they would be staying.[34]

Indian Christians and non-Christians often walked miles to attend a camp meeting at which Goucher and Foss were present. At one such gathering for the Kumaon District Conference, overlooking Naini Tal and the Himalayas, some of the 2,000 people in attendance had walked more than thirty miles. One teacher brought forty-six women and girls who had walked 100 miles on rough paths over nine days; each woman had carried twenty-five pounds of baggage on her head, and each girl ten pounds. At the same meeting, Goucher and Foss attended a picnic lunch in sight of the Pindar Glacier and several peaks of more than 20,000 feet; that evening, there were over 250 guests at dinner, but Goucher noted, "only 4 of us had chairs, table, fork and spoon."[35]

Indian Christians also looked forward to the bishop and the minister baptizing them, the culmination of their spiritual odyssey. At one area mela or religious festival, Goucher baptized half of the 225 people waiting for them. Another time, he was asked to baptize an Indian family who had been starving, had come to a missionary for help, and then converted. First Goucher cut off the man's topknot, signaling his break with Hinduism. When he asked the little girl's name, her father said, "Whatever you like, sahib." John recorded in his diary, "I baptized her 'Miryam,' i.e. Mary, for my wife."[36]

At times, Goucher was the one seeking out Indians in their schools or churches. When he inspected the mission properties and schools in Budaun, near Bareilly, he was told he was the first American, except the missionaries, to visit the town. While there, he walked a mile off a road to visit a village school, which he found decorated with large cotton shawls, rugs, and what he described as "a beautiful picture with some English letters on it which read 'Fine Wines from Corsica and Naples.'" Goucher and Foss also visited Pau, a village of outcast sweepers, several miles from Bareilly. They helped the residents lay the cornerstone for and mark the outline of a small church to be built on the edge of a mango grove. The pair placed bricks of dried mud and straw into a shallow trench where one corner would stand.[37]

For the service that followed, nearly four dozen people sat on the ground inside that outline, the men and boys separated from the women and girls by an ad hoc purdah, or screen, made up of three beds turned on their sides. Some children, Goucher wrote, "were clad only in their complexion or robed in a smile." These converts, encouraged by a missionary and an Indian pastor-teacher, had faced persecution from their Hindu neighbors but were ready for baptism. Goucher described the scene:

> The crowd, hushed by the unusual ceremony, looked on with wonder and reverence. The candidates answered the inquiries with apparent appreciation of the great responsibilities and privileges involved. The women, close veiled, trembled like aspen leaves as our touch shattered the last vestige of caste relationship which bound them to the old order of things, and with solemnity and gladness we administered the sacrament.... They were sudras [the lowest caste] no longer.

He wrote in his diary, "No service which I have performed in India has impressed me more than this."[38]

Later, at a talk he gave to the Church Extension Society, Goucher reflected on the impact this simple church—and what it stood for—made on him. He compared it to the Taj Mahal, which (having seen it) he called "the most wonderful of all human architectural achievements." But that tomb of the seventeenth-century Mughal emperor Shah Jahan and his favorite wife had required thousands of men and millions of rupees to build. It would never be equalled, but as with the remains within, "the corroding tooth of time" would eventually cause it to crumble and be forgotten. The building in the mango grove, he went on, might have a mud floor, no furniture or windows, and only an opening for a door, but "the luster of the humble church shall brighten as the eons pass" because it was "an inception of divine love and related to eternity." Goucher the church builder saw this small house of worship as a template, to be reproduced "in one form or another in all lands."[39]

On the road, Goucher wrote, a "large opportunity was given me," and he was barraged with "the usual, varied, and almost innumerable receptions and invitations to speak." He later reported that while in India, he preached at least ten times and gave more than 120 addresses of various kinds. On one occasion, he spoke at a service where Europeans, Americans, and Indians of twelve castes participated; he also gave a Thanksgiving Day speech at a camp meeting where his tent was located under a large banyan tree that was "full of parrots in the mornings and jackals howled about at night." At the universities, Goucher might address 400 to 500 young men, half to two-thirds of whom spoke English; he noted a great desire among upper-level students to learn English as a way to get ahead. By the end of his trip, he commented that a visitor to South or East Asia could "travel with greater ease and have better access to information" speaking English than any other single language.[40]

Of course, things could get lost in imperfect translation. Speaking in a remote area where his words were being translated into Hindustani, he said a boy "must not be like a stamp in having his back licked and stuck in a corner." Indians regarded licking stamps as an "unworthy custom," and Goucher's point was lost, despite his translator's several attempts to frame it.[41]

In Madras, the dedication of two special projects awaited the travelers' arrival in mid-December 1897. In the morning, Goucher turned on the steam and electricity to start the machinery at the long-awaited Methodist Publishing House. His dedicatory address focused on advances in printing technology over the centuries, and the importance of this new enterprise to education and providing jobs locally. That night, he and Bishop Foss laid the cornerstone for a new girls' orphanage, sponsored by the Women's Foreign Missionary Society and led by Grace Stephens, who also oversaw several girls' schools. The two men had been entertained by dozens of Stephens' students the day before, and Goucher described her work as encompassing "the almost naked sweepers and outcaste school to the [secluded] zenana school for girls, some of them dressed in silks and jewels." After the cornerstone was in place, the orphaned girls marched around the pair, singing a welcome song and chanting "Goucher, Goucher" and "Bishop, Bishop." They bedecked the men with tinsel and rose garlands and sprinkled them with rose water. Stephens had her own reason to celebrate. She recently had received word that there was no funding to continue the project. But Goucher gave her an early Christmas present of $1,000 ($29,400) to put up the first story, and the New York branch of the WFMS promised to raise the rest. As Stephens later told him, "This is such a help. Your donation turned the whole current of our work! Were it not for what you did and said, I would not have dared going further with the building."[42]

Following the cornerstone ceremony, there was a great tamasha or entertainment. Goucher recorded it attracted about 2,000 people, and was said to be "the most distinguished and representative gathering ever convened in Southern India in the interest of missions." Attendees included government officials, judges, missionaries of various denominations, school children, adult men, and nearly 300 women, who sat behind a purdah shielding them from public view. Goucher was impressed by the turnout and the spectacle and also the reason for it. He jotted down his impressions: "The pavilion cir. 120' x 90' beautiful. Flags and [electric] lights cir. ½ mile in three directions, towers, arches, etc., illuminated and all done and paid for by a Hindu gentleman to show his appreciation of the work our church is doing for the poor of India."[43]

✳✳✳

Goucher took seriously the Board of Managers' directive to familiarize himself, "by personal inquiry," with educational work in

India and financial matters in India and Malaysia during his travels. He talked with missionaries and teachers, presiding elders and pastors, and workers of the Women's Foreign Missionary Society; he met with conference finance committees and looked into treasurers' reports. Through these interactions, he wanted to "strengthen so far as I can the confidence of the workers in the field in this administration and methods of supervision of the Church and Missionary Society." His success is confirmed by a letter John Robinson, a missionary and editor of *The Indian Witness*, wrote Mary Goucher to assure her that her husband was "looking and feeling very well indeed." Robinson went on, "The missionaries greatly appreciate the counsel and information which Dr. Goucher so ably furnishes. It is really surprising to us how intelligently he has grasped the great outlines of the missionary enterprise in India, and how familiar also he is with the details of our work."[44]

Goucher had more in mind than his assigned research, however, and he wrote in his diary, "I have several things I wish to see accomplished." One was to implement better organized and more uniform educational standards in South Asia. To that end, he invited the principals and headmasters of all the Methodist colleges and high schools to join him in Lucknow during the Central Conference to discuss issues of mutual interest. Knowing the Missionary Board could no longer cover expenses for a burgeoning base of students and converts, he also urged India's far-flung conferences to become self-supporting by asking each church member or probationer to contribute something they could afford—cash, labor, or in-kind services—to assist their pastors, teachers, and Bible women.[45]

Goucher didn't just spend time with American missionaries or Indian nationals; he also enjoyed "exceptional opportunities" for educational and sociological discussions with British colleagues and administrators, and received "many courtesies from those interested in such subjects, and from officials of high rank." At the end of January 1898, Lord Bruce, 9th Earl of Elgin and viceroy and governor-general, invited Goucher to Government House in Calcutta. He found the viceroy "an affable man, much more so than most Englishmen usually," as well as "business-like and direct." They spoke about the Methodists' work, and Goucher related that Lord Bruce "detained me for a considerable time talking over educational problems in India." Goucher later told a reporter he was impressed with the colonial power's role in "securing the practical peace and protection" for India's 283 million people with an army of less than 80,000. He praised "the magnificent work" it was doing in "developing a nation out of the segregated and contending tribes it found in Southern Asia," where there seemed to be "nothing in common and nothing which is generally considered fundamental to civilized existence in such quantity and quality as to be built upon."[46]

Following the meeting with Lord Bruce, Goucher and Foss boarded a ship for Singapore to attend the Malay Mission Conference. En route, they stopped first in Rangoon, then capital of Burma (Myanmar), where Goucher inspected mission properties, spoke at several schools, and saw elephants hauling teak from a forest to a lumber mill. On the second leg of the voyage, they stopped in Penang. Goucher inspected several church properties and schools and was pleased to find them already self-supporting. Before the ship reached Singapore, however, a drive shaft broke, and it drifted for twenty hours while the crew attempted repairs. Finally arriving early one mid-February morning, the pair went directly to a church where Goucher spoke via translator to a group of people from Siam (Thailand) and Sumatra and some Dijaks from Borneo; that night, he preached to an English congregation. Ever the naturalist, Goucher also made time to visit the Lotus Botanical Gardens in Rangoon; the Penang Waterfall Garden, featuring orchids and unusual birds; and the Botanical Garden in Singapore, which boasted more than 650 varieties of palm tree.[47]

✳✳✳

Japan was the next major destination. Goucher and Foss sailed from Singapore with an overnight stop in Saigon, the capital of French Cochinchina; they traveled the next 900 miles to Hong Kong on a South China Sea steamer, giving Goucher time to reflect on the personal and spiritual impact of his journey to this point. On a small note card which he stuck in his diary, he wrote, "There have been no other three years in my life in which I have had so many distinct or intense innovational expression of positive gratitude to God for his dealings with me and the evident leadings of His Providence as during the last four months." From Hong Kong, the ship proceeded north to

Shanghai; there the travelers spent the night on solid ground, enjoying the amenities of the Astor House near the Bund waterfront district.[48]

Early in March 1898, the pair finally reached Kobi and secured the necessary Japanese visas. In Yokohama they were joined by Julius Soper, who accompanied them to Tokyo, where they found the kind of warm reception they had often received in India. Goucher and Foss were met at the train station by students and faculty of the recently renamed Aoyama Gakuin, who marched with them to the campus, which would be their headquarters. There, girls attending the WFMS school greeted them "in dress parade as they entered the grounds" and sang songs of welcome. Of the visitors' two-week stay, Soper said, "The Japanese vied with each other in doing honor to them, and in every way possible showed their heartfelt appreciation of the help received from Dr. Goucher in various ways, as well as the deep interest he has taken in Japan."[49]

The pair were feted at numerous parties. Professors, students, and alumni of the Aoyama Gakuin college, academy, and theological school gave a reception, where representatives of each group spoke and toasted the "distinguished guests." Goucher and Foss responded in kind. They were given a small banquet in the city's Botanical Garden, sponsored by several Japanese men John and Mary had helped financially when they were graduate students at Johns Hopkins. Another evening, the father-in-law of one of them hosted a Japanese dinner and traditional tea ceremony for them. Soper reported, "Dr. Goucher was more expert in the use of chop sticks than Bishop Foss, and he could sit 'a la Japanese' more easily" at age fifty-two, than his "elderly and fatherly" companion, all of sixty-four. This ease with Japanese seating was a help when a Japanese friend entertained Goucher at a restaurant where he was served over thirty-five dishes. The travelers also made several sightseeing excursions, and Soper noted that "very few ever saw more of Japan in so short a time."[50]

While in Tokyo, Goucher collected information about Aoyama Gakuin. He met with members of its Board of Managers and others, and inspected the twenty-five-acre campus and buildings, which had been damaged in the 1894 earthquake. He spoke to groups of boys and girls at the academy and college levels and addressed an Alumni Association reunion. He also took part in other church-related activities, both in Tokyo and Yokohama. He preached at Japanese and English services, helped baptize several young people, inspected mission properties, and spoke at the commencement of the Women's Biblical Training School. He talked with Methodist missionaries and with representatives of other denominations in Japan, inquiring about conditions and the prospects for future expansion. As his friend Soper wrote in an article, Goucher "knows how to get information, and knows how to use it, and when to use it after secured."[51]

Departing at the end of March 1898, Goucher retraced the route of his arrival, with the faculty and students from Aoyama Gakuin accompanying him to the train station to give him "a loving send off." He joined Foss in Yokohama, and they left on the *Empress of Japan* for Vancouver. According to Goucher, the ship carried only sixty-four first-class passengers (he and Foss among them), but nearly 100 Japanese and more than 500 Chinese travelers in steerage. Goucher recorded in his diary their latitude and longitude as they moved across the Pacific, and he went below decks to view the ship's engines; relishing statistics, he estimated they made 1.75 million rotations during the voyage. Since leaving home the previous October, the two men had spent sixty-six days on some body of water, but Goucher said he had suffered "not 10 minutes of sea sickness." Back in the United States, he told a reporter he returned in good health, noting he had passed no less then twenty-three bubonic plague inspections in India.[52]

Accustomed to travel by train and ship, Goucher proved comfortable with other modes of conveyance on the trip. Elephant rides became commonplace for him in India. To celebrate Bishop Foss's birthday, Goucher joined his travel companion and Bishops Thoburn and Joyce for a ride on an elephant named Bagwanti. (The event was memorialized in the photo shown at the beginning of this chapter.) Goucher reported that "the elephant became quite angry and the mahout (the driver) could scarcely control her." He also rode on camels to visit some remote villages and see the countryside. When his party traveled from the plains to the mountains of North India, they left the train to board a tonga, described by Goucher as "a 2-wheeled cart drawn by 2 horses on the run and changed every 3 or 4 miles." They went the remaining way up to Naini Tal, in the shadow of the Himalayas, on dandas, which Foss called "peculiar chairs swung between poles and carried on the shoulders of coolies . . . and replaced by relays every three or four minutes." Later in Penang, Goucher had his first ride in a "ginriksha" [sic] and a sampan. When stopping in various ports, he frequently traveled between ships and shore via lighters or flat-bottom barges.[53]

Despite his six months of travel, Goucher was an active correspondent, writing letters and replying to mail that eventually reached him. During a quiet time on one ship voyage, he noted writing eighty-three letters. His family and Baltimore were also never far from his mind. In Calcutta for Christmas 1897, Goucher sent a telegram that morning with holiday greetings for his wife and daughters; owing to the time difference, it arrived at 2313 on Christmas Eve. He was impressed that Mary had the telegram in hand an hour and a half after he had sent it, half a world away.[54]

Goucher also maintained his connections with the Woman's College while away. In one case, the contact was more as a parent than as president. (Janet Goucher had begun her first year at the school not long before her father sailed.) Tennis courts were built shortly after Bennett Hall, the athletic facility, had opened, and an annual tennis tournament between freshmen and sophomores began in 1893. With Janet's class in the contest, Goucher wanted to be able to follow the matches from the other side of the world. He had prepared coded messages before he left on the trip, and asked her to cable him to indicate which class won each round. He also had contact during his travels with Woman's College students—past and future. In Japan, he met two recent graduates who had become missionaries, perhaps from hearing Goucher speak of the country during their college years. On his return journey to Baltimore, he accompanied a missionary's daughter, who was on her way to attend the college where her older sister was currently a student.[55]

❋ ❋ ❋

When Goucher finally arrived home in mid-April 1898, having covered 33,000 miles, he wrote, "As a result of my travels I have concluded that the country in the most prosperous condition for healthy living is the United States; the most beautiful place Maryland; the best, Baltimore, and my home in the heart of the best. All that now remains is to look into the smiling faces of the college girls tomorrow morning." The students undoubtedly were happy to see him again, but they also looked forward to seeing what new exhibits he had brought back for the Goucher Hall museum. Their counterparts had been surprised a few years earlier when they returned from the Christmas holiday to find an exhibit of Korean court clothing and accessories (originally brought over for the World's Columbian Exposition, commonly known as the Chicago World's Fair), along with artifacts from Japan, donated in recognition of the Gouchers' contributions to education in that country. On his just-concluded trip, Goucher acquired other curios for public and private display, including: coral, shells, and sponges; old coins and manuscripts; a sacrificial knife; armor; two elephants' feet (one converted into a wastepaper basket for his study); a purdah; the tanned skins of several flying squirrels; the head of an ancient stone idol; and the spike he had pulled from the bed of nails in India. He especially prized the skin—nearly eighteen feet long from nose to tail—of a tiger shot in North India by the warden of the Royal Hunting Lodge and Reserve. The tiger had killed a number of people, and the warden declined payment because it "had fattened on your Christians" from a village with a Goucher School.[56]

At home, Goucher completed his detailed report to the Board of Managers of the Missionary Society, relating the status of properties, schools, debts, and self-sufficiency initiatives in South Asia. He characterized the trip as one of the "great privileges" of his life, and concluded that Methodist activities there fostered "remarkable vitality, almost boundless opportunity, and magnificent results." While some aspects of administration were open to criticism, he considered them "not evidences of weakness, but incident to rapid growth, changing conditions, and the magnitude of the problem." At each outpost, he said, one could find "a score or more of other things which command our approval and challenge our admiration." He praised the consecrated and self-sacrificing missionaries and the "eager, teachable, and growing" church memberships he had observed. Those he wrote about were pleased with his report. John Robinson wrote from India, "We consider it to be absolutely fair, impartial, and at the same time statesmanlike in its grasp of the situation."[57]

The Woman's College students were not the only ones glad to have Goucher home again. An article in *The Baltimore American* declared,

"There were hundreds in Baltimore almost as delighted to see him as his family." He was likely embarrassed by the paper's assertion that "his long absence, his extensive travels, his divers character of interesting experiences, have all tended to invest him with additional charm which is equaled only by his natural magnetism." Yet he soon was facing the same issues—and the personal stress—he had left behind the previous autumn.[58]

A history of the college states that in public, Goucher always spoke with optimism about the challenges facing the school, but in his November 1898 report to the Board of Trustees, he talked candidly about resuming the burden of facing its financial difficulties. Being away had given him time to think. To illustrate the severity of the situation, he made a rare comment about his own support of the college:

> The aggregate contributions which I have made in buildings, on current expense account, and other matters pertaining to the necessities of the Institution have averaged more than $25,000 a year ever since the College was started. I only speak this to say that I cannot risk the permanent impairment of my health by the continuance of such onerous duties as have devolved upon me in the past. . . . . Personally I have carried the burdens of the Woman's College of Baltimore from its inception to the present time with all cheerfulness and to the full extent of my mental and financial ability.

Now, owing to demands of "other educational and benevolent enterprises" with which he was identified, he could no longer contribute so much. Even so, he assured the trustees, "My sympathies and my interest have not abated in the least."[59]

Goucher admitted that he had not hesitated, up to that point, to extend the college's liabilities. When the enterprise had begun, he reminded them, they faced a stark choice:

> To expend simply the moneys in hand and start with a school with limited faculty, inadequate laboratories and meagre facilities for advance work, unworthy to be called a college, and thus add another to the long list of schools of large pretense and small possibilities, or to borrow money to equip a first-class institution.

The latter option had brought the school to the current "front rank of excellence," but Goucher now felt it would be "suicidal to its future and unjust to its creditors" to continue to run up deficits beyond those already incurred.[60]

Once again he appealed to the trustees to help raise funds to cover immediate expenses, and he reminded them of what was at stake: "He that educates a boy secures the education of a person; he that educates a girl secures the education of a family." Goucher offered to resign as president if the trustees could find a successor "to bring to the enterprise larger ability and greater efficiency than the present incumbent." But the Board of Trustees demurred, likely realizing the value of Goucher's name recognition; his wide reputation in educational, civic, and church circles; and his fundraising connections.[61]

The board determined to find a way to ease his worries. Previously, Goucher's friend and college board chair Lyttleton Morgan had assumed the unpaid role of financial agent, overseeing special fundraising efforts. Since his death in 1895, this position had been vacant. The Finance Committee of the board acknowledged Goucher was overtaxed: "So great are the demands of the work of the College now grown to such vast proportions that it may well be considered whether one man should longer attempt to conduct all the work which up to this time he has done without aid." They recommended hiring another financial agent to serve under the president's direction.[62]

As the 1890s ended, both Goucher and the board were encouraged by anticipated assistance from the Twentieth Century Thank Offering campaign, proposed by the Methodist bishops to begin on New Year's Day 1899, and to run for three years. Half the $20 million ($589 million) goal was to go to the Church's schools, colleges, and universities; other shares would fund such organizations as hospitals, orphanages, and old age homes, or help pay off individual churches' debts. Goucher was among the well-known bishops, clergy, and laymen appointed to the national commission organizing the campaign. He also worked with the Woman's College trustees to try to raise one million dollars (approximately $29 million) of the campaign's education goal to retire the college's debt and increase its endowment. They asked the Baltimore Conference to make this effort a special focus of its thank-offering appeals, and it agreed, appointing a committee to oversee fundraising. Goucher tried to ensure the men kept the college's needs in mind by frequently hosting them for dinner meetings at 2313.[63]

At the Fall 1900 meeting of the board, trustees passed a formal resolution of thanks to the college's president:

> During the eleven years of his incumbency of the office as indeed before, and in the inception and establishment of the enterprise, his labors have been characterized by the most assiduous industry, by patient and consistent care of its interests, by generous contributions and by untiring energy in the direction of all its multiplied affairs. This has been done without other compensation than the consciousness of service in the noble cause of Christian benevolence and education and the knowledge of the help given to many who through the college have been equipped nobly for the labors and conflicts of life. The fruits of his service will form one of the brightest pages in the history of American colleges.[64]

Goucher's work at the Woman's College, however, was far from over.

John Goucher in his study,
2313 St. Paul Street, Baltimore, Maryland (1901)

Courtesy of the Goucher College Library,
Special Collections and Archives, Baltimore, Maryland

A NEW CENTURY

Chapter 15
(1901-Fall 1906)

─────────◆◀─────────

*Life is a very serious business. . . . The most precious of all
possessions is power over self, power to withstand trial, endure
suffering — calm reliance upon God and truth in scenes of darkness.*[1]

To students at the Woman's College of Baltimore, their president
always appeared cheerful and confident. Professor Lilian Welsh
praised Goucher's "invariable optimism, courtesy, consideration,
and friendliness," and she once said that while she had seen him
"many times under trying circumstances," never was "his serenity
disturbed." Living each day through faith and prayer, Goucher had
his own philosophy, which he chose as his motto for a calendar the
college produced to mark the beginning of the twentieth century: "No
tomorrow can mar today." As its first decade unfolded, Goucher would
need that wisdom more than ever, for soon he would be tested in both
his personal and professional lives.[2]

As president, he remained the public face of the institution and a
steadfast champion of women's education. But while Goucher had the
satisfaction of overseeing the college's growing academic reputation,
its burden of debt — which at one time ran as high as $800,000 ($23.6
million) — weighed on him mentally and physically. The board's
Finance Committee commended the president's "heroic energy" in
halving that figure by 1900, and the trustees expected his "valuable
services" in securing more funds would soon set the college on a solid
financial footing. Goucher and other trustees sought to call attention to
the college's financial needs, but response to appeals was weak beyond
the usual donor circle. It fell to these leaders to continue shouldering
the burden, through personal gifts and loans, offers of collateral for
bank loans, and also in Goucher's case, waiving his salary and college

travel expenses. As an Indian missionary friend (and the parent of two Woman's College students) wrote in sympathy, fundraising "must make your burden well-nigh intolerable."[3]

The Board of Trustees feared Goucher would again collapse from the strain, and as before approved his "going off to rest . . . until he felt able to resume his work." Mary had recurring health problems as well. At the end of January 1901, the couple took another cross-country trip, this time to southern California, hoping the warmth and sunshine might bring some relief. While officially this was a rest trip, Goucher seized opportunities to promote educational and church work. An article in the *California Christian Advocate* said he "entertainingly" addressed the students at the State Normal School and the University of Southern California near the end of February, and that a large gathering of ministers received him with "intense delight" when he spoke for more than an hour on his experiences with missions. Goucher was then optimistic about his recovery, writing from Los Angeles to a Baltimore friend, "I am slowly improving and hope to be home and at work again before the last of the month."[4]

But he was overly optimistic. Goucher returned home but missed the Baltimore Conference's annual spring meeting for the first time since joining in 1869. Recognizing his absence, members sent a resolution of appreciation and "sympathy in his affliction," and word of his illness spread among other Methodist leaders. One bishop wrote him in April 1901, "I hear you have been sick—so I reach out my hand and with my heart in it. Sickness has its lessons as well as health, only let us learn them quickly." In May, the college trustees reiterated their concern: "In the apparent view of the President's health, we advise him to take a vacation for such a time as may be necessary for his complete recovery."[5]

As summer arrived, John and Mary took their daughters to Wales and England, joined by John Grier Holmes, Goucher's old school "chum," and his family. Janet Goucher had just graduated from the Woman's College where her sister Elizabeth would start in the fall. Elizabeth recalled that her mother was still "in delicate health," but on the brighter side, "She and Father had a kind of Indian Summer honeymoon as a foil to their daughters' activity, through all those weeks from June to September." The travelers finally stopped in

London, where Goucher was among 600 Methodist delegates from around the world at the third decennial Ecumenical Conference. He was also to give a speech on the status of American Methodism.[6]

While in London, Elizabeth said the two families "chose different financial levels." The Holmeses stayed at the posh Claridge's Hotel in Mayfair, while the Gouchers (who could easily afford a luxury hotel) rented an apartment overlooking the Horse Guards. The two Holmes boys, she said, preferred these more modest accommodations and "came often to make riotous 'high tea' at the big round table in the sitting room." The families also had different sightseeing strategies. Elizabeth testified that "Uncle John was quite dependent on a 'curier' to make reservations and lead the way, regardless of expense." But her father proved to be "a super guide on his own," and he encouraged his daughters to be equally independent. Rather than hire a London tour guide, Goucher gave his daughters maps of bus routes, so they could explore the city on their own while he attended meetings.[7]

✳ ✳ ✳

On returning to Baltimore in the fall of 1901, the Gouchers went to Alto Dale, and Mary remained in the country rather than making the customary seasonal move back to town. John again took up his duties as president of the Woman's College, but he also had to tend to business at Morgan College. Before John had left for England, Francis J. Wagner, Morgan's president since 1888, had retired due to ill health; as president of the Board of Trustees, Goucher had to find the school a new leader at a particularly challenging time. The college was facing increasing debt and a growing student population. It had only one academic building, which was crowded and mortgaged, and no facilities for other collegiate activities, such as athletics. Nor were there funds to increase either the number of faculty members or their salaries. Goucher needed someone experienced in education, who had vision and a willingness to assume the risks attached to leading an African-American college in a city and state that still harbored southern sympathies.

Through his Japanese connections, Goucher thought he knew just the man: John O. Spencer, whose teacher's salary he had paid at Tokyo's

Anglo-Japanese College in the 1880s. Spencer also had been dean after it was renamed Aoyama Gakuin, and on returning to the United States in 1899, he had become principal of a school in New York. Knowing his credentials and drive, Goucher convinced him to take the job. A Morgan College history calls recruiting Spencer "another one of [Goucher's] acts of wisdom" on behalf of the institution.[8]

Not everyone saw Goucher as a champion of African Americans, however. He considered the reunification of the Methodist Episcopal Church and the Methodist Episcopal Church, South—the branches that had split over slavery more than a half century before—to be one of his life's "commissions." But he knew how hard it would be to overcome decades of racial, social, and religious divisions. There had been earlier attempts to establish more congenial relations, but only in 1894 was some progress made. As a fraternal delegate that year to the southern General Conference, Goucher made what he called a personal suggestion, that a Pan-American Methodist Conference, with representatives from both groups, schedule regular meetings with the goal of clearing up misunderstandings and attempting to secure "a comity of relations." The southern brethren agreed, proposed a tentative plan for federation, appointed members to a joint committee to discuss further action, and requested that the 1896 northern General Conference do likewise. Goucher was among the northern branch's nine representatives on this Joint Commission on Federation.[9]

A history of American Methodism records the charge of this eighteen-member group, which first met in Washington early in 1898 and later held some meetings at Alto Dale:

> [It was] to work, not for organic union, but for a type of federation in which both churches, while retaining their own identities, would coexist side by side. Whenever possible, actual overlapping would be eliminated, and a united thrust would be made whenever or in whatever way this was deemed practical. . . . What the plan envisioned was indeed a long stride beyond fraternal relations that then existed between the two churches.

How—or even whether—to incorporate African-American conferences and church members into any new arrangement was a subject of debate on both sides for many years.[10]

In his London speech in September 1901, Goucher spoke of the benefits of this new federation movement but also raised the possibility of a union of "various colored Methodists" to form their own church of 1.7 million members. For black parishioners, Goucher said in his talk, the union would "multiply their opportunities and responsibilities which make for manliness [and] command a large increase of influence and respect." Such an institution, he among others quietly held, might also help overcome southern Methodists' objections to renewed ties with their northern brethren. At the meeting of the General Missionary Committee in Pittsburgh two months later, Goucher again stated that it might be better for all if the African-American Methodist conferences united with other black Methodist churches (the African Methodist Episcopal Church, the Colored Methodist Episcopal Church, and the African Methodist Episcopal Zion Church). According to a news report, Goucher said that "while he was a friend of the colored man, he could not help but know that it is at this time impossible to successfully conduct mixed schools, colleges, churches, especially in the South. . . . It is not the fault of the black man; it is his misfortune."[11]

Goucher's longtime involvement with and support for the Centenary Biblical Institute and Morgan College did not insulate him from criticism in his home city. One black minister likened the proposed separation of black and white Methodists to a pending Jim Crow law in Maryland, intended to racially segregate train and steamship travel. In a sermon, the preacher said that the state was attempting to impose "the same conditions which Rev. John F. Goucher hopes to bring about in the Methodist Episcopal Church [which], so far as it is represented by such men, has become the oppressor of the humble and the poor." But in addition to the other reasons stated, Goucher endorsed a united black Methodist Church because he believed it would strengthen African-American church leadership and grow its membership, free from white paternalistic oversight. He had once urged the audience at a black Washington Annual Conference meeting to take advantage of whatever educational and religious opportunities presented themselves, so they would "not have to demand recognition but command it." Despite the black minister's accusation, Goucher was among those in the Baltimore Conference who condemned the Jim Crow bill. He continued to be sought out by African Americans and to speak at black churches and meetings. One group of black youth commemorated his work on their behalf by establishing a John F. Goucher chapter of the Epworth League at their church.[12]

✳ ✳ ✳

Meanwhile, financial difficulties still loomed at the Woman's College. When its board met in November 1901, the Finance Committee recommended that the trustees act on Goucher's suggestion to pay off the debt, believing it "would be the greatest relief that could come to him and would do more than anything else could to lighten his responsibilities and cares." The anticipated one million dollars from the Twentieth Century Thank Offering was not coming in as planned, despite appeals from Goucher and others to the Baltimore Conference and its congregations. One trustee pleaded: "We owe it to one another, as well as to the College, which is the child of this Conference, so necessary to the Church," to offer adequate support. Yet only approximately $300,000 ($8.6 million) was raised, an amount that was distributed in small sums over the course of the campaign and did little to alleviate the financial problem. Ongoing expenditures aside, the college was spending $300 annually per student while charging $125 in tuition. Scholarships, fellowships, and tuition rebates for daughters of ministers and missionaries and for those going into teaching or missionary work added to the strain. The debt continued to grow.[13]

Again, the trustees sought to relieve the pressures on Goucher, which included Mary's deteriorating health, by granting him "the privilege to be present or absent . . . as may suit his convenience" over the following months. He did not cut back, however, on his extracurricular activities as churchman or Baltimore civic leader. As guest speaker one Sunday at First Church, he sermonized, "There is no provision in the economy of God for an aimless man—no man can drift into excellence." He believed in the power of prayer to provide strength and assistance to those in distress, but also that individuals must lend a hand to those in need. He gave the example of a young boy who heard his father and another man discussing the difficulty of a neighbor in feeding her family; the father prayed for help and comfort for the poor woman. The boy, knowing their own larder was full, asked his father, "Don't you think you could help Mrs. Smith without bothering God."[14]

That was Goucher's own way. He had long been involved with charitable work, but more and more the city's leaders asked him to join organizations and committees addressing local and as well as national needs. He was appointed a member of Baltimore's Permanent Relief Committee, which included the presidents of the Johns Hopkins University, the city's Board of Trade, the Chamber of Commerce, the Merchants and Manufacturers' Association, and the Association for the Improvement of the Condition of the Poor. The committee worked to provide help in the wake of natural or man-made disasters, such as the deadly Fall 1900 Galveston hurricane, which killed 8,000 to 12,000 people along the Texas coast; and the fire in Jacksonville, Florida, in the spring of 1901, which burned nearly 150 city blocks, destroyed more than 2,300 buildings, and left 10,000 survivors homeless. Locally, late in 1902, the committee looked into alternative sources of heating and cooking fuels in the face of a looming coal shortage that would particularly affect the city's poor. The committee recommended that charitable groups such as the Charity Organization Society of Baltimore (of which Goucher was also a member) purchase large quantities of fuel to sell at cost to the needy.[15]

During this nominal time of rest, Goucher also attended several meetings related to missions. As a Methodist publication once noted, "His long study of the general subject of missionary movements, and his modest liberality, peculiarly fit him in head and heart to take up any subject in the whole range of effort." In February 1902, he traveled to the Toronto Conference of Foreign Mission Boards in the United States and Canada, chairing a session on education in missions, especially in China. His knowledge of that country and others in East Asia had been praised earlier in a letter from David H. Moore, bishop of the region: "It never came to me before *en bloc* how large a portion of my 'diocese' you had actually (potentially) opened. I desire greatly to have your statement as a matter of history—your personal relations to West China, Korea, and Japan, and to the others, if so related."[16]

A month later, Goucher hosted the Methodist Joint Commission on Federation at the Woman's College. One continuing topic of discussion which was close to his heart was reducing waste in manpower, time, and money, in home and foreign missions. That summer, as a member of a sub-committee, Goucher helped draft an agreement for a mission venture between the northern and southern branches that had been in the talking stage for six years—the merging of two established publishing houses into one Methodist Publishing House of China, to be located in Shanghai. Bishop Moore had urged him to undertake this project: "Everywhere in China and Japan I find traces of your presence and great business sense and ability, and . . . I beseech you, who more than almost any other man on the Board [of Foreign Missions] understands the field, to lend this your best counsel and your strongest support." Goucher was elected as one of six directors of a Joint Board of Control to oversee the publishing house's operations.[17]

Goucher didn't stop fundraising for missions either. While in Toronto, he spoke at a convention of the Student Volunteer Movement for Foreign Missions (SVM). Organized in 1886 as an outgrowth of and partner to the college and university YMCA programs in the United States and Canada, it encouraged students to study about missions and pledge themselves to enter the field. Thousands were attracted to service, inspired by the slogan, "Evangelization of the World in This Generation." Goucher recognized the movement's potential: "The triumph of Christianity in this dawning century will be intellectual and spiritual. These have been joined together in divine wedlock; let no man put them asunder." But while he believed in the SVM's goal, he was aware of financial obstacles to achieving it.[18]

Painting by numbers, Goucher told the convention that only forty percent of the United States's eighteen million evangelical Protestants had donated anything to missions the previous year, about eighty cents per donor on average. He stressed the need for proportionate giving among both the rich and the poor to support the SVM recruits, and called for still more support: "Consecrated money is needed for the transportation and subsistence of the thousands of eager and qualified young men and women who have consecrated themselves to the rescue of the perishing millions, if their brethren remaining at home will only hold the lines." Citing additional figures in a later speech about the SVM's financial needs, he pointed out that the people of the United States spent—or rather "wasted"—twenty-two million dollars a year ($624 million) on chewing gum. Such a sum directed to missions would "almost save the world."[19]

Similarly, he had been appointed a member of the Open Door Emergency Commission, charged by the Methodist Board of Bishops to "awaken" congregations to the urgency of missionary work worldwide and the need for additional collections. In this role, he spent several months helping to organize a 2,500-delegate convention in Cleveland in October 1902. At the convention itself, after days of speeches showing the "open doors" awaiting missionary support, Goucher oversaw the final financial session. He told the audience they needed to raise $250,000 ($7.1 million) that evening from individuals, districts, and congregations; he pressed delegates, "Look at the cards which have been placed in your hands, take your pencils, raise your hearts to God, and so write that you may have His approval upon your sacrifice, upon this expression of your devotion, upon your cooperation with Him in the great work of the world's redemption." By the end of the program, more than $300,000 ($8.5 million) had been subscribed, a sum the Missionary Society's president called "the largest spontaneous pledges and gifts ever made at one time in the history of efforts to spread the Gospel throughout the world."[20]

✳✳✳

With so much to do in 1902 while he was supposed to be resting, Goucher continued to have health flare-ups. Suffering from a severe bout of inflammatory rheumatism, he missed the annual meeting of the General Missionary Committee in New York that November. The organization's leaders sent him a letter expressing appreciation for his dedication to missions, for his time and money, and for serving as an example of "fidelity to an accepted trust, in confirming the faithful and stirring up the neglectful." Bishop Foss wrote to express his disappointment at Goucher's absence, but urged his friend "to be quiet at home, working your brain with moderation and your offending ankle not at all, until you have fairly recovered from this trouble." Foss recognized Mary's illness as well, assuring her husband of "her constant interest in my prayers for her convalescence and, if God please, her complete recovery."[21]

When the Woman's College trustees met later in November, Goucher again pressed the debt issue and reminded members the college urgently needed to raise $500,000 ($14.2 million) to "secure the institution as it is against any possible disaster in the future."

Acknowledging that he had carried out his presidential duties "under painful limitations" in the preceding months, he told the assembly:

> You generously passed a resolution a year ago offering me
> leave of absence for such times as might be necessary to
> conserve [Mary's] health. This was greatly appreciated but
> I have not been absent from my work a day on account of
> her health, and either in my office or with my stenographer
> in my home, I have been able to meet the most urgent needs
> of the college work except in one particular. I have not been
> able to canvass for money, or leave home for many services
> which, if my strength had permitted and the limitations had not
> prevented, might have been of great value.

In response, the trustees expressed appreciation for Goucher's services to the Woman's College and the Methodist Episcopal Church and offered "profound regret at his illness and that of his devoted wife." The board again gave him "entire freedom from services and duties so far as he can secure it."[22]

Goucher did not have long to make any changes in schedule. An article in *Zion's Herald* noted that for several years Mary had been "gradually declining from malnutrition," indicative of several potential underlying but unspecified medical problems. For a year, she had been mostly housebound at Alto Dale. Even so, her death early on December 19, 1902, was unexpected. Dean Van Meter stunned the college chapel audience with the announcement, just as students were preparing to leave for the Christmas holidays. In a sympathy letter to Goucher, Professor Joseph Shefloe captured what Mary meant to the college community and gave a moving tribute to some of the qualities that endeared her to many:

> Mrs. Goucher's well ordered store of knowledge, her taste,
> experience, and judgment, gave assurance alike to students
> and faculty who were eager to seek her advice in well-founded
> confidence of ready and willing response. . . . [She] preserved
> throughout her whole life a girlish lightness of heart and
> openness of affection which made her presence a constant joy
> to her friends. In her home and at social gatherings, she was
> a delightful companion. She possessed that comparatively
> rare faculty, an adjustable mind. . . . Her genial, amiable,
> sympathetic, pure character drew us all to her.

The funeral was held at Alto Dale, two days before John and Mary would have celebrated their twenty-fifth wedding anniversary. Two hundred friends, associates, and Methodist clergy from the mid-Atlantic states attended, and although the family requested no flowers be sent, the winter gloom was broken with tributes of red, pink, and white roses, lilies of the valley, ivy and violets—all Mary's favorites.[23]

Mary Cecilia Fisher Goucher was buried at Druid Ridge Cemetery, with only her family and a few close friends present. (The pall bearers had been drawn from the college's longtime faculty.) The cemetery was on the site of the former Turner farm where her husband had boarded during his first ministry, and where the two had met at her nineteenth birthday tea party. A newspaper article reported that when the couple had visited the newly established cemetery two years before—and perhaps anticipating this parting soon to arrive—Mary said to John, "Here I first met you. When I am called home, I want you to leave me just where you found me." A story about their marriage noted that her "love was his pole star"; with her death, the two hearts that many said "beat as one" were finally separated. As Bishop Earl Cranston later recalled, "For the husband it was—beyond the agony of their parting—God's call to double responsibility in caring for all they had planned and planted together." Despite his grief, Goucher immersed himself again in work and travel.[24]

✳✳✳

His most pressing concern remained eliminating the college's debt. Goucher was known by Methodist leaders for his fundraising acumen, and a few months after Mary's death, Bishop Frank Warne wrote from Singapore to solicit John's endorsement for a church-wide effort to raise funds for missions in celebration of the bicentennial of John Wesley's birth: "The success or failure of this suggestion, I know, will largely be settled by your attitude. If you can approve and push, the call will be made, and if it is, I believe the church will respond." Despite Goucher's talent for fundraising in wider arenas, he was unable to persuade the Baltimore Conference and its congregations to make the Woman's College a philanthropic priority. Neither the city nor the state gave support, although over the years the college had offered Maryland students thousands of dollars in tuition support. While the college's young alumnae were loyal to their alma mater, they usually had limited financial resources. As Goucher noted, some still lived at home with parents, others were starting their own households, and those who were employed were likely paid less than men for similar work. Despite his best efforts, he told the trustees with seeming frustration at the end of 1903, "No systematic, persistent or organized effort has been made to provide for the indebtedness." He appealed to them to take the lead, but on February 7, 1904, the prospects for additional funds literally went up in smoke.[25]

That day, a fire of unknown origin that started in downtown Baltimore spread to engulf seventy city blocks, destroying more than 1,500 buildings and 2,500 businesses in thirty hours. The total damage was estimated at more than $150 million ($4.1 billion). While the Woman's College was outside the disaster zone, its actual and potential benefactors faced large financial losses and an uncertain future at a particularly critical time for the college. All the lay trustees on the board, Goucher said, were affected by the fire. Not only were they unable to make new gifts, they could not even make their customary annual contributions to help cover expenses and relieve debt.

Yet Goucher remained optimistic, at least publicly. He told a reporter, "There is not the slightest doubt that the institution will obtain the funds it needs to put it on a basis where deficits will be a thing of the past." He was heartened by a resolution from the University Senate of the Methodist Episcopal Church within days of the fire, offering prayers and sympathy to the people of Baltimore and to their colleague John Goucher. The signatories pledged that "we will each of us render him and the Woman's College all the assistance in our power in preventing calamity to the institution." At the same time, Goucher also attended a meeting of the College Presidents' Association, where he laid out the financial difficulties. He had never solicited funds from Methodists outside the Baltimore–Washington area before, knowing that every institution represented at the meeting depended on local support. But out of respect for the college's reputation, or its president's, those in attendance agreed to extend broad support. The group unanimously recommended that the General Conference and the Methodist Board of Education endorse helping raise the half-million dollars needed to keep the college viable. By the end of February 1904, Goucher received more encouraging news: the trustees of the estate of H. A.

Massey, father of his Toronto friend Chester Massey, pledged $50,000 ($1.37 million) to relieve the debt, provided the remaining $450,000 could be raised elsewhere.[26]

The fire disaster finally spurred an organized effort to erase the debt. The goal was to secure the full amount in gifts and pledges by June 7, 1906. Goucher set to work, using fundraising techniques any modern college president would recognize. He used his powers of reason and persuasion to encourage gifts from ongoing supporters, both lay and religious. He gathered names for potential new donors from friends around the country and made solicitation calls on his travels. Once he invited a few friends over for dinner to discuss the college's financial situation; by the end of the meal, an additional $90,000 ($2.5 million) had been pledged. Another time, Goucher entertained several Methodist bishops at 2313, and although he made no direct solicitation, $45,000 ($1.25 million) was pledged that evening. He made another appeal at the annual meeting of the Baltimore Conference, which agreed to raise $50,000 ($1.4 million). Owing to his ongoing contacts with other denominations, several religious leaders in the city, both Christian and Jewish, joined in his efforts. Goucher also reached out to academic leaders including Harvard president Charles W. Eliot, who once called the college "the best equipped college for women," and Woodrow Wilson, then president of Princeton University, whose daughters were attending the Woman's College.[27]

Goucher also solicited help in New York from the General Education Board, created in 1902 by John D. Rockefeller to promote education in the United States, regardless of race, gender, or creed. In October 1905, Goucher applied for a $100,000 grant ($2.8 million), noting the need for funds from outside the Baltimore region. The Woman's College, he said, was the only institution south or west of Philadelphia that maintained "the high standards and efficiency of the great eastern colleges for women." It would be "disastrous to the wider educational interests in an important and considerable area of our country where it has an exceptional influence" should the school fail. He pointed out the impact the college had had on education for girls and young women nationally, noting, "The far reaching and constructive educational work of the WCB outside its halls has been greater possibly than even that done within." Since its opening, students had come from more than 500 secondary schools around the country. More than half of those schools had raised their standards and strengthened their programs so their graduates could qualify for admission. As Goucher told representatives of the General Education Board, all these schools' students benefited, whether they attended the Woman's College or not.[28]

At the November 1905 trustees' meeting, Goucher reported that $245,000 ($6.8 million) had been pledged, contingent on the full half-million being raised, with less than seven months to go before the deadline. He continued to press his case on many fronts. He had already gone to New York to approach philanthropist Andrew Carnegie, who early in 1906 promised $50,000 ($1.36 million), provided the remaining funds were secured. Goucher wrote Carnegie to thank him for his pledge: "Coming as it does at the time of our great crisis, it will so hearten the friends of the college as to make success assured." Goucher also approached supporters of more modest means. As the Woman's College prepared to graduate its fifteenth class, he told the alumnae, "To let [the college's] usefulness be crippled or its development arrested would be an unspeakable disaster." He asked them to give whatever they could afford and to encourage their classmates to follow their lead. All in all these women contributed nearly $10,000 (more than $270,000).[29]

By May 1906, the final month of the campaign, Goucher and associates had raised $415,000 ($11.3 million) toward the goal. While ninety-eight percent of the college's initial support had come from Baltimore, this time the majority of donors came from elsewhere. Some contributions came from Methodist bishops themselves or their appeals to others. Sixteen of them signed a note of encouragement at this final stage:

> We have watched with great concern your brave and persistent efforts to secure the funds needed for that purpose and have rejoiced in your success as from time to time reported to us individually. . . . After giving twenty-three years of your own service without salary, and of your means without stint, to found and carry forward this noble enterprise to the enviable place it now holds among the great schools of the world, we are not surprised that the hearts of the people have been opened to receive your plea for the rescue of the Woman's College's from its present peril. . . . We do not wonder that you come to

us with the question "What more can I do?" With a leader less courageous, less industrious, less trusted by the church, we should almost despair of success. But we dare not contemplate the consequences of failure. [30]

The Baltimore business community, in general, had not been as responsive, perhaps waiting to see if Goucher and the trustees would raise the necessary funds on their own. Now that the deadline drew near, they must have come to realize the impact losing the Woman's College would have on the local economy and civic pride. In mid-May, business leaders finally heard Goucher's appeal firsthand when he addressed members of the Merchants and Manufacturers Association. *The Baltimore Sun* reported, "His remarks made a deep impression on the business men who heard him," and they agreed to inform other local trade groups of the college's needs. With the June 7 deadline just ten days away, Mayor E. Clay Timanus called a public meeting of about 100 men, representing "every interest and element possible," to hear Goucher make his case yet again. His comments drew much applause, but when the subscription cards were passed out, the results were disappointing. A committee of ten prominent businessmen made one last push, personally appealing to their acquaintances for last minute subscriptions.[31]

Goucher did not let up in those final days. Following his meeting with the Merchants and Manufacturers, he was reported to be leaving the city again, "to enlist outside aid, as, having gone so far with the work, he did not wish to fail almost on the eve of accomplishment." On June 1, he received a discouraging letter from the General Education Board, turning down his request for a grant, but he delayed writing back for two weeks, claiming to have been "so occupied with rounding up the $500,000 indebtedness of the Woman's College as to not have a minute's leisure for any purpose other than looking after those things which imperatively demanded attention."[32]

✳ ✳ ✳

At commencement exercises on June 5, Goucher announced that on the eve of the deadline, $580,000 ($15.7 million) had been subscribed. The college was now free of debt, $70,000 had been added to the endowment, and $10,000 was pledged for a special purpose. *The Baltimore Sun* reported, "The words were greeted with long applause by everybody present on the stage and in the audience, and caused visible emotion in members of the college." Goucher said that contributions, coming from around the country, ranged from fifty cents to $50,000. While he singled out a number of major donors, he was mindful that "some of the sums which seem smallest represent the largest sacrifice and express keenest personal sympathy." (In many cases, his extensive connections had been the deciding factor. As another *Sun* article noted, "In almost every case those appealed to by President Goucher and who responded so liberally were personal friends.") Frustrated as he often was with their tepid support for the college, he thanked local citizens for coming forward in the end. In his remarks, he compared the city to a southern gentleman: "It is like Baltimore to have acted so graciously. Baltimore has sustained its reputation for chivalry—it has treated the college like a lady as a woman's college should be treated. Girls can't go out and hustle."[33]

Goucher further reflected on the college's early days. When the Woman's College had first been proposed more than twenty years earlier, reactions ranged from indifference to those "not unlike that accorded to a girl baby in caste-curst India." Now its prospects looked bright:

> The experimental stage of the Woman's College is past; her probation has been accomplished; she has been justified by her graduates, commended by specialists, approved by patronage and endorsed by that subtle and most genuine of commendations—imitation. . . . There is very much yet to be done, not by changing the ideals for which she has wrought, but by enlargement and healthful development of that which has been commenced with so much promise. The maiden has attained her majority, eager to serve, with a high and clearly defined commission, an attractive personality, rare prestige, and demonstrated efficiency.[34]

Describing the college as a "maiden," he drew an implicit comparison between the school and its alumnae, as well as the expectations for those receiving diplomas that day.

A *Baltimore Sun* editorial, appropriately written on Goucher's birthday, praised the fundraising campaign's success: "The splendid work of this magnificent college, its value to the state, to the city, and in fact the country—for all can enjoy its advantages—are well recognized, and that is the reason why all rejoice in its prosperity." On reading it, Bishop Henry Spellmeyer of Ohio wrote Goucher to exclaim: "What a grand achievement! And the church knows you are the only man among us who could have done this splendid work!" A Methodist publication called the kind of personal attention to Goucher that he sought to deflect: "To this college he has given the unselfish devotion of twenty of the best years of his life, taking no salary, giving of his time and private means without stint. Today, amid the congratulations of the entire Church as well as of Baltimore, he has at least his partial reward."[35]

The campaign concluded, Goucher wrote his longtime friend Rev. Frank Porter: "It is a matter of profound gratitude that divine guidance and human cooperation have secured to the Church the permanent establishment of this great Institution. It faces almost boundless prospects and we are praying that it may have grace to occupy them for the Master." Such cooperation began at home; he had quietly contributed enough money—for his own subscription and to cover pledges made by others—to help ensure the goal was reached.[36]

As the 1906–1907 academic year began, Goucher told a reporter, "The financial condition of the Woman's College is excellent." Enrollment was strong, with students coming from all over the United States, as well as Japan, China, India, England, Mexico, Canada, and Puerto Rico. Goucher also claimed that sixty-four percent of entering students graduated, about twice the rate of the country's leading men's colleges. Campaign funds would be used to retire the debt, but he acknowledged that "like almost all educational institutions, we are still in need of funds to branch out"; any new funds coming in would be "devoted to innovations."[37]

Despite his earlier health sabbaticals, the long fundraising campaign had strained Goucher's never robust health. In May 1906, about a month before the deadline, he asked the trustees for another leave of absence. They approved a year's sabbatical, but he said his duties prevented him getting away before fall. He had been invited to attend the fiftieth anniversary of Methodist missions in India, as well as the Centenary Conference in Shanghai, celebrating 100 years of Protestant missions in China. As long as he was going—it had been nine years since his first around-the-world trip—he also planned to visit schools and missions on Java and in Japan, Korea, and elsewhere in China. He told a reporter this jaunt would be taken "as a complete rest from the duties of my position" at the Woman's College. With its finances more secure, he could leave the college's administration and academic program in the hands of his capable dean and partner, John Van Meter.[38]

Goucher had been recommended as a candidate for bishop again in 1900, and mentioned as a likely nominee in 1904 as well. A *Zion's Herald* article that year noted, however, "In his great modesty [Goucher] would deplore his name being suggested for any office in the gilt of the church," and a Baltimore newspaper said he "had to work to keep from being made a bishop against his will." Nevertheless, in the Methodist publication, his nominator touted Goucher's qualifications:

> His name is a household word throughout the missionary world, his time, thought, money and effort being freely given to this cause. He has a genius for organization, and his great executive ability, his magnetic personality, his marvelous tact, along with his genial, tender, brotherly spirit, would make him an admirable general superintendent.[39]

But such a broad array of skills made him even more valuable to the Methodist Episcopal Church as an independent agent, as his next nine-month international journey would demonstrate.

John Goucher (far right) and his daughters with
Bishop and Mrs. Cyrus Foss in Egypt, November 1906

Courtesy of the Baltimore-Washington Conference Archives,
Lovely Lane United Methodist Church, Baltimore, Maryland

AROUND THE
WORLD AGAIN

Chapter 16
(Fall 1906-Summer 1907)

━━━━━━━━━━━━━━━━━━━━◆◆━━━━━━━━━━━━━━━━━━━━

Whatever may be the difference in appearance, in dress, in manners, in color, in essentials, we are much alike. Allowing for individual idiosyncrasies, we are very similar. The circulatory system is the same in all of us, so there is a similarity of soul. Life is the normal adjustment of the soul to God.[1]

One Friday at the end of October 1906, Goucher left Alto Dale before 8:00 A.M. to drive to the Woman's College of Baltimore to sign letters he had dictated the day before, tend to some official financial matters, lead the chapel service, and put some silver in the vault at his home across the street. By 11:00 A.M. he was saying goodbye to friends at the train station, bound for New York where he would meet his daughters. He had left his family behind on his previous global jaunt, but this time he was taking Janet, Elizabeth, and Eleanor—then twenty-six, twenty-four, and twenty-three—along on their first major trip together without Mary. Twenty-four hours later, they, along with Bishop and Mrs. Foss, boarded the *Koenig Louise*, of the North German Lloyd line, for a rainy two-week crossing to Naples, a city he was visiting for the sixth time.

The party soon boarded another vessel for Egypt. In his diary, Goucher noted that Alexandria had greatly improved since he and Mary had visited eleven years before, and Cairo had grown since his last two visits. He again visited the Sphinx and climbed Cheops, but this time with his daughters. Mindful of the important people and dates in his life, he also wrote a personal reflection on November 16: "This is the anniversary of my father's birth and his marriage." Although Goucher enjoyed showing his daughters the sites of ancient Egypt, he found it "a great relief to get out of the Babel of Port Said" on the *Barbarossa*, and to sail through the Suez Canal en route to Aden (then under British control, now in Yemen) and Columbo, Ceylon (Sri Lanka). He colorfully described one evening—"an emerald sun on the Red Sea"—but they also ran into more rainy weather. They spent Thanksgiving 1906 on shipboard.[2]

While on the *Barbarossa*, Goucher received a terse telegram from the Woman's College: "Trustees overwhelmed latest gift." Five days before departing Baltimore, he had sent a letter to the board's treasurer signing over to the college the deed to his house at 2313 St. Paul Street "in fee simple and without conditions." Although the suggestion was not legally binding, he recommended the house be held and used as an administration building, unless the trustees felt it could serve another purpose. If they decided to dispose of the building and land, he asked that the proceeds be set apart as a permanent endowment, the income to be applied at the board's discretion. An appraiser for the college said the house was "in first class condition" and, in his opinion, "the best finished house in Baltimore."[3]

Other members of the board did not learn of the gift until after Goucher had sailed. The letter and deed were accepted at its November meeting, and the trustees wrote him more expansively, "It was altogether in keeping with your quiet and unostentatious way of doing generous things that you so timed this additional benefaction to the College that when it was announced you should be far beyond the reach of our immediate thanks. . . . But we cannot consciously permit your modesty to silence our gratitude." They advised Goucher, "In accepting this trust we are ever mindful of your home life, of the sacred memories and happy years that cluster about the mansion," and they thought it was in the school's best interest for him to remain at 2313, where he and Mary had entertained and influenced "friends and strangers alike." In a unanimous resolution, they invited him to use the house as his in-town residence as long as he lived.[4]

A *Baltimore Evening News* editorial—"Citizen Goucher"—called the gift "only the last link in a chain of benefits which he has been conferring upon that institution throughout its existence." Until the recent fundraising campaign, the editorial went on, few knew "how vitally the College has been dependent for its prosperity upon both the liberality and devotion of its President." The paper spoke for everyone in Baltimore in thanking a fellow citizen who had "done so much for his city as Dr. Goucher."[5]

❋❋❋

While he was being hailed in his home town, Goucher was also experiencing a kind of homecoming on returning to India. During his two months there, he would revisit cities he had seen on his 1897–1898 trip: Bombay and Baroda, Delhi and Calcutta, Agra and Allahabad, Mutra and Madras, Moradabad and Lucknow. As before, crowds would welcome him at train stations with music, banners, torches, or firecrackers, and he would be greeted by missionary or church friends known to him personally or as correspondents. By his own calculation, he would give on average one speech a day. He had been charged again with visiting several annual conferences and assessing and addressing their educational and financial needs, but on this trip, he also would be attending the Jubilee of the India Mission, to be held in Bareilly.[6]

After Goucher's arrival in Ceylon, his first major stop was Madras, where he attended a missionary meeting. Under monsoon conditions, hundreds of urban and rural adults and children from thirty-two castes came together to march in a tamasha, or public procession, before the meeting began. (It ended with fireworks.) Goucher was pleased with the progress Grace Stephens had made in breaking down personal and educational obstacles for girls and women since he had laid the cornerstone for the girls' orphanage on his last visit. She had expanded zenana work, carried on among the segregated upper class Hindu or Muslim women, into seven districts. Five hundred students attended high-caste schools, and there were more than a thousand poor girls in village schools. Goucher spent a full day visiting her various schools and posing exam questions to students. Before breakfast, he met with the orphanage's seven grades, who welcomed him with a garland of flowers and a velvet cap and slippers with silver details. He in turn presented each girl with a small package of sweets. According to *Zion's Herald*, "The recipients were enthusiastically happy and Dr. Goucher's face shone, though he knew it not." Later he examined students at one of the high-caste girls' schools, where a few years before a sign on the door had proclaimed, "No man can enter here." He was given an American flag worked in beads by zenana women. In the evening, he visited village schools; at one he was presented with a beaded pen and ink stand and some paper. In every case, he felt the girls had "passed in good form."[7]

Stephens persuaded several local men to let Foss and Goucher visit a group of zenana women. The latter wrote in his diary that Bishop Thoburn had been permitted to visit the previous year provided he didn't speak or move, which earned him the nickname "Sahib doll." But Goucher was permitted to say a few words, "the first time a gentleman had ever done such a thing in Southern Asia." He saw other signs of progress on this visit: Many high-caste women or girls now were sitting outside the purdah (screen), and even those who still sat behind might pull it down to shoulder height to look over. He also saw a group of low-caste children performing for a high-caste audience, which included the daughter of an Indian chief justice and the wife of the prime minister to the maharajah of Cochin. She placed a garland of flowers around Goucher's neck after he spoke.[8]

Goucher had been warned that Stephens' work was not universally accepted by the Hindu community. A few months before his arrival, William F. Oldham, missionary bishop of Southern Asia, had written him about the plight of a woman Goucher had met in Madras in 1897, who, after being isolated in her zenana for fourteen years, had begun assisting Stephens in her work. Now, Oldham reported, a Hindu man had dragged her out of a cart and abducted her in a closed carriage. "The Hindus had always said that they would take her, but ten years is a long time, and she, with her frank, fearless ways, supposed the Hindu hatred had abated." Oldham looked for little help from the police, with "the stone wall of Hinduism against all government actions," and he feared she might be tortured.[9]

Perhaps that story, along with a compelling report from missionary Jesse Fisher at the Bombay Conference, prompted Goucher to make a new pledge on this visit. Fisher had said his most pressing concern was to reach the secluded village women on his 150-mile-long circuit. Contacting him later, Goucher offered $250 ($6,500) a year for four years to support six women—two Bible-readers and four assistants—and to purchase bulls and carts to take them on their rounds. That sum figured in some additional funds for materials the women could hand out, and to set up and support twelve Sunday schools. In return, Goucher asked for a report on progress and expenditures every six months. He wrote Fisher, "I esteem it a great privilege to be able to do this.[10]

Goucher was also particularly interested in the status (and the graduates) of the North India village and boarding schools he and Mary had supported for twenty years. By 1902, they had invested more than $100,000 (approximately $2.7 million) in schools and scholarships, contributing to an estimated 50,000 conversions to Christianity. That prompted one missionary to write Goucher, "You have done for the cause of education in India what no other man has done. There are preachers and teachers and men in office and business all through the Empire but for your munificence would be sweeping the streets or making cheap shoes in some vile smelling mohalla [neighborhood]." But after two decades of carefully monitoring the results of his experiment, Goucher had no longer felt able to stay involved personally or to provide ongoing support; he had ended his direct funding for the 120 primary schools where students were taught in the vernacular. Now he learned the consequences of that decision:

> I was told that within 5 years after I withdrew our school work
> from the North India Conference there were 7,000 less boys
> in school. Dr. Dease told me that when my schools and our
> scholarships ceased there was a noticeable decrease in the
> quality of men coming to the Theological Seminary in Bareilly
> and their preparation was much lower, neither being so high as
> they were 5 years ago and before that.[11]

Nevertheless, Goucher Schools remained well-known and respected in India. When he and his daughters reached Moradabad, headquarters of the boarding schools, they were greeted by boys and girls leading two torchlight processions. The next day, one student gave a flowery but impassioned speech about their benefactor:

> This is an occasion of special joy, which is particularly meant
> for us. The great swimmer in the river of generosity has exalted
> us today by putting his auspicious feet in our midst for the
> happy sight of which our loving hearts were eager and our

impatient eyes were watching. . . . It is impossible for us to count the pearls of your kindness and to describe the slightest part of your goodness.[12]

Goucher was proud of his graduates and enjoyed learning about their lives. In Bareilly, he arranged a dinner for forty "Goucher boys" who had once received his scholarships. Eating with his fingers and listening to their tales, he found "good cheer, good speaking and good work done." He threw a similar dinner for about two dozen former students who were members of the Northwest India Conference, and was gratified to hear some had government or commercial jobs that enabled them "to live comfortably, educate their children and support the church liberally."[13]

The end of Goucher's support for Goucher Schools did not signal an end to his support for Indian education. He renewed a pledge he had made in 1898 for primary schools around Raipur, in the central part of the country. As missionary George Gilder wrote, "You were the first friend God raised up for this great and promising field . . . and you have stood by it ever since." Goucher continued to aid ten area schools into the early decades of the twentieth century. Before he came to India this time, Goucher had pledged $100 (approximately $2,700) a year for five years—renewable thereafter for another five—to open summer schools around Meerut, north of Delhi, and in Naini Tal, near the Himalayas. One missionary later told him, "To have the assurance all these years that the school could go on is something for which we are very thankful." Goucher also strengthened ties between Lucknow and Baltimore during a visit to Isabella Thoburn College. He announced he would fund annually a four-year scholarship for a student from that institution to attend the Woman's College of Baltimore. It would be awarded in alternating years to an Indian student and to a daughter of a Methodist missionary. Many of these young women would return to work in India after graduation.[14]

✳ ✳ ✳

Between educational missions, Goucher and his daughters saw many colorful sights in India, visiting bazaars and mosques in various cities. They spent Christmas in Ajmer, then traveled northeast to Jaipur, where they saw the maharajah's palace and the calling of the sacred alligators in his well. From there, they rode several miles by elephant to see the sixteenth century Amer (Amber) Fort, "one of the most picturesque episodes thus far in India," in Goucher's assessment. But revisiting some spots evoked unpleasant memories: At several stops he saw thousands of Hindus bathing in the unwholesome Ganges, and various temples and shrines he visited caused him to comment, "Everything is so gross, so mercenary, so heartless."[15]

The Goucher family was treated, however, to an event he called "one of the most impressive I ever saw." The large ceremonial gathering for the Agra durbar brought together the British viceroy of India, Lord Minto, and the amir of Afghanistan, who had traveled from Kabul for this official reception. Also attending were Viscount Kitchener, commander-in-chief of British forces in India, and the lieutenant-governor of the United Provinces, along with several ruling maharajahs and nawabs (provincial viceroys or leaders). Massive temporary compounds—at least 800 tents for the amir and his entourage alone—were erected to house the dignitaries, political officers, and their staffs for the week-long event. The American consul had telegraphed the chairman of the Committee on Invitations to include the Goucher group "among the most distinguished citizens of the U.S." That endorsement, Goucher said, "brought me special invitations for myself and party for everything of interest." By special order, they were allowed entrée to restricted-viewing areas.[16]

One day at the durbar, 30,000 troops, drawn from all of the country's military services, lined up in a semi-circle on a broad plain to be reviewed by the viceroy, the amir, and the military commander. The Gouchers had choice seats not far from where the three men observed the parade from horseback. Brass bands played an assortment of tunes—"Marching Through Georgia" and "My Old Kentucky Home" among them—and there was a thirty-one-gun salute. As one spectator reported of the troops passing in review: "The great semi-circle got into motion. Blue masses were followed by green, green by scarlet, and the sun glinted merrily on thousands of moving bayonets."[17]

That evening there was more pageantry. In the Grand Chapter of the Orders of Knighthood, the viceroy invested the amir with the Knight Grand Cross of the Bath, and various other titles and insignia were awarded. The ceremony was held in the Diwan-i-Am, or Hall of Public Audience, built by Shah Jahan in the first half of the seventeenth century as part of the Agra Fort. Goucher described the 200-foot long room as specially decorated for the occasion with rich rugs leading to the dais, where the viceroy sat to make the investitures. Goucher observed that concealed electric lights, "giving a diffused and soft light like accentuated moonlight, gave a weird brilliancy to the scene." Attendance was limited to those on a Government House list, including Goucher and his party, and the Indian princes and their retinue.[18]

He found the reception that followed in the Khas Mahal section of the fort "even more picturesque," making Goucher feel as if he had been transported back to the time of Shah Jahan, builder of the Taj Mahal. In his diary, Goucher described the people he saw—Indian princes "sparkling with jewels," women in "full-court dress," British soldiers in "their brilliant and varied uniforms," and "native guards looking like bronze or ebony statues." He summed it up by saying, "The careless freedom and startling contrasts, the oriental splendor and suggestions of mystery, which pervaded every turn and the whole scene made it an evening long to be remembered."[19]

While Goucher enjoyed this lavish pomp and ceremony, he felt more at home with the simple activities and fervor he had found the week before in Bareilly, celebrating the fiftieth anniversary of Methodist missionary work in India. In his view, the Jubilee not only affirmed Christianity's impact on Indian lives, but also challenged the Church to do even more. He wrote in his diary, "The exercises were interesting from start to finish, increasing in significance and suggestiveness as they proceeded."

As at the durbar, hundreds of tents had been pitched as temporary living quarters, which one observer said "presented the appearance of a military camp." Eight motley tents had been cobbled together to make an auditorium large enough for 3,500 spectators, and services were held in English and Hindustani. There were greetings from representatives of other Protestant denominations and Methodist missions; presentations by visiting bishops and churchmen; business meetings where mission and school finances and fundraising were discussed; and an exhibition of items handcrafted by students, and of

Bibles in various dialects printed at the Methodist Publishing House. There were social events, parades, a Watch Night gathering on New Year's Eve, and even two weddings—one of a missionary in Burma and his newly arrived American bride, and another of two Indian converts who had met at a Methodist school.[20]

Goucher attended the Jubilee as an official representative of the Board of Foreign Missions (formerly the Missionary Society). Many already knew him. Introducing him, one speaker said, "Because of his friendship for India, he is well called by our Indian Christians 'our beloved Indian friend.'" Lilavati Singh, the faculty member whom Goucher had supported at Isabella Thoburn College, welcomed him on behalf of the educated women of the country. She told the crowd, "There are some whom we have already learned to know by face, as well as to honor by name. . . . [Dr. Goucher] has earned his right to a place in our midst by his love of India." Paying tribute to those missionaries living and dead who had contributed so much to her homeland, she said there were "none whose devotion to the missionary cause has been more unwearied, whose response to our needs more generous, and whose mind and strength were more unstintingly given to this great work" than John Goucher. In his own opening remarks, he reiterated his support for Indian women; while the conversion of the first Muslim man was "marvelous," he said, the conversion of the first Hindu woman was even more valuable.[21]

For Goucher, the Jubilee's final day, the first in 1907, was the most notable. The morning was filled with what he called "a series of living pictures," showcasing the breadth of the missionaries'—and his own—efforts to expand Indians' religious, educational, and social opportunities. The first Tibetan boy who had converted recited John 3:16 in his native tongue; both low- and high-caste boys from small village schools recited the Lord's Prayer and the Ten Commandments; so did schoolgirls, ages four to fourteen, many already married, engaged, or even widowed. Several Himalayan boys had walked ninety miles to the nearest train station, on their way to the event; with a blind chorister conducting, they sang a hymn in their own dialect. Young nurses from the Medical Training School attended, as did boys from the Industrial School, bringing samples of the rugs and wood and brass work they made. Several Indian men and women, who had been trained in Christian schools and now led schools or colleges themselves, spoke on the value of their educations. The morning ended when hundreds of students stood to acknowledge who had received bachelor's or master's degrees, graduated from a theological school, or attended a Methodist-sponsored high school. Goucher's reaction to this three-hour display: "I have seldom been so impressed in all my life."[22]

The rest of the day was devoted to the Epworth League rally, opening with a parade of 3,000 young people from more than sixty chapters, plus boys and girls from orphanages, men and women from villages and cities, preachers and teachers, missionaries and foreign visitors. The marchers sang and carried chapter banners, starting on the street that ran through the camp and from there snaking through the town until they reached the tabernacle tent. Speaking to the hope these young people would change the world and advance the Christian message, Goucher on the final evening told the crowd, "It is a sign that this Jubilee celebration reaches its climax on January the first, and not on December the 31st. It is not so much a eulogy as a prophesy. We are not here to write an epitaph, but to interpret a commitment given of God to us."[23]

A few weeks later, as he left India, Goucher wrote in his diary that his two months there had inspired him profoundly. While he was a man of numbers, India's progress was "more noticeable in those things which cannot be tabulated or placed in figures." He noted shifts since his last visit in "the social relation, the educational development, the mobilization of thought, the accessibility of Christian influence, changed attitude, conscious inadequacy of the old and demand for the new." As a missionary board member, he was energized to encourage more support for India once he returned home. At the moment, however, he was eager to move on to his next destinations.[24]

✳ ✳ ✳

As January ended, Janet, Elizabeth, and Eleanor remained another week in India with the Fosses, while Goucher sailed to Rangoon, where he spent two days attending events led by both Methodist and Baptist missionaries. He did some shopping as well, ordering two Assam silk suits to be delivered before he left. He also dined with a

Woman's College alumna whose husband was the secretary of the area YMCA. He soon was back on the water, headed for Penang, Ipoh, and Kuala Lumpur, now part of Malaysia. More than two decades before, the South India Conference had appointed a missionary to Singapore, and from there, missions had spread to other cities on the peninsula. The region soon boasted its own mission conference, which grew to include Java, Sumatra, West Borneo, and Sarawak.[25]

A *Baltimore World* article written several months later stated that of all the places Goucher visited on his nine-month trip, he was most impressed with the Malay States, owing to marked improvements there. He saw "much evidence of statesmanship and great evidence of economic development," including a railway line that had grown between his visits from less than thirty miles to more than 400. He was also impressed by the area's extensive commercial development; it was the world's primary source of tin, and there were thousands of acres of rubber trees.[26]

Goucher was enchanted with the flora and fauna he saw in every corner. Kuala Lumpur made him wax poetic in his diary:

> Single leaves [of palm trees] might serve as sun shades for a picnic party or make an ample canopy for a monarch's couch fringed the jungle, . . . while beyond, great sweeps of forest which rival the sea to billowy waves of living green, sweep over rugged mountain sides or nestling hills in stately grandeur. Here and there where a patriarch of the forest or one of his initiates has exhausted his vitality in maintaining the carnival of beauty, graceful ferns and exquisite orchids drape its nakedness and conceal its decay. A wealth of blossoms, brilliant as tropical sun can paint them, accentuate the landscape with their startling beauty, while butterflies which baffle description in the variety of their form and color throw the spice of their brilliant and graceful dance upon the ravishing scene.[27]

The Malay Peninsula offered Goucher an unusual adventure on this trip as well. Having enjoyed roaming the woods on his uncle's farm as a boy and camping in the wilderness as a young man, he was surely excited to trek into the jungle to meet members of the aboriginal Sakai tribe. He wrote several diary pages about this excursion, where he was accompanied by H. L. E. Leuring, a missionary who spoke two of twelve recognized Sakai languages. Goucher described the Sakai's "precarious life." They lived on jungle fruits and roots, a little rice and squash they raised in "out-of-the-way places in the mountains," and small game—namely rats and squirrels. Their scant clothing was made from bark and augmented with "cheap jewelry and decoration." The women pierced their noses and ears and painted their faces with thick red stripes. The Sakai Goucher met had come down from the mountains to pick durian—a tropical fruit, sometimes growing a foot long and weighing four or five pounds—which he wrote contained "within its most unpromising shell a most delicious custard."[28]

Goucher and Leuring traveled about thirty miles from Ipoh by train, to meet a car which took them to Tapah. From there, they rode in a shandidan, a covered cart pulled by a "plucky little poney [sic]" from Sumatra. The mountain and jungle scenery they saw along the way, Goucher exclaimed, was "wonderful in its profligacy and beauty." During the day they encountered several groups of Sakai— they were scattered across the landscape—including one chief and his followers. John made friends with the women and children by giving them beads, and he gave the leader a pair of blue glasses, which Goucher said "carried with them a sense of dignity and appreciation which proved potent." In return, the chief split a durian, which the men ate companionably. After their snack, he assembled his clan and "to their amusement," Goucher took their picture; then the chief told the visitors where they might find the next "company." Each group passed the visitors on to the next, or offered a guide to point out a carefully hidden path. Goucher discovered one method the Sakai used to conceal themselves from intruders: "One of the guides gave us away by making a peculiar noise and I saw in the distance all the girls and women fleeing to the dense jungle."[29]

That warning signal aside, Goucher said the Sakai welcomed them "with great frankness." Both sides seemed to enjoy these encounters. On the afternoon they shared, he wrote, the Sakai "shot at marks with their blow pipes. They set snares to show us how they caught rats and other small game. They showed us how they prepared bark for clothing, let us go into their 'duk' [house], laughed much at things we did or said and proved friends." The two Westerners met another chief, who was ninety years old. Although Goucher thought his clan might object to being photographed, they were "less adverse than I thought they would be." Goucher and Leuring returned to Tapah in time for dinner, capping "a great day."[30]

Of course, Goucher made time for some church work as well. He judged that the Methodists had taken the lead from other Protestant groups in the region, with ongoing projects in English, Tamil, Chinese, and Malay, and about 1,200 students in church-sponsored schools. One area of concern, however, was the scourge of opium addiction among the general population. There was an anti-opium movement among the Chinese residents and missionaries in various Malay cities, hoping to bring an end to continued sale of the drug. Goucher was asked to speak at one such prohibition meeting, but his schedule did not permit it.

While in Ipoh, however, he had a look at two of the area's largest "opium joints." As he noted, local regulations at least gave addicts a safe place to maintain their habit: "No opium joint can be in any house, any part of which is used for something else. There must be at least one spittoon for every two persons and clean bamboo mats for each and the rooms must be well ventilated, etc., etc." Addressing the Missionary Training School the previous year, Goucher had denounced Great Britain's role in promoting this menace: "The introduction of opium into China by the British government seems to have been an act of unmitigated selfishness, as reprehensible an exercise of power by a great nation as history records. Its immediate effect was dissipating, enslaving, a deadly curse." Still, Goucher felt British influence wasn't entirely negative: "[I]n the providence of God every port and all of China is not only open to commerce but to Christianity; and this oldest, largest, and most stolid dynasty on earth is in a ferment with the leaven of a new life."[31]

A two-day stop in Singapore gave Goucher enough time to inspect mission properties, revisit the Botanical Garden, develop his photographs of the Sakai, and purchase some old Siamese coins he wanted to repurpose as buttons for his new suits. His next port-of-call was Java, the most densely populated island in the Malay Archipelago and home to native Malays, Chinese, Indo-Europeans, and Babas (male descendants of early Chinese settlers who had intermarried with Malays). Java was then part of the Dutch East Indies, and Goucher observed that the island had "all the conveniences of modern civilization, a most carefully developed system of agriculture, [and] an intelligent and industrious people." But Dutch colonials had left the natives uneducated and "strongly neglected from the missionary standpoint." When the first Methodist mission opened in 1905 around Batavia (Jakarta) and Buitenzorg (Bogor), there were only about 15,000 Christians among the millions of islanders.[32]

Rev. J. R. Denyes had been sent to open the mission, and he and Goucher had corresponded about both the prospects for spreading Christianity, and of acquiring the funds to make it happen. Goucher saw Java as "an excellent base of propaganandism [sic]" for Borneo and Sumatra as well. With his encouragement, the young people of the Pittsburgh Conference's Epworth Leagues promised a multi-year pledge of support. Denyes asked Goucher to do whatever he could to ensure these funds were not diverted elsewhere and to promote sufficient support from the general missionary fund. By the time Goucher arrived on Java nearly two years after this correspondence, Denyes had organized several small churches with Malay, Chinese, and Baba congregations. He was delighted by Goucher's visit and asked him to preach at various locations; then he would be able to give "firsthand testimony" about the progress being made there to the donors in Pittsburgh and the Board of Foreign Missions in New York.[33]

The missionary planned further outreach to the Malays, who were primarily Muslim. The introduction of Islam there had been different from elsewhere, as Goucher explained in his diary: "Java is the only country which has been conquered by the Mohamedans [sic] without the sword. It was visited by Mohamedan traders who resided at the Court, found favor with and converted the king to Mohamedanism. And the kings Islamized the island or their people by edicts, etc." Just a week before Goucher's arrival, Denyes had opened a small school for Muslim children, located on a 16,000-acre tea, coffee, rubber, and cinchona (quinine) plantation. It was owned by a Christian family but employed more than 3,000 Muslims, who also lived on the property. Goucher was eager to visit the school and the estate, so he, Denyes, and Leuring set out on a rainy, fifteen-mile journey, partly by carriage and partly on foot, to the Gunung Gede region, situated between two volcanoes and now part of the Mount Gede Pangrango National Park. When they reached one of the mountain passes, Goucher took stock of how far he had traveled already and what was still in store. He wrote in his diary that this location was "the most remote point I am to reach this trip"—some seventy miles below the equator—and thus he could say he "started for home" once he left the area, heading east.[34]

Back in Buitenzorg, Goucher preached at a Chinese Watch Night service at the mission church, with Leuring translating. It was his second time celebrating New Year's 1907, once on each side of the equator. Denyes had been renting the building, but its location was unsatisfactory and it was too small for his growing congregation. From a business standpoint, Goucher thought Methodists should own rather than rent property, and he and Denyes looked at one affordable building; it was vacant and thought to be haunted. Goucher formed a plan to finance the purchase, promising a personal donation of 2,000 guilders, about half the cost; he persuaded another American he had met on Java to pledge another 250. That total, plus money Denyes had set aside for rent and a reserve fund, equaled enough to meet the sale price. Goucher had helped fund another "first" among missionary ventures: The church-and-school building became the first Methodist-owned property in what Denyes called the Netherlands India District of Java, Borneo, and Sumatra.[35]

While John was in the middle of his stay on Java, he was reunited with Janet, Elizabeth, and Eleanor. The family became tourists, sightseeing and shopping at various markets and stores. Goucher loved nature in the wild but did not mind bringing some home. He became friendly with the curator of the Botanical Garden, who collected more than fifty rare specimens of butterflies and beetles for Goucher to send to Baltimore, for private display or the college museum. He also found a French merchant who kept pythons and other live snakes, and killed them and tanned their skins to make leather goods to order. Goucher had a pair of slippers made from one snake skin he particularly liked, and bought "a fine skin for the college." Advised that "Tjisarora pea berry coffee," grown on the side of the volcano on the estate he had just visited, was the best on Java, he bought nearly seventy pounds to be shipped home.[36]

✳✳✳

Now China and Japan beckoned. Over the next four months, Goucher would travel between these countries several times, tending to various church and educational projects. The Gouchers arrived in Hong Kong on March 1. Until now they had been staying mostly at the homes of friends or missionaries, and they treated themselves to a luxury hotel. In Hong Kong, they found "much mail needing our attention," John noted, but there was still time to shop for curios and to sightsee. Anyone who has visited Hong Kong will agree with Goucher's assessment of Victoria Peak: "The view . . . is one of marvelous beauty and some of the walks and rides of unsurpassed beauty." While he had preached to many audiences during this trip, he added another first when he filled in for an English military chaplain, facing about 400 soldiers and sailors whose attendance was mandatory. "I was glad to do my best to make it worthwhile," he said. It seemed to go well. "The change in their attitude and close attention after the first five minutes or so was marked and hope meant they were being profited."[37]

The Gouchers took a side trip to Canton, traveling overnight by steamer. Disembarking at mid-day, they proceeded directly to the wedding of Anna Edmunds, a 1901 college classmate of Janet, to the secretary of the Hong Kong YMCA. Janet helped with the decorations and flowers. Perhaps thinking of home and Janet and Anna's alma mater, Goucher noted what time it was in Baltimore as this "simple but impressive" wedding took place.[38]

The next day, Janet wrote in her diary that they took advantage of "Canton from start to finish." They traveled around the city in sedan chairs, each carried by three coolies. Goucher recorded his impressions of this "ancient and remarkable city":

> [Canton] is said to number 1,600,000, 250,000 of these living in sampans on the water—literally a floating population—in which they are born and die, sleep, live and perform all their duties.... The streets are narrow, usually paved with stone, over crowded, lined with shops and thronged with huksters [sic], coolies, children, goods, pedestrians and flies. I never visited any other place which so impressed me with population, people everywhere, people feeding [sic] upon people, living off each other. In India, the masses lived off the soil. Here are shops everywhere, food, cloths, furniture, everything exposed for sale, everybody making, selling, buying, carrying or using....

[T]hey are born in swarms, grow up in multitudes and find a subsistence somehow.

The family traveled, he added, "miles through the streets, surrounded by a crowd any moment and any place we would stop to buy or look—all good natured and no one in a hurry but the burden bearers." After visiting various temples and meeting the city's American minister, they boarded a night steamer to return to Hong Kong. They were back for only a day before heading to Foochow.[39]

Goucher's ties to that city went back more than twenty-five years, to when he and Mary had first offered funds to build churches in the area and to help establish the Anglo-Chinese College. Now he was able to assess some results. The Goucher party stayed with a missionary whose sisters-in-law were students at the Woman's College of Baltimore, and the American consul gave them an official welcome dinner, where they met diplomats from several countries. Goucher also had a reunion with Dr. Hu King Eng, a guest at Alto Dale in 1884. She was the granddaughter of the second Methodist convert in China and daughter of one of the first Chinese to be ordained a Methodist minister. After studying medicine in the United States, sponsored by the Women's Foreign Missionary Society, Dr. Hu returned to her homeland in 1895, the first Chinese woman doctor in South China with Western medical training. She remembered her visit to Alto Dale, which she had called "a genuine American farm." Goucher was pleased to see her again; he toured the old Methodist women's hospital she had run since her return, and looked at the site for its replacement.[40]

Members of the Foochow Conference especially wanted Goucher to see what they had accomplished in the Ngu-Cheng District, a rarely visited region about forty-five miles away. He changed his schedule to make the trip, although "it crowded my time in Foochow and took me away from my daughters." It was not an easy or comfortable trek. Goucher and another missionary first headed to Kushan Mountain in sedan chairs carried by coolies. On the other side, they boarded a houseboat, which was battered by a storm during the night and sprung a large leak when it scraped bottom. After a sleepless night on the water, the travelers resumed their journey in sedan chairs.[41]

It was worthwhile to Goucher to see firsthand how his contributions had helped strengthen Christianity in the area. Several converts had become preachers, including the grandson of a man who had donated the land for one Goucher-sponsored chapel in 1881. The congregations had grown in size and fervor, and the Ngu-Cheng District was self-supporting, paying preachers' salaries and sustaining local church operations.

At one church, Goucher preached to more than 850 members and probationers, mainly farmers and their families. Many years before, it had been Dr. Hu's father who had translated Goucher's name into Chinese, and those living in the area already knew him as Ko Yok Hang. "When I was introduced they all rose up and gave me their peculiar bow," he noted. Local Chinese officials later presented him with gifts—old copies of Chinese classics, the 150-year-old ancestral tablet of the pastor's fifth grandfather, a fifteenth-century vase taken from a temple converted into a Methodist church, and an old idol.[42]

The churches Goucher had funded were successful, but now missionaries told him they needed more buildings to serve and increase the number of converts. As soon as he returned to Baltimore, he would make a five-year pledge to build fifteen new churches in three of the Foochow districts. The "Goucher Chapel Gift," as it came to be called, promised $100 (approximately $2,600) for each church, and financed the construction of one church a year in each district, over the five-year period. As was his custom, he required congregations to contribute additional necessary funds.[43]

* * *

Immediately after returning to Foochow from this side trip, Goucher left his daughters behind once again to sail for Shanghai. His arrival was delayed because of dense fog, and he had only one night in the city before heading on to Japan. At the end of March 1907, he was greeted in Tokyo by old friends Julius Soper and Honda Yoitsu, who was then president of Aoyama Gakuin. The institution had changed since Goucher's last visit. In 1899, the Japanese minister of education had begun to enforce the laws that prohibited religious instruction in government-recognized schools. At the time, Soper had written Goucher that this restriction would affect the middle and primary divisions, but not the college. Aoyama Gakuin elected to remain a Christian school, thus losing government sanction and its attendant privileges, and some students as well. But two years later, other political winds favored the school. Students in the Academic Department were freed from military conscription and granted the same admission privileges to upper level government schools as other Japanese middle school students. Another missionary wrote Goucher, "Thus we are better off than when we relinquished government recognition. . . . [It] now feels more secure to lay foundations for permanence and enlargement."[44]

Those foundations were both literal and figurative. Before Aoyama Gakuin could expand, it had to rebuild facilities damaged in the 1894 earthquake. Ten years after this disaster, Honda had notified Goucher that the institution had reached an education level almost equal to publicly supported schools "without compromising our principle," and he included a sketch of plans for a new Goucher Hall. More detailed drawings by a Japanese architect followed, and Honda "earnestly requested" that his friend examine them carefully and give his approval. As when the school was founded, Goucher offered his own funds and solicited other donors, an effort the institution's Board of Managers said "placed us under still greater obligation" to their benefactor. By the time of his 1907 visit, the new Goucher Hall was nearly completed, and John spoke at several events, including the first held in that building—the Aoyama Gakuin commencement ceremony. Another evening, he attended a banquet for 200 guests sponsored by the Alumni Association, celebrating the college's twenty-fifth anniversary. John had missed the dedication of the original Goucher Hall in 1887, but spoke at this one's dedication.[45]

Goucher maintained a busy schedule in Tokyo. One reason for his being there was to deliver an address at the conference of the World's Student Christian Federation. Established in 1895, it brought together a dozen national and international Protestant student organizations, representing over 100,000 students and their professors. Its goal was to strengthen and expand those organizations, deepen the students' spiritual lives, and enlist them in global evangelization. For the first time, the convention was being held in Asia, in a non-Christian country, but it drew more than 625 representatives from twenty-five countries. Goucher was pleased the majority of delegates came from his "much fruit" countries of India, Japan, China, and Korea. He also was proud that eight delegates came from the Woman's College of Baltimore—twice as many women as from any other college in the United States.[46]

Goucher's address was titled "Christianity and the United States," part of a series in which others spoke on Christianity in Great Britain, France, Germany, India, and Japan. In his talk, Goucher drew a distinction between Christianity (which to him meant evangelical Protestantism) and the Church, which he called the former's "more or less immature, and at times, distorted body." He claimed that Christianity accounted for "the discovery and settlement of America, . . . determined our governmental organization, and has been the dominating influence in our national development." As the twentieth century progressed, the United States was seeing its influence grow as a military and industrial power. To his international audience, Goucher gave a glowing description of America and Americans, rooted in Christian influences:

> Within its borders has been developed a great nation
> with 80,000,000 self-governing citizens, whose industry,
> intelligence, initiative, public spirit, courage, and self command
> are unsurpassed. Its high ideal of manhood, its moral stamina,
> even-handed justice, aggressive home policies, and frank,
> uncompromising relations to foreign nations have made it a
> world power, honored in all lands.[47]

In his few days at the conference, he gave several other talks to young people. He spoke to 500 high school and college-age girls on "Christianity in the Home," to nearly 700 university students on "Adjustment in Life," and to a large Sunday congregation comprised of students and delegates. Many federation members were also heavily involved with their countries' YMCAs. Goucher held a private meeting with his friend John R. Mott, the federation's general secretary, and nine national and international YMCA secretaries, to discuss policies and develop a program for "aggressive work in Asia," laying the groundwork for Goucher's increased involvement in the region in future years.[48]

The Japanese welcomed this five-day Christian conference, and Goucher noted they left "nothing undone to make its entertainment notable." Leading Tokyo citizens and several members of the nobility sponsored gatherings for delegates. The minister of foreign affairs gave them a party at his official residence, and the emperor opened the Hama Palace grounds for a reception; Goucher said the "walks, lakes, arborial [sic] effects and views were beautiful and a continual surprise." In his diary he vividly described a different kind of beauty he spied at another garden party at the end of the conference:

> Possibly the most beautiful sight was the Japanese women in
> their exquisite costumes and graceful positions as reflected
> in the water. Never before have I seen women whose clothes
> seemed to be so completely a part of themselves. The shadings
> and form, their gentle movements, quiet colorings, and musical
> voices seemed to blend with the scenery and accentuated by
> gay banners and flowers seemed arranged for color effect,
> made a scene never to be forgotten and very difficult to equal.
> This was the most beautifully dressed company of women I
> ever saw.

He added that while the Japanese women were the most beautifully attired, the most brilliantly dressed women he had ever seen were the several hundred zenana women he had viewed, unobserved, in Madras in 1897. He judged the most gorgeously dressed company of men and women to have been at the Agra durbar, where many were "robed with barbaric splendor."[49]

He did more personal socializing as well. One evening, Goucher gave a dinner for the Woman's College delegates who lived or worked in Europe and Asia. Other guests included Lilavati Singh from Isabella Thoburn College, who was attending the conference. One alumna maintained, "Our President considered it too golden an opportunity to be lost," to gather them all together, and "with his accustomed hospitality summoned us all to partake of a truly Japanese feast and entertainment." Despite the rain and cold outside the inn, "Dr. Goucher's easy cordiality put us back at once into the beloved atmosphere of undergraduate days."[50]

With daughters of his own—and *in loco parentis* to several hundred college girls—Goucher wanted to witness how the Japanese observed "Girls' Day." He was invited into both the "foreign and native" quarters of one home to see how the festival was celebrated with elaborate dolls, representing the emperor and empress, court attendants, and commoners, accompanied by miniature furniture and accessories. Still, he wrote in his diary, there was "no more serious problem in Japan than the school girl problem." He saw that Japanese attitudes about educating girls were changing, but he found them to be "in a transition state without religion, without a chaperone, without fixed social standard or a comfortable environment." He viewed expanding YWCA programs as one way to help girls and to offer moral stability.[51]

Goucher was not in Japan only for parties. Before Goucher left Baltimore, Julius Soper had written him, "In everything pertaining to Aoyama Gakuin, we try to keep you posted." But it was better still to confer with him in Tokyo. A few months before Goucher arrived in Japan, the ownership of the property and the management of the institution had been transferred from the Methodist Board of Foreign Missions and the original Board of Managers to an incorporated eighteen-member Board of Trustees. Half of them were to be Methodist missionaries in Japan and the other half Japanese Methodists. The new trustees called a special meeting with Goucher to discuss future growth, with an eye toward attaining university status, just as Goucher had proposed in the early 1880s. He also devoted one morning to talking with President Honda and Dean Ishizaka about conditions at the college.[52]

Starting in the afternoon and often ending late in the evening, Goucher was occupied "receiving callers and conferring with committees" concerning both the boys' school and the girls' Aoyama Jo Gakuin. Jennie Vail, a longtime missionary and teacher at the college, told Goucher she had overheard two Japanese teachers talking about his speaking skills—"*Goucher san no hanashi.*" When she asked Dean Ishizaka about the comment, he said, "Yes, Dr. Goucher speaks so well," adding, "He's—what do you call it—so penetrative—you say just a little and he knows all—I think he knows Japanese affairs better even than missionaries, not only past but future.[53]

After two weeks in Tokyo, Goucher started for the mainland to attend the China Centenary Missionary Conference in Shanghai. As he traveled via Yokohama, Nagoya, Kobe, Osaka, Hiroshima, and Kyoto to reach his ship in Nagasaki, he stopped to indulge some of his varied interests: He watched a match involving 300 sumo wrestlers; preached to a Japanese congregation of the Methodist Episcopal Church, South; viewed cherry blossoms; and spent time in parks, temples, and curio shops, where he found "some very good things, remarkably cheap and rare." While in Nagasaki, he attended the South Japan Conference and spoke to a crowd of about 400 medical students, doctors, and faculty at the Imperial Medical College.[54]

His daughters, whom he had last seen in Foochow, had arrived in Nagasaki a few days before him. There seemed to be some mutual irritation about travel arrangements. Goucher felt they could have reunited sooner if his daughters had not stopped in Nagasaki, "as they had been told by someone I wished, instead of coming to Yokohama as I expected and suggested." That mix-up led Eleanor to write a plaintive letter that reached Goucher in Hiroshima: "I am very sorry you did not arrange to be with me tomorrow—my first and only birthday in attractive Japan." But all three daughters took rickshaws in the rain to greet their father's train when he finally arrived, and tensions seemed to abate, in John's view at least: "But we are all well and very glad to be together again."[55]

※※※

Returning to Shanghai at the end of April 1907, the family stopped at the Astor House, and John devoted much of his time to the thirteen-day Centenary Conference, held in the city's Town Hall. According to him, 1,500 delegates attended, representing eighty-three Protestant societies working in more than 500 Chinese cities. Invited to sit on the speakers' platform at the opening session, he gazed out at the audience: "I thought I never looked into the faces of as many people at one time who represented so much personal sacrifice, sustained courage or constructive power, and their quiet, unobtrusive manner was as marked as their dynamics." No Chinese delegates were admitted to the conference, however, so he spoke at one of the evening meetings that the YMCA had set up for those excluded. Goucher felt the conference's program was generally interesting, but complained the arrangements were "hardly up to date." Perhaps comparing it to the recent successful Indian Jubilee, he thought the organizers had "tried to cover too much ground, not properly recognizing the historic character of the occasion."[56]

For Goucher, the main benefit of the conference might have been meeting with delegates outside the formal sessions, to discuss matters of importance to him or to give them advice. He attended a planning meeting on young people's missionary work in China, and he presided at another, arranged while he was still in India, to discuss setting up a Chinese Sunday School Union. More than a dozen Korean missionaries attending the conference also consulted with him, and adopted a plan to extend the work of the Young People's Missionary Movement to Korea.[57]

From a business and a religious standpoint, Goucher was interested in Methodist-union missionary enterprises, a subject he discussed at a meeting of Methodist delegates. He also checked on the joint Methodist Publishing House in Shanghai he had helped organize a few years earlier. But he was perhaps most interested in possible joint educational ventures in which Methodist and other Protestant mission schools might share resources and expand Christian influence. He met with Centenary Conference delegates to discuss the possibility of merging the Methodist university in Nanking (Nanjing) with two other institutions in the area, to form a more comprehensive university. West China interested Goucher as well. He had been involved with the Methodist mission there since its inception in the early 1880s, and most recently, he had given $5,000 ($139,000) to help open a boys' school in Chengtu. In 1905, eight missions in West China had organized a Christian Educational Union to coordinate and oversee primary and secondary schools; the Shanghai Conference let West China delegates consult with Goucher about further unification and the potential development of a union university in their region. Although the Nanking and West China projects were both put on momentary hold, once back in Baltimore, Goucher would keep watch as both institutions prepared to open within three years.[58]

Once the Centenary Conference was over, Goucher began to wind his way back to Japan, where he was to take part in another historic event: the establishment of the Methodist Church of Japan, formed from a union of Japanese missions of the northern and southern branches of the Methodist Episcopal Church and the Methodist Church of Canada. Prior to this trip, he had been working behind the scenes from Baltimore to bring about the merger, and Merriman Harris, the resident bishop for Japan and Korea, credited him with being "one of the prime movers in bringing this to pass." When Goucher was in Tokyo in early April, he had met with the commissioners, appointed by the three home missionary boards, to help finalize the organization.[59]

The missionaries, along with Japanese ministers and laymen, had urged him to return in mid-May, for the last annual Japan Conference of the Methodist Episcopal Church before the new General Conference officially voted on church union. Jennie Vail had written in April to press him: "Your work with the Japanese would have much weight—and in the peaceful adjustment of perplexing problems, your presence would be a power.—Of course this has been said to you again and again; but when they are really trusting the 'blue-eyed, red-bearded foreigner,' his presence would be welcomed." Bishops Cranston, Harris, and Foss insisted it was Goucher's "duty" to be at the two conferences, though he had plans to travel from southern to northern China and then on to Korea. But he "changed them as requested" in order to return to Tokyo.[60]

First, however, Goucher and his daughters traveled by steamer from Shanghai to Wu Hu, where he inspected the Methodist hospital and some church property. Eleanor and Elizabeth were to spend a few days in that city before returning to Shanghai; Janet, who had been suffering for some time with a bad cold and possibly pleurisy, would remain with friends to rest until Goucher returned from Japan six weeks later. John meanwhile traveled from Wu Hu to Nanking to visit both Methodist and Presbyterian school properties, and to meet more Woman's College alumnae before rejoining his younger daughters in Shanghai.

After he returned to Alto Dale, Goucher would tell a *Baltimore World* reporter that when he arrived in China, "I was astonished at the transformation which has taken place there among the millions. It appears to be greater than any revolution." He explained that the system of Confucian education that had been "entrenching itself for ages among the people" had been "almost entirely annulled." Following the defeat of the anti-western Boxer Rebellion in 1900, in which much property was destroyed and many lives lost, the weakened Qing dynasty began to consider reforms. In 1905, by edict of the empress, the viceroy or governor-general of each province was to establish schools along western lines. (That edict also abolished competitive but uniform civil service exams for government posts in the imperial bureaucracy.) Now, said Goucher, the Chinese displayed an eagerness for western knowledge that seemed "almost pitiable," a change that made mission-sponsored schools and universities more valued than ever.[61]

He saw the impact of a turn from the old ways when he visited Nanking's deserted, 20,000-stall Examination Hall, and he found similar halls in other provincial cities "falling down to give way for modern educational institutions." Goucher described what he saw as the old system's drawbacks:

> The cast iron nature of [China's] educational method has interpreted and developed her immobility. [Her] youth have been denied that domestic training which is the heritage of western civilization. The mental vitality which this ancient people has retained is not by reason of their education but in spite of it, for its spirit in all grades was imitative and servile. Even though there may be many in the same school, each pupil memorizes, recites and writes in a class by himself. The natural outcome of their education has been to stunt their genius and drill the faculties into a slavish adherence to venerated usage and dictation [62]

Goucher contrasted that with the new scheme: There were western-style schools, at all grade levels, in all of the eighteen provinces, and no one could pass any competitive exams without first taking "the required course of modern learning." Education for girls was spreading rapidly, and in the growing number of public girls' schools in Peking, no student with bound feet could gain admission. As more students took part in advanced studies abroad, the World's Chinese Student Federation brought them together through "modern education, translations and publications, a common language, and mutual practical association, etc. etc." These new developments were so momentous, he remarked later, "It seems that the Celestials are beginning to wake up and make up for lost time."[63]

＊＊＊

Once the Gouchers met back in Shanghai, the family split up yet again. Eleanor sailed for Korea with missionaries just returning from the Centenary Conference, while Elizabeth accompanied her father to Tokyo, where John was again officially welcomed to Aoyama Gakuin by students, faculty, alumni, and friends. At the campus, he viewed the boys' athletic exercises and a girls' archery competition, plus a military drill "when all the boys marched past and saluted and then drew up and gave the Japanese banzai [cheer]." Several Japanese men honored him at a thirty-course dinner with ceremonial dances; all of them had studied or traveled in the United States, had enjoyed John and Mary's hospitality—and more than likely had received financial help from the Gouchers.[64]

The majority of his time, however, was filled with committee meetings, speaking engagements, interviews, and sessions of the last Japan Annual Conference and the newly formed General Conference for the union Methodist Church of Japan. As the Annual Conference's business concluded, Goucher was pleased when the missionary appointments were read out: Amy Lewis, an 1896 graduate of the Woman's College, was assigned to head the girls' Aoyama Jo Gakuin. He had been in Japan to welcome her when she had first arrived as a missionary teacher in 1898, and now he congratulated her on her new position. He later met with her to discuss raising the school to college level; he also spoke to conference delegates to "sell" the need for such an institution and the plan to realize it.[65]

Goucher noted that with the pending transition to one united church, there was still "considerable anxiety experienced (maybe I should say solicitude), by both missionaries and native brethren as to the final shape of the basis of union." To help ease concerns, he and two of the attending bishops spoke with the missionaries and answered questions. The gathering, he said, was "spirited, harmonious, fraternal and every way profitable." The first General Conference, held in the chapel at Aoyama Gakuin, was composed of sixty-six missionary and lay delegates—only nine of them Americans—drawn from the three Methodist groups. It formally approved the organization of a union church for Japan, and Honda Yoitsu was elected as bishop. A report

274

of the conference noted that with his selection, the new church "was launched under Japanese leadership, with the missionaries as workers and friendly advisors." Goucher believed in such self-determination. In an address he was asked to make to the delegates, he talked of the opportunity and responsibilities that came with this milestone for Japanese Christians. He became a popular source of information about the new Methodist Church of Japan, giving nine interviews one day in less than six hours.[66]

His work accomplished in Tokyo, at the end of May 1907, Goucher left Elizabeth with friends and set off on an unusual scenic route for Peking: He traveled through territory that had figured in the Russo-Japanese War two years before, when Japan had shown its emerging military might by defeating Russia in a battle over influence in Korea and Manchuria. The Russians had long wanted a warm-water port on the Pacific for military and commercial reasons, and in March 1898, the Chinese gave the Russian Pacific Fleet a twenty-five-year lease on the Liaotung (Liaodong) Peninsula and Port Arthur in outer Manchuria. This decision angered the Japanese because the area had been ceded to Japan by treaty after it won the Sino-Japanese War; that agreement was later rescinded, owing to intervention by Russia and other western powers. Although the Russians and Japanese signed an agreement in April 1898, recognizing Korean independence (with King Kojong as emperor) and pledging not to interfere in Korean politics, both sides maintained connections in that country.

Tensions continued to escalate as the twentieth century began. Russia and Japan had both sent troops as part of an international force to quell China's Boxer Rebellion, but after that, the Russians kept troops along the Korean border in Manchuria, which the Japanese read as a threat. Russians had also crossed into northern Korea, bought land, and established a trading post. Despite negotiations between the rivals to acknowledge Russia's sphere of influence in outer Manchuria, and Japan's in Korea, talks broke down early in 1904, and war soon broke out.

As in the war with China ten years earlier, Japanese forces proved to be better trained and disciplined than those of their larger opponent. Some eighteen months later, the combatants signed a peace treaty, mediated by President Theodore Roosevelt, at Portsmouth, New

Hampshire. Manchuria was restored to China, although Japan then leased the Liaotung Peninsula; Japan was given control of Korea and the southern half of Russian-held Sakhalin Island. Russia was spared paying reparations, but its quest to expand to the east had been stymied. In his diary, Goucher described the victor's growing influence in Asia since the Sino-Japanese War: "Without losing a single ship or single battle, Japan broke down the power of China, made a new Korea, enlarged her territory and changed the whole political face of the East. Then she fought for her life with Russia and not only gained the right to life [but] assumed a place among the world powers."[67]

As a student of history, Goucher seized his chance to view the disputed terrain for himself. He was especially interested in the area around Port Arthur, where the Russian fleet had been destroyed as the war began, and where a later Japanese siege ended in Russia's surrender. Before he left Japan, he was joined by a new travel companion, George Heber Jones, a missionary in Korea. The pair sailed from Kobe, along the Inland Sea, to Shimonoseki; there they took lunch at the inn where the 1895 Sino-Japanese peace treaty had been signed. After what Goucher called "a restful sea voyage," they reached Dairen (Dalney, Dalian), and were met by the American consul. Goucher saw the ongoing work to improve the harbor and rail facilities, but also "evidences of the Russian occupancy and the looting in their retirement on every hand."[68]

The next day, Goucher and Jones took the train to Port Arthur. When Goucher arrived, his first thoughts were not of war but of the Woman's College of Baltimore, and he went to the telegraph office to cable a message to the seniors, who were holding their Class Day. As he later surveyed the scenes of battle, he was reminded of a similar day he had once spent at Gettysburg: "This day gives greater emphasis to endurance, persistence, patient, detailed effort, recklessness of life. The fervor for a courage that fought in the open, impetuous, majestic courage." But he prayed that God would keep these two countries from further conflict.[69]

Goucher and Jones, joined by a former Japanese army officer who had participated in the siege, toured the scarred countryside and climbed to the top of one contested hill, where they saw the masts of sunken Russian ships in the harbor. During their tour, they collected bullets and buckles—"insignia of death," Goucher called them—and he "wondered at Mars' cruelty and courage." He abhorred war but gave the Japanese credit for vanquishing the Russians. He acknowledged their courage and discipline during the five-month siege of the port, as well as "such cunning and skill, such courage and persistence as cannot be imagined unless seen." The Russians, he felt, had been their own worst enemy; their incompetent leaders had failed to plan adequately, stocking enough champagne and vodka for three years, but too few medical supplies. He also noted Russia's misplaced priorities, spending eighteen times more rubles on the army than on schools.[70]

When Goucher and Jones returned to Dairen to set off for Peking, they followed the path of Japan's earlier war with China, eventually coming to Shan-hai-kwan, where the Great Wall's eastern extremity meets the sea. Their train passed through the wall, and after the travelers checked in at their hotel, they walked atop the Great Wall, coming upon a fort which flew the Union Jack. Goucher had no doubt that "with John Bull sitting on the sea," the British would hold that spot despite any future difficulties. The following day they reached Peking, where Goucher divided his time among the usual speaking engagements, inspections of Methodist properties, and sightseeing excursions. He also celebrated his sixty-second birthday; he received a number of telegrams and letters from family and friends, and bought himself a 400-year-old picture from the Ming dynasty to send home.[71]

Tientsin—home of the Isabella Fisher Hospital that John and Mary had founded more than twenty-five years before—was the next stop. Several missionaries called to talk with Goucher about their work— "past, present, and future." He listened to their accounts of living through the Boxer Rebellion, and they gave him a few "Boxer relics" for his collection. At last Goucher and Jones began their circuitous voyage to Korea by various ships, making a stop on the Chinese coast and one in Japan before landing at Pusan (Busan) in the southeast. From there they took the train to Seoul.[72]

❋ ❋ ❋

Before Goucher had left Baltimore, Bishop Harris had told him of Korea, "Do not dare leave this little country out of your itinerary."

He arrived for the first time in the Land of the Morning Calm just as the country was enduring further subjugation by Japan. In a span of a few months in 1905, Japan had cemented its influence: The United States signed a secret agreement with Japan, acknowledging Japanese dominance in Korea and American control over the Philippines, acquired at the end of the Spanish American War. Great Britain and Japan renegotiated a previous alliance that also acknowledged Japan's role in Korea. Finally, in September, the Treaty of Portsmouth, ending the Russo-Japanese War, ceded control of Korea to the victor. When the Korean prime minister refused to sign a treaty that made his country a Japanese protectorate, Japanese troops entered the ministry and stamped the treaty themselves.[73]

Prince Ito Hirobumi, who had become Japan's first prime minister in 1885, was appointed as resident-general of Korea, overseeing Japanese interests; Korea's Emperor Kojong became a figurehead. In June 1907, Goucher reported "two delightful conversations" with Ito in Seoul. The resident-general might have known of his visitor beforehand, owing to Goucher's connections in Japanese educational circles; they might even have met in Tokyo during Goucher's 1898 visit, when Ito was serving his third term as prime minister. Goucher's interest in Japan gave him credibility that helped him deal with the Japanese government on behalf of Methodist missions and schools in Korea.[74]

Goucher also noted "an interesting call" he paid on Emperor Kojong, who was sending secret envoys to The Hague Peace Convention in hopes of regaining control of Korea. (Japanese delegates blocked them from presenting their case, and Western representatives ignored the envoys.) Within a month of Goucher's leaving the country, Japan would force the Korean government to sign a new treaty giving the occupation power complete control over Korea's internal affairs, installing Japanese officials in all ministries and dissolving the Korean military. Even as Goucher regretted the country's fall, he felt Korea's leaders had brought it on themselves:

> While many like myself think Korea has lost its autonomy, it was inevitable, as she has wasted her opportunities, and by attempting to administer the government under the false assumption that the people belong to the sovereign instead

of the sovereign to the people, they have become deficient in aggressiveness, initiative, courage, resourcefulness, and confidence, so that it was necessary that she be under the direction of Russia, China or Japan.

With the new Japan-Korea Treaty in July 1907, Emperor Kojong was forced to abdicate in favor of his son Crown Prince Sunjong, and he was confined to one of his palaces.[75]

His political contacts aside, Goucher's prime motive for coming was to attend the Korea Mission Conference of the Methodist Episcopal Church and of the Methodist Episcopal Church, South. The two groups met both independently and together, discussing educational and evangelical issues and possible joint ventures. Politically all was chaos, but Korea was also in the midst of a religious revival that saw the conversion of thousands to Methodism and Presbyterianism. Mass revivals had been successful in Wales and India, and Korean Christians hoped for similar results. In 1903, a small group of missionaries had met for prayer, confession, and repentance; from that spark, the movement spread to other mission centers and then the entire peninsula. At the end of 1906, nearly two dozen Methodist and Presbyterian missionaries, as well as a group of Korean Christians, met for daily prayer in Pyengyang (Pyongyang), Korea's third largest city. When Goucher visited in 1907, thousands were converted, and the revival would continue another three years, a boon to the expansion of Christian churches and schools. It also provided an outlet for nationalistic sentiment during the Japanese occupation.[76]

Visiting Korea, Goucher was finally able to see all four of his "much fruit" countries on one journey. But after eight months of travel, it was time to turn toward Baltimore. From Korea he sailed back to Shanghai, where Janet found him waiting on the dock when she arrived from her recuperative stay in Wu Hu. They set off for Japan to meet Elizabeth and Eleanor, who was returning from her own stay in another part in Korea. Eleanor recently had written her father: "It will be so good to get together again on the boat because you must confess that we have not been together as much as we all had hoped." The three daughters had great affection for their father: Janet had written a letter to Goucher, filled with "with heaps of love" and signed "Bairn," her childhood nickname; in her own letter, Eleanor admitted she had grown "very Father sick" while she was off in Korea. Even so, she aired some complaints: "[W]e all 3 wish we could only please you more but little differences of opinions seem to come in the way.... [I]t has been very unfortunate that we have not always agreed on things but we do not talk enough to each other to always understand actions and thoughts."[77]

Eleanor also hinted at the not-unusual role these grown daughters had assumed of watching out for their widowed father: "I know it is not nice to you to have us suggest your few little things you do that we do not approve of but Mother dear used to do so and now that we have lost our <u>dearest</u> friend and you are so busy thinking of work you forget at times what you are doing—you have told me that several times." Still, she acknowledged the pleasure she drew from his "dear letter," and she signed her own, "Lovingly, your devoted and want to mean more to you, Maidie." (She would get her wish. Unlike her sisters, Eleanor never attended college or married; in later years, she would become her father's frequent travel companion, and helped him host myriad visitors to Alto Dale and 2313.)[78]

The reunited family spent the early part of July in Tokyo. Elizabeth decided to remain in Japan to work until the following spring; the experience would help in her future career as a missionary teacher in China. The remaining three Gouchers headed to Yokohama to catch a trans-Pacific steamer for Victoria, British Columbia, and then Seattle, arriving the last week of the month. From there they traveled by rail along a northern route to Chicago, and finally to Baltimore. Meticulous about records and figures, Goucher had noted in the back of his travel journal his location on each day of the trip and the number of miles covered traveling from one location to another. On this second global trip he logged over 41,000 miles—more than 23,000 on water and almost 14,000 on land—and spent a total of fifty-eight days in India, sixty-one in China, and fifty-six in Japan.[79]

After the long months away, Janet wrote in her diary of gazing on Alto Dale, a place they all must have missed dearly: "It is almost unreal in its beauty." *The Baltimore World* reported John's arrival, quoting him as being "glad to get here." He was, the article pointed out, no typical tourist: "No Baltimorean in late years has covered the wide expanse of territory that Dr. Goucher passed through in the last nine months, and some of the ground he trod on is rarely included in the itinerary of the globe-trotters." But with the rigors of travel barely behind him, Goucher was at his desk in his office at the Woman's College the next day.[80]

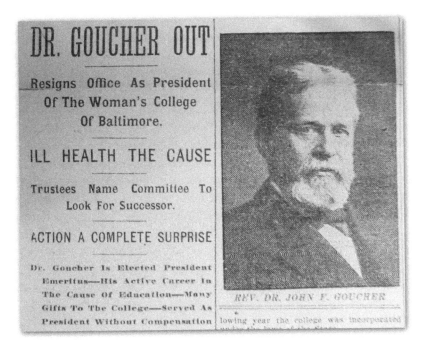

DR. GOUCHER OUT

Resigns Office As President
Of The Woman's College
Of Baltimore.

ILL HEALTH THE CAUSE

Trustees Name Committee To
Look For Successor.

ACTION A COMPLETE SURPRISE

Dr. Goucher Is Elected President
Emeritus—His Active Career In
The Cause Of Education—Many
Gifts To The College—Served As
President Without Compensation

REV. DR. JOHN F. GOUCHER

lowing year the college was incorporated

The Baltimore Sun, November 22, 1907

*Courtesy of the Baltimore-Washington Conference Archives,
Lovely Lane United Methodist Church, Baltimore, Maryland*

RESIGNATION

Chapter 17
(Fall 1907-1908)

━━━━━━━━━━━━━◆◆━━━━━━━━━━━━━

Love is not a fancy, but the great transforming, constructive force of the universe. Lovableness is not an accident, but an achievement, a characteristic of true education.[1]

Goucher had taken this international trip as a break from the stresses of his duties at the Woman's College of Baltimore. But *Zion's Herald* noted, "It was no rest whatsoever, he being in continual attendance upon conventions and conferences, as well as prominent as adviser and speaker on many subjects." When the new academic year began in September 1907, the college's president found his load no lighter than when he left. The celebrated debt campaign had not relieved the institution's financial strains all at once. Much of the $500,000 raised was in pledges, not cash, and donors had up to five years to fulfill their promises; by the time Goucher returned from East Asia, only a third of those pledges had been paid. To cover operating expenses, college trustees continued to give personal loans or approve additional borrowing.[2]

The president gave his annual report at the November meeting of the Board of Trustees: During the nine months he had been away, no new money had come in to the treasury, and the previous academic year had added $50,000 ($1.3 million) to the deficit. On his return at the end of July, Goucher quickly set up business meetings—from Boston to the west coast, and from Toronto to the far southern United States—in hopes of turning up "considerable financial returns" for the college, to eliminate or at least reduce the deficit. But, he reported, because his health had become "so limited," he had to cancel all such appointments scheduled before January 1908.

Goucher urged the trustees to address these financial challenges: "If the Woman's College is worthwhile it is tremendously worthwhile, and if we believe this we should make her care our business, and care for her with as much devotion, plan for her as sagaciously, work for her as industriously, and support her as generously as we do our secular businesses at least." Drawing an analogy to his experience as a father, he told them, "A great college, like the growing daughter, requires increased outlays to provide for the necessities of her healthy development." He made several concrete suggestions: develop a list of annual contributors, increase the endowment, increase the tuition and/or board, expand the number of students, and modify the charter so the college could be supported by more than one conference, as Dickinson College was. To underscore the importance of the Woman's College and its mission, Goucher touched on a theme from his own life: "We owe more to our Mothers, our wives and daughters, and the womanhood they represent than we have ever repaid or recognized."[3]

With that report out of the way, Goucher then read a letter that a *Baltimore Methodist* editorial would say struck the assembly "like a thunder clap": he announced his resignation. Briefly reviewing his own contributions to the Woman's College, Goucher told the trustees:

> In a few weeks it will be a quarter of a century since it was my privilege to suggest the establishment of a College, in the city of Baltimore, for the higher and thorough Christian culture of young women as women. For seven years, by public address, by personal interviews, by correspondence, and through the press, and as Chairman of various committees, I gave the launching of this enterprise all the time and energy I could spare from the exacting demands of a heavy pastorate. For eighteen years I have occupied the office of President, and the interests of the Woman's College have been my chief and absorbing concern. I need not add, my faith in its future and interest in its work are unabated, but for many months the condition of my health has been a matter of serious concern to the physicians I have consulted and they insist I must have protracted and complete rest.

> Recognizing that the best interests of the Woman's College require more vigorous direction than I shall be able to give, and that there can be no more favorable time to change its Chief Executive, I hereby present my resignation as President of the Woman's College of Baltimore, the same to take effect at the close of the present academic year, or as much earlier as you may be able to arrange for the work of the Office.[4]

One indicator of Goucher's poor health: he cancelled his appearance at an all-college reception that evening and returned to Alto Dale. Unaware of his resignation, some 350 elegantly dressed students were enjoying the party when word began to spread through the crowd; according to a story that would run in *The Baltimore Sun*, "Soon there was no other topic of conversation." There was much speculation about the nature of Goucher's illness, but Janet Goucher, then an alumna trustee, assured everyone her father was "just weary— terribly so—and must get a rest. . . . The responsibilities of the institution are too much for him." The day after the resignation, the *Baltimore News* reported the usually accessible Goucher was "very much under the weather at present and unable to see anyone."[5]

The trustees reluctantly accepted his decision, and an official tribute, later incorporated into the board minutes, chronicled his role in the college's evolution from their perspective:

> The history of the Institution, from its beginning, has been the record of your achievement. To intelligent foresight you have added incessant toil; to lavish generosity, vigilant care; and to all these a leadership which has placed the College within twenty-five years of its inception in a position second to none for the distinctive education of women.

As capstone to that tribute, they named Goucher president emeritus, so "your name may remain associated with the Institution; and that you may feel entire freedom in counsel and cooperation in furthering its interest and development." They assured him the honor was not intended "to embarrass you by any burdensome sense of continued obligation for service which may be beyond your convenience or strength." Still, they kept him close. He was given office space on campus and a seat on the Board of Trustees; under their earlier agreement, he would continue to live across the street at 2313.[6]

Public and private reactions to Goucher's resignation flowed in from many quarters. William Hersey Hopkins, his predecessor as president, wrote to say he felt as if he were "walking in a kind of unpleasant dream" since hearing the news. "To think of the college apart from your direction and responsibility is well nigh impossible." The *Pittsburgh Christian Advocate* concurred: "It will be difficult to think of the Woman's College without Doctor Goucher at its head. He and the College have seemed to be so entirely one that to divorce them seems almost a violation of the law governing such matters." Chancellor James R. Day of Syracuse University, however, knew the burdens his friend shouldered and observed, "It gets in upon not only the nerve but the very bone and it must be a sweet Elim to a man to wake up and feel that he has not the active care and endless details of a college presidency." W. A. Candler, former president of Emory College in Atlanta and bishop of the Methodist Episcopal Church, South, offered Goucher a restorative change of scene, telling him, "Come, go with me to Cuba, and we will have a good time. Then come back and stay with us through a Georgia spring time, and you will feel like a new man."[7]

Goucher received a very different invitation from the other side of the world. From Tokyo, Jennie Vail proposed he take over the presidency of Aoyama Gakuin, an office vacant since Honda Yoitsu was named bishop of the new Methodist Church of Japan. Vail wrote, "It is impertinent even to think of 'Dr. Goucher' [as president], and yet you have loved this school and planned for it, and your resignation makes it more possible for you to steer our ship for awhile." He also heard from alumna Amy Lewis, who sent him a sympathetic note from Aoyama Jo Gakuin. She let him know that Elizabeth, working with her at the girls' school, was worried about her father so far away.[8]

The Woman's College community expressed its dismay at Goucher's decision in a school publication that acknowledged the behind-the-scenes challenges he had faced:

> If old records dared to speak, they would divulge the secrets of his quiet, unobtrusive generosity. We would all know then that our beloved president has never failed to tide us, individually or collectively, over every wave of fortune and misfortune that has come into the current of our existence. He has been keen and farseeing in his judgments and quick in action in times of emergency.

A history of the school likewise credits him with never letting his worries intrude on daily life at the college. Lilian Welsh, who had known him from early in his presidency, later said of those strains:

I doubt whether any of our faculty knew until after Dr. Goucher's resignation the overwhelming financial burden he had constantly borne. When the responsible head of an institution sees year after year the income fall far short of the outgo, when he sees all possibilities for growth and expansion sacrificed in order to keep the college going, it takes rare qualities of mind and soul to present to the public a never failing optimism. This Dr. Goucher always did.[9]

The true measure of his tenure was the college's tangible growth. There were three buildings when he became president and nine when he resigned, and the college owned six acres of land. Faculty and administration had increased from eighteen to forty-one. There were forty college-level students at the beginning of his tenure, and more than 340 enrolled during his last year in office. The first graduating class he presided over had five students; at his last commencement in 1908, he would confer sixty-one degrees. In all, he had welcomed nearly 725 young women as alumnae.[10]

Zion's Herald reported it wasn't just Methodists and the Woman's College community who regretted his leaving, but "men of all denominations and in every walk of life." The Midwest's *Central Christian Advocate* called his resignation "a national event," echoing a *Baltimore News* commentary: "He can take with him into his retirement the consciousness of having, under most serious difficulties, done an important and lasting service—one that has spread, and will continue to spread great benefits among the young women of this country." Another article compared Goucher's role at the Woman's College to former president Gilman's at Johns Hopkins: "Each proposed something new in the educational field, each devoted himself with tremendous energy to the task of transforming his dream into an actuality, and each lived to see his work splendidly successful."[11]

With his resignation came renewed discussion of making Goucher a bishop. The quadrennial Methodist General Conference was to be held in Baltimore in May 1908, and one local minister voiced the feelings of many that Goucher would be elected if only he would allow his name to go forward. Chancellor Day—who had been elected a bishop in 1904, but had declined the office to continue running Syracuse University—encouraged Goucher to accept, despite his previous demurrals. "If I had my way, I would have you in the Episcopacy, an office which would afford recreation, for you are adapted to travel, and to fields where your statesmanship and magnificent wisdom could go on in the service of the church and humanity." *Methodist Review* editor William V. Kelley wrote Goucher, "I once told the mother of your children that the only fault I had to find with her husband was that he is not numerous enough: We need three of him, one for the Woman's College, one for chief Missionary Secretary, and one for the bishopric." But Kelly recognized that now, Goucher would likely prefer to pursue his varied "commissions" in his own way.[12]

※ ※ ※

Following his resignation, Goucher maintained an active calendar in 1908, despite health issues. For the sixth time he was elected a delegate to the General Conference, and he was also a delegate and guest speaker at the founding of the Federal Council of Churches (now the National Council of Churches) in Philadelphia; that partnership of thirty-two religious organizations addressed such social issues of local import as temperance, immigration reform, and the exploitation of child labor. He continued to travel regularly to New York for meetings of the missionary Board of Managers. As William F. Oldham, missionary bishop for Southern Asia, told him, "The Church at large accepts your judgment of missionary situations almost without question." Goucher also had a reputation as an education expert. The recently appointed corresponding secretary of the Methodist Board of Education in New York, Thomas Nicholson, asked Goucher for help in light of his extensive practical experience: "I should highly prize your advice and suggestion as to what our Board ought to do and what the greatest things before us—which are really feasible—are."[13]

The talk on "Christianity and the United States" Goucher had delivered in Tokyo was published as a book after his return and received widespread praise. The dean of the Biblical Department at Vanderbilt University wrote to say he would cite the article's facts and figures in his classes, and he thought all state and federal legislators should read it. The general secretary of the Baptist Forward Movement for Missionary Education told Goucher it was to his knowledge "the best brief compendium of the facts and figures of the forces of

Christianity in our country." And the corresponding secretary of the Methodist Board of Sunday Schools wished a copy could be given to every fledgling minister. The superintendent of the Presbyterian Sabbath-School Training rhapsodized: "I find it a treasury filled with gems, gold and precious stones—cut and polished and arranged after the pattern of an expert in rare diamonds of rich and exquisite forms." He concluded, "All of us Americans thank you for showing the moral worth of our nation to the world." Another church friend offered a more personal reaction to the book: "There is only one thing that produces a feeling tinged with sadness to say the least and that is that the picture of the author shows the wrinkles so prominently." He wrote of Goucher's now-public health problems, "I am not surprised in the least, for I have been expecting them. I told your dear wife before her departure to the blessed home that the work you were doing would tell very soon."[14]

※ ※ ※

Goucher maintained his ties to missionaries in the countries he had visited in 1906–1907, and they continued to seek out his guidance and (often financial) assistance. He had been back from that trip only a few weeks when he received an update on perils to Indian girls and women, a longtime concern. Grace Stephens wrote there was "trouble and persecution" in the high-caste girls' school where he had recently given the exams. In Madras, Hindu men were going house to house, threatening parents with disgrace and expulsion from their caste if they allowed their daughters to attend school. They even dragged away any girls attempting to enter the school. Despite these difficulties, Stephens told him, instruction and baptisms continued, and the girls he had met "do not forget you." Goucher also heard regularly from Jesse Fisher, who noted that the money Goucher had pledged for visiting Bible readers remained the only funds supporting work on behalf of women on his missionary circuit. But he reported some Goucher-funded progress:

> The work has brought the women up to the same plane as men.
> . . . In many cases the women take the lead. . . . Before we
> began the work among women the common expression was
> 'What can women do? Prepare bread for their husbands. That

is all.' I never hear that anymore. . . . Wife beating is common in India. A man beats his wife as he would his ox or ass. The teaching has overthrown it among Christians. Men are now ashamed to be known as a wife-beater.[15]

In China, the idea Goucher had discussed at the Centenary Conference, to form a union university in Chengtu, was beginning to take shape. As Goucher resigned his presidency of the Woman's College, the Board of Foreign Missions asked him to serve on a newly created board for the proposed institution in West China. Its members would help coordinate efforts between missionaries in China and Methodists and other denominations in their home countries to solidify plans and raise necessary funds. Goucher accepted the offer.[16]

He also read reports on the churches being built in the Foochow region, thanks to money he had pledged. Local districts appointed committees to determine where churches were most needed, and one stone church seating 400 was completed within a year of Goucher's return home. Missionary Harry Caldwell, who had seen Goucher in Foochow and visited him in Baltimore, said other area congregations were begging for their $100 to begin construction, and several delegations requesting funds had to be turned down. Caldwell wrote, "I am sure you never invested a portion of your consecrated money where it would yield more immediate and greater results than in the erection of these houses. . . . When the fifteen 'Goucher Churches' are erected we will be in much better condition than this work has ever known before."[17]

After Goucher's soujourn in Korea, George Heber Jones assured him, "Your visit still lives in our memory. You did us good." But, he added, "When you left us we had little idea that we were to be plunged into such trials as have been ours." Now that Korea was under Japanese rule, there had been "bloodshed and terror for a time," followed by "intense political excitement." At the same time, owing to the ongoing revival movement in the country, the mission lacked sufficient personnel to serve all the new converts. Another Korean missionary pleaded with Goucher to find more workers: "You have a wide influence and you were our founder. WE MUST HAVE HELP." Bishop Merriman Harris also wrote, acknowledging the recent political upheavals, but bringing the good news that there were now

120 students enrolled at Pai Chai Hakdang. On the advice of Prince Ito, the Japanese resident-general, the government also had given the mission a valuable half-acre plot of land inside the East Gate on which to build a hospital—a project Ito and Goucher might have discussed during his recent visit.[18]

Even missionaries in Africa, a continent where Goucher was not so heavily involved, sought his assistance. Because John and Mary had given funds to start the East Africa mission in the 1880s, Erwin H. Richards, head of the Methodist mission in Inhambane (Mozambique), still referred to Goucher as the "Mother" of Africa, just as he called Bishop William Taylor the "Father." Richards applied his own plea: "Our East Coast work expects you to continue in full recognition of all your children."[19]

The plan for village schools that the Gouchers had instituted in India became a prospective model for other missions, and Richards had previously asked Goucher how to raise money for similar schools in Africa. "You advised me safely and I followed it carefully," Richards told his mentor, and he had been able to open fifteen schools at one station. By 1908, his work was growing, but the only financial aid he received from the mission office in New York was his salary. Richards intended to use a home furlough to reach out to as many Methodist conferences as possible for support. He again asked Goucher for advice: "Write me directing me in the safe way of procedure. I am certain the Continent of Africa will owe you an ample debt of gratitude."[20]

One way many missionaries raised money was by selling local crafts and curios to individuals in the United States. Items Richards had gathered to sell included a bark blanket, dolls, a hippo hide, a complete witch doctor's outfit, and a kaross—a cloak he claimed was made from more than two dozen gray jackal skins. Goucher the collector sent money for some curios for his own collection and persuaded one American buyer to pay $125 ($3,300) for the kaross, even though the asking price was $50. Richards wrote in appreciation: "You are an excellent character for doing the unexpected in a most profitable fashion. You talked and wrote $75 worth into that kaross."[21]

Goucher was still being asked for larger contributions. In 1903, he had donated funds toward establishing a boys' school in Chengtu, West China, but on joining the Board of Governors promoting the new union university there, he was asked for another gift toward the $50,000 ($1.3 million) the Methodist Episcopal Church had committed to the project. Joseph Beech, who had recruited him for the board, confessed, "I know something of how liberal you have been everywhere round the world and how many calls you must have, and for these reasons, and because we are asking so much in service I have feared to present this additional request." But Bishop Oldham, who still remembered "with deep gratitude" Goucher's early-1880s gift for the Anglo-Chinese College in Singapore, did not hesitate to ask him to become one of five trustees who would each "give or find" $10,000 ($265,000) for the school. A pledge in that amount or "any amount that may seem best to you," Oldham told Goucher, ". . . would not only greatly gratify me and help the proposed object, but it would strengthen me with others whom I approach."[22]

By now, keeping track of his numerous donations became a complex job in itself. Over the previous decade, and on his more recent global journey, Goucher had pledged (and was now paying out) several thousand dollars for various educational and church projects in South and East Asia. He also continued to help defray annual expenses at the Woman's College and Morgan College. As a hands-on donor, he followed where his monies were used, and that required sending payments at different times of the year to different countries, with fluctuating international exchange rates. Those waiting for funds might write to thank him, but also to inquire where their money was. One missionary helpfully volunteered, "Your own private check will serve to get the money just as well as a draft. Our bankers cash either." Another supplicant probably reflected other missionaries' thinking: "Now I do not want to be guilty of proving a nuisance, by troubling you needlessly. If therefore you will of your indulgence, let me know when each year I should send you the reminder you were good enough to ask me to give you, I shall be obliged." For Goucher, balancing philanthropic and personal financial commitments would prove even more challenging in the future.[23]

Goucher looked forward to his retirement as president, and he helped choose his successor at the Woman's College. Wanting his input, the trustees put him on a three-member national search committee, which considered more than fifty candidates. In May 1908, Methodist minister Eugene Allen Noble—a former hospital superintendent and then principal of the Centenary Collegiate Institute in New Jersey—was elected the college's third president; he assumed his duties in early July. *The American Star* commented on Goucher's role in the transition: "The change signifies that the man who took the college into his care as an infant has raised it to a strong, self-dependent maturity, and he can now turn it over to others in confidence that he made the future of the Woman's College, Baltimore's one higher institution for the education of woman, safe and sure."[24]

Now Goucher was free of daily responsibilities at the college, and he was ready for new challenges to join the ongoing projects that still held his interest. Soon the outdoor-loving explorer would undertake an expedition many might consider more taxing than relaxing—the one that began with a shipwreck.

John Goucher (center) with Prior Economos Eugenios,
Monastery of St. Catherine at Mount Sinai,
March 1909

*Courtesy of the Baltimore-Washington Conference Archives,
Lovely Lane United Methodist Church, Baltimore, Maryland*

FRESH AIR ADVENTURE

Chapter 18
(Winter 1909)

$\blacktriangleright\!\blacktriangleleft$

Life is intensely practical. Conscience, like the heart, is never entitled to a vacation.[1]

As 1909 dawned, Goucher was in Carthage, Missouri, visiting his brother David and sister Ella and her husband. David's wife Bell had died the previous October, when Goucher was in a Rochester, New York, homeopathic hospital for several weeks having two hernia operations; he had been "an acute sufferer" for several years. He had not been well enough to travel that fall to join the bereaved family members, but on New Year's Day, John and Eleanor were there to place wreaths on Bell's grave, and on those of his beloved mother and father.[2]

To aid his recuperation, his physician had urged him to have "complete and protracted" rest in the fresh air and especially to "let all mental work alone." Goucher's idea of taking his doctor's advice was to leave for Egypt in late January with his hiking and camping companion S. Earl Taylor; they planned to follow the exodus route of the Israelites, reaching Jerusalem in time for Easter. They would continue on to Damascus and Beirut, both then part of Syria, returning to Baltimore at the end of May. Goucher had arranged through a friend in Beirut for the necessary animals and supplies for the arduous journey. Crossing the Sinai Peninsula to Petra was potentially dangerous, so he and Taylor did some target practice at Alto Dale with a Winchester rifle and Colt automatic pistol John had purchased for the trip.[3]

The crash of their steamship *Republic* with the *Florida*, as described in the Introduction, captured the attention of the world press for several days. (Three years later, another ship of the White Star Line, the *Titanic*, would also draw international attention.) Goucher might have considered himself blessed; two passengers on the *Republic* had been killed, one of them in a cabin recommended by Goucher's travel agent. Once back on shore in New York, he expressed gratitude for what he saw as divine help in saving the lives of some 1,600 passengers and crew from both ships. He also praised "two agencies of man serving in perfect accord"—the technological advances of watertight compartments and the wireless telegraph: "How mighty is science after all and how great and wonderful are the strides it is making in the preservation of life."[4]

When the ships collided, thousands of gallons of water began pouring through a hole into the *Republic*'s engine room. Were it not for twelve collision bulkheads—quickly closed, isolating the engine room from the rest of the hold—the ship would have sunk in minutes, instead of remaining afloat for nearly forty hours. After the *Republic*'s passengers had been transferred, first to the *Florida* and then to the *Baltic*, three other ships that had responded to the *Republic*'s radio distress calls towed the crippled vessel toward shallower waters. One after another, the bulkheads finally broke under pressure and the watertight compartments filled; the ship sank in about 300 feet of water, south of No Man's Land near Martha's Vineyard. Captain Sealby and his second officer remained on board and were rescued just as it sank beneath the waves.[5]

The *Republic*'s Marconi wireless system, then a relatively new addition to naval communication, was crucial to the rescue. From his own wrecked cabin near the crash zone, the young Marconi operator began sending out the signal "C.Q.D," which meant "All stations, Distress." With the ship's electricity out, he relied on battery power. The signal was weak and its range limited, but a Marconi station picked up the calls at Nantucket, about sixty miles away; the operator there relayed the message to other Marconi-equipped ships. The *Baltic* responded and returned the evacuees to New York on the afternoon of January 25; the heavily damaged *Florida* limped into port a few hours later.[6]

In press interviews, Goucher was quick to praise the bravery of the captains and crews of all three vessels involved. He also noted the different reactions of those traveling on the two damaged ships: "The steerage passengers on the *Florida* were excited," he said—understandably enough, as they had recently survived an Italian earthquake; they "were not calculated to withstand the shock of the sea danger well." The *Republic*'s passengers, however, "were all people of culture, [who] had that remarkable gift of poise which acted as a steady press upon nerves that were almost breaking but did not."[7]

While Goucher was modest about his own role in the rescue, a Baltimore editorial praised him as a local hero:

> Dr. Goucher, president emeritus of the Woman's College, not only gained credit for himself, but reflected credit upon the city that holds him in high esteem as by his signal act of chivalry and self-abnegation in the trying hours of the *Republic*'s disaster. The circumstances were those of great fatigue, as well as great danger, but this college president, who has always preached the doctrine of manly graces combined with modesty, bent to the oar and refused to be relieved as boatload after boatload of passengers were conveyed from ship to ship.[8]

For his part, Goucher would only comment, "I did only what I conceived as my duty; that was all." But his travel companion Taylor testified, "One woman after another came up to Dr. Goucher and thanked him for his kindness." The many letters he received congratulating him on his safe return included one from Woman's College professor Lilian Welsh: "I knew you would give moral strength and spiritual comfort to your fellow passengers, but I did not for a moment think of your giving physical assistance in the work of rescue. . . . Nothing has affected me so deeply as the fact that you helped man a lifeboat. I can see you smile and say, 'Why not?' Yes, being you, why not?"[9]

After docking in New York three days after his departure, Goucher caught a train to Baltimore. He already had telephoned his Thomas Cook travel agent to book passage for another trans-Atlantic crossing barely forty-eight hours later; arriving at the Baltimore station Monday evening, he made a reservation for a sleeper compartment on the Tuesday night train back to New York. The ordeal of the past few days would not make him cancel his travel plans.

Goucher had called his daughters when he disembarked in New York, and they awaited his arrival at 2313. He passed the rest of the evening talking with them, fielding telephone calls from well-wishers, making to-do lists, and assigning shopping duties to restock for his trip. Goucher ended the day giving "special thanks to Our Father for safety and His peace continued."[10]

The next day was a frenzy of shopping to replace clothing and gear lost with the *Republic*. Goucher was asked if he intended to pursue reimbursement from the White Star Line for lost luggage. He replied laughingly, "I hadn't thought of anything like that because I was thankful to escape with my skin." (Although he would reconsider.) Tuesday afternoon, he and Janet went to Alto Dale to pick up some items; Baltimore merchants, who enjoyed his patronage and respected him as a city leader, came to his aid. Every one of them he approached, Goucher said, gave him "right of way," and by 6:30 that evening, everything from clothing to new eyeglasses had been delivered to his house in town. He spent the evening packing, receiving callers, and answering the telephone. By midnight, he was headed back to New York to resume the trip he felt was "absolutely necessary" for rest.[11]

✳ ✳ ✳

The following morning, January 27, 1909, Goucher met Taylor for breakfast, and after talking with a lawyer about collecting damages for their lost possessions, they embarked for England on the Cunard Line's *Lucania*, one of the in-bound ships that had responded to the *Republic*'s distress calls. Exhausted, Goucher spent two-thirds of the first three or four days at sea sleeping, and stayed in his bed ten or twelve hours a day for the remainder of the trip. But on February 2, the day Eugene Noble was to be installed as president of the Woman's College, his thoughts turned back to Baltimore. Before leaving, Goucher had composed a letter for the new president, which was read at Noble's installation, "a touching part of the ceremonies" according to a news account. Goucher had written, "While my presence is in no sense necessary to assure you of my confidence . . . it is a matter of keen regret to me that I am to be absent." He continued, speaking from the heart and his own experience:

> Permit me to congratulate you that this work with which you are intrusted [sic] is large, varied, and intricate enough to tax the ability of the wisest and strongest; that it is so vitally related to the conditions fundamental to the highest development

of society and the race as to be worthy of the complete consecration of the most richly endowed, that it is so manifestly under the generous guidance of God as to justify unwavering confidence in its future.

Goucher also wrote in his diary that he devoted much prayer to both Noble and the college on that installation day. He believed "the need for [the college's] influence and development and prospects for success are almost boundless."[12]

When Goucher and Taylor arrived in London, John did some last-minute shopping, buying "riding britches" and "securing many little things which we will need at the Army & Navy store." By the second week in February, he and his companion were sailing on another ship through the "Isles of Greece" to Port Said. They traveled on to Cairo, arriving a day ahead of their original schedule. They were met by Goucher's Beirut friend E. Franklin Hoskins, who had made their next travel arrangements. The three men crossed the Suez Canal in a small boat to meet the caravan that would be their movable home for the next two months.[13]

That "home" consisted of two sleeping tents; kitchen and dining tents, staffed by a cook and a table boy; and a lavatory tent. Daily operations were overseen by Milhem, the commissary, who acted as dragoman or interpreter, and who arranged for the thirty-nine campsites where the group would stop along their route. They were accompanied by Sheik Hammadi, leader of a nomadic Bedouin tribe. Hoskins (writing of the trip in the *National Geographic*) said the nomads wandered in search of food and water and "lived largely on supplies from Egypt and the proceeds of escorting groups of pilgrims to [Mount] Sinai."[14]

The "old Sheik," as Goucher called him, oversaw the twenty camels and fifteen cameleers that navigated the difficult terrain of the Sinai Peninsula, which was then under British control. Egypt had been an vassal state of the Ottoman Empire since the mid-nineteenth century, governed by the khedive, a viceroy of the sultan. By 1882, Great Britain had established its presence in the country to maintain political stability following an anti-European uprising; the khedive kept his position, but a British consul-general oversaw financial and governmental matters, making the country, in effect, a protectorate. Ten years later, the sultan granted the khedive the right to administer the Sinai; the British, seeking to ensure a buffer from any Turkish attempts to control the Suez Canal, unilaterally declared the boundary between Egypt and Turkey farther east on the peninsula. In 1906, under threat from the British navy, the sultan finally signed an agreement establishing an administrative demarcation line between Egypt and the Ottoman Empire. Delineated by a series of more than ninety masonry and iron pillars, the boundary ran in an almost straight line from Rafah on the Mediterranean, to Akabah (Aqaba) on the Red Sea.[15]

In his article, Hoskins described the landscape of the Sinai Peninsula as "a vast desert relieved by a few oases along the seacoast and deep among the network of rocky valleys." The party carried water barrels, but Goucher reported they once rode seventy-seven hours before finding a fresh supply. His "special camel" was named Um Barak, and they spent hours together each day. Goucher often included a notation in his diary such as, "Started at 7:15 A.M. and camped at 4:05 P.M. having 8 hours on our camels," or "We camped at 4:44 in site of a beautiful bay, after 9 hours on our camels." When the caravan reached the Gulf of Akabah, he recorded traveling about 350 miles in twenty days, 109 hours of which he spent riding Um Barak.[16]

Nature presented some challenges along the way. When the party first set out on February 19, a sirocco—a hot, dry windstorm— immediately delayed them twenty-four hours. Hoskins wrote that baggage outside the tents was nearly buried; inside, everything was covered with "fine yellow particles of desert sand." Goucher found it all "uncomfortable but interesting." Camping a few days later, the three friends had tea and then walked a mile or so to the Red Sea for what Goucher called "a delightful bath." But very late that same night, a sudden sea-squall blew his tent over as he slept on his cot. The seasoned traveler took it in stride: "I lay still as the Arabs re-erected [the tent], then gathered up my toilet articles, etc., out of the sand and slept until morning." Goucher noted this coincidence in timing: "The blow was at 2:30 A.M. the morning of [February] 23rd, just one month from the shipwreck which was at 5:30 on Jan. 23."[17]

On March 8, the caravan passed the 1906 boundary between Egypt and Turkey, and the caravan now faced other potential dangers.

The faltering Ottoman Empire had become known as the "Sick Man of Europe," as its sphere of influence dwindled. In 1878, soon after he assumed power, Sultan Abdul Hamid II had suspended a new constitution and dismissed the first Ottoman Parliament. He set up a system of palace spies, rewarded corrupt officials, restricted the press, incited hatred between Muslims and Christians, and jailed or killed real or perceived enemies. (In his diary, Goucher estimated the "Old Sultan" was responsible for the death of a person every fifteen minutes during his thirty-two years in power.)[18]

Early in the twentieth century, a group known as the "Young Turks," driven underground by the sultan's despotism, promoted government reform and modernization. Under its official designation as the Committee of Union and Progress (CUP), the group encouraged rebellion, aided by the Ottoman Empire's Third Army, originally established in the Balkans and then headquartered in Salonica, central Macedonia.

The CUP and the troops led a successful revolution in July 1908, forcing the sultan to reinstate the constitution and hold elections for a new parliament. Franklin Hoskins, who had lived in Syria for a number of years, wrote several newspaper articles describing the excitement the revolution engendered:

> If a prophet had appeared in July and announced that within a month the famous and infamous "camarilla" known as the "Palace party" [courtiers or favorites surrounding the ruler] would be broken up and scattered forever, no one could have believed.
>
> From time immemorial public gatherings of all kinds have been prohibited, and now, for the first time in the life of the present generation, crowds gathered at the open places . . . and speaker after speaker delivered impassioned addresses on the iniquities of the passing regime and the long sought liberty.[19]

Amnesty was granted to political exiles, the spy system was abolished, and daily newspapers went uncensored for the first time in more than three decades. The old regime was not ready to give up, however. The sultan sowed seeds of discontent in Parliament late in 1908, and plotted its overthrow with the help of the ruling class.

This chaos caused a loosening of government control at the far end of the Ottoman Empire that Goucher and his party would be crossing. Bedouin tribes, headed by sheiks, settled disputes among their own and represented the tribe before the provincial government. These independent agents often approached travelers in a menacing way, demanding money for safe passage. In helping plan their trip, Hoskins had undoubtedly warned his friend about uncertain situations they might face, hence that target practice at Alto Dale.[20]

As a precaution, the governor of the region had assigned his military assistant, a Turkish major, to meet the travelers at Akabah. (The governor, who was in Damascus at the time, had sent telegrams to various outposts, extending "every protection and courtesy" to the Goucher–Hoskins party.) After crossing the Sinai desert, they no longer needed camels, which were replaced by horses and pack mules that Hoskins had arranged for in Beirut. They arrived fifteen minutes before the travelers, the new animals bearing fresh provisions, charcoal, and two boxes of oranges from groves at Jaffe. There also were letters from home; Goucher welcomed news from his daughters, "my three dearest." Hoskins noted, "There was great joy in the camp that night."[21]

The major offered to have several soldiers accompany the group, although Goucher felt they could take care of themselves, if they could "refuse without offense." Early the next day, however, as the caravan prepared to leave Akabah, two sheiks and their Bedouin followers arrived. Hoskins explained their sudden appearance: When a traveler arrived in the area, "the news is sped by means as mysterious as the wireless, and hungry fellows with their lean camels hasten from every tribe and wrangle . . . over the right and privilege to share in their transport of the traveler and his outfit."[22]

The sheiks threatened the party's safety unless a fee was paid, but Goucher refused to deal with them. The major then sent word that he could not allow the party to leave until its security was assured. Goucher suspected the military man was either intimidated by the sheiks or wanted to share in the bounty, and he called the situation "an interesting case of Turkish intrigue, duplicity and incompetency." Since the caravan was ready to go, the three travelers told the major they would be leaving unless he gave them written orders to stay—and then they would report him to the governor. As Goucher wrote in his diary, "We won out."[23]

After waiting three hours in the sun, the caravan set out after lunch, but the Bedouins insisted on sending the two sheiks along after them. Perhaps realizing the risk to himself if anything happened to the travelers, the major assigned up to two dozen soldiers to accompany the party along the route. Goucher and his companions declined to pay any fee or recognize in any way the sheiks following them; he called them "a bad lot and [they] mean ill." One of the sheiks, named Aly, continued to approach the party and even tied a goat to a tent stake as a peace offering. The travelers again refused to deal with him directly, but through their commissary, they paid for the goat and gave it to the soldiers for their dinner. When the caravan reached its next main camp, the persistent sheik demanded a toll of three pounds per animal and one pound for each person for having conducted the party safely thus far. Goucher called this "a bluff at which the officers wink and perhaps divide." Sheik Aly "got nothing from us, not even a salaam."[24]

The party continued on to Petra, where they spent a week. There three sheiks, including the chief one in the region, tried "to hold us up," as Goucher wrote in his travel journal. "After some altercation, we told them we would have nothing to do with them, unless they called at our camp when we were at rest, and then we would talk it over with them." Learning of the governor's edict of protection, the leader tried to make amends by presenting them with a lamb, asking for a good report of his behavior. When the group prepared to leave Petra, Goucher related his final encounter with the sheik:

> He again called this afternoon to say goodbye. We served him coffee and gave him a good time, but no baksheesh. When told by Dr. Hoskins that I have 3 daughters at home, he said to me, 'Give me one of your daughters for wife and then our relations will always be that of brothers and mostly friendly.'

Although these encounters with various sheiks passed without violent incident, a few days later the party was reminded of their uncertain position. Some pilgrims returning on foot from Mecca asked to sleep near the caravan because they had already been robbed four times by bandits. A few months after the trip ended, Hoskins would write Goucher with a proud description of their handling these encounters in the desert: "We Jesse Jamesed that part of the country."[25]

✳ ✳ ✳

This trip was as much a spiritual journey for Goucher as a restorative trip. It enriched his personal experiences of faith and prompted him toward reflection. On March 21, he wrote in his travel diary: "Forty years ago today was the first Sabbath I spent on the Baltimore Circuit as Junior Preacher and today has been full of memories and thanksgiving." Now he could finally look upon some of the ancient Biblical sites that he had read about and studied for so long. An early stop on this pilgrimage was Mount Sinai, where the party was welcomed at the Eastern Orthodox Monastery of St. Catherine, on the site of a fort built by the Emperor Justinian in the sixth century. Goucher saw the site of the burning bush, and like other pilgrims, climbed the approximately 3,700 "steps of penitence" carved into the rocks above the monastery, approaching the summit of Jebel Musa (Mount Moses). He wrote that he stood at the top and "read the account of God's giving of the law to Moses and greatly enjoyed the record and my meditations." He also recited the Ten Commandments aloud, and claimed Taylor could hear him distinctly 500 yards in one direction and 900 in another, despite a "contrary breeze." The library at St. Catherine's was the oldest in the Christian world, and Goucher spent several hours studying early Greek manuscripts. Before leaving, their party drank coffee and ate quince jelly with the prior, Economos Eugenios. (Taylor captured the event in the photo at the beginning of this chapter.)[26]

At other stops, Goucher took pleasure in reading the Old Testament, matching Biblical events with their actual locations:

> Have been traveling along the Red Sea a good part of the day through what has been identified by many as the Wilderness of Sin. If so, here Israel was fed with quails, which were blown from Africa in great quantities and picked up when tired, just as one was picked up by one of our Arabs and brought to us. Here also the provision of Manna commenced.

> Went to the principal high place this AM, cir. 500' above the level of our camp [at Petra], and read the Bible references from Edom, from Genesis to Malachi, with thrilling interest and great profit.

> This morning we rode over to Nebo [the mountain on which Moses died]. . . . Such is the course of the Jordan, the bay of the Dead Sea . . . and the positions of the mountains as make the land of Canaan from Dan to Beersheba including Jerusalem and Bethlehem easily visible. On Nebo we read the later chapters of Deuteronomy with peculiar interest.[27]

At times, after inspecting a site, Goucher disagreed with the accepted Biblical interpretation. He described in his diary a visit to Mount Hor, supposedly where Aaron, brother of Moses, had died.

> I accepted for the time this tradition [of Aaron's burial place] as true and gave myself up to the natural meditations and thoughts suggested by Numbers 20.14 [and following verses] and greatly enjoyed the excursion. Our horses got lost on the wadi side and I walked from the 'Tomb of Aaron' at the top of the edge to Petra, where the Roman road from Gaza entered, in 1½ hours and from there to camp in ¾ of an hour.

The long walk back gave Goucher time to mull over what he had seen: "My judgment is very clear that this is not where Aaron died."[28]

When the group finally reached the Jordan River and crossed into Canaan at the beginning of April, Goucher moved on from contemplating the Old Testament story of the Exodus to the New Testament accounts of Jesus' final days. They spent Palm Sunday near Jericho; Goucher pondered how "the ancient walls of this almost forgotten city fell at the blow of Israel's trumpet in the time of Joshua." He wrote of "the heart stirring intent" of this site from which Jesus started to Jerusalem and his death. Goucher even determined that departure's probable date—Friday, March 31, AD 30. "How wonderfully the record has refreshed my soul today."[29]

The Goucher–Hoskins party rode their horses through Jerusalem and camped on the west side of the city. Like many tourists, the men visited sites of religious significance to Christians, Jews, and Muslims.

They rode around the Mount of Olives and out to Bethlehem; they saw the Western Wall and "studied the plans of the Temple." They were also granted a special permit to visit and photograph the Haram al-Sharif. On Good Friday, they, like other pilgrims, walked to Calvary along the Via Dolorosa and "read the record of this day." Goucher had a severe headache on Easter Sunday, so he stayed in his tent. He did not attend church, but he found the day spent alone "most profitable in its quiet suggestiveness and deep impressiveness."[30]

The following day, rain was expected; Goucher and his party struck camp and stored everything under cover. The men checked into a hotel for the night, the first time since leaving Suez more than seven weeks earlier. With a proper desk in his room, Goucher caught up on correspondence, writing sixty letters and postcards. Over the next week, the party continued north on horseback from Jerusalem to Tiberias on the Sea of Galilee, again solemnizing sites along the way with Biblical readings. Goucher and his friends bid goodbye to their retinue and animals at Tiberias before boarding trains to Damascus and then to Beirut, where they spent their last few days in the Middle East. Continuing his record keeping, Goucher noted that over the previous month, he had covered about 650 miles on horseback, spending over 160 hours in the saddle.[31]

The three men arrived in Damascus on a Saturday, as political turmoil in the Ottoman Empire reached a peak. About ten days before, Sultan Abdul Hamid's Reactionists had begun a counter-revolutionary action in Constantinople against the Committee of Union and Progress. "Things are very strenuous here in Damascus," Goucher wrote. He said a massacre of Christians in the city was planned for the next day, but the French minister had sent for the leader of the city's Muslims, threatening him with hanging if anyone were killed.[32]

Goucher, Taylor, and Hoskins called on the American consular agent in Damascus, who secured from the governor-general of Syria and the marshall of the Fifth Division of the Turkish army assurances of the men's "safety and comfort" as they traveled on. Both the American and British consuls shared private and official dispatches with the men, updating them on the conflict; Goucher felt it was "a great privilege to be so favored in these strenuous times." Soon after arriving in the city, he wrote that the Progressives had "overthrown the Reactionists, captured the barracks, and compelled the retirement of the Old Sultan." This change caused "much rejoicing here among many," as there had been "great fear and business was paralyzed" during the upheaval. They were reassured of political stability when they were en route to Beirut. Two high officials boarded the train and entered their compartment to let them know a new sultan had been chosen: Reshad Efendi, brother of Abdul Hamid, was to become Sultan Mehmed V.[33]

When they reached Beirut, Hoskins enjoyed a reunion with his wife and children. After roughing it for weeks, Goucher and Taylor suddenly had "two or three times as many invitations for dinner, luncheon and teas" than they could accept before leaving for home. Goucher attended a reception thrown by the victorious Committee of Union and Progress, and was guest of honor at a dinner given by the American consul general. For the first time on this trip, Goucher spoke at chapel services, at two girls' schools and a college. After riding camels and horses for a thousand miles, Goucher and Taylor were treated to a different style of ride—in an automobile. With Hoskins and his wife, they drove over fifty miles to Sidon, about two and a half hours each way. They visited a silk worm farm and stopped at an orange grove, whose Muslim owner insisted they take two bushels with them for their upcoming sea voyage. As their trip wound down to its final days, Goucher wrote in his travel diary with satisfaction: "We have had an exceptionally delightful time, and far more profitable than we had anticipated. We have not had a monotonous moment nor an incident to mar our delight since leaving New York."[34]

On May 2, 1909, after saying goodbye to the Hoskins family, Gouchr and Taylor boarded a steamer for Naples—with stops at Rhodes, Constantinople, Smyrna, and Athens—to meet their ship for New York. The men had one last chance to witness the revolution that had been swirling around them. At Constantinople, they hired a guide to visit "the barracks, palace and places showing evidences of the struggle." Already the new regime had made changes, and a military escort was no longer necessary. Goucher and Taylor were able to go "anywhere we desired and unmolested, visiting the mosques and bazaars freely, and photographing in the streets with no questions asked."[35]

Once in Naples, they took a day trip to Rome, where Goucher could see the progress of the Methodist mission properties he had inspected on previous trips. He reminisced about earlier visits, the first more than thirty years before, and wrote of "renewing my acquaintance with old friends—the Forum, Colosseum, Pantheon, etc., which I have studied and enjoyed in other days." From Naples, Goucher also made a side trip to Pompeii. The armchair archeologist was "much pleased with the improved method of conserving the ruins, i.e. leaving everything found in excavating as nearly as may be in the original position." Before leaving Naples, he purchased two very old souvenirs—a 2,000-year-old Tuscan scarab and an intaglio, or carved gem stone, from about 200 B.C. These objects, along with Egyptian spears and swords and ancient Babylonian seals he had also picked up on the trip, went into his collection of world artifacts back home.[36]

Goucher and Taylor arrived in New York on May 27, exactly four months after leaving on their second attempt to cross the Atlantic. In addition to souvenirs, photographs, and memories, Goucher brought his meticulous written record of the trip. At the end of his diary for 1909, he included the location of each camp they had pitched, along with the elevation and temperature at each stop. He recorded covering more than 16,000 miles, broken down into travel on water, rail, camel, and horse, as well as "autos, carriages, street and electric cars." He estimated the cost for this trip as 1,265 British pounds ($6,200 in 1909, and more than $150,000 a century later). At journey's end, that outlay seemed worthwhile, for Goucher noticed a steady improvement in his health.[37]

He returned to Baltimore ready to undertake new tasks. His friend William V. Kelley had predicted on his retirement from the Woman's College: "The work of your life up to date is very great, Dear Dr. Goucher, in magnitude and in quality—its total value is immense. You will add to it, when you are well rested; and in future years you will have leisure to put on your work some of the finishing touches you have doubtless dreamed out in your mind." Over the next dozen years, Goucher would do just that, as he solidified his position as an international educator and statesman of the church.[38]

President Eugene A. Noble
has the honor to announce that
by order of the Board of Trustees and
by act of the General Assembly of Maryland
the Corporate name of
The Woman's College of Baltimore
has been changed to
Goucher College

Baltimore, Maryland
March the fifth
nineteen hundred and ten

Courtesy of the Goucher College Library,
Special Collections and Archives, Baltimore, Maryland

A LIVING MONUMENT

Chapter 19
(Winter 1910)

━━━━━━━━━━━━◆◆━━━━━━━━━━━━

The two most important things in this world are life and education.
. . . Without education, there would be no development. Everything
would remain in status quo or deteriorate.[1]

As Goucher passed through his sixties and seventies, he thrived on new intellectual and physical challenges. This "short compact man, whose white hair and beard grow with the compactness with which the whole man is formed," stayed involved with civic causes, the two Baltimore colleges he had long supported, and the national and international committees and boards of which he was a member. In his final dozen years, as his friend Kelley foresaw, Goucher focused on the two passions that had gripped him since his youth and were a centerpiece of his years with Mary—missions and education, especially in East Asia, where he had been a pioneer.[2]

The year 1910 brought milestones: Goucher's sixty-fifth birthday and the twenty-fifth anniversary of the Woman's College of Baltimore. That year the trustees assured ongoing recognition for his efforts by renaming that institution Goucher College. As far back as 1893, one professor had complained the title "Woman's College of Baltimore" was not distinctive enough; other women's colleges, often with much inferior standards, had cropped up using similar names. Others found that generic title "discordant, unadaptable, unrhythmical." A few years later, when he was proposing Norse names for the residence halls, Joseph Shefloe told alumnae he had suggested naming the school in honor of Mary and John Goucher. Its president took a dim view of that suggestion, but in 1898, students took up the idea of a rebranding: "We are a first rank college with a third-rate name." Their suggestions included Calvert College, in honor of Lord Baltimore; Goucher College, "for our honored President"; and even Fisher College, "for the much loved wife of our President." No action was taken, but the idea of naming the college for the Gouchers continued to arise from time to time. A *Baltimore Sun* article noted that whenever Goucher was presented with it, "with characteristic modesty, he strongly objected and the matter was dropped."[3]

Goucher's retirement as president spurred renewed talk of a name change. The Student Government Association sent a petition to the Board of Trustees in May 1908, again pointing out the inadequacy of the current name and requesting a new one be chosen, preferably Goucher College. Were that name not an option, they requested "some other individualistic and characteristic" title. Early in June, members of the Alumnae Association paid tribute to Goucher at their annual meeting: "We are increasingly sensible, in our various walks of life, of the debt we owe the college. In this debt, which we gratefully acknowledge, we count your genial spirit, your wise sympathy and your high aspirations for us who now offer you our affectionate loyalty." They sent their own resolution to the trustees after Goucher reluctantly consented to putting his name on their alma mater. As he once told a friend, "I never like to speak about myself, either in public or in private," but according to an official college publication, he finally gave in "when he felt that those who loved the college and had its most vital interests at heart demanded this concession from him."[4]

Not everyone liked the new name. Some questioned whether it was necessary at all. A few chapters of the Alumnae Association threatened to withdraw if the change went through, although a majority of graduates felt the naysayers were "assuming a personal interest point of view and forgetting the larger interest of the College." Other observers—perhaps even Goucher himself—wondered if naming a college for a particular individual "would be perpetuating a monument to a man and not to an education," thus limiting donations. A *Baltimore Sun* article wondered if the Johns Hopkins University, founded nine years before the Woman's College, would have received more gifts had it not been named after one person.[5]

Even John Van Meter, who had worked closely with Goucher since the idea for the school was first raised, told the students who had signed the resolution, "No change of name is desirable. . . . You must count me on the opposite side." This declaration seemed a sign of growing friction between the two men who had worked together so long—the stay-at-home dean who had run the college on a daily basis and the globe-trotting president who was its public face. One could detect an earlier touch of asperity in Van Meter's reply to a 1907 inquiry for details about Goucher's international itinerary: "It is not his custom to allow his associates in work to know his movements. They must guess at them." Many years later, Van Meter laid the blame for their growing estrangement on Goucher, saying it were as if his old friend "had slammed a door in my face and turned the key."[6]

At a special meeting in June 1908, where trustees were to debate and vote on the name change, several spoke out in favor; Van Meter again opposed it, fearing it would hurt the college's interests in the Baltimore community. His stated reason echoed old and unfounded allegations of ulterior motives, dating back to when Goucher first donated the land: "While Dr. Goucher has many friends in the city who would be glad to honor him, he also has enemies, made in the course of business transactions, who would seize the opportunity to attribute such action to his own strategy and to selfish motives." Trustee R. Tynes Smith later noted another ongoing animosity toward Goucher "on the part of some of his associates." Goucher's "rather rapid and remarkable advance to prominence," Smith felt, had "engendered a feeling of jealousy and envy which has degenerated into actual, and sometimes active, enmity." He admitted that Goucher, like everyone, "has his weak points [and] his optimism sometimes goes to the brink of rashness." But Smith added, "[It] is this very optimism which has been the mainspring in his accomplishment of some pretty big things."[7]

Longtime trustee and donor Benjamin Bennett also spoke up at the meeting, saying "the temper of the community was unfavorable to such a [name] change and would probably do harm," though not for the reasons Van Meter or Smith stated. While the words "of Baltimore" could give the false impression students were primarily drawn from the local community, some who opposed the change thought the original name added luster to the city's reputation. Van Meter appealed to Goucher, sitting with the other trustees, to end the discussion. When the board's secretary made a motion to withdraw the proposal and expunge the discussion from the minutes, everyone suspected Goucher had quietly made the suggestion.[8]

Instead, a motion was carried to defer action until President Eugene Noble's first official meeting with the board in November. A news story confirmed Noble's own endorsement: "My greatest asset as your president is that I am the successor of Dr. Goucher." But he also understood it would require modifying the charter, and it was better to delay action in order to address other needed modifications at the same time. Noble appointed a five-member committee to review the matter with him, and after a year's deliberation, he made his report to the board. On February 2, 1910, a special meeting was held—"as solemn as a funeral and a wedding combined," according to one person who was there— to vote on the propositions before it.[9]

The first motion was to change the name to Goucher College. Van Meter, whose opposition had only grown more intense, later related his version of what transpired: When Noble put forth the motion, Goucher "rose immediately and declared vigorously that if this change was proposed with the expectation that its adoption would induce him to continue and enlarge his gifts to the college, it was a mistake." He declared his chief interest had "always been on missions" and he now planned to devote himself to that area. He did not "forbid or decline the honor that the article sought to thrust upon him," but with that, Goucher grabbed his hat and coat from the chair next to him, left the room, and did not return.[10]

His remarks and exit, Van Meter said, "created a sensation." The new president reminded the trustees of the college's precarious financial situation and urged them to pass the motion. He believed Goucher would never let the college that bore his and Mary's name go under, but would continue to support it, either personally or by encouraging others to donate. Van Meter, persuaded, withdrew his objections. Following further deliberations, Noble later told alumnae, the motion for the institution to be known as "Goucher College" passed unanimously.[11]

The meeting that had begun in the afternoon stretched into the evening, and ended too late for the vote to make the morning newspapers. Nevertheless, Shefloe, that longtime advocate of the name change, learned of the outcome as soon as it occurred and spread the news himself:

How I thrill in remembering the circumstances which gradually led up to the action of the Board of Trustees that memorable evening, when, at ten o'clock, Dr. Widerman [a trustee], by special prearrangement, slipped out of the meeting for a moment to tell me the most gratifying news that I was now a <u>professor in Goucher College</u>! Within one hour I had telegraphed this news to Mrs. Shefloe [in New York], and to alumnae in Boston, Chicago, Des Moines, Kansas City, and San Francisco, etc. The next morning, at seven o'clock, Dr. Goucher received a telegram from Mrs. Shefloe, addressed to <u>Goucher College</u>—the <u>first</u> communication to be received thus addressed.[12]

When an alumna teaching at the Leland Stanford Junior University in California received Shefloe's news, she immediately wrote Goucher expressing her personal satisfaction—and that of other alumnae she knew—that "our college will go down to the world in name, as well as in deed, a memorial to the guidance and inspiration and sacrifice of yourself and Mrs. Goucher." In the next issue of the college magazine, Noble reassured alumnae, "Nothing is lost, and much may be gained by this vital movement." He reminded them of their personal associations with Mary and/or John, and the connotations the new name would hold for them: "memories of hospitality, of rare, sweet courtesy, of wise words spoken, of generous giving, of cheering encouragements, of uplifting sympathies, of strong manhood and ideal womanhood; and Goucher College will be the 'Open Sesame' to some of the rarest and most helpful recollections."[13]

Current students who had lobbied for the change felt vindicated:

We, who for over twenty years have been well-nigh nameless, who have suffered hopeless confusion with institutions of similar name but inferior standing, who when the world bestowed upon us the title 'Ladies College of Baltimore' have inwardly raged, while we outwardly pitied an ignorant public, we at last have had a name conferred upon us. And as for that name . . . is it not mentioned always . . . with a loving thought of those who bear and have borne it?[14]

As a further sign of support, early on the second morning after the trustees' decision, students donned academic caps and gowns and marched in procession from Goucher Hall to 2313, singing out the new name in a quickly revised college chant. Hearing their approach, Goucher came to the front door to thank them for the visit. Then, according to *The Baltimore Sun*, "very heartily rang out the fresh young voices in cheer, 'Goucher, Goucher, Goucher!'" That evening, he welcomed seniors, soon to receive redesigned diplomas, to a reception at his home and presented each with a red carnation in recognition of their class color and class flower, one of his traditions.[15]

Goucher also heard from Chancellor Day from Syracuse University, who hailed this recognition for his friend and "the grand woman who cooperated and coordinated with you in that marvelous work":

> It is a great thing educationally to have the name of a man who
> has done so much for the education of women live not only
> in enduring stone but [in] living, active personalities. I never
> thought much of marble tombs or granite shafts but I think such
> a memorial as this is every way worthy and has a language that
> will live as long as the centuries endure. Nothing too great and
> good can come to you.[16]

Goucher accepted the honor but did not let it (or anything else) interrupt his work. A few days after the trustees' announcement, he was in New York for meetings when he was struck by a car while crossing a street. He bandaged his badly sprained wrist and completed his business before returning to Baltimore. With his arm in a sling, he immediately left town again, this time for a month's speaking tour that took him west to Denver and Salt Lake City.[17]

Passport for John Goucher, January 1911

Courtesy of the Baltimore-Washington Conference Archives,
Lovely Lane United Methodist Church, Baltimore, Maryland

A NEW CAREER

Chapter 20
(Mid-1910-Mid-1911)

━━━━━━━━━━━━━━━◆◀━━━━━━━━━━━━━━━

Be true to your best self and high possibilities. Be worthy of self respect, worthy of the confidence of your fellow-men, worthy of the approval of God.[1]

As Goucher had told the college Board of Trustees in February 1910, missions interested him above all else, and now he had the time to focus on them. That spring, he delivered a series of five lectures over four days: *Growth of the Missionary Concept*. The *Philadelphia Record* reported of them, "Dr. Goucher has traveled far and observed closely, and the opinions he advances are informative on the matter about which there is much indifference and misunderstanding." He lectured first at Syracuse University, and then, over a period of a month, at Northwestern, Ohio Wesleyan, and Wesleyan Universities.[2]

The lectures, which *The Methodist Quarterly Review* called "crisp" and "compact," were titled "The Impossible," "The Improbable," "The Imperative," "The Indispensable," and "The Inevitable." The *Times-Picayune* provided a synopsis:

> He examines the arguments of the superficial observer who thinks the evangelization of the world impossible and those of the more careful observer who regards the solution as improbable. He shows that it is imperative that we should co-operate with the Divine Leader. . . . That Christ has assumed the world's salvation as his special mission makes his relation to it indispensable, and is the guarantee that the complete solution of the problem is inevitable.[3]

As in his 1882 Missionary Sermon, Goucher proclaimed the United States the leader in world evangelization. He offered as reasons its geographic position "in the highway between the Pacific and Atlantic"; its relationship to both Europe and Asia; its "marvelous history, in which the hand of God can be seen in every stage"; the character of its Anglo-Saxon people, with their "genius" for Protestant Christianity; and the vitality and evangelistic spirit of Christian churches and other institutions that were "reaching out and laying hold of the strategic points of the world." These talks, which devoted particular attention to China, were meant to encourage the college and university students who heard them to pursue missionary work and to garner financial support for the missions. The 1910 lectures were so well received, they were published as a book the following year. A review in the *California Christian Advocate* stated that Goucher was not only well qualified to speak on missionary work, he had "the power to transfer his feelings and convictions to the printed page" as well. (A biographical sketch of Goucher two decades later, however, said his writings were "slender both in bulk and importance.")[4]

In June, Goucher would deepen his commitment to missionary work when he traveled to London and then on to Edinburgh to attend the 1910 World Missionary Conference (Edinburgh Conference). Those meetings would help shape his work and travels in the years to come. Goucher was among the 1,200 delegates, drawn primarily from the major Protestant denominations and missionary societies in the United States and Northern Europe; a few came from newly formed Christian churches in South and East Asia, and there were hundreds of unofficial visitors. One attendee noted men and women of every race and color and of all walks of life and political persuasions were there, "from the Archbishop of Canterbury to the native Christian from the hill tribes of Assam" in India. One delegate commented it was "a rare sight to see the crowds eager to pay 50 cents each for tickets to missionary meetings." While two earlier ecumenical conferences in London in 1888 and New York in 1900 had examined Protestant missionary endeavors worldwide, the Edinburgh Conference focused on missionary work in non-Christian countries. The clarion call of the period—"Evangelization of the World in This Generation"—echoed in the reports of the eight commissions, each the product of two years of research. Goucher had served on a commission of special interest to him: Education in Relation to the Christianization of National Life.[5]

After ten days of meetings, notable for a spirit of cooperation among the various denominations and missionary societies, delegates voted to form a Continuation Committee to further research issues raised, and to foster greater efficiency in and coordination of missionary work. John R. Mott, whom Goucher knew from his work with the Student Volunteer Movement and the World's Student Christian Federation, had chaired the Edinburgh Conference and was chosen to chair this new committee of thirty-five members. The group, to be based in New York, was charged with forming nine special sub-committees, including one on Christian Education in the Mission Field. Goucher was chosen to chair its American section, which was to concentrate on Asia and the Levant (the countries along the eastern Mediterranean); the European section would focus on Africa and India. Soon after the Edinburgh Conference adjourned, Goucher assembled his group to define the scope of its work. He would continue to involve himself with Methodist committees and projects he had long supported, but now his charge called for extensive interactions with other Protestant missionary and educational efforts.[6]

After Edinburgh, Goucher remained in London for a few days to chair a meeting of the West China Union University (WCUU) Board of Governors. Following the China centenary events he had attended in 1907, four Protestant mission boards from the United States, Great Britain, and Canada had established a joint educational enterprise in Chengtu; each was responsible for funding the purchase of land and the construction of a building in which to hold classes, and for providing housing for students and faculty. The Board of Governors, comprised of three representatives from each mission board, would oversee policy and administration and the university's development. Goucher, involved with the organization from its early stages, was elected chair. In March 1910, ten students attended the first classes at the university.

Writing on stationery from his London hotel, Goucher penned a description of the university's opportunities and its future, personifying it (much as he had once done in describing the Woman's College as a "maiden"): "The WCUU is but an infant, which means its wealth is in the opportunities, not in its achievements. For this Infant is well born and has distinguished relations. It has a vigorous cry and is born to large inheritance." In six months' time, he would visit the infant university in person. In years to come, those who presided over its growth would say Goucher came to regard it as "one of his children," and they were "happy to look to him as one of our fathers."[7]

A 1911 *Baltimore Sun* editorial asserted that "a casual observer" who saw Goucher overseeing farm work at Alto Dale "might [imagine] that his only anxiety" was the yield of the crops and the price they would get. But such an observer would be "entirely mistaken because this Rev. Dr. Goucher has his mind on enterprises related not to bushels or dollars, but to the uplifting of human kind of many tongues in many climes and within the boundaries of many longitudinal circles." His new role in promoting Asian schools and missions for the Continuation Committee was almost a whole new career. He would honor the pledges he had already made in India, but the primary focus of his work now shifted to East Asia, after three decades of supporting work there.[8]

✳ ✳ ✳

Within three months of the Edinburgh Conference, Goucher set off across the Pacific, on his third trip to Asia. As ever, when conducting work for the Methodist Episcopal Church, and as he would when conducting interdenominational business, Goucher paid his own travel expenses. His daughters Elizabeth and Eleanor came along; Janet, who had married Henry Clay Miller in September 1909, stayed in Baltimore. En route to Japan, the ship stopped in Honolulu, where Goucher was hosted by Korean émigrés and spoke at a Korean school. His friends Soper and Ishizaka met the family when they arrived in Yokohama in mid-October 1910. The next day they traveled to Tokyo, and as on previous visits, Aoyama Gakuin students and teachers greeted him at the train station.[9]

Over two weeks in Japan, Goucher combined research for his Continuation Committee with activities at Aoyama Gakuin. In Tokyo, he also met with Premier Katsuro Taro. The month before Goucher's arrival, Japan had annexed Korea, and in their meeting, Katsura attempted to justify that move to his visitor. Owing to Japan's rise in East Asia over the previous fifteen years, he told Goucher, "heavy responsibility is resting on Japan's shoulders in fulfilling its heaven bestowed mission." Korea, meanwhile, "had not been capable of governing herself and in past caused Japan to engage in two great wars." Following the Russo-Japanese War, the premier assured his guest, "she became Japan's protectorate but [that] never was satisfactory so she was annexed which I believe was best for Korea and best for all and it will no doubt bring a very happy result to the people of Korea." Katsura said his government expected to enforce uniform laws in both countries and to establish the same system of education in Korea as in Japan. He asked Goucher to convey to missionaries in Korea that "the same privileges allowed to the Christian education work in Japan will be allowed in Korea also."[10]

At the end of October, only a few hours before Goucher and his daughters left for Korea, he met with Terauchi Masatake, the country's new governor-general, who would become Japan's prime minister in 1916. The meeting provided a useful introduction between the two men, who would each exert influence over Japanese and Korean religious and educational affairs in the coming years. The Goucher party finally arrived in Seoul in time for the opening celebration of the silver anniversary of the Methodist mission. While Goucher characterized Japan as "the leader of the Far East in Arts and Sciences and material progress," he considered Korea the "leader in Spirituality." Twenty-five years after Appenzeller and Scranton had established the mission in that country with the Gouchers' backing, the Korea Annual Conference boasted seven districts; 50,000 members, probationers, and inquirers; and 6,000 boys and girls enrolled in Methodist schools.[11]

Goucher's ten-day visit revealed the new political dynamics. Katsura had assured Goucher the Japanese education system would be established in Korea, but the government expected Korean schools to steer students away from their own language and customs, to foster "such national spirit as will contribute to the existence and welfare of our empire," as one official later explained. Japanese authorities regarded with suspicion church-sponsored schools influenced by foreign missionaries, fearing they encouraged independent thinking and nationalist sentiment. Realistic about Japanese dominance and wanting to prepare young Korean Christians to assist their countrymen, Goucher created several scholarships for students at Pai Chai Hakdang, allowing a few young men to take upper level classes at Aoyama Gakuin in Tokyo before beginning courses in its Theological School.

Goucher later explained his reasoning to the treasurer of the Board of Foreign Missions: He was "anxious that the [Korean] leadership of our Church should be familiar with the Japanese spirit, Japanese language, [and] should have a chance of studying the Japanese government in the home land and have much more advanced preparation than was possible in Korea." Although he believed it was usually best to educate students close to home, young men could not pursue higher religious training in Korea under the current government. Goucher was told that no Korean parents would send their sons to Japan to study, but all his scholarships were used over the next dozen years.[12]

Seeking firsthand information on the status of the Korean missions, Goucher traveled to remote parts of the country. As one missionary later wrote him:

> You did what so few, who are interested in missions, think of doing—you left the beaten track and went out to see the work among the interior towns. So many who come to see the work never get beyond Seoul and Pyengyang, and leave with the idea that they have seen all phases of the mission work. They miss a great deal, because they will not be persuaded to do as you were so willing to when you were with us.[13]

By the second week in November, John, Elizabeth, and Eleanor Goucher had moved on to China. Here, too, there had been political developments. Emperor Guangxu had died in 1908, followed a day later by Empress Dowager Cixi, the country's de facto ruler for a decade. On her deathbed, she chose Pu Yi, who was less than three years old, to be the next emperor, under the regency of his father Prince Chun. The weakness and unpopularity of the Qing dynasty led to a series of uprisings, which were ultimately unsuccessful. Despite the country's unsettled state, Goucher detected an energy that had been lacking before. He later described China's recent evolution:

> Her condition has ceased to be one of inertia and is rapidly becoming one of momentum. Her past is a question of arrested development, not incompetence. She is belated, not incapable. . . . She is no longer looking backward but forward. She has ceased marking time and is moving with a swinging stride in an unfamiliar way toward an uncertain future; expecting from other nations the inherent rights of a peer.

He also considered China's future:

> Changes in the 'Celestial Empire' are being made so rapidly
> and are so stupendous and far-reaching as to be almost
> incomprehensible. . . . No one can consider the ultimate
> humanity, no matter at what angle he seeks to approach,
> without seeing the Dragon lies athwart his meditations and
> he is forced to recognize that China must be reckoned with
> as a determinative factor. She is wrestling single handed with
> a series of crises—governmental, social, economic, ethical,
> educational. Her struggle and its outcome involve national
> crises of the utmost gravity.[14]

In Peking, Goucher found a welcoming letter from Wilson S.
Lewis, resident bishop of China at Foochow: "There has been large
expectation of your coming, and I realize that this note of mine is
but one in the chorus of welcome that greets you." By the end of
November, the family had moved to Shanghai. One of Goucher's
responsibilities there was to inspect the Methodist Publishing House
he had helped establish almost a decade earlier. He was pleased to see
that the plant was "overcrowded with business" and that a "steady,
growing demand" would require an expansion of operations before
long. He quickly enacted a plan to make it happen. While in Korea, he
had seen printing equipment that had gone unused for several years.
Now he dispatched three letters soliciting help.[15]

Goucher wrote missionary W. A. Noble in Seoul to inquire if
he intended to reopen the printing business, or if it might be more
practical to have the printing done in Japan. If so, it would be best
to sell the unused equipment for cash. Writing on the same day to
Homer Eaton, general agent of the Methodist Book Concern in New
York, Goucher noted the growth at the Shanghai establishment and
suggested the Board of Foreign Missions appropriate the Korean
hardware if Noble had no use for it. In the third letter, he contacted
A. B. Leonard, corresponding secretary of the board, to inform him
about the Shanghai press's needs and the potential availability of the
Korean presses, which were "merely stored and rapidly deteriorating."
He warned that "a few more years of disuse and rust will leave you
nothing but scrap iron." Despite his query to Noble, Goucher knew
the Seoul printing operation would likely remain dormant. He told

Leonard, "Of course you know and understand that since Japan has annexed Korea the censorship is much more severe than ever, and if any book is published in Korea which has even a sentence which they disapprove of the whole edition is confiscated, and it will be some time, if ever, before any but Japanese establishments will have any freedom in this respect." Sending the printing equipment to Shanghai and reimbursing the Seoul mission, he wrote, would benefit all sides.[16]

✳✳✳

As December 1910 began, Goucher set out on an eagerly anticipated visit to West China. He and his daughters met James W. Bashford, the first resident bishop of China (stationed in Peking), and Frank Gamewell, Methodist superintendent of education for China, and his wife; the group departed on a long, arduous trip west on the Yangtze River. On the first leg of their journey, the weather was cold and rainy, and there were no fires to warm their living quarters on the boat. On their arrival at Wuhan, it was so damp Goucher passed on attending service in a church with a stone floor and walls, fearing for his daughters' health. From there they caught another boat for the four-day trip to Ichang (Yichang), a starting point to reach further inland. On this leg they were joined by scores of laborers bound for work on the Ichang-Chengtu Railroad.

The longest part of the trip—nearly twenty days on the river—took them to Chungking. On this leg, Bashford, the Gouchers, and the Gamewells traveled on two houseboats lashed together, each eighty-one feet long and thirteen wide, with masts climbing nearly fifty feet. Honoring the Sabbath, the party did not travel on Sundays, despite the attendant delay, but Goucher paid the boatmen for these days off. Bashford said this gesture afforded an opportunity for the workers to learn Christian values "by example." Observing the family from Baltimore up close, the bishop wrote, "I marvel at the graciousness of Dr. Goucher in his family life. He is a model." Along the river, they passed through picturesque gorges and over miles of rapids. Bashford found it "the swiftest and most comfortable trip" he had ever made from Ichang, but there were harrowing moments. The Gamewells' boat struck a rock, and a half-day was lost to repairs; the rope securing the Goucher boat broke twice, each time sending the vessel drifting down rapids. Goucher later received a letter from Bishop Lewis, giving thanks for the party's "escaping the greatest perils" of the trip. Perhaps knowing Goucher's tendency to discount dangers, he added, "You may not have seen them, but I assure you they lurked in the muddy waters of the Yangtze."[17]

After spending New Year's Day 1911 afloat on the Yangtze, the group arrived in Chungking, a city of 800,000, where Bishop Bashford presided over the fourth annual session of the West China Mission Conference. Missionaries reported on the challenges and successes of the preceding year, and informed Goucher about their efforts to create union schools—at the primary, middle, senior, and normal or teacher-training levels—among several Protestant denominations operating in Chungking. By mid-January, the party was transported nearly 200 miles overland via sedan chairs, with each traveler perched in an enclosed seat that bearers carried by bamboo poles. Joseph Beech, missionary superintendent of the Chengtu district, once noted that this mode of transport "costs about the same per mile as the Twentieth Century Limited"—the celebrated New York–Chicago express train—but "with far less comfort." Beech often traveled that way himself; his district, over 100 miles long and sixty wide, covered Chengtu, two other walled cities, and about 140 towns and villages. It took a missionary two weeks to make a circuit of the mission stations, on foot or carried in a chair.[18]

After nine days along the "Big Road," the party at last reached Chengtu, a city surrounded by nearly ten miles of walls and the seat of the viceroy of Szechuan Province. Goucher at last saw the initial stage of West China Union University and met with those working there on the joint enterprise. He made what Bashford called "a remarkable address" to the missionaries concerning the results and aspirations of the Edinburgh Conference; he also preached at a Chinese service through an interpreter.

While Goucher did his education fact-finding on behalf of the Continuation Committee, he also considered taking on more personal commitments. While in West China, he announced various pledges for schools and churches in the country, totaling nearly $20,000 (approximately $500,000). Earlier he had given some funds to the Methodist Board of Foreign Missions toward its commitment to

WCUU, but he now pledged an additional $7,500 ($193,000) to buy land. He promised Beech $500 (more than $12,000) per year for five years to establish a group of Chengtu day schools modeled after the Goucher Schools in India; to help train teachers, Goucher offered $1,000 ($25,700) toward founding a Union Normal School for Women in the area. He also pledged $500 per year for five years to establish day schools in Nanking and Nanchang, plus offered $600 (approximately $15,000) per year to support a teacher at one of them. On top of the hundreds of dollars he had already donated to build churches in the districts around Foochow, he now pledged funds toward six more.[19]

Although he sought to reach wider audiences with these donations, Goucher also knew the difference he could make in the life of a single child. He offered to support, through to the university level, a boy from Suining, one of the districts in the West China Conference, and he left funds so his schooling could begin right away. The boy was illiterate when he began classes, but a few months later, missionary J. O. Curnow reported, "YOUR boy LO TSAI-KAO is doing well," and he sent a sample of his writing, with a translation. Curnow gave an optimistic description of the boy's potential: "He is a 'rough diamond' but he is likely to be susceptible to the lapidary."[20]

At the beginning of February 1911, the party reversed course to return to Ichang, and conditions were occasionally hazardous. As Bashford observed, "Parts of the road [from Chengtu] . . . pass over hills on which the slipping of the chair carriers would throw the chair 30 to 50 feet down an embankment." The bishop related an incident on the way back to Chungking that could have had serious consequences: The men carrying Goucher's chair got into a quarrel and dropped it. But Goucher, who spoke no Chinese, "never lifted his eyes from his book." Expecting a tongue lashing, the bearers "were struck dumb and quietly picked up the chair and walked in silence." After ten days of being borne aloft, the group again boarded boats on the Yangtze. They had spent more than nine weeks in the Szechuan region since leaving Ichang in mid-December.[21]

Shortly after Goucher left Chengtu, Joseph Beech wrote to thank him for his visit and noted its impact: "Your name is often used as an argument in itself when we are trying to do things that mark an advance. It is more and more evident that you came at the right time and brought the right message and influence." It also helped that as Goucher left the province, he sent the first installment on his pledge for Chengtu schools, allowing Beech to open seven inside the city walls and one outside.[22]

Now the travelers split up, the Gamewells heading to Shanghai, the Gouchers and Bashford to Nanking, then Foochow. A report from the Edinburgh Conference had recommended establishing several union schools around the country rather than a single national university, and Goucher spent a good part of his time in China promoting these ventures. Although the Continuation Committee was behind him in his efforts, as *The Baltimore Sun* would explain, "In every gathering of men in which [Goucher] is a factor, his clearness of vision and his persuasive eloquence cause him to dominate . . . not because of any electrical influence, but by reason of the lucidity of his arguments, his provision, and the accepted unselfishness of his motives." He had discussed a joint university in Nanking during his 1907 visit, and now the school was a reality. Its president, A. J. Bowen, asked him to attend a meeting of its Board of Trustees in New York later in the year, since Goucher knew more than any of the trustees about the university's work, problems, and opportunities, having "studied the matter on the field."[23]

Foochow still lacked its own union school, and Goucher called for an interdenominational conference to plan for and discuss the feasibility of higher Christian education in the region. A research committee was formed, and years later, Edwin C. Jones, president of what became Fukien Christian University, recalled its first meeting one chilly night in March 1911. Goucher stood by the fireplace as they mulled over the union's seemingly insurmountable problems. There was one usual difficulty: they needed funds for ongoing expenses, only partially covered by user fees. Goucher told the assembly "in his quaint way" that he knew someone who might make up half the shortfall—himself, most likely—if the missions raised the other half. As the committee worked out details after Goucher left, Jones said their plans "would have borne little fruit" without "the seed sown" by their visitor.[24]

As a longtime supporter of higher education for women in the United States and India, Goucher wanted to promote it in China and

Japan as well. As he told missionary Lydia Trimble, founder of the Woman's Christian College of Foochow, "No appeal can be more urgent." Woman, he later wrote her, was "the strategic personality of the human race; the determinative factor in the educational, social and ethical standards of every community; and the creator of the atmosphere of the Home, which is the uniting factor of Christian civilization." When the Goucher family returned to Tokyo in April on their way home, he called together representatives of the various missions to discuss higher education for Japanese women, and made certain before he left that a committee was appointed to look into opening a union college in that city.[25]

By late Spring 1911, after nearly eight months abroad, and having given more than 100 talks on issues relating to Christian education in the three leading East Asian countries, Goucher and his two daughters were back home. *The Baltimore Sun* once again hailed him as an "educator, traveler, distinguished theologian, and constructive philanthropist" and highlighted his international work. The article especially praised the recognition he had brought his home town: "It is doubtful if there exists anywhere another character that is a counterpart to that of John Franklin Goucher, who has not only spread his own name over the entire world—with no intention of doing that thing—but who has made Baltimore known in many a crevice of this old globe that never would have been aware of the Monumental City had it not been for Dr. Goucher." He was not home long, however, before he was drawn back into affairs at the college that now bore his name.[26]

TWENTY-FIVE YEARS OF GOUCHER'S WORK

What The College Has Done To Help Women Of Every Section Of Country To Higher Ideals And Usefulness.

At the request of THE EVENING SUN, Dr. John F. Goucher, after whom Goucher College was named, has prepared the following statement of how the institution was founded, some of the difficulties it has passed through, the work it has accomplished and the reasons that should prompt the people of Baltimore at this crisis in the career of the college to rally to its support.

Dr. Goucher's article is, indeed, worth reading. It is a statement of facts as they are—of needs as they exist. It is as follows:

"Progress is not absolute, but relative. It is not to be measured by position, but by distance from the starting point and approach to the goal. When the project of founding in Baltimore a college for women was first broached it met with much passive and active resistance—the inertia of indifference and the opposition of disfavor.

"Several months were spent in studying the best institutions of the kind, consulting with many of the most representative educators of the country and formulating an ideal and plans for the institution. The educators and business men consulted were almost unanimous in their disapproval of the attempt. This disap-

a reserve, the income from which assists in meeting its expenses.

"Every institution of higher education belongs to one of three classes—it has ample endowment, a considerable debt, or is a fake institution, as no institution of higher education can possibly maintain its work by its tuition fees.

"It costs the trustees of Goucher College an average of about $355 a year for the tuition of every student it receives. It charges $150 a year. This is about the average of the Johns Hopkins University, Wellesley, Vassar, Bryn Mawr and other institutions of like grade.

"There have been 2,355 students in attendance an aggregate of 6,339 years. If you add to the difference between cost and receipts for tuition, the rebates given to teachers and the daughters of ministers, the scholarships and the fellowships, Goucher College has given to its students in free tuition $1,733,999. This fact accounts for the debt of the college. To have made such generous contributions in tuition may not be considered good business, but life is more valuable than gold and character is more precious than rubies. Every institution of higher education is a benevolent institution.

"The college has given in free tuition to its 344 students from the State of Maryland during the 2,512 years of their attendance $899,998, but has never received any municipal aid from the city nor State aid from Maryland. It asked for a reasonable grant from the Legislature last winter, not a dollar of which was for land, buildings, equipment or endowment, but to pay for a part of the tuition of the Maryland students attending the college while it is trying to meet its present crisis. This was refused, and the Maryland students in the college cost the trustees this year $40,488 more than they pay.

"The refusal of the Legislature is more surprising since the population of Maryland includes 6,896 more fe-

The Evening Sun, Baltimore, Maryland
March 15, 1913

*Courtesy of the Goucher College Library,
Special Collections and Archives, Baltimore, Maryland*

RECALLED TO WORK
IN BALTIMORE

Chapter 21
(Mid-1911-Mid-1913)

━━━━━━━━━━━━━━◆◀━━━━━━━━━━━━━━

Duty is more than a theory and helpfulness is not a pastime.
Character is no chance nor transient product . . . and destiny is not
an arbitrary assignment.1

During Goucher's absence, President Noble made a candid statement to the trustees—later published for the community to read—about the difficult financial situation at Goucher College. Of the more than $500,000 ($13.6 million) pledged in 1906, only a little more than $300,000 ($7.7 million) had been collected four years later, and the annual deficit was running $40,000 ($1 million) a year. While Noble said he did not wish to lay blame, he told the board, "No college can be assured of permanence or can perform its academic functions . . . if it assumes liabilities which it cannot easily meet, or bears the galling yoke of debt." He felt the school needed at least one million dollars ($25.7 million) to remain open and ensure its future through a wisely-invested endowment.[2]

Even as Noble issued this warning, vindication came for the spending decisions the president emeritus and the trustees had made over the years. In 1911, the Bureau of Education of the Department of the Interior ranked Goucher College among fifty-nine Class I universities and colleges in the United States (out of 581 under consideration)—and one of only six women's colleges so ranked. As Bryn Mawr president M. Carey Thomas would point out, "No one who is not in the college world can realize the full significance" of this high ranking, as Goucher was competing with older, larger, better endowed schools, most of which only admitted men. Years later, a *Ladies Home Journal* article would point out the irony: Goucher

College "had reached the unique state of being financially bankrupt at the same time that it was one of the most intellectually solvent colleges in the country."[3]

After only three years in office, during which he had been unable to fix the school's financial problems, Noble resigned as president in June 1911 to assume the same position at Dickinson College. Goucher College was now rudderless in a crisis, and the board appointed a committee to examine the situation and look for a successor. John Goucher was named to that group, and unsurprisingly, the trustees tried to persuade him to take his old job. As *The Baltimore Sun* reported, "A decided sentiment developed that if Dr. Goucher would again take up the reins nothing better could happen for the institution." As soon as the faculty learned of the possibility, there was "manifest enthusiasm and a general demand" for his reappointment. Realizing the obstacle this suggestion posed for the search committee, Goucher made it clear he was unable to accept:

> While I am naturally deeply interested in the welfare of the college, I do not think it would be advantageous if I accepted the offer of the committee. Probably for a few years I might be able to attend to the duties and after that I am sure the continued work would injure my health. . . . What is most desired is a younger and more vigorous man who will be able to devote a number of years of his life to guiding the institution along the way which has been marked out. Numerous changes at the head do not make for the success which we are all seeking for the college.[4]

At this point, the search committee decided to select an interim president—John Van Meter, who had just retired, exhausted after more than twenty years as a teacher and administrator. Goucher visited the former dean as he enjoyed a much-needed vacation, and despite their former differences, convinced him to come to the rescue in this emergency. As a college history notes, Van Meter "loved the College too unselfishly to desert it at such a time of peril." Although he anticipated he would serve just a few months, Van Meter held the position for two critical years.[5]

At the moment, solving the school's financial problems was more pressing than finding a new president. After Noble resigned, the board assigned several trustees, including Goucher and Van Meter, to come up with a plan to erase the debt and increase the endowment. With what a friend called "a breaking heart," Goucher had already spoken about the crisis to the Board of Bishops, as he had done in the previous campaign. The bishops made personal donations and asked Bishop Wilson Lewis, visiting from his post in China, to remain in the United States to help raise the needed one million dollars. He induced five men to pledge $60,000 ($1.5 million) each as a nucleus to spur other contributions—including John Goucher, who had previously told college trustees to expect no further major donations from him.[6]

His funds were not unlimited, however, and this new commitment seemed to impinge on at least one of the pledges Goucher had recently made in China. He had paid his first installment toward the Nanchang day schools, but several months later, the district school superintendent wrote in surprise, "I could scarcely believe that you meant to cancel your pledge to us." But the missionary conceded that Bishop Bashford had made him understand "the burden which you have had to assume again in connection with Goucher College." He resumed his payments within the year, and the Nanchang project quickly grew to ten schools with more than 150 students. In the end, Goucher honored his commitment for the five years he had promised, and donated an additional sum to purchase land.[7]

Even as Goucher's time and money turned again to Goucher College, his focus remained on missionary work. He was barely three months back from East Asia when he set off in September 1911 for the Netherlands to attend the first International Study Conference on missionary training. From there he crossed the channel to London to attend meetings on missions and education, conducted by the European Section of the Continuation Committee. Back in the United States, he made several trips to New York before the end of the year for meetings concerning the West China and Nanking universities and the Board of Foreign Missions. In this last group, a missionary once acknowledged, Goucher often served as a "Big Friend in Court" for those in the field who needed extra funding for their work.[8]

For example, Arthur D. Berry, dean of the Theological School at Aoyama Gakuin, was facing a large deficit that might require slashing department size by half. He wrote Goucher in November 1911, "I am sorry to shove this burden upon you but I have nowhere else to turn for help but you and Providence. And as far as our school is concerned I feel that you and Providence are about the same thing." Goucher duly obtained a special grant from the General Missionary Committee and added some of his own money. Berry responded that on hearing of it, "I suddenly felt as though I had had a furlough and all my weariness was gone. How fine of you to take the burden of that deficit on your own shoulders and bear it for me." Later the dean again asked Goucher "to present the case and speak for us," in hopes the grant might be renewed. Berry bolstered his request by reminding Goucher that his scholarships for Korean students meant Aoyama Gakuin now provided "higher theological training for Korea as well as Japan."[9]

✳ ✳ ✳

As 1912 began, Goucher was again plagued by physical ailments "brought on by over work." He had had months of severe stomach problems, and he traveled to St. Francis Hospital in Pittsburgh at the end of January for two more hernia operations. David Goucher had just died, but ill-health prevented his brother from attending the Missouri funeral. Goucher called the first operation "almost painless and a success," although he found himself unable to eat for ten days. Finally, he sent for the New York physician who "had been in charge of my stomach for about four years," who was able to ease his problem and prepare him for the second operation three weeks after the first. After spending more than six weeks in the hospital, Goucher recorded his "weight in the buff 126½ pounds"—he had lost twenty since he arrived. He wrote his friend Frank Porter that he was "greatly improved in health, with the prospect, as soon as I regain my flesh and strength, . . . of being in better physical condition than I have been for many years." Another friend later noted, Goucher "mastered the art of recuperation in the same methodical manner as he does every other duty."[10]

Returning to Baltimore in mid-March, Goucher hoped for a few days' seclusion to catch up on correspondence. Instead, he was immediately dispatched to New York on behalf of the Goucher College Million Dollar Campaign. He told a *Baltimore Sun* reporter he was "confident" that with time, the money would be raised, and that it was critical that Baltimoreans who valued the school offer their support. The college wasn't eager to relocate, he said, while admitting that emissaries from two locations—one an unnamed university outside Chicago—had been "offering most tempting terms" to prompt such a move.[11]

Goucher was disappointed when the Maryland legislature denied the trustees' request for an appropriation of $100,000 ($2.5 million), to be paid in two annual installments. The school was not asking for "a gift," he pointed out: Over nearly twenty-five years, the college had offered Maryland women several hundred thousand dollars in scholarships and fellowships, and had subsidized other costs not covered by tuition. Goucher said later such generosity might not be considered good business, but "life is more valuable than gold and character is more precious than rubies. Every institution of higher education is a benevolent institution." The denial especially irked him because the college had never before asked the state for support, while over the same period, the legislature had appropriated nearly $900,000 for two private men's institutions—the Johns Hopkins University and St. John's College—and nearly $700,000 for the private, co-educational Washington College, Western Maryland College (now McDaniel College), and the Maryland Institute (now MICA, Maryland Institute College of Art). Yet of all Maryland schools, only Goucher and Johns Hopkins had been federally rated as Class I institutions.[12]

Nearly a third of the million-dollar goal had been pledged by only five contributors, and the Campaign Committee, including Goucher and Bishop Lewis, resolved to raise $400,000 ($10.1 million) from donors in Baltimore and Washington and another $300,000 elsewhere ($7.6 million). Goucher and Lewis attended the May 1912 General Conference in Minneapolis to stress Goucher College's national as well as local impact. Lewis told him at the time, "I want you to know that I reckon the days and weeks spent with you in this struggle as among the happiest in my life. There are very few men that have found as deep a place in my heart as you have. I regard the building of Goucher College under the circumstances as the greatest achievement in our church in your generation."[13]

Meanwhile the Campaign Committee hired a fundraising consultant to organize teams of solicitors. Van Meter, who knew all the alumnae, spearheaded a drive among them; the graduates also helped the campaign by writing letters—"What Goucher Has Done for Me"—that were printed in newspapers and spurred others to give. Under Lilian Welsh's direction, a committee of Baltimore women made what the 1938 college history calls "systematic and persistent" weekly appeals. At a College Women's Rally in December 1912, Baltimore's college-educated women gathered to urge public support. The main speaker was Bryn Mawr president M. Carey Thomas, a Baltimore native. She and Goucher had sparred a dozen years before in speeches at the annual convention of the Association of Colleges and Preparatory Schools of the Middle States and Maryland, held at the University of Pennsylvania. Both were strong advocates of single-sex higher education for women, and both believed women merited the same rigorous education as men. But where Thomas believed women's colleges should teach courses just as men's schools did, Goucher (and Van Meter) favored a woman-centric focus in academic classes:

> Woman approaches a subject differently from man . . . and if she masters a subject, even though she masters it more thoroughly, she will do it in different ways and by different processes and she will use her aquirements [sic] differently. . . . Woman is more highly organized, more sensitive and sensible, more limited and intense in her functional relations to the race. It is not a question of who is greater or less, [or] who can attain the most.

Thomas had sometimes questioned practices at the Woman's College, but she recognized the quality of the alumnae who had enrolled in Bryn Mawr's graduate programs. She also respected the college's Class I status. Hence her offer of support at this critical time.[14]

✳✳✳

Goucher was often on the move in 1912. His East Asian projects brought him to New York nearly two dozen times for meetings related to the Board of Foreign Missions, the publishing house in Shanghai, and the Board of Trustees of the University of Nanking. At other conferences he helped plan a union Japan University and discussed joint educational enterprises in Korea. As chair of the Board of Governors of West China Union University, he was engaged in another major fundraiser for construction and the endowment; that campaign required travel to Toronto as well as New York. Goucher also led a meeting of his American Section on Christian Education in Asia, in advance of the second meeting of the full Continuation Committee that fall.

In addition, Goucher got to see some of his Asian contacts on his home ground. He hosted lunch for Nitobe Inazo, a late-1880s graduate of the Johns Hopkins University and then a faculty member at Tokyo's Imperial University. Nitobe was lecturing at Hopkins as one of the first Japanese exchange professors under the auspices of the Carnegie Endowment for Peace. Goucher also invited William P. Eveland, the newly appointed missionary bishop for Southeast Asia, to stay at Alto Dale. "You have a very beautiful home life and one is the better for a touch of it," the bishop wrote in thanks. "I was glad too for the talk with you. I wish that I knew as much about the work in my new field as you do." Goucher minded those closer to home as well. On his calendar, he noted that November 3 marked twenty years since he had hired Robert Green, his African-American driver.[15]

Goucher keenly followed the 1912 presidential race. He had always voted Republican—eleven times since graduating college in 1868—but this time, he told some newspapers, he planned to vote for Democrat Woodrow Wilson, whom he knew as president of Princeton, governor of New Jersey, and father of two Woman's College graduates. Goucher had been satisfied with the presidency of Republican Theodore Roosevelt, who had been vice president when William McKinley was assassinated in 1901; he served as president for three years and then was elected to a full term in 1904. He did not run in 1908, but Goucher thought it "a serious deviation from the unwritten law of this nation" to elect a man to what he considered a third term. He also disapproved of the rift between Roosevelt and President William H. Taft, both of whom had sought the 1912 Republican nomination. When Roosevelt lost, he organized the independent Progressive Party (also known as the Bull Moose Party), dividing the Republican vote. Referring to the sitting president or the former president (or perhaps both), Goucher found it "very humiliating to see the President of the United States in a personal scramble for renomination. . . . It seems below the dignity of the office for the President to engage in vituperative expressions concerning an opponent."[16]

With the Republicans in disarray, Goucher viewed the Democrats as "the real party of progress," telling *The Baltimore Sun*, "I feel that I owe it to my country to break away from the political affiliations of the past and support the man and the platform that I truly believe are for the welfare of my country." He called Wilson "a safe, sane, progressive leader," who would "mightily advance the cause of civic righteousness" and enter office "absolutely uninfluenced except by his desire to advance the people's interest." Goucher said he would cast his vote for Wilson "with the greatest pleasure."[17]

Meanwhile, Goucher College's Million Dollar Campaign continued to drain his time and energy. As 1913 began, the school had raised approximately $650,000 ($16 million), but trustees announced that continuing financial pressures ensured the college would close if its goal were not met by April 4. Another relocation bid had come in, this one from American University, and rumors circulated that if the school did leave town, the Catholic Church might buy its buildings. At the end of January, Goucher went to New York for meetings on Japan and China. Bishop Lewis and other trustees joined him to plead with Methodist bishops, ministers, and laymen, in hopes of meeting their goal of raising $300,000 outside of Baltimore and Washington.[18]

Those two cities were still $200,000 ($4.9 million) short of the trustees' target, which came as no surprise to Goucher and Van Meter, who had both made such pleas before. In a long article in Baltimore's *Evening Sun* that reviewed the institution's history—from early indifference to its growth and academic rise, even as it accumulated debt—Goucher appealed to the Baltimore public while chastising it for its lack of support:

> The present crisis, with its insistent and unanswerable appeal for immediate relief, has met with such unjostled deliberation as gives evidence that Baltimoreans keep their benevolent impulses under such exact control . . . This is a striking illustration of persistence of generations of inherited tendency strengthened by continual cultivation.[19]

Goucher was equally blunt about the lack of support for the college from the South in general (Baltimore lying below the Mason–Dixon line). He noted that in colonial times, fledgling southern educational institutions looked to the king or English parliament for support, while northern ones were started through personal philanthropy and "maintained by local cooperation." Since then, he maintained, with rare exceptions, no leading educational institution had been started in the South except "by persons from, or educated in, the North." The article ended with Goucher again warning, "If Baltimore does not care enough for the continuance of the college in the city to provide the $200,000 necessary for its success," it would close by summer.[20]

An intense final push came in the last six weeks. Pamphlets argued for the college's financial benefits to the city, pointing out how much would be lost if it closed. The front page of *The Methodist* proclaimed, "Goucher College Must Be Saved!" Women of all denominations gathered for a mass prayer meeting. A fundraising rally of girls from public and private high schools featured Woman's College alumna Jesse Woodrow Wilson, who read a letter of support from her father. Baltimore citizens and civic leaders came through in the end. Mayor James H. Preston invited several hundred prominent men to City Hall to organize final fundraising efforts; civic organizations such as the Greater Baltimore Committee encouraged their employees to participate. Banks and street cars displayed placards, and local newspapers ran editorials.[21]

Some of the smallest last-minute gifts provided the most encouragement and inspiration: A Jewish factory worker contributed three dollars ($74), saying he wished he could give $3,000; three young girls, perhaps aspiring to attend the college one day, brought in five dollars ($123) from a sewing circle they had organized. A black Methodist congregation sent in fifteen dollars ($370), "given in the best spirit of helpfulness," even though a *Baltimore Sun* article noted "they cannot hope to send their own children there." African-American workers at the college faced the same restriction but nevertheless came forward to help: Two men who operated the elevators each contributed ten dollars ($247) for the cause; a woman who had been in charge of upkeep in Bennett Hall for more than twenty years gave the same; and workers in Vingolf Hall, a student residence, pooled their money to donate $1.50 ($37).[22]

When the April 4 deadline arrived, the campaign was still shy of its goal. Canvassing teams returned to the streets and phones during the day. Campaign leaders met in the evening at the Emerson Hotel for a final push, and by ten o'clock that night, only $8,000 ($197,000) remained to be raised. As in previous campaigns, a handful of donors— unnamed but "guessed at pretty accurately"—stepped forward at the last minute to cover the shortfall, bringing the total to just over one million dollars. There were cheers in the hall, and more than a hundred voices joined in singing a spirited doxology. Bishop Lewis proclaimed himself "almost speechless at the successful whirlwind close of this most remarkable campaign," adding, "and above all, let me say the praise of American lovers of learning remains for Dr. Goucher." Goucher deflected any personal recognition and instead turned his thanks to his fellow citizens (even though he had earlier been discouraged by their response): "I have had faith in the college and faith in the people of Baltimore and I am happier now than ever in my faith in both. . . . Baltimore has made a glorious finish. One cannot have too many friends and the college has never been so rich as it is tonight."[23]

The next day, *The Baltimore Sun* gave its own report on the final hours of the campaign: "All during the evening Dr. Goucher had been apparently the coolest man in the room. His confidence never seemed to waver and his appearance unmoved when the completion of the fund was stated." Yet the article acknowledged that "those who knew him best knew that a great load had been lifted from his mind and that no one there was more thankful than he."[24]

At the conclusion of the campaign, his sister Ella, who still called him Frank, wrote out of concern for his health, "knowing how much you and your friend Bishop Lewis needed rest and building up." In the aftermath, Lewis checked in to Michigan's Battle Creek Sanitarium, a health resort that stressed the restorative powers of proper nutrition and diet, exercise, and fresh air. Goucher visited him there and stayed more than a week, perhaps investigating some of these holistic activities for himself; he noted in his diary that his blood pressure dropped by nearly sixty points during his stay. Lewis wrote after Goucher departed, "There is not so much music to this place since you left us. Many of the attractions fled with you." With the college's finances secure for the moment, the president emeritus considered his work there completed, and he was ready to get back to other projects. He told Lilian Welsh he had "done what was in his power to do for the College," reiterating that his primary interests now were missions and the educational opportunities in those fields.[25]

GOVERNOR-GENERAL AND COUNTESS TERAUCHI

REQUEST THE PLEASURE OF THE COMPANY OF

Dr. and Miss Goucher

AT GARDEN PARTY

IN CELEBRATION OF THE THIRTY FOURTH BIRTHDAY OF

HIS MAJESTY THE EMPEROR OF JAPAN

ON FRIDAY, THE THIRTY FIRST OF OCTOBER, 1913,

AT 3 P.M.

A visit to Korea, 1913

Courtesy of Janet Miller Bernet

THE TRANS-SIBERIAN CONNECTION

Chapter 22
(Fall 1913)

━━━━━━━━━━━━━━━━◆◆━━━━━━━━━━━━━━━━

*Every person should live for others, because no person
can live without others.*[1]

In the wake of the college campaign, in late spring and early summer
of 1913, Goucher continued commuting to New York for meetings
of the Board of Foreign Missions and the committees and boards
related to his work in East Asia. John R. Mott, chair of the Continuation
Committee, visited him in Baltimore at 2313, and Goucher traveled
to Florida to address the Epworth League Convention on missions
and West China Union University. In the same period, he squeezed
in two more activities on behalf of Goucher College: He again hosted
the popular Alto Dale Day, attended by nearly 700 students, faculty,
alumnae, trustees, and local ministers. He also helped recruit and elect
the college's fourth president—William Westley Guth, formerly head
of the College of the Pacific. By early August, Goucher was again
steaming across the Atlantic, bound for China, Japan, and Korea by
an indirect route. The Board of Foreign Missions had asked him to
confer with missionary leaders about conditions in those countries and
present a formal report on his return.[2]

In 1911, a *Baltimore Sun* profile had proclaimed, Goucher "packs
a gripsack and steps aboard a steamer with no more ado than an
ordinary man would make in going from Baltimore to New York." On
this fourth tour of East Asia, Elizabeth and Eleanor again accompanied
their father, as did Bishop Wilson Lewis on his way back to Foochow.
Their ship traveled through the North Sea to dock at a port serving
Bremen, Germany; from there they caught the train to St. Petersburg
and Moscow. In the former city, the superintendent of the Russian

Methodist Episcopal Church, which had been officially recognized by Czar Nicholas II only a few years earlier, called his time with the travelers "joyous, blessed days." Their two weeks in Russia brought new sights for the travel-loving Goucher. In early September, the party set off for China via the Trans-Siberian Railway, and he praised the long-distance train service and the interesting scenery as they made their way further east.[3]

In China, Goucher would revisit familiar ground, but political conditions had changed. At the end of 1911, a few months after his previous trip, a series of anti-dynastic revolts had led to a revolution in which a majority of provinces declared their independence from the Qing dynasty. Events unfolded quickly after that. A provisional government based in Nanking and calling itself the Republic of China was proclaimed on January 1, 1912, with exiled nationalist Sun Yat-sen declared provisional president. Boy emperor Pu Yi abdicated the following month through the influence of General Yuan Shih-kai, leader of the imperial forces. By March, Yuan had replaced Sun as provisional president, returning the capital to his military stronghold of Peking. Previously, provincial officials had been appointed by the emperor, and power flowed from the central government; now each province elected its own governor, who controlled his own army.

Early in 1912, Bishop Bashford had written to warn Goucher that many parts of the country were awash in "ambition, greed and fear," as warlords exerted greater control in the absence of an effective central government, demanding protection payoffs from Chinese and Westerners alike. Chengtu was under control of a bandit chieftain, and the bishop told Goucher, "The best street in the city, where you made purchases last winter, has been completely looted." The recently opened West China Union University had to suspend operations, and missionaries temporarily fled. Although democratic elections for a National Assembly were held early in 1913, Bashford described the assembly's 800 members—"some of whom could not read or write, a majority of whom were young and some of whom were expected to be paid for their support of measures"—as "simply an impossible group of men for the inauguration of a Republic." The rivalry between Sun and his Kuomintang (KMT) party and Yuan escalated over the following months. As Goucher's party was passing through China that September, Yuan used his military muscle to have himself elected to a five-year term as president. He dissolved both national and provincial assemblies as Sun Yat-sen called for a second revolution and fled to Japan.[4]

Despite these upheavals, Elizabeth would be staying in China, teaching at the Nanking Woman's College under the auspices of the Women's Foreign Missionary Society. She had spent time assisting at a Japanese girls' school on the family's previous trip, and once back home, took courses at Teachers' College, Columbia University. Goucher had wanted to be a missionary himself, and as one writer would later comment, Elizabeth's vocation "must have been one of his supreme satisfactions." It was a mixed blessing, however; save for visits, Elizabeth would remain abroad, far from the Goucher family circle.[5]

October 1913 was divided between visits to Japan and Korea. Along with John's usual rounds of meetings with missionaries and educators, dinners with dignitaries, visits to schools and speeches (thirty-two in Korea alone), Goucher immersed himself in discussions in each country about opening union universities, which usually began as colleges. In a speech at Clark University in Massachusetts the year before, Goucher had asserted such enterprises yielded dual benefits: "Businessmen desire that their investments shall have two qualities in particular, security and productiveness," and interdenominational institutions "furnish these in large measure." They also appealed to the "loyalty and liberality" of Christians and brought "blessed influence upon the supporting Churches in the home land."[6]

Goucher arrived with a plan to unite the Methodist, Baptist, and Episcopal schools into one Japan University based in Tokyo. But when a meeting was held, the role of Aoyama Gakuin in such a joint enterprise was of concern to Methodist missionaries and the Japanese involved with the institution. The union school might require a larger campus, and Aoyama Gakuin's president, Takagi Mizutaro, said the school was opposed to any relocation of "the Methodist center." Others expressed skepticism at the feasibility of Goucher's plan. After he left the city, representatives of the three missionary societies met to discuss it again but could come to no agreement on how to proceed. On Goucher's part, as much as he believed in the principle of union work, he did not to want to harm Aoyama Gakuin's relationship with the Japanese government or risk loss of privileges it had been granted over the years.[7]

A possible union university in Korea faced different obstacles. On a visit a year earlier, John R. Mott had reported that the country's Japanese rulers exerted "a strong insistence on outward forms of expression of loyalty to the government." A few months before Goucher's current trip, he was "deeply grieved" to learn the fate of his Korean friend Baron Yun Chi-ho, who had been among more than 100 men arrested in 1911 under suspicion of being sympathetic to the Korean independence movement and of making an assassination attempt against Governor-General Terauchi. Baron Yun, the only member of the royal family educated in the United States, and at one time the only Christian on Emperor Kojong's Privy Council, was among six alleged conspirators ultimately sent to prison in what became known as the Korean Conspiracy Case.[8]

Goucher stated in a March 1913 *Baltimore Sun* interview that Yun's trial was "the result of unfortunate circumstances and the attitude of the military administration in Korea." He saw no reason, however, "to believe that [it] was less fair than any in Japan or Korea." Yet he echoed Mott's concerns about Japan's demands for public displays of loyalty, allowing that the same military administration had crushed any Korean organizations "as a first step toward assimilation." He pointed to a further ramification of the conspiracy charges: "The Japanese officials have been especially suspicious of the Korean Christian meetings." It was hard to convince the authorities that hymns such as "Onward Christian Soldiers" were apolitical. The military "consider[s] them dangerous, not because they are Christian, but because they think they have significance" when sung by independence-loving Koreans.[9]

At such a tense moment, Goucher's connections with the Japanese government and the military administration in Korea proved helpful. Several years earlier, Methodists and Presbyterians had united to set up an academy in Pyengyang; on his 1910 trip, Goucher had helped establish the Christian Educational Federation of Korea. Its purpose was to unify standards; eliminate waste and duplicated effort in the various missions; and work within the Japanese government's regulations, which had left higher education open to expansion. Both denominations wanted to ensure any university-level institution opened in Korea would be Christian, not secular. Nevertheless, there was an important dividing point: Should such a school be located in Pyengyang or Seoul? Some thought the established joint academy in the former city could be raised to a higher academic level. Seoul, however, was Korea's political (and Christian) capital, with extensive rail connections enabling students to travel there from the hinterlands. In addition, Pai Chai Hakdang already offered some college classes.[10]

The issue had yet to be resolved when Goucher arrived, and he gave a speech declaring that the time for a decision had come. Horace Underwood, a Presbyterian missionary who had been in Korea since 1885, reported that Goucher spoke of "this time and place as 'strategic'" and that "the psychological time to approach the government" was now. As Goucher would tell another missionary audience, he realized his own weakness for procrastination when one of his workmen at Alto Dale said, "Doctor, I think you find it easier to plan your work than to work your plans." Even so, he understood the wisdom of "Do it now" as a business principle and warned, "How the Devil does get the upper hand on many a big man by saying 'Wait till you can do something big.'" He advised instead, "The way to begin is to begin."[11]

Toward that end, he had dinner twice with Governor-General Terauchi to discuss university plans. Underwood later informed the head of his home mission board that Goucher surprised him by bringing up the question of the school's location "on his own initiative." Speaking for the government, Terauchi decreed the school should be located in Seoul. With that decided, the Joint Committee on Education in Korea, whose members were appointed by the North American Methodist and Presbyterian mission boards, approved the plan for a Christian college in Seoul, with the denominations sharing expenses.[12]

Instead of continuing his trip around the world, Goucher backtracked. He had planned his trip so his return to Europe—again via the Trans-Siberian Railway, with a stop in St. Petersburg—would coincide with the third annual meeting of the Continuation Committee in The Hague in mid-November 1913. (The first gathering had been held at Auckland Castle in England in 1911, and the second at Lake Mohonk, New York, the following year.) Queen Wilhelmina of the Netherlands provided a special train to take attendees to lunch at her summer palace in Apeldoorn, and she gave Goucher a private audience; he said they had an "agreeable talk." She knew of his travels to Dutch-colonial Java and was interested in his impressions of the island and missionary work there. He and Eleanor then spent a few days in and around Frankfurt, where he visited the Martin's Mission Institute, recipient of an endowed fund for scholarships and library books that John and Mary had established more than thirty years earlier. After making a rough Channel crossing, they reached London, the final stop on their 30,000-mile, nearly four-month trip.[13]

In London, Goucher had a full slate of meetings concerning the Continuation Committee. He also met with British architect Fred Rowntree, at work on plans for the West China Union University campus. (A 1922 resolution by the WCUU Senate credits Goucher with financing the Methodist share of the property's cost.) A professor at WCUU's successor, Sichuan University, describes Rowntree's "unique design and layout" as mixing "mysterious eastern beauty" with western style. John was likely as drawn to Rowntree's architectural vision as he had been to Stanford White's plans for First Church and the Woman's College of Baltimore many years earlier.[14]

As John and Eleanor sailed for home from Queenstown, Ireland, on December 19, 1913, he was mindful of the import of that date— "11 years after the death of Mother," meaning Mary. He took time to reflect on the people he had lost:

> But among the innumerable blessings with which the Lord
> hath enriched my life, . . . the ones of which I am increasingly
> appreciative and for which I am increasingly grateful, day by
> day, are my Parentage, my Conversion, and my Wife. . . . Their
> memory and their influence bide in my consciousness with
> unclouded sweetness and the presence of their Lord and mine
> grows more real.

Goucher also wrote several prayers of thanksgiving. In one, he told God he was waiting in "patient expectancy" for His "fourth great blessing, Thy call for me to join Thee and the loved ones who rejoice in Thy unveiled presence." Meanwhile, he pledged whatever time he had left to "fill to the full with loving loyalty the measure of service Thou dost entrust me with."[15]

Father and daughter arrived at 2313 on Christmas Eve, but one could never be certain Goucher would stay home for long. As one Methodist interviewer later acknowledged, it would be no surprise to learn that "the trunk is again packed, and that our friend is again upon extended travels in service to his King."[16]

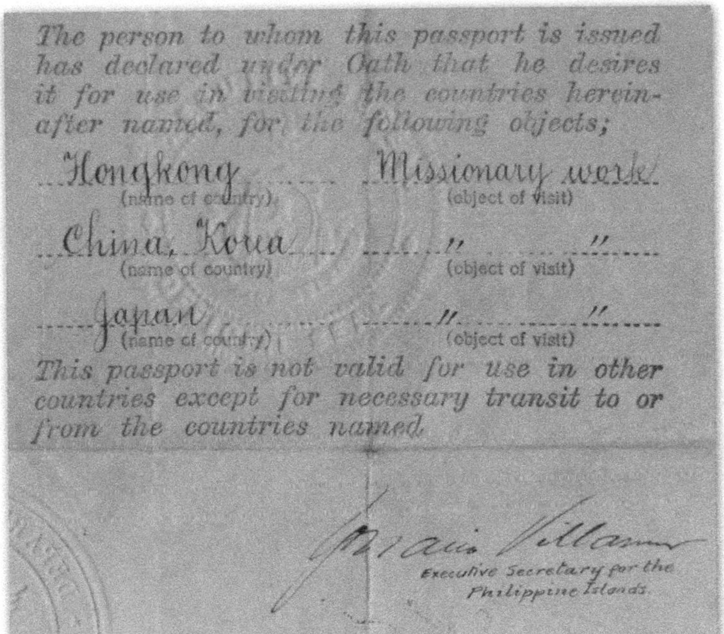

The person to whom this passport is issued has declared under Oath that he desires it for use in visiting the countries hereinafter named, for the following objects;

Hongkong (name of country) Missionary work (object of visit)

China, Korea (name of country) " " (object of visit)

Japan (name of country) " " (object of visit)

This passport is not valid for use in other countries except for necessary transit to or from the countries named.

Executive Secretary for the Philippine Islands.

Portion of passport for John Goucher, August 1913

Courtesy of Janet Miller Bernet

ASIAN CONFLICTS, ASIAN UNIONS

Chapter 23
(1914-1915)

━━━━━━━━━━━━━━◆◆━━━━━━━━━━━━━━

Permanent peace cannot exist where there is oppression. The size of the army is not the most important factor on determining victory. The great decisive battles of the world, when judged in the light of their results, have always been won for humanity.[1]

With so many Goucher-supported educational ventures in Asia and new opportunities to explore, in late September 1914, only nine months after his previous trip, Goucher again set off for the East. He had originally planned to attend meetings of the Continuation Committee in London early that month, then take the Trans-Siberian Railway to China as he had the year before. But World War I had broken out that summer, and those meetings had been cancelled. He would cross the Pacific instead.

Earlier in 1914, Goucher had traveled to New York nearly twenty times to handle business, give speeches, or attend events. Frequently he left home on the midnight train to make an early morning meeting, returning later the same day; at other times, he would spend two or three days in the city on work related to the Board of Foreign Missions or the several Asian union universities he was assisting. At the end of February, he left chilly Baltimore for a working vacation in Daytona and Miami. During that week away, he spoke about education in Asia and enjoyed rides in a motor boat and a hydroplane, speeding along at sixty miles per hour. On March 3, he recorded some happy news from home: He had become a grandfather for the second time—a baby girl, Janet Fisher Miller, who joined her older brother, known as Junior. Called Fisher by her family, she later said Goucher liked to call her "Miss J. F." because they shared the same initials.[2]

Goucher remained committed to educational opportunities for all, emphasizing that "development from infancy to manhood is determined by education. Instruction is construction." In the twentieth century, he saw education becoming more available around the globe, although he noted a "diffusion of opportunity" in the "belated" nations of Asia. In a report, he pointed out that a high percentage of Asian converts were illiterate, "not willfully so, nor from lack of capacity," but because they lacked access to basic instruction: "Hence, the tremendous, unavoidable necessity for greatly increasing facilities for Christian education." His fall trip would give him a chance to review progress of schools already operating in China, Korea, and Japan and to promote new ones.[3]

In Korea, missionaries and educators awaited his arrival, knowing he had been doing preliminary work on their behalf. Soon after Goucher had returned from his 1913 trip, Horace Underwood wrote that the government had selected two potential sites in Seoul for a university campus. But there were rumors the governor-general might be replaced. Goucher urged Underwood to secure the best site "at the earliest possible moment," because in Terauchi's absence, "negotiations may be seriously retarded." Back in Baltimore, he began assessing needs and resources and securing funding for buildings and equipment. Goucher reached out to one likely prospect, John T. Underwood, Horace's older brother and the founder of the Underwood Typewriter Company: "I told him if he would constitute himself a committee of one to provide the $100,000 ($2.4 million), I would constitute myself a committee of one to secure the other $75,000 ($1.8 million)." When the businessman said that was too much money for him to raise from his contacts, Goucher replied, "You need not solicit the $100,000, you can have the privilege of paying it, and I cannot pay the $75,000 but I would undertake to raise it."[4]

In June 1914, Bishop Lewis wrote that he, Underwood, and representatives of other denominations in Seoul had unanimously decided that the university's affairs should be conducted under the auspices of the Educational Section of the Continuation Committee, which Goucher chaired. There were fears that the Japanese in Korea were becoming hostile to establishing Christian schools, and his colleagues in Seoul hoped Goucher would take the lead in securing backing from the home missionary boards and the occupation government. Lewis urged his friend to personally conduct these negotiations:

> All agree that no man has ever come to Seoul who has received anything like the attention from the government that was freely accorded to you. Since you left the country, references have been made by the officials here which clearly indicate that they look upon you as representing united Christendom in Christian education matters. It is therefore of the utmost importance that this impression be deepened by the method of conducting our negotiations with the government.

Lewis strongly advised Goucher to "make this work your first business" on the upcoming trip.[5]

By the time his ship left San Francisco at the end of September, the war had spread to the Pacific. In August, Japan had followed its ally Great Britain in declaring war on Germany, which held territory in China's Shantung (Shandong) Province and had colonies on several Pacific islands, including Samoa and New Guinea. There was some concern that Goucher's ship, carrying barbed wire destined for Russia, might be intercepted and detained by a German warship, but he arrived in Japan without incident. During his short time there, Goucher again discussed forming an interdenominational university before moving on to Korea, where plans were more advanced. Goucher wrote Bishop Earl Cranston to tell him that prospects for the union college in Seoul had improved, owing to "the kind consideration which government officials gave to the project I was enabled to present to it." He added, "What seemed to be a condition of disaster was arrested." His stop in Korea was also brief, but he promised to return in the spring of 1915, after spending four months studying the state of educational and missionary affairs in China.[6]

Goucher was drawn to education in China both because the challenge was so enormous and the potential for improvement so great. As he would note after his visit, "No other people in all the world have so persistently and for so long a period exalted learning." Yet only two percent of school-age children in China were being educated. Under the new Yuan government, funds began to be diverted to provincial primary schools, and many temples were being turned into classrooms. Nevertheless, Goucher estimated a million additional schools were still needed.[7]

On site, Goucher noticed how missionaries' conversion strategies in China had changed in the last few years. The individual appeal for salvation, while still important and carried on "without abatement," had offered converts a way to escape eternal punishment and reap personal blessings, which Goucher found a "narrow and selfish" motivation. Now, he added, personal salvation was seen as part of an enlarged ministry and in a broader social context, as "a call to become a larger asset in one's family, an evangelist in the community, a dependable and constructive citizen in the nation." The new approach, he saw, was "communistic," promoting the common good and looking toward "Chinese transformation as a Christian nation." But Goucher cautioned Westerners on the ground against ethnocentrism:

> In seeking to understand oriental problems occidental culture may prove to be a liability rather than an asset. This is likely to be the case unless the occidental holds in strict abeyance many of his habits of thought, accepted standards of excellence, hitherto unquestioned convictions, and uses his mind as an instrument for unprejudiced investigation. This is especially true in his approach to Chinese problems, for China is a land of exceptional magnitude, apparent contradictions, and continual and colossal surprises.[8]

❋ ❋ ❋

In mid-November 1914, Goucher was set to join Bishop Bashford on their second trip to West China, intending to "inspect and counsel" in the cities between Chungking and Chengtu, and "meet the officials who are interested in . . . advantages of education." Again, they would take a long boat trip up the Yangtze River, followed by an overland trek in sedan chairs. Frank Gamewell, having survived the Boxer Rebellion, had warned Goucher before he left Baltimore that successive upheavals had led to "widespread brigandage," making it "impossible to travel in many parts of China." The route that Goucher and Bashford were planning to follow was "badly infested with marauding bands" committing daily robberies.[9]

Indeed, Chinese officials tried to dissuade them from making the trip west. On due consideration, however, Goucher believed "the path of duty seemed so manifestly in this direction that we proceeded according to what we believed to be the guidance of the Spirit." In an echo of his experience in the Middle East five years earlier, magistrates in various districts along the way insisted on giving the travelers an escort—anywhere from two to twenty-five men—through lawless territory. But while they heard reports of robberies every day, "No harm came nigh us and we were able to do the work which we had undertaken, the results of which seem thoroughly worthwhile."[10]

Conditions in Chengtu had stabilized some. West China Union University was open again—with departments in arts, medicine, theology, and teacher training—and local officials were less resistant and more sympathetic to Christian enterprises. The highest provincial authority had closely reviewed Rowntree's map of the campus and used his personal influence to cut through local red tape. One missionary reported that even President Yuan had donated money of his own.[11]

Goucher stepped up his personal commitments as well. He had been supporting several Goucher Schools in Chengtu since his 1911 visit, but there were continual new requests for money. One missionary admitted, "I know that the calls upon your funds are 'Legion,' but at the same time I know your interest in this line of our work." Now Goucher drew up a proposal to create a Primary School Unit for Szechuan, to include four junior primary schools and one senior primary school, all to be located close enough to WCUU's Normal School to serve as labs for aspiring teachers. He sought the "highest efficiency in teachers and scholars," with "quality taking precedence over quantity in every detail." To encourage the best students, he created competitive scholarships, open to those completing the junior primary level; criteria included academics, deportment, ability, leadership, and health, and winners received three years of free tuition at the senior school.[12]

Following the template he had laid out for schools in North India in the 1880s, Goucher presented a detailed operations plan and appointed a local oversight committee. Daily activities would include Bible readings, prayers, and hymns alongside the academic curriculum. His five-year pledge would cover salaries for teachers and assistants, the purchase of tracts of land large enough to include playgrounds, and construction costs. The buildings, he specified, were to be "well lighted, well ventilated, thoroughly sanitary throughout, . . . properly equipped and well built of good material, but as inexpensive as may be in order that they may serve as models for similar buildings." He put a limit on his funding, however. He expected the schools to become self-supporting as quickly as possible, but certainly by the time his pledge expired.[13]

It was Goucher's hope that students who passed through the Primary School Unit would, in time, be admitted to West China Union University. He had similar expectations for the students at the Chungking Union High School, which he had helped organize three years before. "To unite the two institutions more perfectly," he created additional competitive scholarships at that high school to cover a year of junior college at Chungking, followed by two years at WCUU. One university administrator wrote him in approval: the plan would attract "the best men" and strengthen the ties between the two schools.[14]

By mid-January 1915, Goucher and Bashford began their return trip, taking a leaky houseboat down the Yangtze. On board, Goucher wrote Bishop Cranston, outlining the circuitous course he would follow over the next six months. He had promised to return to Korea, and there were "urgent demands" for him to come to the Philippines. He also needed to revisit Japan for a few more weeks "in the interest of their great educational scheme." He still wanted to visit "a number of educational centers in China as well, such as Peking, Nanking, Foochow, Kiukiang, Nanchang, Tsinanfu (Jinan), Soochow (Suzhou), etc."[15]

Goucher's first stop after West China was Foochow, the home base of his friend and fellow fundraiser Bishop Wilson Lewis, who had asked for a consultation. Attending a meeting of the interdenominational, university planning committee he had helped organize in 1911, Goucher found that in the interim, union medical, theological, and teacher-training schools had been established as potential affiliates of the new university. Several ongoing schools in the area, such as the Methodist Anglo-Chinese College, were ready to furnish students. He urged that the Fukien Union College of Liberal Arts be established as soon as possible, to be in a position to serve a growing population distant from other university centers. Goucher said that the many

Fukien residents migrating to the Malay Archipelago also created an opportunity to help shape development there as well. As an impetus to launching the school by the upcoming Chinese New Year, Goucher pledged to cover a share of the first two years' operating budget. A missionary would tell him later, "I am quite sure that without your presence and your generous help we could not have organized." (Goucher would become a trustee of the new university, known as the Fukien Christian University.)[16]

In mid-March 1915, Goucher and Lewis set sail for Manila to meet with Bishop William Eveland, who faced a shortage of money and manpower for mission work in the Philippines. He, too, had asked Goucher for a consultation: "I would like to see things through your larger experience and clearer and more mature vision and judgment." Goucher attended two days of the Philippine Islands Annual Conference, where his advice was not so warmly received by some; given the mission's strained resources, he recommended that the Methodists limit their working territory. At least one missionary contacted the secretary of the Board of Foreign Missions, complaining that Goucher had not explored any territory except Manila, nor "did he seem to be much interested in Philippine Islands work." But the writer admitted, "I find no fault with this since he is so much interested in other fields."[17]

✳ ✳ ✳

By April, Goucher made his promised return visit to Korea. The union school had finally opened as Chosen Christian College (now Yonsei University), with Horace Underwood as its president and nearly fifty students enrolled for the spring term. As the first semester began, Goucher and Bishops Lewis and Harris gave "inspiring messages" to the students housed in temporary classrooms rented from the YMCA. The college was operating under new educational ordinances, announced by the Japanese at the end of March 1915, that affected the several hundred missionary-sponsored schools in Korea. As outlined in Tokyo's *Official Gazette*, the government-general proclaimed that "not only government and public schools but also private schools, whose curricula are fixed by provisions of law, shall not be permitted to give religious instruction or conduct religious ceremonies." Director Komatsu of the Bureau of Foreign Affairs in Korea further explained the government's view in the *Seoul Press*, "[W]e are resolved to maintain an absolute independence in our policy and system concerning national education, which we formulate and put into effect by ourselves without foreign influence or assistance."[18]

But there was some leeway in the Korean ordinances. Private schools which held a government permit before the regulations took effect had ten years to either conform or close their doors. As for Chosen Christian College, it was too late to secure the necessary papers before opening, but the grace period did apply to the John D. Wells Training School for Christian Workers in Seoul. The new college was able to operate under its permit. Nevertheless, Director Komatsu left no doubt about Japan's longterm educational plans: "[I]t is the purpose of Japan to assist, guide, and lift up the Korean people lagging in the race of civilization, and make them not only good and intelligent but also loyal subjects of the Empire both in name and reality."[19]

Lewis and Goucher also spent two days in Seoul attending the Korea Annual Conference. The mission property John and Mary Goucher had financed in 1885 was worth $150,000 in gold in 1915—equivalent to more than $3.6 million a century later. Goucher was pleased with the success of Pai Chai Hakdang, later observing it had "built itself into the community, its scholars have included hundreds of children who have given themselves to Christianity and have gone out as leaven to leaven the whole community." The school's current needs were a major topic at the conference. When Goucher was there in 1913, he had attended a meeting of the mission's Finance Committee that debated an expansion, including a new academic building, dormitory, athletic field, and additional property. About a quarter of the money was to come from local subscriptions and the rest raised from donors in the United States. Goucher had approved the plan, and Bishop Lewis had agreed to help raise funds for the academic building. Now he told the assembly that owing to war conditions, he could not make good on his offer. He agreed, however, to borrow $10,000 ($243,000) for the project if someone would pay the interest on the loan.[20]

In addition to giving what the meeting's minutes called a "splendid address," Goucher agreed to cover that interest for two years. He also pledged to donate any interest saved through early repayment of the loan to the development of the athletic field. With those commitments made, the conference adjourned on the second day for members to attend the groundbreaking for what would be known as the East Building (now the Appenzeller/Noble Memorial Museum). Wearing a black skullcap in place of his trademark hat, Goucher wielded a pick axe to begin the new construction.[21]

On this trip, Goucher also reconsidered the three-year scholarships he had instituted in 1910 for Pai Chai students to attend the Theological School at Aoyama Gakuin. Arthur Berry, who administered the awards in Tokyo, had recently informed him that two of the scholarship students had failed their exams twice and were ineligible to take them again. Berry asked if he could still use the money to support the pair for another year, to spare them the shame of returning home early as failures. Goucher replied that the scholarship fund was "established to secure excellence" and standards should not be compromised. Even so, to help the students, he agreed to pay up to half the amount he had given them the year before. He stipulated, however, that his name "must not be known in connection with it by anyone but yourself." He wanted to protect the integrity of the scholarships: "If [my name] were known, [this] assistance would associate with that fund and would prevent the fund accomplishing the very thing created for by condoning failure to meet requirements." Nevertheless, he also included a $200 donation (nearly $5,000) to the scholarship fund in his letter.[22]

After spending time at Pai Chai Hakdang, Goucher decided to modify the competitive-scholarship rules for Aoyama Gakuin to better serve "the urgent need for an educated Christian ministry in Korea and in view of the historic and potential relation of Pai Chai to the development of leaders." Rather than support two students at a time, beginning the following year, the scholarship would cover five students. Each recipient would need to sign a pledge to serve as a minister in his homeland for as many years as he received funds; otherwise he would be obliged to refund to the Theological School any scholarship money for time not served.[23]

Alice Appenzeller, daughter of Pai Chai Hakdang founder Henry G. Appenzeller and a teacher at the girls' Ewha Hakdang, wrote Goucher after this visit to Korea: "I want to tell you how much good you did while you were here. . . . I have gone about my task in this little corner with renewed courage since then."[24]

※ ※ ※

Over the next two months, Goucher kept zig-zagging among the three East Asian countries. He headed to Shanghai for two weeks of meetings related to the Continuation Committee, the Educational Association of China, and the East China Central Conference. He returned to Tokyo for a meeting concerning the union school now to be known as the University of East Asia. Goucher believed that the Japanese, in contrast to the underserved Chinese, were becoming the most educated people in the world, saying they would soon have the smallest percentage of illiterates and the largest percentage of school-age children in school. He also found Japan more open to Christianity than it had been in thirty years.[25]

Then he was back in Korea once more, before traveling to Nanking. Bishop Lewis later told Goucher one of his "most distinct and far reaching services rendered in China" on the trip was to meet with representatives of the University of Nanking. "You visualized policies for the institution that took deep root in the heart of those who are at the center of things." (Novelist Pearl S. Buck would teach at this university, starting in 1920.) Goucher had a personal reason to visit the city: His daughter Elizabeth, whom he had not seen in more than a year, was due to join the faculty at the new Ginling College, the first institution in China to offer bachelor's degrees to women. She had written him in Baltimore, addressing him as "precious Father of mine," to say how much she looked forward to the reunion: "Oh! I just stop and pinch myself to know if it is I, anticipating even dimly having you to myself and in just the surrounding I love most to be with you." She signed it with her childhood nickname, "Your Lassie."[26]

Goucher's seventieth birthday passed on June 7 before he set off across the Pacific on the same ship he had arrived on, reaching Baltimore at the end of July 1915. On his return, Joseph Beech wrote him from Chengtu: "Welcome back to the United States once more—I hardly know if I may say 'homeland' to you—the seas claim you a good share of the time." Goucher had given 600 lectures or formal addresses during his more than nine months abroad, and Beech recapped some of what the traveler had accomplished on his trip: "From reports that have come, you have had a remarkable journey and have been at the strategic center—or carried it with you—a large share of the time."[27]

In later speeches, Goucher praised the "extraordinary revolution" he had seen in his travels in China:

> If one considers the time required; the territory and population involved; comparatively small amount of bloodshed; radical governmental change; establishment of international relations; progress in organizing essentials for stability; and the progress made in developing a new national conscience, it is without parallel in human history.

He described the new republic's "rainbow flag," whose colored bars symbolized China's five predominant ethnic groups. He characterized the Chinese people as individualistic, with few common ideals and suspicious of centralized government. Nevertheless, when Japan presented China with its "Twenty-One Demands" early in 1915 (as Goucher was returning from West China), the Chinese realized that "isolation meant absorption and if they did not hang together they would hang separately." Among the demands, Japan wanted control over the Shantung Province, Mongolia, and Manchuria, and sought to prohibit China from leasing further territory to other foreign countries, negating the "Open Door" policy that benefited the United States and other Western nations. Another demand called for China to accept Japanese advisers to oversee its political, financial, and military affairs, making the country a de facto protectorate.[28]

Suddenly, Goucher said, "as with a single bound, these particularistic factors and factions [in China] merged their interests and became radically communistic." As anti-Japanese feeling spread, the Chinese were "reaching together towards the fuller, freer life of a limited Republic, and with a new nationalism and a new patriotism." He called President Yuan Shih-kai "perhaps the greatest statesman of them all in the last fifty years," possibly because Yuan and his administration encouraged Christian educational work in China. But the president was unable to unify a country rife with provincial divisions and power struggles among warlords, even as Japan threatened military action. At the end of May, Yuan was forced to accept a revised list of thirteen demands. (The one requiring Japanese advisers was dropped.) Nevertheless, Goucher foresaw the day China would be "one of the world's great republics."[29]

The relationship between Japan and Korea was causing consternation in many circles as well. From Aoyama Gakuin, Arthur Berry wrote Goucher in August 1915, expressing "much concern over here over the misunderstanding in regard to the educational situation." The home missionary society in New York worried that Japan's new regulations limiting religious instruction in Korean schools might hinder fundraising for Japanese schools. Berry told Goucher, "Of course you will be able to set many of the fears at rest and point out that whatever has been done in Korea, the opportunity for Christian education work in Japan proper has never been so bright before." There also were rumors that Japan and the United States were headed for conflict. Many Americans disapproved of Japan's attempt to limit foreign access to China and expand its regional influence, as well as its ongoing occupation of Korea. In a *Zion's Herald* interview after his trip, Goucher rejected the idea that Japan wanted war: "The press, the people, those in authority, all declare the suggestion utterly foreign to the real sentiment of the Japanese toward us of the western world." Because he was known in both American and Japanese educational, religious, and even diplomatic circles, Goucher's opinion had some weight.[30]

Goucher also reported he had detected only "the remotest quivers" of the world war then raging in Europe, although he did see a falloff in contributions to Asian missions, retarding the expansion of Christian education. Any delays in establishing God's Kingdom in that region were due not to resistance or indifference on the part of "the belated nations," but to a lack of vision and a reluctance to give "in the Home lands." Quoting Alexander Hamilton on the fledgling United States, Goucher urged Christians to support these efforts: "It is ours to be either the grave in which the hopes of the world shall be entombed or the pillar of cloud which shall pilot the race inward to millennial glory."[31]

Perhaps in reaction to the political, social, and military turmoil around the world, Goucher also urged schools everywhere to teach ethics as part of a comprehensive education. His words would be just as timely a century later:

> Higher education must include the education of the highest elements of one's nature. Wherever arsenals and battleships are of greater consequence to a nation than churches and schoolhouses, its development will be perverted and its duration limited. Whenever amassing of wealth and seeking political position are more emphasized as national characteristics than the attaining of character and the maintenance of personal and official integrity, that nation is facing social corruption and disintegration.[32]

John Goucher and Bishop Earl Cranston,
first session of the Methodist Joint Commission
on Unification, Baltimore, Maryland
December 28, 1916 - January 2, 1917

ON THE HOME FRONT

Chapter 24
(1916-1918)

———◆◆———

Every act of selfishness, every unkind word, every ungracious thought is evidence of crudeness, unhealthfulness or deformity of spirit. Every neglect to sympathize with the suffering, to help the needy according to opportunity, evidences a thriftless spiritual life, criminally wasteful of that which is essential to the soul's enrichment.[1]

Despite Goucher's long and demanding trip to Asia, on his return in July 1915, a reporter found him looking "as rested as though he had spent the last ten months quietly at his lovely Pikesville home instead of covering in that time more than 41,000 miles in the East and Far East." Even then, Goucher said that "another such journey is not out of the realm of the possible." By November he was off on another, shorter excursion: a 7,000-mile train ride to Los Angeles and back to attend the General Committee of the Board of Foreign Missions. In February 1916, he set off for a new destination—Panama.[2]

Goucher was an official delegate to the Panama Congress on Christian Work in Latin America, an interdenominational, trilingual conclave of more than 300 representatives from across the Americas and from England, Spain, and Italy. Modeled on the 1910 World Missionary Conference in Edinburgh, it was primarily for Protestant leaders, although Roman Catholics were also invited. Its purpose, according to one article, was "to consider the moral and religious conditions of Latin America with a view to bringing into cooperation the religious forces of the whole hemisphere." The opening of the Panama Canal had drawn both "Latin and Anglo-Saxon culture" into the "most intimate commercial, economic and political relationships," affording "both an opportunity and a duty" to religion. Goucher supported such cooperative efforts and was invited to speak at an evening session. After the meetings, a Committee on Cooperation in Latin America was formed, whose aims mirrored the Edinburgh Continuation Committee. Goucher would subsequently become a supporting member when its secretary had difficulty "finding friends to carry the budget." The officer said if Goucher could give the committee "a leaf out of your large book of experiences, it would be of great help."[3]

John Goucher had been president of the Maryland Bible Society since 1909, and it had sponsored a translation of the Bible into Arabic, which Goucher had given to a few leaders when he was in the Middle East that year. One reason for his going to Panama was to witness the laying of the cornerstone for the Bible House at Cristobal in the Canal Zone. The Maryland branch had pledged $50,000 toward the building—called a "sermon in stone"—in honor of the American Bible Society's centennial. It faced the canal and addressed Goucher's hopes for international outreach: The Bible House expected to give hundreds of thousands of Bibles to sailors on ships passing through, "reaching dwellers in many lands using this great water way of nations."[4]

After Panama, Goucher's international travels were put on hold as World War I intensified. (He did, however, make his way to Toronto, mainly to lead meetings of the Board of Governors of West China Union University.) He continued to make shorter trips, including almost monthly excursions to New York on behalf of the Board of Foreign Missions, or to attend meetings related to his East Asian interests or other church committees. In addition, he spoke at church conferences in Cincinnati, Richmond, Altoona, Washington, and elsewhere, and attended the 1916 General Conference of the Methodist Episcopal Church in Saratoga. He squeezed in some fishing during meetings in Florida and Michigan. At home in Baltimore, Goucher was drawn into a public conflict that involved a critical change for Morgan College. He had asked to step down as president of its Board of Trustees in June 1912, but members, citing their "honor and respect . . . and high appreciation" for his nearly thirty years of leadership, had asked him to remain in office. He did so, but the decision brought him additional stress and unfavorable publicity as the trustees and President John Spencer sought to move that burgeoning institution to a new campus.[5]

✳ ✳ ✳

Morgan College was still housed in a single building, on the site John and Mary had provided more than three decades earlier. When Spencer had become its president in 1902, he felt "no great encouragement," owing to the college's physical constraints and financial woes. Goucher and other trustees had promised their support if he developed an expansion program. Spencer began raising money, in particular by reaching out to churches in the black Washington and Delaware Conferences, but he knew the college required a larger infusion of capital. In 1907, he approached Andrew Carnegie, who pledged $50,000 ($1.3 million) for construction if the college and its friends raised matching funds for an endowment. Over the next five years, Spencer raised that sum, but it seemed imprudent to invest Carnegie's money in the current building as enrollment grew beyond its capacity. As Spencer wrote in his memoirs, "It was agreed that in order to meet the needs of the College for the immediate future, and especially for the more distant future, a large and well selected site would be necessary."[6]

Foremost among the obstacles to a move, however, was the strict racial segregation that had permeated city life since the late nineteenth century. Before the Civil War, black residents were scattered throughout the city, but beginning in the late 1880s, several factors conspired to foster segregation. Black migration from rural Maryland gave Baltimore the second largest African-American population of any American city. Increased industrialization caused the mostly poor migrants to settle close to their jobs, while railroad construction near the harbor forced hundreds of African Americans to find other places to live. Already-crowded alleys became breeding grounds for disease, especially tuberculosis. An influx of European immigrants, many of whom refused to work with blacks, brought increased competition for jobs and created new ethnic enclaves. At the same time, new modes of transportation—first horse-drawn trolleys, then electric streetcars and automobiles—allowed more affluent white Baltimoreans to move to the healthier, safer suburbs.[7]

During the first decade of the twentieth century, as whites moved out of town, their houses became available for affluent blacks to buy or rent. As an example, when the Johns Hopkins University moved north from downtown in 1901, prime faculty and student housing opened to African Americans. There was pushback, however. In June 1910, when black lawyer W. Ashbie Hawkins purchased a white woman's house on McCulloh Street, the unofficial racial dividing line, many whites felt a barrier had been breached. Hawkins then rented the house to his law partner, George W. F. McMechen, who in 1895 had been Morgan College's first graduate. McMechen told the press he was looking for larger and more comfortable quarters, not trying to force his way into a white neighborhood. But *The Baltimore Sun* warned that the city was under a "negro invasion," and reactionary whites formed the McCulloh Street-Madison Avenue Protective Association. McMechen was subjected to vituperation and vandalism.[8]

This white citizens' revolt prompted Mayor John Barry Mahool in December 1910 to sign an ordinance, passed by the City Council, dividing every street into "white blocks" or "colored blocks." No black person could move into a block where more than half the residents were white, and vice versa. Furthermore, racially monolithic blocks were required to stay that way. Over the next two-and-a-half years, courts would overturn the law twice, but it was amended to pass constitutional challenge late in 1913. Jim Crow laws passed a few years earlier already segregated public transportation in Maryland. Now there was segregation in housing, as well as restrictions on blacks building schools or churches in white neighborhoods (or the reverse). The stated rationale for these restrictions—"preserving peace, preventing conflict and ill feelings between the white and colored races in Baltimore city, and promoting the general welfare of the city"—became a rallying cry for those opposed to Morgan College's move.[9]

Communities mobilized opposition to Morgan's relocation to their areas. One site considered was Mount Washington, just north of the city on the rail line along the Jones Falls Valley; one resident called it "one of Baltimore's oldest and most conservative suburbs." The proposed forty-three-acre property included fields and fruit orchards and an old stone lodge, and there was a small black settlement and church nearby, as well as a few new homes being built for middle-class blacks. Spencer and Morgan trustees wanted to devote half the property to the new campus, reserving the rest to build more housing for African Americans.[10]

When the college's interest became known, one white homeowner contacted Goucher, praising him as "fair in your convictions" while cautioning him that the college's move into "the heart of such a village as Mt. Washington would be a reflection on your good judgment." An opposition group mailed 1,500 letters to residents and organized a rally "against negro invasion." Representatives of the area improvement association also wrote Goucher in September 1913: "The mere suggestion of locating Morgan College at Mount Washington, especially if this were followed by the grouping of a negro settlement around the site of the college has aroused the most acute indignation among the citizens of this section." These fretful citizens urged him to "exert your influence to prevent the consummation of a project so inimical and so detrimental to the best interests of our community." The city's mayor, James Preston, added fuel to the fire, predicting that the black institution would depress property values.[11]

At the same time, another property was available in Baltimore County, about fifty acres not far from Alto Dale. Again, the Morgan administration proposed devoting half of that tract to the new campus, to be partially funded by the Andrew Carnegie gift, and the rest to "a premium residential community for African Americans." More than 150 residents in the surrounding areas held a mass meeting and sent Goucher a resolution opposing Morgan's buying land in the heart of "one of the finest suburban neighborhoods of Baltimore,"and decrying the "threatened despoliation of this section." The signatories "respectfully urged" the trustees to consider "the strong sentiment existing in the city and State against the imposition upon any neighborhood occupied largely by white residents of a negro institution." An editorial in *The Baltimore Sun* also castigated the college trustees for considering such a move: "If [the trustees] have any such purpose seriously in mind, they must be utterly blind to their own interests or careless of public sentiment. We do not believe they could do anything which would more injuriously affect the usefulness and development of the college, or which would so intensify race prejudice among the better classes of respectable white people." The paper further suggested the trustees should "call an immediate and peremptory halt on this project. They have dallied with it too long already."[12]

Undeterred by this pushback, the board continued to pursue the purchase, with the assistance of several African Americans Spencer had recruited. At the June 1914 meeting of the Morgan trustees, Goucher reported progress from the committee researching the site, and he appointed additional members to sell the building at Fulton and Edmondson Avenues and prepare to secure the new property. By the end of the summer, however, bank financing fell through and World War I loomed. As Spencer would note with disappointment, "The chosen site could not be purchased and the search was continued."[13]

In 1915, the United States Bureau of Education, having looked into Morgan's operation, commended its work but recommended that it "speedily secure an adequate site in Baltimore." Goucher and Spencer both stressed "the urgent need of immediate action" at the June 1916 Board of Trustees meeting. Another committee was appointed and authorized to select and purchase new property and dispose of the old "as soon as satisfactory arrangements can be made." There was an additional reason for an immediate push: Morgan's fiftieth anniversary was coming in 1917, and trustees were planning a $150,000 ($3.3 million) fundraising campaign for the college and its affiliated schools in Princess Anne and Lynchburg. It was Spencer who finally found the school's new site, about seventy acres in Northeast Baltimore, on Grindon (now Cold Spring) Lane between Harford and Hillen Roads. Known as Ivy Mill, it had been the site of a grist mill dating to the late 1700s and then a quarry. A black family was living in part of the old mill, and a Baltimore County school for black children occupied the remaining space. About ten African-American families lived on the site. The property also included the Ivy Mill Hotel, a tavern with rooms to let, and about twenty other buildings, several adaptable to college needs; the size of the plot left room for expansion.[14]

Again, Spencer and the trustees wanted to reserve part of the tract for a new community, as Goucher explained, "wherein colored persons who wish to rear their families in the presence of a high ideal, free from ordinary and low temptations, in a clean, social atmosphere, with healthy surroundings may have the opportunity to strengthen their conditions." Morgan Park, as it became known, had the potential to house several hundred black families, including college faculty and staff. Early in 1917, Goucher met with Mayor Preston to inform him of the plan; the mayor agreed it would "do a great deal to assist the movement for securing better homes for the colored people of Baltimore."[15]

The *Afro-American* newspaper highlighted two reasons for a housing shortage: "Not only has the segregation law 'bottled up' Baltimore's colored population, but there has been a considerable influx here from the South in recent months on account of the big labor demand." The *Baltimore News* reported that the majority of the city's nearly 90,000 African Americans "must seek its habitations where the white, even the poorest whites, will no longer live." Indeed, city Health Department statistics confirmed that the black mortality rate was twice as high as the white, and three-and-a half times as high for deaths from tuberculosis. The mayor pointed out that the spread of contagious diseases "jeopardizes not only the lives of the colored people, but also the lives of the white people with whom they are brought into close daily contact." Public action was called for.[16]

At the end of February, Mayor Preston invited more than 100 leading citizens to a City Hall conference "to discover any practicable remedies" to the housing and health crises. Preston wrote, "The unsanitary housing of many of our colored people and the congestion within the areas in which they reside are developing breeding places for disease. This constitutes a serious menace to the general health of our city." *The Baltimore Sun* reported, "It is felt that the present limits in which the negroes are segregated by ordinance are becoming too congested and that other means of securing housing for them will have to be provided." Goucher spoke at the meeting, estimating that Morgan's intention to build new housing would benefit 20,000 African Americans. He predicted the project would create a domino effect: "Homes vacated by those moving into them would be available for others unable to locate in the colony, and their domiciles in turn, would be occupied by another group, thus making improvement all along the line."[17]

In a draft document on Morgan's plans, Goucher explained further what was at stake for Maryland, Baltimore, and its black population should housing conditions not improve. Under better conditions, the city's African Americans, "under wise Christian leadership," could be "a valuable asset to the State, contributing to its industrial development, increasing its revenues, assisting in the maintenance of law and morality by attaining to self-respecting, industrious, dependable, and useful lives." But the city housing ordinance had "placed a limitation upon the development of homes for its colored citizens, which retards their virtuous development and is a serious menace to the future of the race and threatens the city and state." At the mayor's meeting, with an audience of potential sponsors, Goucher suggested that all the Morgan College plan lacked was approval of "thoughtful and courageous men" who were interested in improving the city, and were willing to provide security for the school's financial investment in the development. He told reporters the next day, "We have lived with the evil [of poor housing conditions] so long," but the trustees needed to be certain "the men who do the thinking for Baltimore" were willing to support a modern, African-American suburb adjacent to the college.[18]

Very few black men had been invited to the conference, and those only as observers. The reason given was that the property affected was largely owned by whites—although the mayor promised a follow-up meeting with black representatives. The African-American press reacted skeptically to the conference and Goucher's proposal. An *Afro-American* reporter observed that Preston and conference participants were as well intentioned "as any meeting of that kind could be," but compared it to "the play of Hamlet with Hamlet left out." His readers, after all, were as deeply concerned about the housing crisis as anyone in Baltimore. Another article in the same issue maintained that Goucher's proposal "for relief of the colored people in the seggregation [sic] district is probably all right as he sees it, but it is far from being all right as the colored people see it." The article predicted that few would take advantage of "his very kind effort," as suitable housing already existed in the city; the "true solution" to African-American housing problems was "to get rid of the obnoxious segregation law."[19]

Preston's conferees recommended he appoint a committee to offer suggestions to alleviate housing conditions, and Goucher was among twenty men named. The constitutionality of Louisville, Kentucky's housing segregation law was currently before the Supreme Court, and its decision would also affect the Baltimore law. Shortly after forming the committee, the mayor wrote its members, "The colored people are making a great deal of noise about the Segregation Ordinance. . . . It looks to me like they are trying to change the little movement which has been started for better housing, into an opportunity to affect the public mind about colored segregation." Preston told Goucher and others that he was delaying any official meeting with African Americans until the case was decided.[20]

President Spencer, representing the Morgan trustees, meanwhile proceeded to negotiate the purchase of Ivy Mill. Much like Goucher and Frysinger in Princess Anne thirty years earlier, he made visits to the property under cover of darkness or bad weather to keep his intention secret. Over the preceding nine years, Spencer had looked at more than fifty prospective locations in the city, suburbs, and surrounding counties. As a later history of the college notes, "In each case, as soon as the purchaser became known, opposition developed." So too this time. White residents from several neighborhoods adjacent to Ivy Mill asked the trustees to reconsider, saying the purchase would depreciate property values and bring homeowners financial hardship. A letter from one community association summed up the feelings of the nearly 3,000 area residents:

> We respectfully submit that this Honorable Board is aware of the fact that white and colored people will not fraternize or intermingle, and that to establish a colored institution or colony in the midst of and contiguous to this thickly settled white community would create a condition which would continually occasion ill feeling and enmity between these two people.[21]

One area resident wrote Goucher to argue, "If Morgan College and Colony were very desirable neighborhood features that would attract whites within their vicinity there would not have been any protest to former prospective sites." If the college did proceed with its plans for Ivy Mill, he predicted, "It will be a case of the whites selling their properties to the trustees for the use of the colony or a case of the whites arming themselves and destroying property and life. Which of the two it will be remains to be seen." Another writer urged (with no punctuation to slow the flow of his irate thoughts), "Think it over Doctor consider our position as well in the matter you would not yourself tolerate such a proposition in your own community." *The Baltimore Sun* weighed in, saying one group of residents had "blood in its eye for any invasion of its 99 percent, pure white community by a Negro institution, colony or settlement of any kind or character" and would "fight any such invasion to the last ditch." Opponents even tried to bribe Spencer.[22]

On the other hand, officers of the Neighborhood Improvement League, representing segregated black areas in West Baltimore, wrote

Goucher of their "profound interest in [Morgan College] and the present plan," urging the trustees to proceed. If they failed, "it would mean DEATH to any future plan of expansion for the institution for the future. It is purely a matter of selfishness on the part of those who oppose it." Goucher thanked the group for its "frank statement" and promised to present it to the Board of Trustees. The board, he wrote with some understatement, had received a number of letters, "but not all are exactly in the same spirit."[23]

Morgan dean William Pickens also wrote to apprise Goucher of "the colored people's attitude toward the new college site." While he and others had suggested the black community "'sit tight' and say nothing inflammatory [sic]" to provoke white reaction, their silence should not be taken as a sign of indifference. "A disappointment of this interest . . . would be next to a disaster and would retard the college for a generation to come. . . . The few property holders are faced by imaginary dangers, but the risk and danger of holding back the colored people of Baltimore for fifty years is very real."[24]

The president of the Epworth League of the Washington Conference, representing 6,000 young African Americans, also wrote to thank Goucher for "the interest you have manifested in the well being of the colored race." She went on, "Their hope [is] that you will continue to be a friend tried and true in the future, as you have been in the past and that your labors for the uplift of all the races will be approved by the Most High, whom you love so well and serve so faithfully."[25]

On May 31, 1917, the Board of Trustees voted unanimously to approve the relocation plan and pay $60,000 ($1.1 million) for the Ivy Mill tract, which remains part of the Morgan State University campus. The next day, a notification letter was sent, over Goucher's signature, to several dozen interested parties, and it appeared in local newspapers within the week. He stated that the trustees had weighed the views of those who "criticized and even protested" and those who "highly commended" the plan. They had read all of the mail, conducted interviews with concerned individuals and groups, and discussed the plan with numerous parties, giving "an interested and unhurried hearing to all who have asked it."

> The responsibility of the Board of Trustees is primarily civic and not sentimental and their motive is the largest helpfulness to the largest number. The interests involved in their action are not confined to any particular community or to any racial unit even though including one-sixth of the population of the City and of the State. These interests are vitally related to the health and development of the City of Baltimore and to various other economical and ethical questions which reach far beyond the State of Maryland. . . .
>
> [The trustees] carefully reviewed the entire problem in all its bearings, so far as they were able, and concluded, all present voting in the affirmative, that there is no valid reason why they should change their program; but on the contrary, their civic and moral obligations require them to proceed with the enterprise . . .[26]

The opposition responded swiftly, with much resentment focused on Goucher as president of the Board of Trustees. Several improvement associations sent him a joint letter reiterating their position: "You cannot be ignorant of the harmful antagonism which is engendered by an effort such as yours to exploit your theories of race equality. . . . Nor can you be ignorant of the fact that natural racial prejudices and sentiments cannot be eradicated by such an arbitrary 'strong armed' method." In the associations' view, the State of Maryland should no longer offer any aid "to a body which proposes to so indecently ignore the natural and just sensibilities and even prejudices of so large a body of people." If the college held fast, these neighborhood groups offered to raise money to buy the land from the trustees and scuttle the plan.[27]

Aggrieved individuals wrote Goucher as well. One of the milder letters praised his "deep interest in the civic welfare of our community," but asked him not to deny the area the privilege to enjoy "life, liberty and the pursuit of happiness." A more vehement missive began, "Shame! on the Christian men of Baltimore, who think more of the Negro than their own race, that they would place a Negro Colony and College in the middle of a white community." The correspondent said she had written Goucher before, but her appeal "fell on deaf ears and a cold heart." Now she asked, "Where is your civic pride and moral obligations we would like to know. Answer Dr. Goucher—how would you like it in the vicinity of Goucher College or your country home;

would you submit to such an invasion." In ignoring the opposition, she felt, the trustees had only exacerbated racial tensions. She added, "The Negro would be far better off, if theorists would let them alone."[28]

After Goucher's letter explaining the board's action appeared in one morning newspaper, a neighborhood resident wrote that afternoon asking the paper to print his rebuttal letter to Goucher as soon as possible. As Spencer wrote to the board president, "In the strange doings of these people they seem to think it perfectly proper to give letter, resolution, etc. to the public before presenting them to our Board." The newspaper writer claimed Goucher's letter was "noticeable for its broad generalities and lack of application to the particular question at issue." He then proceeded to reframe each of Goucher's claims to bolster his own case. He concluded:

> You have had much to say of ethics in this matter. Do you consider it ethical to place your own race at a disadvantage in order to exploit a dream of advancement of the negro? If so, you must be dead to all sense of right or justice. . . . You must align yourself with either your own race or that of the negro. It is for you to choose. [29]

Goucher's and the trustees' resolve galvanized neighborhood activists. They held public meetings and raised several thousand dollars to cover legal fees to fight the purchase and development. Several families filed a petition with the Baltimore County Circuit Court in early August, claiming a decline in property values and "irreparable injury" if Morgan were allowed to move into the area. They also charged that the college did not have authority under its charter to buy and develop land for housing. The Circuit Court unanimously denied the petition, finding that the charter granted Morgan the right to "have, hold and acquire" land and property for the purpose of supporting the school and carrying out its plans. For any college, selling or leasing unneeded land was "one of the most usual and approved methods of investment." (In 1918, the state Court of Appeals upheld the lower court's decision.) Pushing further, protesters asked the Judiciary Committee of the Maryland legislature to revoke Morgan's charter. Spencer responded: "No institution—educational, religious, commercial or charitable—is safe if [opponents'] arguments prevail." The committee unanimously rejected the request. Undaunted,

Morgan's foes then introduced three other bills in the legislature. All of them failed.[30]

Legal wrangling aside, there was much to celebrate when Morgan College turned fifty in late November 1917. Earlier that month, the Supreme Court had found the Louisville housing segregation law unconstitutional, in effect overturning the Baltimore ordinance. The $150,000 fundraising goal had been reached, and relocation plans were proceeding apace. Anniversary events included an "automobile pilgrimage" to the new site, followed by a mass meeting that evening at which Goucher reviewed the history and influence of the school since its days as the Centenary Biblical Institute: More than 5,000 students had studied there, nearly 1,000 of them becoming teachers; many other graduates had become ministers, doctors, and lawyers. In words similar to those he had once used to describe the growth of the Woman's College of Baltimore (although now with a masculine reference), he told the crowd that Morgan "had gone through the period of infancy, youth, and early manhood." It was now ready to "enter upon a riper period of usefulness" with its move.[31]

By 1918, the Board of Trustees was finally ready to tap the $50,000 Andrew Carnegie had pledged years earlier. World War I had caused a surge in building costs, however, and that amount was no longer sufficient. Spencer appealed to the Carnegie Corporation, which donated an additional $46,000 ($723,000) for the campus's first new building, to be named Carnegie Hall. Plans also proceeded for the housing that would surround the college. Goucher signed a deed transferring nearly twenty-five acres from Morgan College to a separate company responsible for developing Morgan Park, which would be divided into 137 lots with building restrictions. The area would become home to such luminaries as civil rights leaders W. E. B. Du Bois and Carl Murphy, and musicians Eubie Blake and Cab Calloway.[32]

A few years later, Bishop Earl Cranston would sum up the scope of Goucher's longtime relationship with Morgan College: "He was more than a mere contributor—he was the ever accessible and reliable defensive and aggressive friend and promoter, sharing in its administration and planning largely for its future development."[33]

✳✳✳

During the same period, Goucher was involved with another major push in which African Americans played a pivotal role. Long committed to fulfilling his sixth "commission"—to work for the unification of American Methodists—he had been a member of the Joint Commission on Federation for many years. He had told the 1908 General Conference that organic union (as opposed to federation) between the northern and southern churches was still not feasible, and that "a deliberate courtship would accomplish more than a precipitate proposal." Representatives of both sides continued their work, and the southern General Conference finally approved a framework for "unification by reorganization" in 1914. A Committee of 60 prepared a similar report for the 1916 northern General Conference in Saratoga. As a committee member, Goucher presented the plan to the delegates, telling them that "the proposed amalgamation" would protect "all interests just as the federal government protects interests of the states, but in the case of federated Methodism, the world and not the nation would be under ecumenical control." According to a news account, following his presentation, "everyone rose to his feet," and the building "shook with applause" as the assembly voted approval."[34]

Future deliberations were to be carried out by a new Joint Commission on Unification—twenty-five members each from the north and south—which held its first meeting in Baltimore at the end of 1916 and met five more times in various cities over the next three years. Goucher, a northern delegate, served as a bridge in discussions with his southern colleagues. As the dean at Vanderbilt University told him, "I do not know any man in your Church who more thoroughly understands the Southern Church and can talk in a more acceptable manner to our preachers and people than you can."[35]

At one meeting, Goucher spelled out to the commissioners what he saw as their focus and responsibilities:

> The Joint Commission is called to serve as an engineer, to discover and organize the dynamics of Methodism, not to reflect its past or present status. We are to serve as seers, as pioneers. Our functions are not to serve as historians. We are not to occupy ourselves with registering theological past. This Commission, as I understand it, is called to see and interpret a vision, not to prepare an obituary. . . . So I take it we are called . . . to form a plan for progress, not for entrenchment, or retrenchment, or for retreat.

Much as he longed for an agreement, he added, he "would rather, far rather, be a party, if it pleased God, to formulating a plan which it may require eight or twenty years for the Church to grow up to, than to formulating a plan which the Church has already outgrown or which it is likely to outgrow before it really becomes effective."[36]

The Methodist Protestant Church, which had separated from the Methodist Episcopal Church in the late 1820s over governance issues, especially the roles of bishops and laymen, was not involved in the Joint Commission. According to a church history, it felt "the Northern and Southern Churches must come to some agreement before unification of the three [Methodist] bodies would be possible." Both northern and southern parties also allowed that "there could be no unification unless each of the churches was ready to make concessions and accept new ideas." The three main issues to be addressed were: the General Conference and its powers; the number and powers of the Jurisdictional or Regional Conferences; and the status of African Americans in the reorganized church. This last issue was a major source of tension at Joint Commission meetings. Several solutions were proposed: The 350,000 African-American members could be left out of the new church structure and asked instead "to unite with some other colored body or Methodist denomination"; they could be an integral part of the reorganized church, but with no representation in the General Conference; or they could have the same rights as white members.[37]

Many years earlier, Goucher had thought the best solution might be a separate, fraternal African-American Methodist Church, alleviating one of the stumbling blocks to northern and southern unity; this idea had been promoted by the 1914 southern General Conference. By the time of the Saratoga General Conference two years later, Goucher supported its recommendation to include black members in one or more Jurisdictional Conferences of their own within a united church. Such a plan, Goucher told his colleagues, would allow African Americans to "study their own problems [so] that they may have their own episcopal supervision within their area; that they may be recognized as an entity and a part of the great Methodist movement; and have the same opportunities and the same responsibilities for meeting their problems as characterize every other of these conferences." He further noted, "[Negroes] have never had the privilege of making their own mistakes. Mistakes have been many, but they have been made for them by others."[38]

At the Joint Commission's first meeting in Baltimore, Goucher proclaimed that he did "not like standing here and talking on the negro question as though that was the only question confronting the Methodist Church." He knew from personal experience that Methodists in South and East Asia, Europe, Africa, and Latin America also had questions about their places in a unified Church. Goucher preferred that the commission discuss any questions of inclusion "on the broader plane" and "not on a particular plane, as though it applied to negroes as altogether different from the rest of humanity." A broader solution, he said, "would not be special legislation, not open to the suspicion of trying to force the negro out of Methodism.[39]

He later told his fellow commissioners, meeting in Savannah in 1918:

> There is nothing in the organic law of the Methodist Episcopal Church, or of the Methodist Episcopal Church, South, which makes the slightest suggestion of legal discrimination against any member of either Church. They are recognized as members whatever their color, whatever their language, whatever their nationality. . . . We should recognize that the Constitution [for a reorganized Church] may not have written into it any special legislation either for or against any class or condition, no discrimination except such as is based upon those things which are removable by the parties themselves.[40]

In addition to granting African Americans their own Jurisdictional Conference, Goucher believed they should be part of a unified General Conference with the same representation as their white brethren. He continued:

> God created all men with the same blood, and God has given to each a different environment, but in spite of race peculiarities, which are inevitable and which may be in a measure antagonistic, He is bringing all men, as His sons, into higher relations of cooperation. Therefore, respecting them as I desire to be respected, I think there should be a proper representation in the General Conference of all American Methodist

organizations throughout the world, as included in the Regional and Sub-regional Conferences.

Goucher noted that the Presbyterian General Assembly and the Episcopal General Convention both had African-American delegates, and "they find the color line is no serious hindrance." In another address he said, "It would be more than a blunder for reorganized Methodism to establish a color line more rigid than other branches of evangelical Christianity working in the same field. . . . It would be bad strategy to do so and unscriptural."[41]

Early in 1920, at its sixth meeting held in Louisville, Kentucky, the Joint Commission finally accepted a proposed constitution to present to the northern and southern General Conferences. It called for six white Jurisdictional or Regional Conferences (later reduced to five) based on geography. There would be one for all African Americans in the United States, who would have proportional representation in the General Conference. Instead of approval for the plan, however, the conferences recommended that a new Joint Commission be formed to reconsider some of the details. That group presented a second draft constitution to the General Conferences in 1924. Both sides adopted it, but the southern group also required approval from three-quarters of its Annual Conferences, which it failed to receive. Goucher had once recommended taking time to formulate a viable long-range plan, but one doubts he anticipated it would take until 1939 for the Methodist Episcopal Church, the Methodist Episcopal Church, South, and the Methodist Protestant Church to finally unite. It was nearly another thirty years before African Americans were fully integrated into the Church.[42]

While at the Joint Commission meeting in Savannah in 1918, Goucher gave an interview to a local paper about another hotly debated issue, women's suffrage: this champion of women's education and father of three daughters opposed it. The topic had engendered spirited discussions in classes when Goucher was college president, but he had discouraged the institution from taking any public stand on the issue. On one occasion, however, returning from his 1907 global trip, he saw an advance program for an upcoming College Night at the Woman's National Suffrage Convention in Baltimore. A number of Woman's College students were listed as ushers for the event. "Very quietly but with evidence of some feeling," Lilian Welsh reported, he inquired who had given them permission to participate. John Van Meter, in charge in Goucher's absence and a proponent of women's suffrage, claimed responsibility. Other leading women's colleges were taking part, and had the Woman's College withdrawn at that point, its reputation might have suffered. In the end, Goucher permitted the students to attend.[43]

In 1918, as the Nineteenth Amendment moved closer to ratification, Goucher remained opposed to women voting. In that *Savannah Press* interview, he spelled out what the paper called his "cogent and concrete reasons." Among them: "The family is the unit of Christian civilization and I consider anything that undercuts home life would be more detrimental to the nation than any benefit which is likely to accrue." He warned that rather than women elevating politics, it might be that politics would instead lower the ethical standard of women. He noted, "The most dangerous element in a republic consists of those who, from indifference or necessity, fail to exercise their franchise"; he feared giving women the right to vote would increase the number of non-voters and not necessarily "increase the vote for furtherance of higher interests for a community." He also felt that some men were trying to hide their own political weaknesses by wanting women to vote on measures "which they say they believe to be right, but yet have not the courage to support themselves." Despite his objections, other northern commissioners at the Savannah meeting favored suffrage, and the southerners, though not in favor, were preparing for it. During the same period, however, Goucher was in step with his Methodist brethren in favoring one other contemporary issue: "I rejoice," he said, "in seeing the progress being made by [alcohol] prohibition."[44]

✳ ✳ ✳

When Goucher was at home during the restricted-travel war years—at 2313 or Alto Dale—he was often entertaining or providing a meal or bed for friends or foreign visitors. One associate said the country home became "the rendezvous of Christian leaders of the whole world." Eleanor Goucher reported that one month, she and her father hosted 100 overnight guests. Goucher once reflected that "the great need in the world is to strengthen fellowship in home life," and he immersed himself with his family when not traveling. In the summer time, Janet and her children—Fisher (Miss J. F.) and Junior—often came out from the city to stay at Alto Dale. Many years later, Goucher's granddaughter testified he "adored his grandchildren" and called him "a real sweety." He didn't mind if they slid down a banister instead of taking the stairs, and they were free to go "everywhere and could do anything—ride the mules, ride in the hay wagon, and all that stuff." Her brother, three years older, followed his grandfather around "all the time," while she preferred sitting on his lap and hearing travel stories about riding an elephant or camel. She recalled him strolling the estate "looking perfect" in a white alpaca suit, as he checked "to see if everything was working" to his satisfaction. In the evening, they sometimes sat around the fireplace toasting marshmallows—rejecting what Goucher once called "the modern tendency" to be "in the same house without living together." In a sermon he decried another familiar, modern sight: "Persons . . . sitting at the same table without holding communication."[45]

When America entered World War I in 1917, the Wilson administration encouraged citizens to plant "war gardens." Goucher the farmer duly dug up nearly two acres of his Alto Dale front lawn, and Goucher College students helped him plant twenty pounds of potatoes; they also helped him harvest the crop, which he proudly noted yielded more than 250 bushels. His sermon topics also turned to the war: "Here we are dreaming of the day when the boys come home; planning celebrations against the days when the boys are home; thinking tenderly, reverently of the boys who never can come home. Yes, every soldier fit to be honored when he comes home offered [his] all." But he also warned, "It is not yet certain how greatly his country will repay."[46]

The armistice ending World War I finally came in November 1918. While Goucher remained true to his Methodist roots and deep Christian faith, his extensive travels and the recent global conflict caused him to rethink religious traditions he might once have dismissed. In a heartfelt sermon delivered as the war's end drew close, he proclaimed:

> There is no such thing as a Methodist religion or a Papist religion or a Lutheran religion. These, all, are merely windows toward the same Sun of Righteousness, doors into the same

holy presence. Seriously, I believe there is but one religion on earth; and whoever is really religious has warmed his soul at the <u>One</u> Fire. To use Laymen Abbott's beautiful definition: 'Religion is the life of God in the soul of each man.' Of that life there may be more or less. To help deepen that life, there are denominations many, each with its special accent and ministry. But religion is essentially one. The devout soul of 1,000 years ago and the devout soul of today; Roman Catholic, Quaker, Methodist—yes, Buddhist and Mohammedan (in so far as they are true to their light) are full brothers by the same father whose life in the soul of a man is religion.[47]

Japan's Third Class Order of the Rising Sun,
conferred on John Goucher in November 1919

*Courtesy of the Baltimore-Washington Conference Archives,
Lovely Lane United Methodist Church, Baltimore, Maryland*

A HALF CENTURY
OF SERVICE

Chapter 25
(1919-Mid-1920)

◆◆

Man's enrichment is through ministry, and helpfulness
is the only patent for greatness.[1]

The year 1919 was a significant milestone for Goucher: it marked
the fiftieth anniversary of his ·entering the ministry. As an active
minister he had led churches and congregations, but during his life, he
also embraced the broader concept of ministry—serving and caring
for others. The Board of Trustees of First Church, with which he had
been closely affiliated for almost forty of those years, issued a public
statement, touching on what he had accomplished at home and abroad:

> Your brotherliness, your devotion to duty, your clear and
> statesmanlike views of men and affairs, your administrative
> ability, your loyalty to the church, your spirituality, and lowly
> walk with God have called forth our most reverent regard. Our
> beautiful House of Worship, and our great [Goucher] College
> will abide as among the lasting monuments of your Christian
> faith and vision, your toil, sacrifice and success. You have
> used your heart and brain, your voice and pen, your means and
> influence unselfishly and for the advancement of the Kingdom
> of God in the world.[2]

That summer in Columbus, Ohio, Goucher would help celebrate
another milestone—the hundredth anniversary of American Methodist
missions. It seemed appropriate that events were held in Ohio, where
John Stewart, an African-American itinerant minister, had begun
his pioneering missionary work with the Wyandot Indians in 1819.
A joint production of the northern and southern church branches and
the Colored Methodist Episcopal Church, the Columbus exhibition—

dubbed a religious "world's fair"—attracted over a million visitors. There were more than 16,000 exhibits representing thirty-seven countries, highlighting both domestic and foreign missions with "an emphasis on the humanities, education, religious, moral and spiritual progress," according to *The Methodist Year Book.* An article in the souvenir program noted the timeliness of the celebration as "our brave boys are coming back" from World War I, and "when hearts are filled with a common gratitude for the blessings of the past and with a common passion for the evangelization of the whole world" in the years ahead. The centennial was a rallying point for renewed commitment to (and recruitment and fundraising for) missions.[3]

At the same time Goucher had been working on the Joint Commission for Unification, he had also served on the Joint Centenary Commission that planned this three-week, multi-million dollar event. As the director of exhibits, he oversaw the conversion of eight large buildings—where livestock and farm implements were displayed at the Ohio State Fair—into international pavilions. Vignettes and presentations of life around the world were part of the program, and more than 500 people—some indigenous to the countries depicted but most American actors in costume—were recruited to take part. Artifacts, parts of buildings and actual villages, a slice of desert life, and exotic animals such as elephants, camels, and water buffalo, were brought to Ohio from far-flung points of origin. The souvenir program listed several scenes a visitor might see walking through the pavilions, "transported in a wink of an eye":

> In India, one sees a child-wife leaving her home . . . surrounded
> by her relatives and friends who walk beside her to the Zenana
> or home of her husband to be. . . . [F]rom a distance down
> the Peking or Nanking Road comes a gorgeous procession of
> dragon worshippers. In Latin America, it is market day
> . . . On to sunny Japan, the land of exquisite gardens, Korea,
> Malaysia and the Philippines, each one varying to some extent
> in manners and customs but all abounding in beauty, life and
> color. Devastated Europe, appalling in all its hopelessness and
> the suffering through which it has passed is seen through the
> crypt which is all that remains of a ruined Cathedral. . . . In our
> own America one is struck by the many intensive problems to
> be met in Home Mission work. . . . We see the organizing of a
> frontier church taking place in a school house where a cow-

puncher is the ring-leader of the enterprise. Rural problems, and those in the mining town are being met by the church as is shown in a series of short demonstrations.[4]

In his history of the fair, Christopher Anderson explains, "Visitors at the Centenary Celebration were then able to view the successful expansion of the Methodist Church into domestic and foreign mission fields. Inside the pavilions of the exposition audiences witnessed the civilizing influences wrought on native peoples by missionaries affiliated with the Methodist missionary societies." Having seen so many of the scenes depicted first hand, Goucher was uniquely qualified to help ensure authenticity. To Anderson, it all gave fairgoers "a glimpse of foreign lands and distant people invisible to many in America outside the pages of missionary periodicals or magazines such as *National Geographic*."[5]

✻✻✻

Despite his personal travel embargo during the war, Goucher had stayed in touch with missionaries and educators in Japan, Korea, and China, and remained involved with his projects in those countries. As ever, his foreign mailbag contained both praise and pleas. At Aoyama Gakuin in 1916, there were plans to add a new academic building and two dormitories. One missionary wrote to thank Goucher for his long-range thinking: "Your insistence on our having prepared a plan of the grounds has proven very wise. . . . [The new buildings] fit into the scheme already prepared." But two years later, school president Takagi Mizutaro reported that college enrollment was down and the institution faced financial trouble, "no matter we have your yearly support." He appealed to Goucher to make certain that Aoyama Gakuin, ever closer to government certification as a university, would benefit from mission-centenary fundraising back home.[6]

Goucher had followed progress at Pai Chai and Chosen Christian College in Korea as well. As a firm believer in balancing a strong body and educated mind, he wanted Pai Chai to have the athletic fields students had long needed. On his previous visit he had marked off the potential size for soccer and baseball fields, and principal Hugh Cynn, who visited Goucher in Baltimore in 1916, sent him blueprints of the

400

proposed facilities. Goucher wrote his own check and solicited a few other donations, and missionary Arthur L. Becker told their friend early in 1918, "By your aid, the athletic field was made the best in Seoul." Although enrollment was high, Pai Chai was in debt. Becker asked Goucher for extra financial support: "We know this adds another burden but having no one else to whom to look for relief, and knowing that you are personally very anxious that Pai Chai become a great factor in our Korean Mission work, I am sending you this appeal."[7]

After attending the opening of Chosen Christian College in 1915, Goucher was asked to continue his support from Baltimore. As Horace Underwood reminded him, the school still lacked papers of incorporation, a scholastic charter, and a permanent site; he asked Goucher to intervene with the Board of Foreign Missions in New York. "It is a shame," Underwood admitted, "to burden a man already overburdened as you are, with added work, but you are the one 'who does things,' who accomplishes, and so I write assured you will do what you can." It's not clear whether Goucher's influence was a factor, but the college received its charter in 1917 and moved to its new campus a year later, with ninety-one students enrolled. Adding to his other committee memberships, Goucher was chosen to serve a two-year term on the Cooperating Board for Christian Education in Chosen, representing the Methodist mission board.[8]

Missionaries in China had also continued their appeals to Goucher during the war years. As one explained, it was "because of your long interest in the Chinese problem, your extensive travels in that land, and your knowledge of its needs and opportunities, that you have a warm hearted interest in the welfare of this mighty people, and will do all you can to promote their progress in Christian life." Goucher maintained his support for the union Fukien Christian University, his schools in the Nanchang District, the scholarship students he sponsored in Chungking, and the junior and senior primary schools near West China Union University. After a visit to Chengtu in 1917, Bishop Wilson Lewis reported that the buildings and grounds for the "Goucher Units" were "models I hope will be copied throughout our area in China." Another missionary alerted him that the war had made the exchange rates less favorable. Although he was striving to get "the best returns from [Goucher's] gold," workers were growing anxious as funding fell short and prices kept rising. Missionaries in China, as elsewhere in Asia, kept looking to their benefactor to increase his own donations or help find more donors.[9]

***

A few months after his seventy-fourth birthday in June 1919, Goucher began a new round of international travel. Over a seventeen-month period, he would make three trips—including another around-the-world journey— spending thirteen of those months away from home and traveling more than 65,000 miles. At the end of September, after a four-year hiatus, John (with Eleanor as his companion) left Baltimore on his sixth trip to East Asia, visiting Japan and Korea twice each, with an extended stop in China in between.

On his visits to Japan—late in 1919 and at the end of the following February—he attended the General Conference of the Methodist Church of Japan and spoke to promoters of the World's Sunday School Convention, to be held in Tokyo in the fall of 1920. He also looked into the possibilities in northern Japan for a Christian union university and for Methodist missionary and educational opportunities. While Goucher was in the north, President Sato Shosuke (who had received financial support from John and Mary while a graduate student at Johns Hopkins) invited him to speak at Hokkaido Imperial University. He addressed a crowd of a thousand students and a hundred faculty members, who, one listener said, "greeted him with such an overflow of enthusiasm as was never witnessed before."[10]

He was accustomed to such warm welcomes at Aoyama Gakuin where, as usual, students, faculty, and administrators hosted receptions and showered him with gifts. Goucher, in turn, threw a dinner of his own, a small one for his Korean scholarship students studying theology there—"all fine fellows." He also paid a personal call on Honda Tei, widow of Honda Yoitsu, the former president of Aoyama Gakuin and bishop of the Methodist Church of Japan, who had died in 1912. Years earlier Goucher had heard from a missionary that Honda had gone into debt, supporting a sick son and poor relatives on his modest salary. After Honda's death, Goucher quietly stepped in to help his wife and provide for the son's education. Thanking him for his visit, the widow wrote, "As a benefactor of Aoyama Gakuin and intimate friend of my husband, you are always in my remembrance. . . . For my sick boy, you gave me much money, and I am very grateful for your kindness." (Her son died soon after Goucher's visit.)[11]

On arriving in Tokyo in October 1919, Goucher had an interview with Premier Hara Takashi, who knew of him through Sato, his boyhood acquaintance. The two men discussed education in Japan and conditions in Korea. Hara reassured Goucher that the Japanese government wanted to maintain good relations with the mission in Chosen and were "earnestly trying" to treat Koreans the same way it treated the Japanese. The premier called Goucher "a good friend of Japan," and asked him to continue explaining "the conditions, the attitude [of the Japanese] people, [their] thoughts, ideals . . . in [a] true and sympathetic way in America."[12]

A month after that meeting, Japan formally conveyed its gratitude for Goucher's forty years of involvement: The emperor, at the request of his cabinet ministers, conferred on him the Imperial Decoration of the Third Class Order of the Rising Sun, the highest honor bestowed on a civilian—Japanese or foreign—in recognition of distinguished service to the country and its people. *The Baltimore Methodist* noted that Goucher's first impulse was to decline the honor. Missionaries and friends, however, persuaded him that "such a decoration, by a non-Christian emperor, was a recognition of the service of Christianity and the value of Christian education to the state too marked to be allowed to pass." Striking as the medallion was—with a ruby red center and radiating golden rays depicting the Land of the Rising Sun—Goucher preferred not to show it, keeping it packed away in its lacquered case. When he later gave a dinner for church dignitaries in Baltimore, they teased him that this much-heralded medal must be a myth, since no one had seen it. "In sheer self-defense," the same article said, the honoree was "compelled to display the splendid symbol and meritorious ornament."[13]

By December, John and Eleanor Goucher began their ten-week stay in China, visiting Peking, Kiukiang, Nanchang, Shanghai, and Nanking, where they joined Elizabeth. Several West China missionaries had warned him that Szechuan was "disturbed by robbers," and the "Big River" and the overland "Big Road" he had traveled on previous trips were often closed. The central government remained weak, and warlords caused ongoing disturbances in the provinces. President Yuan Shih-kai, whose leadership Goucher had praised on his previous visit, had died in 1916; Sun Yat-sen had returned from Japanese exile in 1917 and re-instituted the Kuomintang Party in the south. In addition, what became known as the 1919 May Fourth Movement spurred Chinese nationalism and protests against Japan's being awarded the former German stronghold of Shantung through the Treaty of Versailles. Goucher sent a friend a 1920 New Year's greeting from China, "the land of disorder and destiny." Despite the political disruptions, he found "such an eagerness for counsel and such large opportunity for constructive influence."[14]

Goucher recorded seventy-three speaking engagements in China: at an assembly for students at Ginling College, where Elizabeth was teaching; at meetings in Peking of the Church's Eastern Asia Central Conference; and for various church services and prayer meetings. In Shanghai, he again inspected the Methodists' publishing house and took part in a meeting that explored a possible Methodist-Presbyterian joint publishing venture. As a result of his winter travel, Goucher developed a severe cold and cough, which kept him housebound for several days; even then, visitors flocked to see him, and there was "much conversation about Chinese matters." He was welcomed at receptions wherever he went; in Peking, he was guest of honor at a dinner given by members of his old Dickinson College fraternity, Sigma Chi, who were living in the area. Although unrest in Szechuan Province prevented Goucher's visiting Chungking or Chengtu, he received reports from several West China missionaries at the Central Conference; the governor of Szechuan, visiting the capital, called to see Goucher, and he returned the visit.[15]

Nearing the end of their trip, John and Eleanor returned to Korea. The Korea Annual Conference had met during his brief stop the previous fall and offered a resolution expressing appreciation for his generosity in founding the mission and for continuing to be a friend and supporter. On this second visit, Goucher checked the expanded educational opportunities for women at Ewha, and once again visited Pai Chai Hakdang and Chosen Christian College. The college had suspended classes during the March 1919 Korean independence demonstrations, in which thousands of students around the country had taken part, and many had been arrested by the Japanese. When it reopened that September, there were only sixteen students enrolled, but the institution was now preparing for its second graduation.[16]

From Seoul, father and daughter returned to Japan, revisiting Tokyo and Yokohama. Goucher also met with Japanese leaders to plan a union college in Fukuoka, on the northern island of Kyushu. In his diary, he listed the number of speaking engagements during his visits to these two countries: seventeen in Korea and sixty-eight in Japan. By the first week of March 1920, he and Eleanor were bound for California. En route home, the ship stopped overnight in Manila, where Goucher spent time visiting several mission properties and preaching to American soldiers stationed there.[17]

After reaching San Francisco, the two Gouchers embarked on five days of train travel to Baltimore, where they were welcomed at Union Station (now Pennsylvania Station) by Janet, her husband, and children. Yet after being away for six months and adding more than 27,000 miles to his travel log, John was planning two more international jaunts within the next few months. In the trip's final diary entry, he wrote, "Before leaving Union Station, telegraphed to NY for the *Empress of Russia* to sail Sept. 23 for Yokohama and for reservations on steamer sailing to London cir. 15 of June."[18]

John Goucher in Tokyo,
October 1920
(*Christian Advocate*, July 27, 1922)

INTERNATIONAL EDUCATOR AND CHURCH STATESMAN

Chapter 26
(Mid-1920-Mid-1921)

━━━━━━━━━━━━━━◆◆━━━━━━━━━━━━━

*And I'd rather go down into history with some of the brightest spirits
who have enobled [sic] the earth—moon-struck, apparently, and
defeated—than to accept compromises and compounds with felony,
which a practical world puts forth as substitutes for victory—on the
specious pledge that half a loaf is better than none.*[1]

In May 1920, before leaving the country yet again, Goucher trekked
to Des Moines, Iowa, for the three-week Methodist General
Conference. He had been elected a delegate for the ninth time
since 1888—a record—and was honored along with the bishops at
a special reception. He attended or spoke at committee meetings on
various topics of personal interest—foreign missions, the state of the
Methodist Church and inter-church work, internationalism, and the
upcoming World's Sunday School Convention. He met with foreign
visitors and gave a talk to the Women's Foreign Missionary Society
about planned union colleges for women in Foochow and Chengtu.
On his way home, he detoured to Carthage, Missouri, to see his sister
Ella and her husband, then in their 80s. He was pleased to see they
were "much better than I expected to find them."[2]

Goucher was home for his seventy-fifth birthday on June 7, but a
week later, he left for Canada—"on my way to England," he wrote in
his diary. In Toronto, he was the guest of his friend Chester Massey
for a few days. He had been invited to speak on his Asian work to
the Toronto Annual Conference, and he reviewed Canadian Methodist
support for West China Union University. A meeting with a women's
group promoting a union college for women in Chengtu kept him

"talking and answering questions for two hours." By mid-month, he was on a steamship to England to lead the annual meeting of the Board of Governors of WCUU. (He would be elected board chair for the eleventh time.)[3]

Goucher learned that work at the university was "prospering," and the board "made enlarged plans for the future." A prospectus distributed at the time noted it was the only Christian higher-education institution serving a population nearly equal to that of the United States. Goucher's endorsement stated: "It is the finest system of organized Christian missionary education in the world." By then WCUU occupied nearly 100 acres, with a professional staff of more than twenty, and 300 students enrolled in its various divisions. Nearly twenty buildings were in some stage of development, and the board planned to raise $500,000 (approximately $6 million) to complete the expansion. Provincial leaders and China's president had pledged funds to help. While in London, Goucher also consulted with Fred Rowntree, the university's architect, on campus plans.[4]

John's trip was not all work. He visited his favorite London tailor to order a winter suit and other garments, and went to Wimbledon for the world's singles and doubles, and men's and women's, championships. He also looked at relics from World War I and attended a pageant featuring 200 airplanes. His curiosity was partly practical: he had booked a flight from London to Paris. As his granddaughter would observe, he was fascinated by anything new and wanted to try it for himself.[5]

On a late afternoon in early July 1920, Goucher boarded his flight on Handley Page Transport, a Bristish airline established the previous year. The aircraft was a war-surplus bomber, a biplane converted to accommodate ten passengers. The ever-curious traveler recorded all of the details he could gather: the size of the engines and propeller RPMs, wingspan, flight speed and altitude, and the route across the water and along the French coast. The 250-mile trip took more than three hours; despite the novelty of it all, he dozed off when he lost interest in looking out the window.[6]

Once settled in Paris, Goucher and a few friends left the city by automobile for a tour of the countryside and to visit some of the well-known battlefields—Meaux, the Marne, and Belleau Wood. He had braced himself for scenes of devastation like those he had starkly described in a sermon: "[A]cross the blood-drenched fields of France and Flanders . . . lives were wiped off by the hundred thousand, like flecks of moisture on a glass." They stopped overnight at Chateau-Thierry, the headquarters of Methodist workers who were helping rebuild nearly three dozen ruined villages in the area. The following day, the Goucher party began a circuitous, two-day trip to see more war-torn areas: Reims, St. Hilaire, the Argonne Forest, Verdun, Chalons-sur-Marne, and Epernay. They also saw the site from which a German howitzer known as "Big Bertha" had shelled Paris, more than seventy miles away. They returned to Paris via the Methodist compound, having driven nearly 350 miles in "three wonderful, interesting days." Goucher was distressed by the destruction he witnessed but heartened by the spirit and determination of the French as they rebuilt their lives. Later, the director at Chateau-Thierry sent him an update and invited him to return to measure their progress. He also noted, "You were one of our first visitors by areoplane [sic]."[7]

From Cherbourg, Goucher boarded a steamer for New York. He spent the last two months of the summer fundraising for Morgan College and making the usual trips to New York for meetings. He also made "many business calls for various church enterprises." Even staying close to home, he covered another 2,500 miles, traveling by train and auto. By mid-September, he and Eleanor were making their second Pacific crossing in 1920 (and their third within a year). As a Japanese missionary once told Goucher, "The Pacific is nothing but a ferry to you, and so you have no excuse for not coming back soon." It was John's seventh trip to East Asia.[8]

Their first stop was Tokyo, where Goucher was a delegate and speaker at the World's Sunday School Convention. His ten days in the city were filled with meetings, interviews, and receptions, including one given by the emperor in the Imperial Gardens. John and Eleanor moved on to Seoul, and during the last half of October, they were entertained at still more banquets and receptions. As Goucher would relate when he returned home, seeing the Korean's "great capacity for religious fervor and feeling," he "had a great vision of the conversion of Japan, China, and the whole East to Christianity largely through the influence of the Koreans." As in the past, seeing progress at Chosen Christian College and Pai Chai Hakdang was a primary interest. The new campus encompassed more than 200 acres, and enrollment had begun to grow again, with nearly seventy students attending. He met with college leaders to discuss developing a department for women, which was "unanimously and enthusiastically recommended." At Pai Chai, enrollment had swelled to more than 475 boys. He inspected the athletic fields he had helped plan and fund and discussed expanding them. He also unveiled a large bronze medallion of founder Henry Appenzeller that had been created in Baltimore.[9]

By the beginning of November, father and daughter traveled overland to China, where they made early stops at the northeastern cities of Mukden, Dairen, and Harbin. They would be nearly two months in the country, spending Thanksgiving with Elizabeth in Nanking, and celebrating "a delightful Christmas" in Foochow with occidental trimmings: a tree, presents, carols, and a large dinner with the missionary community. Goucher had planned to spend several weeks in West China, but on reaching Peking, he received word from friends in Chungking that "it would not be advisable for me to come at this time owing to the unsettled conditions." One missionary had written earlier that the region was in chaos, with factional fighting, "brigands everywhere," and a cholera epidemic that had claimed thousands. As a result, he "reconstructed" his itinerary, noting there were more than enough "urgent requests for me to give cooperation in important phases of work in Manchuria, Foochow, and Singapore." Goucher assured his West China contacts, however, that his visit was "postponed and not abandoned."[10]

This particular trip to China also involved very personal business. While in Nanking, Goucher had the pleasure of announcing to Elizabeth's Ginling College colleagues that she was engaged to B. Burgoyne Chapman, a missionary from Australia. Although Goucher had met him before, he had a chance to have tea with his future son-in-law during a recent stop in Peking. John was pleased that Elizabeth would be returning to Baltimore with him for her wedding the following spring.[11]

Goucher spent New Year's Day 1921 on the South China Sea, bound for three weeks in Singapore, his first time there since 1907. In addition to the usual round of speeches at schools and churches, he met with local missionaries and officials to promote a new Christian college. George Bickley, bishop of Southern and Southeast Asia, wrote after his visit, "I feel confident that your coming and interview with the Governor has helped our college cause in a quarter where it needed a friend." By the end of January, Goucher and his two daughters began their trip home, sailing west to Columbo, Ceylon, where he had stopped fourteen years before on his way to India.[12]

❋❋❋

Although Goucher did not receive official notification until April, it was during this part of his journey that he received his second medal: The president of the Republic of China, Hsu Shih-chang (Xu Shichang), awarded him the Third Class Chia-ho Decoration—induction into the Order of the Golden Grain—for "valuable services rendered the Chinese nation," in education especially. A noted Chinese physician Goucher had met on his travels wrote congratulating him: "This recognition is rather late [in coming], but I trust you will excuse the oversight for our leading men are too busy with politics and often overlook their duty connected with the many quiet and deserving men and women who have done so much for the younger generation." WCUU president Joseph Beech also sent good wishes but suggested his friend accept one more honor: "You must come out to Chengtu and get one from the University with the largest constituency in the world."[13]

On this trip, Goucher wrote one correspondent that he had found "evidences of real progress in Christian education at every point I visited." Even before he returned home, he was keeping track of (and offering advice about) his ongoing Asian projects. In early February, from a ship on the Indian Ocean, he answered a letter from President Takagi of Aoyama Gakuin. To attract the best students, trustees wanted to upgrade the institution to a university, however small, in time for the school's fortieth anniversary in April 1922. The plan to make Aoyama part of a union university no longer seemed viable. Goucher agreed that the upgrade "should be pushed with energy and persistence." But he also expressed the wish that the land he and Mary had purchased four decades before—then valued at $500,000 ($6.6 million)—should not be "alienated from the original purpose for which [the grounds] were donated, namely to establish a Christian University for Japan."[14]

As was his custom, Goucher also offered some practical advice:

> I would think it unwise to plan for wooden buildings as a
> temporary expedient in which to open the University. It would
> be a confession of loss of faith in your constituency and prove
> expensive to maintain and replace. The atmosphere is a largely
> educative influence. Maintain the standard of permanence
> in equipment and quality of work done and facilities will be
> forthcoming, I doubt not. Do not encourage your constituency
> to compromise on either.

He asked Takagi to excuse his lengthy missive—"my interest in the future of Aoyama Gakuin is my only excuse."[15]

In a letter written the same day to C. B. Rape, head of the Chungking High School where he had been providing scholarships, Goucher stressed academic excellence and student leadership. Rape hoped to raise the school to junior-college status, and Goucher seconded those hopes. But, he added, it should not be done "till it can maintain the high standard of your high school. The prime question is quality and not quantity." Since the uncertainties of the mail in China had led to a deficit in the scholarship account, Goucher included a check for $1,100 ($14,500) to cover expenses through July.[16]

After crossing the Gulf of Aden, the ship stopped at Djibouti (in what was then French Somaliland), then traveled through the Suez Canal to Port Said, and finally on to Marseille. Goucher wrote in his diary that on the final leg of the trip, the sea was "boisterous" one day and "placid" the next. He also recorded spending a day reading, walking twelve miles on deck, and pondering "the problems of education in the Far East and Asia." When the Goucher family reached Paris, they enjoyed a few days of sightseeing—"visiting my old friends [monuments] of six previous visits"—before sailing from Cherbourg to New York. They were back in Baltimore in early March 1921. On Goucher's third trip around the world, he had traveled more than 28,000 miles in six months. As he set down his bags, he was already considering a make-up trip to West China in the fall of the following year.[17]

Plaque dedicated in honor of John Goucher's
75th birthday, First Methodist Episcopal Church,
Baltimore, Maryland
(*The Methodist,* March 10, 1921)

*Courtesy of the Baltimore-Washington Conference Archives,
Lovely Lane United Methodist Church, Baltimore, Maryland*

THE FINAL COMMISSION

Chapter 27
(Mid-1921-1922)

───────◆►◄◆───────

*I reckon that life is the material out of which we build for eternity
. . . . Heaven must be earned. Heaven must be built from life here. . . .
Life poorly invested, life spent in pleasure and vanity and commerce
only, is but a step removed from life uninvested.*[1]

Less than two weeks after their return to Baltimore, the Goucher family gathered to celebrate Elizabeth's wedding. The pre-wedding festivities were held at Alto Dale; on March 30, the proud father performed the noon ceremony at neighboring Stone Chapel, with a reception at 2313 in the city. Over the rest of 1921, Goucher observed his customary routine: entertaining visitors, speaking to various groups, attending meetings, and making short trips. He traveled more than a dozen times to New York, tending to the business of the Board of Foreign Missions, West China Union University, Peking University, and Chosen Christian College. Having seen the scars of war firsthand, he also attended meetings promoting peace and disarmament. He went to Washington with a delegation from the Ministerial Union, a group of more than 400 Protestant ministers from the Baltimore area, to meet with Secretary of State Charles Evans Hughes and offer assistance "in creating sentiment in favor of a Peace Conference." While on his way to Detroit and Toronto, he detoured to Chicago for a convocation of educators from 225 colleges and universities in more than forty states. The group endorsed disarmament and, Goucher said, would "encourage study and discussion of international relations by undergraduates."[2]

Closer to home, he participated in two local church events, as he had since entering the ministry more than a half century earlier—the Baltimore Annual Conference and the camp meeting near Reisterstown. Morgan College's trustees elected him as their president for the thirty-ninth time. As warm weather arrived, he hosted Alto Dale Day for 300 guests, a tradition suspended during World War I. Goucher also immersed himself in a special project he said "constituted my vacation this summer." The water for the estate came from a favorite spring he had dubbed "Egeria," located at the bottom of a hill, and his workers dug a reservoir to conserve the supply and laid pipe to improve flow to the house. He also planned to build what he called a "cairn," an artful stone pile, near the spring to act as a landmark for Egeria's location. As he became more involved in planning the reservoir, he realized such a project would likely interest his grandchildren—in particular seven-year old Miss J. F.— visiting for the summer. He gave her her own small nearby spring, which she said bubbled all the time and was clear enough for drinking. The best part? "It was all mine."[3]

Goucher kept track of personal as well as professional events in his 1921 pocket diary, recording Elizabeth's marriage that spring and Janet's twelfth wedding anniversary that fall. In October, his longtime, African-American employee and friend Robert Green was hospitalized; John noted his several visits to the recuperating patient. After thirty-five years of service, Goucher wrote with sadness, Green "feels his work is done for the present at least and wishes me to find someone to fill his place." As year's end approached, Goucher reflected on his special blessings:

> I think high among my causes for Thanksgiving is the satisfactory relation of the various branches of the family in church life. Henry and Janet are devoted to First Presbyterian and they call them 'a tower of strength.' Burgoyne and Elizabeth are making a record of beautiful devotion to China and highly appreciated by the Board of Missions. And Eleanor is much occupied in gracious ministries through First Methodist Church and Stone Chapel. The Lord is good.[4]

✳ ✳ ✳

As Goucher went about his usual business, others were thinking about his contributions "to all Methodism and even to all Christendom." Soon after Goucher returned from his last international trip in 1921, William V. Kelley, former editor of *The Methodist Review*, approached Rev. Frank G. Porter about writing a Goucher biography, as the subject "is too busy <u>making</u> history that he has no time for <u>recording it</u>." He added:

> It must be forced upon him as a <u>duty</u>. . . . Catch him quick before he gets off again to Europe or Asia on his next errand for the Kingdom. Hold him long enough to get from him the story, the inside knowledge of great affairs in which he has had an active and often leading part. In world-wide missionary work, particularly, he is today one of the most outstanding statesmen and leaders.[5]

Porter, a longtime Baltimore friend and occasional confidante, contacted Goucher about setting up interviews and gathering documents. John replied with his usual reservations about focusing attention on himself:

> It is very trying for me to think of having to do with any account of my life and work. . . . What Dr. Kelley and you want me to do is so foreign to my feelings that I can only slowly bring myself to it. It will require a good deal of concentration and thought, and I am so busy . . . and the trying thing I shall have to think so much about myself, and who can tell what effect it may have on my spiritual life, so subtle are the temptations when one thinks much about himself.[6]

Another old acquaintance, Bishop Earl Cranston, countered such modesty in a letter: "Where most of us simply 'functioned' you have on your own initiative <u>achieved</u>. You have been the world pioneer to your church in her most impressive undertakings." Even so, Goucher told Porter there was too much "extravagance in pinning to some outstanding figure a larger amount of endorsement than logically belonged to him." But he reluctantly agreed that Porter knew him better than most, and in the end he relented: "I will be glad to talk the matter over with you more fully."[7]

One possible reason his friends were pushing the project: Goucher's health was declining. A Korean missionary wrote to commiserate: "You carry the burdens of continents on your heart." For a few years, Goucher had been suffering from severe nosebleeds, sometimes repeatedly over several days, exacerbating his anemia. His doctor had called these episodes "a symptom of overwork," and told him he "must slow up." He was reluctant to take that advice, but in December 1921, he wrote to a missionary in West China who had his own health problems:

> I reached a conclusion sometime since (my friends think I am not a shining illustration of the fact), that it is an evidence of unbelief for a man to work beyond his strength for it implies at least that he thinks God could not get along without him. God is not a hard master, but our acceptance is first according to that which we have and not according to that which we have not.

While Goucher still contemplated future trips, he added, "I think it will be necessary for me to change my plans once more and postpone my visit [to West China] for a year or two."[8]

Knowing of his friend's health issues, William Kelley wrote him at the beginning of 1922:

> I am not surprised that the Cosmos has cried "Halt!" to you. Listening to your activities, going near and far by land and sea, I have expected a collapse. . . . Let me beg you to obey your doctors by taking systematically a good big rest. Give exhausted vitality, long overtaxed, a chance to fill its reservoirs lest you be permanently <u>down and out</u> and in consequence go <u>up and in</u> to the Heavenly Places all too soon for this world that needs you.

Kelley still pushed him to continue working with his biographer: "It is natural for you, indeed inevitable with your nature, that you should underestimate the value of this final crowning service to your Master and His Kingdom."[9]

※ ※ ※

In January 1922, Goucher was drawn into a public controversy between President William Westley Guth and Goucher College trustees on the one hand, and the leaders of the Methodist Episcopal Church and the Baltimore Conference on the other. Guth's party wanted to revise the college charter to make the Board of Trustees self-perpetuating, with no input from any Methodist body in selecting trustees. A decade earlier, a similar amendment had been proposed, leading to a compromise solution, but by 1922, administrators felt it was time, as Professor Lilian Welsh put it, to proceed "in accordance with the modern trend of educational policy and method entirely unhampered by external control."[10]

The college did not have any "denominational or sectarian test" in admitting students or in choosing trustees, officers, or teachers. The original 1885 charter, however, had given the Baltimore Conference the right to approve or reject trustees elected by the board; a 1910 amendment to the charter shifted that right to the Methodist Board of Education in New York. Two years later, a small committee of trustees considered a further revision to eliminate "the veto power of any ecclesiastical body over the Board of Trustees," making it "the ultimate source of authority in all matters pertaining to the college."[11]

At the time, Goucher opposed this change. He "was very clear on the necessity of eliminating any semblance of Conference control from the College, as that narrowed the scope of the institution and did not interpret its breadth and largest opportunity." He was "just as clear," however, "on the importance of maintaining close alignment in its relations to the Methodist Episcopal Church," which had given the college "its inception, its authorization, its official endorsement," and provided for "its organization, maintenance and development thus far in large measure." John Van Meter, a member of the revision committee, complained about Goucher to another trustee: "Nothing seems to suit him but the legal subordination to the Methodist Episcopal Church through some of its representatives." Van Meter considered that arrangement "entirely unnecessary to the character of the College and crippling in its interests."[12]

The debate coincided with the critical 1912–1913 million-dollar fundraising campaign, and out of concern for offending potential Methodist donors, the plan was put on hold until the end of the campaign and Guth had taken over as president. An ordained Methodist minister, he nonetheless endorsed loosening the college's ties to the Church. Within a few months of assuming office, he was ready to move forward with an amendment that would reduce the maximum number of trustees from forty to thirty-three; only eleven would be elected from candidates proposed by the Baltimore Conference and five other conferences, whose selection supposedly was based on their pledges of financial support to the campaign. With a minority of church-designated trustees, funding organizations such as the Carnegie Foundation would be more willing to recognize that the college was not under denominational control.[13]

At the end of December 1913, Guth was eager to get trustees' approval of the proposed charter amendment. Goucher remained a member of the board but had not yet returned from his journey to East Asia, The Hague, and London. The new president, however, did not want to wait for his arrival to hold the vote. Thomas Nicholson, secretary of the Methodist Board of Education, urged caution in dealing with "our friend across the water": "[He] has deep interest in the institution, he has rights; he has invested largely and his continued interest is widespread by a large unpaid subscription [for the campaign]; he has powerful friends who put great store by his judgment; he was the chief factor in framing past charters."[14]

Guth replied that he planned to move ahead without Goucher, and added, "To counsel and advise with the person whom you suggest would put me almost at once at a disadvantage and would imply that I was ready to bend to his judgment." Guth felt "no reason to delay because of the absence of one trustee over another," and he called a board meeting for a few days before Goucher was due to arrive home, eliminating his input. (The amendment was approved by the Maryland legislature in March 1914.)[15]

This early experience between the sitting president and the president emeritus seemed to set the tenor of their future relationship. Guth resisted any influence Goucher might have on campus, and later he even removed a faculty member—Joseph Shefloe—because of his ties to the former leader. The professor told a friend that his nearly thirty-year career at the college was "more than life" to him, and he was certain he owed his dismissal to his close connection to the president emeritus. He also claimed Guth had once ordered Goucher off college property. Goucher wrote a diary entry that might have been indicative of his ongoing interactions with the president: "Dr. Guth asked me to come to his office to be talked to about the college," apparently a one-sided conversation.[16]

A few years into Guth's presidency, Van Meter wrote to another longtime faculty member that the college did "not seem like the same place. . . . [T]he feeling of home and family that I used to have in connection with it has passed." Yet he acknowledged it had become "big and popular and is really accomplishing wonders." By January 1922, Goucher College had expanded its student body and facilities and purchased 421 acres of land for a new campus in Towson, just north of the city. The college also had launched the ambitious "Greater Goucher Campaign" (usually called the "4-2-1 Campaign") to raise $6 million to move the school to the new location and provide an endowment to increase faculty salaries.[17]

Guth, who had resigned his position as a Methodist minister in 1919, also declared it was time the board was free of any denominational control. According to the president and a majority of the trustees, the six Methodist conferences had not sent names of candidates in recent years, as the 1914 charter allowed, nor had they paid their previous financial commitments. (The Methodist contingent questioned whether the trustees, "now or ever, have sought to allot memberships on the board under solely financial considerations.") In mid-January 1922, the trustees asked Senator David G. McIntosh to introduce a bill in the Maryland legislature to amend the charter to reduce board size to a maximum of twenty-five trustees, none to be recommended by Methodist conferences. The faculty, Students' Organization, and the Alumnae Association's Board of Directors sent resolutions of support.[18]

Needless to say, the press was eager to hear John Goucher's opinion, but according to the *Evening News*, "He sent word to a reporter that he had nothing to say on the subject. . . . In the silence of Dr. Goucher both sides in the controversy are a little baffled because of the weight his opinion as to the relation of the college to the church would have." But the paper offered an excuse: "He has not been feeling well of late, and it is thought partly on account of that he has kept aloof from the controversy."[19]

Less shy, the trustees published a statement in Baltimore newspapers—"To the Public of Baltimore and Maryland—A Statement by the Trustees of Goucher College," giving twenty-eight reasons for the charter amendment. Guth also hired a public relations firm in New

York to help publicize the board's position in Maryland and other key markets. Bishop William McDowell and five district superintendents of the Baltimore Conference countered with their own missive addressed "To the People of Baltimore and Maryland and the Alumnae of Goucher College," pointing out "some serious omissions" in their opponents' arguments. At the end of January 1922, the Methodist leaders testified before the Senate Committee on Corporations and persuaded Goucher to make a public statement. They felt his views were important, although a few years earlier, Van Meter had argued that Goucher knew "the sentiments of a small coterie of leaders of the Methodist Episcopal Church and even of some other churches, but he does not know the large sentiment of even the community in which he lives."[20]

Goucher was too ill to attend the Senate hearing, but his written statement was read and published in the newspapers. He reviewed the history of the college's Methodist connections and lamented the current administration's failures to conform correctly "to the provisions of the Charter as amended in 1914." He "deplored" a movement to "sever and destroy" the official relationship with the Methodist Episcopal Church, whose "sacrificial generosity and persistent devotion" had made the school possible: "Those of us who are thoroughly conversant with all the facts are compelled, conscientiously, to protest against and resist such an act of injustice." Ninety-year-old Summerfield Baldwin, a trustee since the college's founding, spoke at the hearing and expressed his concern that the controversy might have a detrimental effect on Goucher's health: "[He] feels deeply the possibilities if this measure is passed even more than I. He is not well now and I hesitate to think of the possibilities if this blow succeeds."[21]

A key constituency—alumnae—weighed in on both sides of the debate. In response to Goucher's remarks, more than 100 alumnae of various religious denominations produced their own public declaration, stating that an increasing number of graduates were not in favor of the proposed change. "Dr. Goucher has made it clear . . . that he is opposed to the Charter change, and we, whose college training has been made possible in large measure by him, should give careful and respectful consideration of his views." Others were of the opposite opinion, as reflected in one alumna's letter: "I grant Dr. Goucher credit for all he did—but his administration is over—so it seems to me quite unsuitable for him to interfere in the present administration's plan for the development of a greater college."[22]

Longtime Goucher colleagues John Van Meter and Lilian Welsh continued to back the amendment but had different reactions to his public statement. Van Meter questioned how the president emeritus could defend the Baltimore Conference's support after all the times it had been slow to offer the college financial assistance. Welsh maintained that Goucher and his Methodist allies were "living largely in the past." She told a member of the Maryland House of Delegates that the old guard "cannot be trusted as educational leaders" to determine what was the best course for the future. In her view, the college had "gained its position as a great independent college for women . . . not because of its connection with the Methodist Church, but in spite of that connection."[23]

The two sides met several times in February, looking for a compromise, but no agreement was reached. Those in favor of the amendment postponed and then abandoned any presentation to the Senate hearings. Trustees recognized a shift in alumnae sentiment, and newspaper editorials were beginning to question the wisdom of antagonizing the Church in the middle of a fundraising campaign. There were also reports from Annapolis that the general sentiment in the legislature was leaning against the bill. In mid-March, the trustees told McIntosh that "for the best interests of the College, further controversy should be avoided"; they asked him to withdraw the bill. *The Baltimore Sun* reported that, consistent with the current charter, the board would allow the designated Methodist conferences to nominate eleven trustees—especially those "sincerely and enthusiastically interested" in the campaign—while affirming the college would continue to be known as nonsectarian and nondenominational. The connection between Goucher College and the Methodist Episcopal Church held fast, and John Goucher could rest knowing of this resolution. (It would be nearly forty-five years before the college amended its charter to remove any Methodist input on the Board of Trustees.)[24]

❋ ❋ ❋

Goucher's health continued to deteriorate as 1922 progressed. He told a colleague in February that his doctor had prescribed bed rest, "made necessary by overwork that has been going on for some past months." Although housebound, he kept in touch with his far-flung projects in East Asia. He checked on the status and payment of his Korean scholarships and increased the number of his West China scholarships. He asked about the requirements (and assets) needed to raise the Chungking High School to the level of a junior college, so he could provide "more intelligent study," and he continued to promote new ventures, such as admitting women to WCUU. A Chinese missionary wrote to say he had heard Goucher was "speaking in its favor everywhere."[25]

A Methodist publication lamented, "His quick step upon our streets is missed for awhile, and it is difficult to grow accustomed to his absence from pulpit, platform and committee gatherings." During his months of illness, various institutions and groups he was closely involved with sent get well wishes. Morgan College's trustees expressed regret he could not attend the winter board meeting "to furnish guidance by your wisdom, and inspiration by your devotion to the great work which you have led so long and so successfully." The secretary of Baltimore's Eclectic Club, an interdenominational group of ministers who often met at Goucher's house, sent "heartfelt sympathy in your prolonged illness." The ministers added their prayers that "you may be speedily restored to your wanted health and activity, not only in our Club but also in the larger field of Christian effort to which you have devoted your fortune and your life in unstinted measure." In April, Ishizaka Masanobu, the former dean and new president of Aoyama Gakuin, offered prayers for a speedy recovery, so the school might be "blessed with your visit in the near future and receive unspeakable inspiration which you left so deeply among us every time you were here." Julius Soper also wrote from Tokyo, relating the institution's progress toward becoming a university and expressing hope this achievement might be "realized in Dr. Goucher's lifetime."[26]

Goucher viewed his anemia and ongoing confinement as temporary setbacks. In early May, he wrote to Frank Mason North, secretary of the Board of Foreign Missions, with regrets at not being able to attend the upcoming New York meeting: "I am still a prisoner. My physician says that I'm improving steadily but it will be several weeks before I am able to go away from home." But as senior member of the board, he had business he wanted to conduct by letter. He appealed to North for support for Aoyama Gakuin, whose chapel and assembly hall had been condemned for safety reasons. North wrote back to say funds were short that year—"the crisis in Aoyama confronts the crisis in the Church." He dampened Goucher's usual optimism, adding, "We must, however, include in our vision things as they are as well as things as we wish them to be."[27]

With the arrival of warm weather, Goucher made his customary move to Alto Dale, and many afternoons he was able to enjoy a car ride around the countryside, with Eleanor as his chauffeur. Although the *New York Christian Advocate* reported he was a semi-invalid, it added, "He is as jovial and sparkling as ever in conversation and betrays the liveliest interest in Church and State affairs." On June 7, he celebrated his seventy-seventh birthday; barely a month later, he was confined to bed. Nevertheless, he still dictated letters and memoranda, and he continued his interviews with Frank Porter for the proposed biography. Their talks were framed around Goucher's six "commissions"—the "definite and distinct calls" from God that had influenced his life's work. In his notes, Porter described their July 11 session:

> Dr. Goucher was stronger this morning than yesterday, and there was suffering but a frequent changing in his position, propped up in bed. . . . Miss Eleanor and Mrs. Janet Miller were more cheerful today. In telling his story the Doctor quietly laughed as he recalled amusing incidents. He talked slowly, with eyes closed at times, and I never hurried him. We (or he) talked two hours and the time seemed short. He did not appear to be weary.

Seeing Goucher in good spirits, Porter noted, "I am sure Miss Eleanor's statement yesterday that her father could not live over a week is incorrect." His physician, however, had told the patient "if he had any matters to attend to, to do so at once." Goucher knew his time was short, but Porter was confident the news brought him "no anxiety." Instead, he would tell those who gathered around him, "I am about to take up my <u>seventh</u> commission. I am ready. It is all right."[28]

In the early morning hours of July 19, 1922, at his home of forty-five years, John Franklin Goucher accepted that last commission, dying peacefully with Janet and Eleanor at his side. As the *Christian Advocate* would point out, he had planned for this passage "as calmly as for any other of his many voyages into a far country."[29]

Courtesy of Janet Miller Bernet

IN MEMORIAM - TRIBUTES AND LEGACY

Chapter 28

———————————◆◆———————————

History is but the lengthened shadow of great men whose influence has given trend and inspiration to society. . . . Those are greatest in the record of the centuries who have been most completely one with God.[1]

Two days after his death, John Franklin Goucher was laid to rest next to his beloved wife in Druid Ridge Cemetery. His life in Baltimore had come full circle: The cemetery sat on the site of the old Turner farm, where more than a half-century earlier Goucher had begun his ministry on the Baltimore Circuit and had met Mary.

A late afternoon service was held at nearby Alto Dale. Methodist bishops, ministers of many denominations, friends from near and far—including three of the first five graduates of the Woman's College of Baltimore—gathered to comfort Janet, Eleanor, and John's sister Ella. Always looking ahead, Goucher had left behind written instructions, indicating whom he would like to take part and help see him to his final resting place. To conduct the service, he chose his longtime colleague Bishop William F. McDowell. The active and honorary pallbearers he named reflected the range of his connections: John Van Meter, fellow founder of (and occasional adversary at) the Woman's College; former missionary to Japan and Morgan College president John O. Spencer; Syracuse University chancellor James R. Day; Frank Mason North, corresponding secretary of the Board of Foreign Missions; and William V. Kelley and Frank G. Porter, who had promoted the unfinished Goucher biography.

He reached out to the Methodist Episcopal Church, South, by naming Bishop E. R. Hendrix, who had helped establish a church and school in Seoul in the early 1890s; Bishop William R. Beauchamp, a fellow member of Sigma Chi and an attendee at the World Ecumenical Conference in Edinburgh; and W. W. Pinson, who had worked with Goucher on Methodist unification. Among the honorary pallbearers were lifelong members of the Baltimore Conference and trustees of Goucher and Morgan Colleges: Charles and Summerfield Baldwin, Henry S. Dulaney, John Alcock, Morris A. Soper, and Bishop Earl Cranston. All in all, the list was a *Who's Who* of Methodist leaders in the city and the country.[2]

Only Bishop McDowell spoke at the simple service. He told the gathering, "We do not need to praise or analyze him among ourselves. He would not like us to do the first, and we are having such trouble with our eyes that we cannot see clearly enough for analysis." But they could measure the value of Goucher's life by its length, breadth, and height. The bishop spoke of the long reach of Goucher's half-century of service and the ongoing influence of his multi-faceted work into the future. He praised Goucher's embrace of "all races and all nations in [his life's] sympathies." His faith, McDowell went on, grounded his earthly work even as it directed his thoughts toward heaven and regular communion with God. Goucher had been involved in so many projects and with so many people, "It will not be an easy thing for us to go on without turning to take counsel with him." That sentiment was echoed in numerous condolence messages his daughters would receive. One friend summed up the views of many: "He was so perennially young in his spirit that I have always thought of him as living always."[3]

✳ ✳ ✳

His death drew comments from around the globe—in the form of letters to the family, obituaries, newspaper editorials, and other published testimonials. There may be no better way to do justice to John Franklin Goucher's character, the extent of his interests, his friendships, and his influence and international reach, than to cite a wide assortment of these remembrances.

The Baltimore Sun paid tribute to his deep connection to his adopted home town:

The Rev. Dr. John F. Goucher, though Pennsylvanian by birth, was identified with this city from so early an age that he may be claimed as a Baltimorean by over a half a century of naturalization as well as of deliberate personal choice. . . . [He] built some of the noblest and most enduring monuments in a city rich in personal monuments. His name belongs in the lasting roll of public benefactors like Hopkins and Peabody, who have associated themselves permanently with educational and moral influences, who have been creators in their day of new sources of light and higher life. . . .

To him [Baltimore] can point with pride as a man who accomplished great things for society, for the world, and for the Church. And Baltimoreans, without regard to creed or race, will place him among those who have rendered distinguished and lasting benefactions to their country and to humanity.[4]

His colleague Frank Mason North wrote in the *Christian Advocate*:

Personally, Dr. Goucher was a polished gentleman, a citizen of the world at home in countries and capitals, but at his best in his own homes in Baltimore, the city of his pride.[5]

A *Methodist Review* article weighed in on Goucher's relationship to his Church:

In every advance in the missionary or educational operations of the church, the quiet man from Baltimore was a potent factor from its inception to its fruition. Never obtrusive with his advice, his counsel was yet sought after by people of all colors and all degrees, from employees and near neighbors to preachers, general secretaries and bishops.[6]

There was also a statement made at a meeting of the Joint Commission on Unification:

In all of his action, in his spirit, and in his temper of mind he stood for unity of the denominations; and he let no opportunity either in action or of speech pass without giving his voice to unification. . . . No man has done more in his day for bringing together of the two Churches than this great man whom we honor.[7]

Commission member Judge H. H. White added a personal note:

> He took me under his wing. I learned lessons of wisdom,
> of courtesy, of wit, of world-wide knowledge, of Christian
> statesmanship, of Christian character, from Dr. Goucher. He
> was a scholar. He was a psychologist. He was informed in all
> branches of art and science with which I have even the most
> distant and rudimentary connection of information.[8]

Methodist publisher John H. Race testified to Goucher's ecumenism:

> Though an intense believer in the polity and program
> of the Methodist Episcopal Church, he was no narrow
> denominationalist. He was broadly catholic. He loved every
> church that exalted the Christ.[9]

Of course, there was much comment from the Goucher College community. A resolution from the Board of Trustees reminded the world of John and Mary Goucher's largesse:

> These gifts . . . are remarkable among educational benefactions,
> both for their size and for their method of bestowal. Without
> them the establishment of the College probably would not have
> been possible, for there seemed to be no one who had at once
> the vision, the means and the generous spirit to make the gifts
> possible [10]

The *Alumnae Quarterly*'s memorial issue took up that theme:

> It is always startling to find that quiet, familiar figures are, in
> reality, honored citizens of the world of great affairs. This is
> especially true of these two explorers—explorers in the sense
> in which Kipling writes of those to whom God whispers his
> secrets, who blaze the way over inaccessible places into new
> fields of endeavor, and who lay the foundation for the building
> of great enterprises.[11]

Other alumnae groups made official statements, such as this one from the Class of 1902:

Dr. Goucher made an incalculable contribution to the education of women the world over. Those of us in Baltimore who received the benefits of his leadership, his devotion, his untiring zeal, are challenged to pass on to succeeding student generations some measure of our gift.[12]

Members of the Class of 1906 added their own remembrance:

He particularly left the impress of his kindness upon the girls whose meagre resources were quietly supplemented by his generous and understanding interest. To us all, the spirit of service, which by word and deed, he impressed upon our lives, has remained as our present permanent heritage.[13]

College colleague Lilian Welsh said:

[Dr. Goucher's] life must be viewed from many angles, because his interests and activities were so varied; his contacts with peoples, with institutions and with social forces that make for human progress were world-wide in their range. Here in College we saw but a part of his life and labors when for a brief period we walked in common College pathways with a common purpose. . . . As I look back with the perspective of added years it appears that his interest in education was that of a pioneer.[14]

Tributes came in from Morgan College as well. President John O. Spencer described his friend:

Patiently aggressive, cautiously progressive, holding tenaciously to the good of all the past, he pressed forward to the better future that finally the best should be realized in human society. He was a practical idealist. . . . An aristocrat in the best sense, he was a democrat in opportunity to all.[15]

Joseph Lockerman, principal of the Colored Training School and former secretary of the Morgan Board of Trustees, spoke of Goucher's crucial role in the college's advancement:

[Morgan's] magnificent vantage ground has not been easily won. On the contrary, it is largely the result of Dr. Goucher's

masterly generalship, combined with his abiding faith in
the value of the highest type of education for all persons of
whatever color or sex, his unquenchable zeal in achieving ends
worthy of his high powers, and the broad Christian sympathy
that enabled him to convert enemies into friends of the school
and impart to them some measure of his lofty wisdom and high
purposes.[16]

A resolution from the Morgan College Summer School amplified
Goucher's importance to the school:

Among the fearless men who, in spite of determined
opposition, urged the cause of higher education for Colored
boys and girls; gave largely of their means for the development
of an institution with such an aim; and continued to be a trusted
and devoted friend to it through all the years; there was none
who surpassed in devotion the late Dr. John F. Goucher.[17]

The Baltimore *Afro-American* gave a more measured view of
John Goucher in its obituary. It said he was "regarded by many as
a believer in strict segregation for the races," noting his early stance
on forming a separate, fraternal African-American Methodist Church.
But the article admitted Goucher had "wielded a far more potent
influence in the lives of the colored people living within the bounds of
the Washington and Delaware M. E. Conferences than many suspect."
He "commanded big influence with the bishops of his church," and
for more than forty years, black ministers often went to him, seeking
help for an appointment to a particular church. The newspaper briefly
acknowledged his longtime leadership at Morgan, "giving his time
and of his wealth to the college."[18]

Goucher's international work drew another set of accolades. As
the *Central Christian Advocate* noted, to Goucher, "The oceans were
but lanes to outposts in the Kingdom of God." Official statements
came from among others the Methodist Episcopal Church in Russia
and Baltic States: "When the history of Russian Methodism is written
his name will also appear there." The North Japan College told Eleanor
Goucher, "Thousands of people both in America and in the Orient
have reason to be grateful that he lived. The good influences that he
started will go on endlessly." And to fellow traveler Frank Gamewell,

writing in the *China Christian Advocate*, "Dr. Goucher was a man of unlimited horizons and accepted Wesley's motto and made the world his parish."[19]

The schools he directly supported offered heartfelt tributes. Joseph Beech at West China Union University told Goucher's family that "there have been very few lives that have been so complete," and the WCUU Senate noted the extent of his influence: "Among other things, Dr. Goucher will be remembered as a great traveler. The continents that have not been covered by him in his travels are very few indeed."[20]

Edwin C. Jones, president of Fukien Christian University in Foochow, wrote Eleanor:

> Your father will be tremendously missed by all of us who knew him, and more than that, the institution will miss his kindly interest and apt counsel which has helped us in many crises in the University's life. . . . Had it not been for the impetus which he gave, the move of the University to its new site would have been much delayed. The work he did on the question of women's education, while it has not developed in exactly the lines we had thought probable, still has borne fruit and will continue in other and probably better ways.[21]

Eleanor also received this note from Kawashiri Seishu, dean of the academy at Aoyama Gakuin, whose students had always made their affection for John Goucher known: "I can sympathize with you in your great sorrow—the sorrow I and a great many Japanese share, for he was our father in many ways. . . . He made such a deep impression on individuals but not only that, he was more himself when among Aoyama boys and girls." John Z. Moore, an acquaintance from the Pyengyang District of the Korea Conference reminisced, "I shall never forget my trip into Manchuria with your father and Bishop Welch some years ago." Goucher, Moore continued, "stood the hardships, the long tramps about Harbin as though he was in the prime of life. He was always saying something to brighten the way. To how many thousands all over the world he pointed a better way."[22]

Bishop Earl Cranston, noting Goucher's reluctance to become a bishop, said, "He did far better in becoming an untitled premier in the missionary councils of the world, the clear-visioned chief of staff in field operations, and the master diplomat of the Kingdom to powers and potentates of all degrees civil and ecclesiastical." *The Baltimore Sun* summed it up: "His field of activity was the whole world. Nothing human was alien to his interest or too remote for a hand that delighted in helpfulness, for a heart that was in love with service."[23]

John R. Mott, then chair of the International Missionary Council and later a Nobel Peace Prize winner, told Eleanor:

> Your father was one of the most vital, creative, and helpful personalities whom I have ever known. I would find it difficult to overstate my appreciation of the profound and far reaching influences he exerted. His was a most productive mind. It proved to be the generating ground of more attainable visions and constructive plans than that of any other Christian leader of his generation.[24]

"How richly and how fully he lived life," Dr. William L. Moss, a teacher and medical researcher, wrote Janet and her husband. "Rich and full because he gave himself for a great cause and that cause was his fellow man." Moss went on:

> He lived life actively not passively. Fearlessly. He was not afraid to dare and do. To play for big stakes. . . . What was the secret of his greatness? First, it seems to me, was the quality of the man. The product perhaps of inheritance and early environment. Second, a great purpose. Third, giving himself wholly to that purpose. I have tried to learn some of the lessons which his life teaches.[25]

Rev. Alfred H. Barr, minister of Baltimore's First (now First & Franklin) Presbyterian Church, told Janet:

> He was different from anyone I ever knew. He was different in the quality of his courage, and ardor and foresightedness and bigness. But it was his <u>sureness</u> that fed my faith and spirit. He <u>knew</u>. How I loved him. He was so kind to me. His counsel was so wise.[26]

In *Zion's Herald*, Boston's Rev. Willard T. Perrin related a personal anecdote of a rare leisure moment he and John had shared in Toronto:

One day I played golf with Dr. Goucher on the links of Dentonia Park. His play gave evidence that he had not wasted much time on this popular sport. One of his drives went beyond his vision behind the trees. At last I found his ball at about half the distance where he was looking for it. . . . He was a Christian gentleman, a charming companion, a priceless friend, and a magnificent leader in the church of God.[27]

His friend Cranston also testified to Goucher's focus and tenacity:

No allurement enticed him, no antagonism unbalanced him, no treachery angered him, no reverse dismayed him, no attack on his line confused him, no treachery angered him, no hostile shaft pieced his armor of perfect calm—which I suppose is another way of saying that he seemed entirely unburdened of self or self-interest. . . . Thus, with self out of the reckoning of results, his vision was clear, his way more open, and his steps firmer as he went steadily forward even in the face of disheartening conditions.[28]

George C. Peck, general superintendent of Maryland General Hospital wrote:

John F. Goucher never would have admitted it, but he was a king, every inch. . . . Modest, unassuming, hiding in velvet glove an iron hand; trustful of men, diplomatic in the best sense; a convinced lover of his kind; a man who 'never turned his back but marched breast forward' to foe or friend, he stepped forward like a king.[29]

Still more local tributes were published. J. M. Gillum, superintendent of the Baltimore Conference's West Baltimore District noted, "In him religion, education and philanthropy got a good chance to show their real value and true worth to mankind." Lawyer J. Henry Baker shared, "His religion was broader than any denomination and his love for his fellow man was boundless. It seems his big heart beat for all mankind, the lowly and the influential." And J. St. Clair Neal, executive secretary of the city's Missionary and Extension Society, wrote, "He strove to give back to God, with interest, all that God had entrusted him with."[30]

Peace advocate Evelyn Riley Nicholson, who would become the first president of the World Federation of Methodist Women, contacted the Goucher family: "He was so gracious, so gentle, so kindly, and so human; so youthful in his outlook on life yet so ripe in experience that to counsel with him was to be lifted up in spirit—illuminated in mind and inspired to 'carry on.'" And as Rev. Edward L. Watson, who had known and worked with Goucher since 1885, told readers of the *Washington Christian Advocate*, "There were no racial barriers for him. He belongs to the world.[31]

✳ ✳ ✳

Half a world away, in Tokyo, Aoyama Gakuin held its memorial service on November 10—Founder's Day, appropriately enough—and faculty and students planted a memorial tree on the lawn of Goucher Hall. President Ishizaka told Eleanor Goucher he also had received telegrams and letters of sympathy from alumni and friends "in distant places in the different parts of the empire." The Goucher College community held its commemorative service in February 1923, with special tributes from all the classes who had attended during Goucher's presidency. The great theme of his life and work was summed up by the Baltimore Conference's Benjamin DeVries: "He thought, lived, and acted in world terms. . . . He was a real brother to all men"—and to all women as well.[32]

A week after Goucher's death, his last will and testament was filed in the Orphans' Court of Baltimore County. He had previously deeded 2313 St. Paul Street to Goucher College, which had granted him life tenancy, and the school could now appropriate the building for its own use. Writing his will in 1917, Goucher had divided his personal property at 2313 and Alto Dale and the Alto Dale estate among Janet, Elizabeth, and Eleanor. He also provided an annuity for his sister and her husband, as well as outright bequests to several longtime employees. With his remaining assets, greatly depleted from decades of generosity to educational and missionary causes, he set up a trust for each daughter, the funds to be passed to her children on her death. If a daughter died without surviving issue, Goucher named several institutions he supported to receive a portion of her remaining trust funds—Goucher and Morgan Colleges, Aoyama Gakuin, West China

Union University, Chosen Christian College, and Fukien Christian University. In a codicil dated a week before his death, he added Pai Chai Hakdang but removed Goucher College. Likely he made this change because he had given such a large portion of his donations over the years to his namesake college, and he was still paying on an earlier pledge. As usual, he weighed where he felt needs were greatest.[33]

Vincent Massey—son of Goucher's Toronto friend Chester Massey and later Canada's governor general—wrote Janet, "The consolation is of course in the work he left behind which will not die." But one might wonder why, with all these posthumous accolades, John Franklin Goucher's name and works were not so well-remembered after all in church, educational, and civic circles in the decades that followed. International and local events conspired to overshadow or even erase his contributions and connections: Chinese Christian union universities suffered during Japan's military expansion into China in the 1930s; World War II disrupted life in all of his "much fruit" countries. The ascendency and control of communism in China stifled religion and reshaped education; the Korean War shattered the landscape and divided a nation. In Goucher's home town, Morgan College was transferred in 1939 from private ownership to the State of Maryland to provide public higher education opportunities for African Americans, then denied admission to the state's white institutions. In the early 1940s, Goucher College began building a new campus in Baltimore County, and by mid-century, it left behind its historic roots in the city.[34]

John Goucher once said, "One of the most difficult feats in the world is to describe anything: nay to see anything uncolored by personal interest or bias; undistorted by the lens of the beholder's eyes. I do not mean that we are dishonest; all I mean is that we are wretched reporters." And so it came to pass that these upheavals and changes sometimes caused the histories of church and educational institutions to be seen in a new light, if not ignored altogether. By the end of the twentieth century, John Goucher's name no longer rang out in many quarters where he had once been well-known and had made a decisive difference.[35]

Still, the Methodist Board of Education's Abram Harris declared when Goucher died, "Only the coming years can ever fully reveal the farsightedness of his generous patronage of schools and universities." In the second decade of the twenty-first century, with increased emphasis on diversity, global engagement, and access to learning, John Goucher's worldwide role in advancing education is being rediscovered and re-evaluated. His farsightedness is still paying dividends at many institutions he established and/or supported and at their successor schools. Sichuan University (once West China Union University), Fujian Normal University (merged with Fukien Christian University), and Nanjing University (which took over the University of Nanking) are important centers of higher education in China. Isabella Thoburn College in India continues to be a leader in women's education. In the South Korea, there is a gamut of educational opportunities with Goucher connections: the boys' Pai Chai School and the co-educational Pai Chai University, Ewha Girls' High School and Ewha Woman's University, and Yonsei University (the former Chosen Christian College). In Tokyo, Aoyama Gakuin now encompasses divisions from kindergarten to university level, while in Baltimore, Goucher College and Morgan State University offer undergraduate as well as graduate programs to a diverse body of students.[36]

A massive, plain granite stone—engraved only with the word GOUCHER—marks his grave at the Pikesville cemetery plot he shares with wife Mary and daughter Eleanor. But John Franklin Goucher's legacy at home and abroad confirms the observation a member of the Baltimore Conference made at his death: "He needs no monument. His monument is everywhere."[37]

HIGHLIGHTS
LIFE OF
JOHN FRANKLIN GOUCHER

───────────◆▶────────────

1845   Born June 7 in Waynesburg, Pennsylvania

1868   Graduated from Dickinson College

1869   Entered the ministry of the Methodist Episcopal
              Church, Baltimore Conference

1871   Received master's degree from Dickinson College

1877   Married Mary Cecilia Fisher on December 24

1879   Birth of first daughter, Eleanor (d. February 19, 1880)
              Donated land and building funds for the Centenary Biblical Institute,
                  Baltimore (later Morgan College, now Morgan State University)
              Donated funds for the Isabella Fisher Hospital, Tientsin (Tianjin), China
              Created the Frontier Loan Fund, Methodist Church Extension Society
              Donated funds for the Japan Mission

1880   Birth of second daughter, Janet

1881   Made two-year pledge to open the Methodist mission in West China
              Donated funds for churches in Foochow (Fuzhou), China

1882   Birth of third daughter, Eleanor
              Made multi-year pledge to open primary schools for
                  boys and girls in North India and provide scholarships
                  for students to continue through high school
              Donated funds to purchase land to establish the Anglo-Japanese
                  College, Tokyo (now Aoyama Gakuin University)

1883   Birth of fourth daughter, Elizabeth
              Became minister of First Church (now Lovely Lane United
                  Methodist Church) and led building campaign
              Elected president of the Board of Trustees, Centenary Biblical Institute

Donated funds to open the Methodist mission in Korea
Donated land next to First Church to establish a college for women
   (the Woman's College of Baltimore, now Goucher College)

1884   Donated funds to buy a site for the Korea Mission
Elected member of the Board of Managers of the
   Methodist Missionary Society, New York

1885   Elected as one of the first trustees of the Woman's College of
   Baltimore City ("City" dropped from name in 1890)
Received honorary doctor of divinity degree from Dickinson College

1886   Examined Methodist missions in Italy on behalf of the Missionary Society
Donated funds to build a church in Pontedera, Italy
Donated funds for an academic building (named
   Goucher Hall) at the Anglo-Japanese College
Donated funds for the first building (named Goucher
   Hall) at the Woman's College of Baltimore City

1887   Birth of fifth daughter, Mary (d. July 11, 1887)

1888   Elected delegate to the General Conference of
   the Methodist Episcopal Church

1890   Elected second president of the Woman's College of Baltimore

1891   Retired as congregational minister in the Methodist Episcopal Church
Offered to pay teacher's salary at Isabella Thoburn
   College, Lucknow, India

1892   Examined Methodist missions in Mexico on
   behalf of the Missionary Society

1895   Enjoyed delayed "honeymoon" with Mary in Egypt

1897-98 Made first trip around the world; first trip to East Asia
Inspected and reported on Methodist missions and schools
   in India on behalf of the Missionary Society
Established annual scholarship for a student from Isabella Thoburn
   College to attend the Woman's College of Baltimore

1899   Received honorary doctor of laws degree from Dickinson College

1901	Chosen as delegate and speaker at the Ecumenical Methodist Conference in London
1902	Death of Mary Fisher Goucher at Alto Dale on December 19
1904-06	Led campaign to retire debt of the Woman's College of Baltimore
1906-07	Made second trip around the world; second trip to East Asia Attended the Jubilee of Methodist missions in India and the China Centenary Missionary Conference Donated funds to build additional churches in Foochow region Attended organization and first General Conference of the Methodist Church of Japan
1907	Resigned presidency of the Woman's College of Baltimore
1908	Named president emeritus of the Woman's College of Baltimore Published *Christianity and the United States*
1909	Shipwrecked en route to Egypt; traveled across Sinai Peninsula to Jerusalem on camel and horseback Elected president of the Maryland Bible Society
1910	The Woman's College of Baltimore renamed Goucher College in honor of John and Mary Goucher Attended the World Ecumenical Conference in Edinburgh, Scotland Elected chair of the American Section on Education in the Mission Field, Continuation Committee of the Ecumenical Conference Elected chair of the Board of Governors of West China Union University (now Sichuan University) Made third trip to East Asia; first trip to West China via Yangtze River Made ongoing financial commitments for educational projects in China Established scholarships for students at Pai Chai Hakdang, Seoul, to attend the Theological School at Aoyama Gakuin
1911	Published *Growth of the Missionary Concept*
1912-13	Worked on successful $1 Million Campaign for Goucher College
1913	Made fourth trip to East Asia, via Trans-Siberian Railway

1914-15   Made fifth trip to East Asia; second trip to West China
           Funded the Goucher Primary School Unit and
               scholarships in Chengtu (Chengdu), China
           Assisted in organization of Fukien Christian University,
               Foochow (now part of Fujian Normal University)
           Assisted in organization of Chosen Christian College, Seoul
               (now Yonsei University)

1916   Attended the Panama Congress on Christian Work in Latin America and
               the cornerstone-laying ceremony for the Bible House in the Canal Zone

1916-20   Elected member of the Joint Commission on Unification of the Methodist
               Episcopal Church and the Methodist Episcopal Church, South

1917   Led Board of Trustees to move Morgan College to a new campus

1919   Awarded Imperial Decoration of the Third Class Order
               of the Rising Sun by the emperor of Japan
           Served as director of exhibitions for the Centennial
               of Methodist Missions, Columbus, Ohio

1919-20   Made sixth trip to East Asia

1920   Traveled to London on behalf of West China Union University;
               made trip to Paris by airplane to visit World War I battle
               sites and inspect Methodist war-relief efforts
           Elected for ninth time as delegate of the Methodist General
               Conference

1920-21   Made third trip around the world; seventh trip to East Asia

1921   Awarded Third Class Chia-ho Decoration by the
               president of the Republic of China

1922   Died at Alto Dale on July 19; buried at Druid Ridge Cemetery

PHOTOS

John Franklin Goucher

1. Lansing, Michigan (1851)

2. Pittsburgh, Pennsylvania (1862)

3. Baltimore, Maryland (c. 1870)

1 and 2 - Courtesty of the Baltimore-Washington Conference Archives,
Lovely Lane United Methodist Church, Baltimore, Maryland
3 - Courtesy of the Goucher College Library, Special Collections and Archives,
Baltimore, Maryland

Mary Cecilia Fisher Goucher

Mary Goucher at Alto Dale
(c. 1880)

Mary Fisher (c. 1860)

Courtesy of Janet Miller Bernet

Elizabeth, Janet, and
Eleanor Goucher (c. 1885)

John Goucher with his grandson at Alto Dale (1914)

Courtesy of Janet Miller Bernet

John Goucher with his daughter, Janet,
at Alto Dale (c. 1905)

At Alto Dale

The Gouchers' residence, 2313 St. Paul Street, Baltimore, Maryland

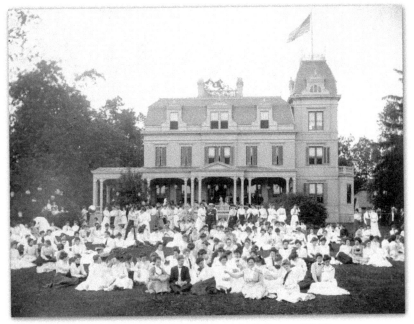

Alto Dale Day for the Woman's College of Baltimore
(c. 1900, John Goucher standing in center)

1. Signboard for Pai Chai Hakdang, name conferred by King Kojong, Seoul, Korea,1887

2. Laying of cornerstone for girls' orphanage,
Madras, India, December 1897
(John Goucher holding trowel)

The second Goucher Hall (1907), Aoyama Gakuin
(destroyed by the Great Kanto Earthquake, 1923)

Aoyama Gakuin 25th Anniversary Founding Memorial Postcard

Courtesy of the Archives of Aoyama Gakuin, Tokyo, Japan

Mary Fisher Goucher (c. 1900)

NOTES

Introduction

1. John Franklin Goucher, "The Financial Cooperation of Both the Rich and the Poor Indispensable to the World's Salvation," February 1902, in *Sermons*, record group 3, box 3, folder 1, John Franklin Goucher Papers, Goucher College Library, Special Collections and Archives (hereinafter Goucher Papers, GCSCA).

2. Diary of John F. Goucher (hereinafter Diary), January 22–23, 1909, box 7, Rev. John F. Goucher Papers, Baltimore–Washington Conference Archives (hereinafter Goucher Papers, BWCA). S. Earl Taylor was secretary of the Young People's Missionary Department of the Methodist Board of Foreign Missions and Board of Home Missions and Church Extension in New York. See also "*Republic* a Handsome Ship," *New York Times*, January 24, 1909, 2. The *Republic* was the flagship in the White Star Line's Boston–Europe route. It was taking its first winter cruise on the New York–Mediterranean service, scheduled to call at the Azores, Madeira, Gibraltar, Genoa, Naples, and Alexandria. On December 28, 1908, Sicily and Calabria in southern Italy, along the Strait of Messina, were hit by a massive earthquake, causing tidal waves and fires. On its previous voyage from Italy to New York, the *Republic* had brought the first refugees from the earthquake to the United States. "Money Loss May Be a Billion; Dead, 200,000," *New York Times*, January 3, 1909, 1; "Big Steamship Sinking, Every Soul Is Saved," *Baltimore Sun*, January 24, 1909, 1.

3. "Story of the Disaster," *New York Times*, January 24, 1909, 1; "*Florida* Was Astray in Fog," *New York Times*, January 25, 1909, 3; "*Baltic* Brings Full Details of Fog Crash," *New York Times*," January 26, 1909, 1. Two passengers on the *Republic* were killed and two injured severely; four crew members on the *Florida* were killed in the collision.

4. Diary, January 23, 1909; "Dr. Goucher a Beacon," *Baltimore Sun*, January 26, 1909, 1. See also "How Bulkheads Safeguard Liners," *New York Times*, January 25, 1909, 3, which noted that if the accident had occurred a few years earlier, without the availability of watertight bulkheads, the *Republic* would have sunk within five minutes.

5. Diary, January 23, 1909.

6. Ibid. Also "Clothes Found by a Stranger," section of article in the *Chicago Tribune*, January 26, 1909, box 1, folder 18, Goucher Papers, BWCA.

7. "How Wireless Saved a Ship," *New York Times*, January 24, 1909, 1; "*Lorraine*'s Search for Disabled Liner," *New York Times*, January 25, 1909, 3; "Big Steamship Sinking."

8. Diary, January 23, 1909; "Mr. Connolly's Criticisms," *New York Times*, February 5, 1909, 6; "*Baltic* Brings Full Details." The *Republic*'s lifeboats

transported only fifteen to twenty passengers per trip so as not to be too heavy. The *Florida*'s lifeboats were also used for transport.

9. "Clothes Found by a Stranger"; "Aged Man Stays at Post," section of article in the *Chicago Tribune*, January 26, 1909, box 1, folder 18, Goucher Papers, BWCA; "American Heroes All," *Baltimore Sun*, January 26, 1909, 2; "Dr. Goucher Manned Oars in Lifeboat," *Baltimore News*, January 25, 1909, box 4, folder 2, Goucher Papers, BWCA; diary, January 23, 1909. Goucher never mentioned in his diary his role in manning a lifeboat between the *Republic* and the *Florida*.

10. "*Baltic* Captain Tells of Search," *New York Times*, January 26, 1909, 2; "*Republic* Sunk; 1650 Rescued Here on *Baltic*," *New York Times*, January 26, 1909, 1.

11. Diary, January 23–24, 1909; "The Rescue in Open Boats," *New York Times*, January 26, 1909, 8.

12. Diary, January 24, 1909; "Dr. Goucher Sends Wireless," *Baltimore Sun*, January 25, 1909, 1.

13. "All Safe Ashore," *Baltimore Sun*, January 26, 1909, 1; "Dr. Goucher a Beacon."

14. Diary, January 25 and February 10, 1909.

15. Diary, March 29, 1907. The second Goucher Hall (1906) at Aoyama Gakuin was destroyed in the Great Kanto Earthquake in September 1923. Part of its foundation was discovered during campus construction in 2008. Fukamachi Masanobu, chancellor of the university, was given an honorary degree by Goucher College that year, and he presented the college with a brick from this historic building.

16. Sanford J. Ungar, president of Goucher College, and I were invited to speak at the November 2002 event at Aoyama Gakuin. In June 2010, we were also invited to speak at an international forum held in John Goucher's honor at Pai Chai University. Both Pai Chai and Goucher College were celebrating their 125th anniversaries that year. There also were speakers from Aoyama Gakuin and two universities in China that considered Goucher a founder and/ or benefactor. I received another invitation to attend the celebratory events for the 130th anniversary of the Korean Methodist Church in April 2015, honoring the arrival of the first Methodist missionaries sent through the Gouchers' generosity. Other Goucher family members with whom I have become acquainted include E. John Bernet and Mary Fisher Bernet (great-grandchildren) and John Goucher Bernet, a 2008 alumnus of Goucher College (great-great-grandson).

17. J. Henry Baker, in "Tributes to Dr. John F. Goucher," *Washington Christian Advocate*, July 27, 1922, 10, record group 3, box 1, folder 19, Goucher Papers, GCSCA.

18. Frank Mason North, "Dr. Goucher's Lifelong Service to Foreign Missions," *Christian Advocate*, July 27, 1922, 925, record group 3, box 1, folder 16, Goucher Papers, GCSCA.

19. Charles E. Guthrie and Benjamin F. De Vries, in "Tributes to Dr. John F. Goucher," 7, 10.

20. William F. McDowell, in "Tributes to Dr. John F. Goucher," 6.

Chapter One

1. John F. Goucher, "True Education," matriculation sermon, the Woman's College of Baltimore, October 9, 1904, 6, record group 3, box 3, folder 21, John Franklin Goucher Papers, Goucher College Library, Special Collections and Archives (hereinafter Goucher Papers, GCSCA).

2. John F. Goucher, undated, handwritten card describing birth of the four Goucher children and locations of family's homes, box 5, folder 2, Rev. John F. Goucher Papers, Baltimore–Washington Conference Archives (hereinafter Goucher Papers, BWCA).

3. Genealogical materials for Goucher and Townsend families, Goucher Papers, BWCA; John F. Goucher, undated, handwritten and typed notes on family history and genealogy, box 1, folder 23, ibid.; Goucher, form for *American Ancestry* (Albany, N.Y.: Joel Munsell's Sons); Goucher, application for membership, Maryland Society of the National Society, Sons of the American Revolution, April 5, 1894, box 1, folder 21, ibid.; Pearl Willard Bruce to David R. Goucher, August 1903, box 1, folder 22, ibid.; Henderson Henry Goucher to John F. Goucher, October 30, 1918, box 1, folder 22, ibid.

4. William McKinley to John F. Goucher, January 11, 1896, and card from President-Elect William McKinley to John F. Goucher, November 18, 1896, box 1, folder 3, Goucher Papers, BWCA.

5. Goucher, notes on family history and genealogy; John R. Dorsey, Maryland Society, Sons of the American Revolution, to John F. Goucher, November 16, 1895, Goucher Papers, BWCA. Goucher was elected chaplain of the Maryland Society, Sons of the American Revolution, in 1895, a year after his application.

6. Goucher, card describing locations of family's homes.

7. John F. Goucher, undated, handwritten note relating to his father's involvement in Lansing, Michigan, Goucher Papers, BWCA; "First Visit in Fifty Years," *State Republican*, August 8, 1903, and "Clears Up Early History," *Lansing Daily Journal*, August 8, 1903, box 1, folder 21, ibid.

8. "When Johnny Goucher Met Lincoln," *Christian Advocate*, February 4, 1909, Goucher Papers, BWCA; Frank G. Porter, "John Franklin Goucher," minutes, Baltimore Annual Conference (hereinafter minutes, BAC), April 4–9, 1923, 380, record group 3, box 1, folder 12, Goucher Papers, GCSCA.

9. Lucy Leatherman Clark, "Letter to the Editor," *Christian Advocate*, February 11, 1909, reprinted July 27, 1922, Goucher Papers, BWCA. Clark was Goucher's sixth-grade teacher in 1857–1858 at the Monongahela Elementary School. An article written about her noted that "among her pupils was an especially bright little boy, 'Johnnie' Goucher, now the famous Dr. Goucher, the founder of Goucher College in Baltimore." *The Observer* (Washington, Pa.), August 15, 1912, box 3, folder 1, ibid. Mrs. J. Sutton Wall to the Goucher daughters, July 25, 1922, Goucher Papers, BWCA; Isaac Yohe to John F. Goucher, February 2, 1908, box 1, folder 7, ibid. In Yohe's letter, he continued his description of Goucher, based on a more recent photo he had seen: "I notice [your hair] is getting thin now but fifty years of study and thought and hard work has wrought the same change in all of us."

10. Ella Goucher to John F. Goucher, September 3, 1859, courtesy of Janet Miller Bernet, granddaughter of John and Mary Goucher.

11. "John Franklin Goucher, D.D.," *Daily Advocate*, May 10, 1894, box 4, folder 2, Goucher Papers, BWCA; Porter, minutes, BAC, 377.

12. Porter, ibid.; John F. Goucher, undated, handwritten card listing important dates and events in his life, box 5, folder 2, Goucher Papers, BWCA; diary of John F. Goucher (hereinafter Diary), October 5, 1869, box 7, ibid.; John F. Goucher, interview by Frank G. Porter, July 1922, box 7, ibid.

13. Janet Goucher Miller to Carlyle Earp, November 4, 1957, Carlyle Reede Earp Papers on John Franklin Goucher, Baltimore–Washington Conference Archives (hereinafter Earp Papers, BWCA). Janet Miller, Goucher's oldest daughter, noted that her father's spending time on his uncle's farm "may have made Alto Dale [the country home and farm of John and Mary Fisher Goucher] such a deep happiness for him." Diary, October 13, 1869, February 5, 1907, June 6, 1920.

14. Goucher's oft-repeated recollection of meeting Abraham Lincoln influenced the career of another young man: Raymond Massey (1896–1983), longtime stage and screen actor. Goucher was a friend of Massey's father, Chester D. Massey, head of the Massey–Harris Company in Toronto and a prominent layman in the Canadian Methodist Episcopal Church. Raymond heard the Lincoln story during Goucher's visits with his father, and it piqued his interest in the president. Later he said, "Every actor, I suppose, wants to play a certain part. . . . I wanted to play young Lincoln and it was a part I would have dropped any other role at any time to do." Massey's portrayal of Lincoln on Broadway (*Abe Lincoln in Illinois*), as well as on film, became a signature role for him. His best-known television role was playing Dr. Gillespie to Richard Chamberlain's Dr. Kildaire. "Abe Lincoln of 45th Street," *New York Times*, October 20, 1938, 161.

15. "When Johnny Goucher"; "Downtown: Abraham Lincoln," *Pittsburgh Evening Chronicle*, February 15, 1861, http://clpgh.org/exhibit/neighborhoods/downtown/down_n121.html.

16. Diary, July 21, 1869.

17. Ibid., December 30, 1869; John Franklin Goucher, report card, Pittsburgh High School, 1863–1864, box 3, folder 1, Goucher Papers, BWCA.

18. James Henry Morgan, *Dickinson College: The History of One Hundred and Fifty Years, 1783–1933* (Carlisle, Pa.: Dickinson College, 1933). Dickinson College was the first college chartered in the new United States and was named in honor of John Dickinson, one of the early governors of Pennsylvania. It suspended operation in 1832 because of financial and organizational difficulties. The college was transferred to representatives of the Baltimore and Philadelphia (then including New Jersey) Conferences of the Methodist Episcopal Church in 1833, by replacing the former trustees with men nominated by those conferences. "Dickinson College," *Christian Advocate and Journal*, June 2, 1864, 172; "Collegiate Department," in *Catalogue of Dickinson College (1864–1865)*, Dickinson College Archives and Special Collections (hereinafter DCASC). The admissions criteria included a testimonial of good moral character and examinations on English grammar and composition, outlines of ancient and modern history and geography, arithmetic and algebra, and Latin and Greek.

19. "Dickinson College, Carlisle, PA.," *New York Observer and Chronicle*, July 16, 1863, 227; "Carlisle, Penn.," *New York Times*, June 17, 1863, 8; "Telegrams

from Harrisburg," and "Our Harrisburg Correspondence," *New York Times*, July 3, 1863, 1; Morgan, *Dickinson College*, 314–318.

20. Carlyle Reede Earp, *John Franklin Goucher*, unpublished manuscript, c. 1960, 8, 21, Earp Papers, BWCA; Morgan, *Dickinson College*, 307, 311–313, 319. An 1863 federal conscription act required males ages 20–45 to register for the draft.

21. Earp, *John Franklin Goucher*, 21–22; diary, February 18, 1869. Goucher's father paid approximately $225 for his freshman year, which included the $40 annual tuition, room, and board, plus several other academic fees: $3 a year to use the library, $8 a year to warm and use the recitation rooms, and $5 to study special languages such as Hebrew, a necessity for Goucher's training for the ministry.

22. Earp, *John Franklin Goucher*, 7, 22; Janet Miller Bernet, interview with the author, December 2004. Holmes was a year ahead of Goucher at Dickinson but left after his junior year to return to Pittsburgh and assume a position in his father's bank. Goucher roomed with Hobart Harvey Smith, "Smithie," during his last two years at college. Rooms cost $10–$12 per year. Students also had to pay for janitorial services and laundry. Goucher and Holmes split the cost of the relatively new gas lighting and rented a stove and bought fuel for it from the college.

23. Earp, *John Franklin Goucher*, 9; diary, March 13, 1869. Faculty wives sometimes supplemented their husbands' meager salaries by inviting two or three students to have meals with them.

24. "The Jones Prizes," in *Catalogue of Dickinson College (1864–1865)*, 33, DCASC.

25. "Religious Instruction," in *Catalogue of Dickinson College (1864–1865)*, DCASC; John Franklin Goucher, "Young People and the World's Evangelization," *Christian Advocate*, December 24, 1903, record group 3, box 3, folder 32, Goucher Papers, GCSCA.

26. Earp, *John Franklin Goucher*, 10. This Mission Sunday School became a full-fledged Methodist chapel by 1869. Several years later, Charles Himes, one of Goucher's professors who became a lifelong friend, gave him an example of the school's impact on at least two of the participants: The two gang members Goucher originally recruited held steady jobs, with one "doing very well as a painter" and the other holding a job as a conductor on the Harrisburg and Potomac Railroad. Charles F. Himes to John F. Goucher, March 16, 1884, box 1, folder 1, Goucher Papers, BWCA.

27. "Constitution of a Sunday-School Society," *Sunday School Series*, no. 2 (New York: Tract Society, c. 1865), Earp Papers, BWCA; "Walks and Talks," *Chautauqua Assembly Herald* (Chautauqua, N.Y.), August 20, 1897, 1, box 3, folder 5, Goucher Papers, BWCA.

28. "Dr. Goucher at Chautauqua: The Baltimore Educator Makes the Principal Address at the Recognition Day Exercises," *Baltimore Sun*, August 19, 1897, 8. The Chautauqua Lake Sunday School Assembly, now the Chautauqua Institution, was founded by Vincent and Lewis Miller, a businessman, in 1874 in southwestern New York State. The program broadened beyond summer classes for Sunday school teachers to include academic subjects, art, music, and physical education. By 1880, "the Chautauqua platform had established itself as a national forum for open discussion of public issues, international relations,

literature and science." Chautauqua continues to offer public programs and study courses in a wide range of fields.

The Chautauqua Literary and Scientific Circle (CLSC) was one of the first attempts at distance learning and the first to offer correspondence degrees. It is the oldest continuous book club in the United States, and local reading circles were established around the country and eventually around the world. From the CLSC grew the Chautauqua Movement, with "circuit" or "tent" chautauquas providing traveling speakers and entertainers. http://www.ciweb.org/about-us/about-chautauqua/our-history.

29. J. Frank Goucher, "Climatic Influences," Junior Prize Contest, Dickinson College, June 24, 1867, record group 3, box 1, folder 1, Goucher Papers, GCSCA; "Dickinson College," *Christian Advocate*, August 22, 1867, 266.

30. Morgan, *Dickinson College*, 419-422; Earp, *John Franklin Goucher*, 8; Merkel Landis to John F. Goucher, March 27, 1905, box 1, folder 5, Goucher Papers, BWCA; Carl A. Hedblom to John F. Goucher, June 9, 1915, Series 1: China, box 1, folder 2, MRL 12: John Franklin Goucher Papers, Burke Library at Union Theological Seminary, Columbia University in the City of New York.

31. Alexander Dallas Bache Smead, "History of the Class of 1868," Dickinson College Class Day, June 23, 1868, 10, 22, 26, DCASC; program of the 85th Commencement of Dickinson College, June 25, 1868, ibid; faculty minutes, Dickinson College, May 23, 1868, vol. 1858–1869, ibid; J. Frank Goucher, "Thought Gravitation," commencement address, June 25, 1868, record group 3, box 1, folder 1, Goucher Papers, GCSCA.

32. "Degrees of Master of Arts," in *Catalogue of Dickinson College (1864–1865)*, and "Master of Arts Degrees Conferred," in *Catalogue of Dickinson College (1871–1872)*, DCASC; Charles F. Himes to J. F. Goucher, April 4, 1871, box 1, folder 1, Goucher papers, BWCA. Although many biographical sketches list 1872 as the date for Goucher's master of arts degree from Dickinson, primary sources indicate that it was conferred at commencement on June 8, 1871.

33. Charles F. Himes to John F. Goucher, June 24, 1885, box 1, folder 1, Goucher Papers, BWCA; George Edward Reed to John F. Goucher, May 31, 1899, box 1, folder 3, ibid. Goucher was also offered an honorary doctor of laws degree from Cornell College in Mt. Vernon, Iowa, but declined it. William King to John F. Goucher, Cornell College, January 20, 1904, box 1, folder 5, ibid. "Dr. Goucher for President," *Daily Sentinel* (Carlisle, Pa.), August 11, 1888, box 1, folder 18, ibid. Dickinson College, the Woman's College of Baltimore, and the Centenary Bibilical Institute (later Morgan College) all received funding from the Baltimore Conference of the Methodist Episcopal Church.

Chapter Two

1. Diary of John F. Goucher (hereinafter Diary), May 19, 1869, box 7, Rev. John F. Goucher Papers, Baltimore–Washington Conference Archives (hereinafter Goucher Papers, BWCA).

2. Ibid., February 18, 1869.

3. Diary of James Whitford Bashford, January 20, 1911, box 2, folder 4, MRL 6: James Whitford Bashford Diaries, Burke Library at Union Theological Seminary, Columbia University in the City of New York; John F. Goucher,

interview by Frank G. Porter, July 11, 1922, box 7, Goucher Papers, BWCA; Mark 16:15.

4. John F. Goucher, undated, handwritten card including major dates and events in his life, June 1868 to March 1869, box 5, folder 2, Goucher Papers, BWCA; James Curns, Presiding Elder, and John Miller, Secretary, Quarterly Conference, Carlisle, Pa., July 4, 1868, Carlyle Reede Earp Papers on John Franklin Goucher, Baltimore–Washington Conference Archives (hereinafter Earp Papers, BWCA). The Quarterly Conference, now called the Charge Conference, was "the traditional business and governing body of the local charge or station." It had the authority to license men to preach. Nolan B. Harmon, ed., *The Encyclopedia of World Methodism*, vol. 2 (Nashville, Tenn.: United Methodist Publishing House, 1974), 1969. Shaddrack L. Bowman to the Pastor and Official Brethren of Christ Methodist Episcopal Church, Pittsburgh, June 29, 1868, Goucher Papers, BWCA. Ministerial assignments were made each spring during the annual meeting of the Baltimore Conference.

5. John F. Goucher, handwritten page, October 1868, box 5, folder 2, Goucher Papers, BWCA.

6. Diary, October 17, 1869.

7. Ibid., February 21, 1869.

8. Ibid., March 3–4 and 9–10, 1869; Frank G. Porter, notes on meetings attended by John F. Goucher, Goucher Papers, BWCA. Porter wrote, "[Goucher] has shaken hands with every President since [Lincoln], and with the exception of two or three, as a member of a Committee or Commission that saw the President by appointment, he had the opportunity for more or less lengthy conversations as well as hand shake."

9. According to Rev. Edwin Schell, the late executive secretary emeritus, United Methodist Historical Society, Baltimore–Washington Conference, a Methodist preacher was sometimes assigned to several churches in an area. If he could visit them all and return home in one day, his set of churches was a station; if visits required him to be away overnight, it was a circuit. The churches in Goucher's circuit were Reisterstown, Pimlico, Stone Chapel, Ward's, Quarries, Mt. Olive, Pleasant Hill, and Mt. Pleasant.

10. Diary, March 20, 1869.

11. Ibid., March 31, April 5 and 7, June 30, and July 8, 1869.

12. Ibid., April 2 and June 12, 1869.

13. Ibid., May 8, June 12 and 14, and November 27, 1869; Carlyle Reede Earp, *John Franklin Goucher*, unpublished manuscript, c. 1960, 190, Earp Papers, BWCA. Goucher noted that he received $40 of his pay in early May, "the first money I've ever earned."

14. Diary, June 7, 1869.

15. Ibid., April 27, June 6 and 27, July 4, August 2, and October 18, 1869.

16. Minutes, Baltimore Annual Conference, March 2–9, 1870, 37, BWCA; ibid., March 1–7, 1871, 24; ibid., March 5–12, 1873, 16; diary, April 7, 1869. Goucher was on trial as a minister for Baltimore Conference years 1869 and 1870; he became a member in full connection in 1871. He was ordained a deacon that year and an elder in 1873.

17. Diary, April 23, July 4, August 1 and 29, and September 25–26, 1869.

18. Ibid., June 5, 1869.

19. Ibid., March 25, April 9–10, October 31, and November 24 and 26, 1869.

20. Ibid., November 6, 24, and 26, 1869.

21. "Keeping the Faith," *Owings Mills Times*, September 15, 1994.

22. Diary, August 18 and 20, 1869. Goucher and those attending the camp meeting were offered ample opportunities for both personal and group meditation and learning. He related the daily schedule for that summer: "The horn blows at 6 A.M. to rise, 6:30 for family prayers. 7 for breakfast, private prayers in camping tents 7:30, prayer at the Stand 8. Preaching 9:30. Silent prayer all over the grounds at 1 P.M., Sunday School or Children's Meeting in some of the tents at 2. Preaching at 3 and again at 7:30." The day did not end there: at 12:45 A.M., when all were in their tents, another horn blew for "secret prayer."

23. Ibid., August 18, 20–23, and 27, and September 2 and 6, 1869.

24. Ibid., April 20, August 24, and December 31, 1869.

25. John Fisher to John F. Goucher, May 29 and June 13, 1873, courtesy of Janet Miller Bernet.

26. Goucher, interview, July 12, 1922.

27. J. Frank Goucher, examination for Elder's Orders in the Methodist Episcopal Church, 1873, box 3, folder 1, Goucher Papers, BWCA.

28. John F. Goucher, "The Church and Education," *Methodist Review*, March 1902, 186, record group 3, box 3, folder 19, John Franklin Goucher Papers, Goucher College Library, Special Collections and Archives (hereinafter Goucher Papers, GCSCA); Goucher, "The Social Equipment of a Pastor," speech for the Itinerants' Club, Baltimore Conference, May 17, 1899, 3, box 4, folder 8, Goucher Papers, BWCA.

29. John F. Goucher, "I Corinthians 10:31," in *Sermons*, record group 3, box 3, folder 1, Goucher Papers, GCSCA; Goucher, "Missions and Education," in *Missionary Issues of the Twentieth Century*, address delivered at the General Missionary Conference of the Methodist Episcopal Church, South, April 24–30, 1901, 144, https://archive.org/details/missionaryissues00methiala; Earp, *John Franklin Goucher*, 210.

30. Untitled news clipping, *California Independent*, February 1901, Goucher Papers, BWCA; Janet Goucher Miller, "Chapel Address," January 8, 1937, GCSCA; untitled news clipping, *Tacoma Ledger*, June 22, 1896, box 4, folder 2, Goucher Papers, BWCA; Rev. Edwin Schell, story related to the author.

31. Elizabeth Goucher Chapman to Kenneth R. Rose, February 16, 1955, box 4, folder 11, Goucher Papers, BWCA; Miller, "Chapel Address"; Goucher, "Luke IX:29," in *Sermons*. Goucher's thought about "no prayerless men" seems a forerunner of the later aphorism that "there are no atheists in foxholes."

32. Goucher, "Social Equipment," 2–6.

33. Earl Cranston, "John Franklin Goucher—Modern Apostle and Civilized Saint," *Methodist Review*, January/February 1923, 11, record group 3, box 1, folder 22, Goucher Papers, GCSCA.

Chapter Three

1. John F. Goucher, remarks for memorial statement for Bishop Cyrus Foss, 1910, box 5, folder 2, Rev. John F. Goucher Papers, Baltimore–Washington Conference Archives (hereinafter Goucher Papers, BWCA).

2. Alexander Dallas Bache Smead, "History of the Class of 1868," Dickinson College Class Day, June 23, 1868, 22, Dickinson College Archives and Special Collections (hereinafter DCASC); diary of John F. Goucher (hereinafter Diary), March 13, 1869, box 7, Goucher Papers, BWCA; Goucher, "Genesis 41:51," in *Sermons*, record group 3, box 3, folder 1, John Franklin Goucher Papers, Goucher College Library, Special Collections and Archives (hereinafter Goucher Papers, GCSCA).

3. "It Was but the Master Calling," *Christian Advocate*, December 25, 1902, 2078.

4. Diary, March 18–20, 1869.

5. Ibid., March 22, 1869; John F. Goucher, undated, handwritten card including major dates and events in his life, June 1868 to March 1869, box 5, folder 2, Goucher Papers, BWCA.

6. Diary, April 3, 1869; certificate of John Fisher's election as a delegate to the Electoral Conference of Laymen, February 5, 1872, box 3, folder 6, Goucher Papers, BWCA. Dr. Fisher became president of the Electoral Conference of Laymen, which was charged with electing two lay delegates to attend the General Conference of the Methodist Episcopal Church for the first time. "Mary Cecilia Goucher," minutes, Baltimore Annual Conference, April 1–7, 1903, 62, Baltimore-Washington Conference Archives (hereinafter minutes, BAC); "It Was but the Master Calling."

7. Dawn F. Thomas, *The Greenspring Valley, Its History and Heritage* (Baltimore: Maryland Historical Society, 1978), 1:374–376; "Mary Cecilia Goucher," minutes, BAC. The Alto Dale property was once part of the estate of Revolutionary War hero John Eager Howard.

8. Diary, May 4, 1869.

9. "Mary Cecilia Goucher," minutes, BAC, 63; Kathryn Allamong Jacob, "Mary Fisher Goucher," 1, record group 3, box 1, folder 6, Goucher Papers, GCSCA; Margot Doss, "A Great Deal of Good with the Money," *Baltimore Sun*, April 2, 1950, SM7; "It Was but the Master Calling."

10. "Mrs. Goucher Is Dead," *Baltimore Sun*, December 20, 1902, 12; Jacob, "Mary Fisher Goucher." Two other noted Baltimore women philanthropists attended the Edgeworth School at a later period: Mary Elizabeth Garrett and Julia Rogers, who were among a small group of women known as the "Friday Evening" group. Among the projects they sponsored were the founding of the Bryn Mawr School for Girls in Baltimore and a fundraising effort to help open the Johns Hopkins University School of Medicine, with the stipulation of admitting women. A bequest from Julia Rogers was used in the early 1950s to build the Julia Rogers Library on the Goucher College campus in Towson.

11. "Mary Cecilia Goucher," minutes, BAC, 63; diary, May 6 and August 13, 1869.

12. "A Christian Home," *Christian Advocate*, March 1, 1883, 134.

13. Doss, "A Great Deal of Good"; John Fisher, last will and testament, August 6, 1877, liber 5, folio 316, Baltimore County Register of Wills, Towson, Md.

14. Doss, "A Great Deal of Good"; Jacob, "Mary Fisher Goucher," 1–2.

15. J. Goucher to John F. Goucher, January 30, 1879; Bell M. Goucher to Mary Goucher, September 9, 1879; and Sarah B. Crosby to John and Mary Goucher, February 23, 1880, letters courtesy of Janet Miller Bernet. Dr. John Goucher recommended the "stomach cordial" he used in his own practice to help with nausea during pregnancy. It combined carbonate of magnesia, salts of tartar, and peppermint oil with water. A large teaspoonful of the mixture was added to two tablespoons of water and given five to ten minutes before each meal. A drop of ipecac was added if the "disgust for food" was worse. Another remedy was a tincture made from a half pint of fine iron scales from a blacksmith's shop added to a quart of cider vinegar. The patient was given several drops of the tincture in a tablespoon of sweetened water after each meal.

16. John F. Goucher to Charles F. Himes, March 29, 1880, box 1, folder 1, Goucher Papers, BWCA.

17. Ella Goucher Bedell to John and Mary Goucher, November 4, 1880, and Bell Goucher to Mary Goucher, November 6, 1880, courtesy of Janet Miller Bernet. Bell, wife of David Goucher, wrote, "I felt so sure a boy was coming that it never occurred to me to think what name would be given if a dear little girl came." Mary C. Goucher to Mary Himes, November 18, 1880, MC2000.1, box 8, folder 15, Charles Francis Himes Family Papers (hereinafter Himes Family Papers), DCASC.

18. Ella Goucher Bedell to Mary Goucher, June 1883, courtesy of Janet Miller Bernet.

19. John F. Goucher, handwritten card, box 5, folder 2, Goucher Papers, BWCA. He later added that the baby died on July 11, 1887, age four months six days. Adelaide Buckley to Mary Goucher, May 26, 1887, courtesy of Janet Miller Bernet.

20. Goucher, "Genesis 41:51"; Earl Cranston, "John Franklin Goucher—Modern Apostle and Civilized Saint," *Methodist Review*, January/February 1923, 22, record group 3, box 1, folder 22, Goucher Papers, GCSCA; Jacob, "Mary Fisher Goucher," 3; John F. Goucher, "The Advisable Differences between the Education of Women and That of Young Men," opening address before the annual meeting of the New England Association of Colleges and Preparatory Schools, October 13, 1899, 6, record group 3, box 3, folder 15, Goucher Papers, GCSCA; Betsy Woollen, "The Life of Dr. Goucher," 15, record group 3, box 1, folder 26, Goucher Papers, GCSCA; "Mary Cecilia Goucher," minutes, BAC, 62.

21. Marjorie Heitkamp, "Alto Dale and Its Relation to Goucher College," January 1931, 1–2, record group 3, box 1, folder 7, Goucher Papers, GCSCA; "Dr. Goucher Home in Pikesville Sold," *Baltimore Sun*, April 18, 1928, 6; Elizabeth Goucher Chapman to Carlyle Earp, March 30, 1964, Carlyle Reede Earp Papers on John Franklin Goucher, Baltimore–Washington Conference Archives (hereinafter Earp Papers, BWCA). When Isabella (Belle) Fisher died in 1890, John Goucher was the executor of her estate; she left Mary nearly $100,000 (approximately $2.7 million in 2014). "Suburbs and County," *Baltimore Sun*, January 12, 1893, 8.

22. Janet Miller Bernet, interview with the author, December 2004; Chapman to

Earp, March 30, 1964. Two longtime family employees were Robert Green, the driver, and Minnie McCauley, a seamstress and companion.

23. Bernet, interview.

24. Mary C. Goucher to Mary Himes, July 7, 1885, MC2000.1, box 8, folder 15, Himes Family Papers, DCASC.

25. Martin Vail to John F. Goucher, July 19, 1886, Series 3: Japan, box 14, folder 3, MRL 12: John Franklin Goucher Papers, Burke Library at Union Theological Seminary, Columbia University in the City of New York (hereinafter MRL 12: Goucher Papers, Burke Library); "Pleasant Afternoon with Dr. and Mrs. Goucher at Alto Dale," *Baltimore Methodist*, September 1, 1898, BWCA; James M. Buckley to John F. Goucher, September 2, 1906, box 1, folder 6, Goucher Papers, BWCA. Granddaughter Janet Miller Bernet also played in "Cricket."

26. "John Franklin Goucher," in *Baltimore: Its History and Its People* (New York: Lewis Historical Publishing Co., 1912), 2:484.

27. "An Enterprising Minister," *Zion's Herald*, September 23, 1887, Goucher Papers, BWCA; F. L. Neeld to John F. Goucher, April 20, 1887, Series 2: India, box 12, folder 18, MRL 12: Goucher Papers, Burke Library.

28. Heitkamp, "Alto Dale and Its Relation to Goucher College," 3; Anna Heubeck Knipp and Thaddeus P. Thomas, *The History of Goucher College* (Baltimore, 1938), 57, 377; shipping manifest from Kai Tsu Sha, General Custom House, Brokers and Shipping Agents, March 2, 1885, and shipping manifest from Kaitsu Gomai Kwaisha, March 3, 1908, Series 3: Japan, box 14, folder 9, MRL 12: Goucher Papers, Burke Library. Dr. Goucher gave a clipping of the Wesley ivy to be planted outside Goucher Hall by the first graduating class of the Woman's College of Baltimore in 1892. It began a twenty-year tradition at the college for graduates to plant ivy, often derived from faraway places such as Malmesbury Abbey, Oxford University, Newnham College at Cambridge University, and Heidelberg University.

29. Bernet, interview; Chapman to Earp, March 30, 1964.

30. "Pleasant Afternoon"; Mary A. Badley to Mary C. Goucher, August 20, 1886, Series 2: India, box 11, folder 1, MRL 12: Goucher Papers, Burke Library.

31. Lucien Clark, in "Tributes to Dr. John F. Goucher," *Washington Christian Advocate*, July 27, 1922, 10, record group 3, box 1, folder 19, Goucher Papers, GCSCA; "A Noble Woman Crowned," *Zion's Herald*, December 24, 1902, 1661; Samuel H. Williamson, "Seven Ways to Compute the Relative Value of a U.S. Dollar Amount, 1774 to present, MeasuringWorth, 2015, https://www.measuringworth.com/uscompare.

32. Goucher, "Luke XII:21," c. 1918, in *Sermons*; Cranston, "John Franklin Goucher," 19.

Chapter Four

1. John F. Goucher, "The Present Position of Methodism in the Western Section," in *Proceedings of the Third Ecumenical Methodist Conference* (New York: Eaton and Mains, 1901), 70, box 5 folder 5, Rev. John F. Goucher Papers, Baltimore–Washington Conference Archives (hereinafter Goucher Papers, BWCA).

2. Diary of John F. Goucher (hereinafter Diary), May 12, 1869, box 7, Goucher Papers, BWCA.

3. John F. Goucher, record of his first four assignments as a minister, box 5, folder 2, Goucher Papers, BWCA; Goucher, handwritten sheet relating to Gilmor Street and Harlem Park Churches, 1878–1881, box 5, folder 2, ibid.; "A Short History of Harlem Park Church," sixty-fifth anniversary, November 10–17, 1940, BWCA; Joseph Garonzik, "The Racial and Ethnic Make-up of Baltimore Neighborhoods, 1850–1870," *Maryland Historical Magazine* 71, no. 3 (1976): 396.

4. Goucher, handwritten sheet relating to Gilmor Street and Harlem Park Churches; Mary Ellen Hayward, *Baltimore's Alley Houses: Homes for Working People since the 1780s* (Baltimore: The Johns Hopkins University Press, 2008), 135.

5. Goucher, handwritten sheet relating to Gilmor Street and Harlem Park Churches; program for the Potato Supper and Parlor Sociable, Harlem Park Methodist Episcopal Church, February 6, 1880, Goucher Papers, BWCA; "Church News," *Baltimore Methodist*, June 17, 1880, 5, ibid. Along with the usual staples of baked, fried, and roasted potatoes, the menu included brown potato soup, potato snow, potato bread, potato pickle, and, for dessert, potato cheese cake and potato pine apple [sic].

6. Arthur C. Day, "Brief Historical Statement," Strawbridge Methodist Church, March 1970, MS 1799, Maryland Historical Society, Baltimore, http://www.mdhs.org/library/Mss/ms001799.html.

7. R. V. Logan, Treasurer of Trustees, July 19, 1881, Records of Strawbridge Church, Bolton Hill, BWCA; John W. Locks, Samuel S. Brown, Isaac Myers, Bethel AME Church, to J. F. Goucher and the Board of Trustees, May 5, 1881, ibid.; Strawbridge Methodist Episcopal Church, Amendment to the Articles of Incorporation, June 30, 1881, ibid.; Day, "Brief Historical Statement"; "From Baltimore," *Christian Advocate*, 1882, 511, BWCA.

8. "Baltimore Then and Now," pictorial review, *Baltimore American*, May 13, 1956, 10, BWCA; David Gilmore Wright, "Conception to Realization: An Historic Building Statement," in *The Restoration of the Lovely Lane Church* (Baltimore: Architectory, 1980), 1:2–3.

9. "Baltimore Then and Now."

10. Wright, "Conception to Realization," 6–7.

11. Ibid., 9.

12. Lewis H. Cole to J. F. Goucher, March 1, 1883, box 1, folder 1, Goucher Papers, BWCA.

13. Wright, "Conception to Realization," 12–16; "National Register of Historic Places—Old Goucher Neighborhood District Expanded," September 26, 1994, Goucher College Library, Special Collections and Archives.

14. Wright, "Conception to Realization," 13; Anna Heubeck Knipp and Thaddeus P. Thomas, *The History of Goucher College* (Baltimore, 1938), 7.

15. "National Register of Historic Places."

16. Wright, "Conception to Realization," 18; minutes of the Building Committee, First Methodist Episcopal Church, August 21 and November 12, 1883, Lovely Lane United Methodist Church Archives. Stanford White (1853–1906) became

known for designing the second Madison Square Garden and the Washington Square Arch in New York City, several buildings at the University of Virginia, and the Boston Public Library. He also became famous for his death: White was shot by a jealous husband, Harry Kendall Thaw, for his affair with Thaw's wife, model and actress Evelyn Nesbit.

17. Wright, "Conception to Realization."

18. Stanford White to John F. Goucher, September 7, 1886, Goucher Papers, BWCA; Wright, "Conception to Realization," 45.

19. Minutes of the Building Committee, September 19–20 and December 14, 1883; January 25 and February 8, 1884; and May 4, 1885; Wright, "Conception to Realization," 3, 20.

20. John Dorsey to John F. Goucher, November 9, 1887, box 1, folder 2, Goucher Papers, BWCA; "Groundbreaking," *Baltimore Sun*, November 30, 1883, 4; Wright, "Conception to Realization," 27.

21. Minutes of the Building Committee, June 25, 1884; Wright, "Conception to Realization."

22. Cole to Goucher, November 21, 1885.

23. Leroy M. Vernon, "Two Dedications in Italy," *Zion's Herald*, January 18, 1888, 18; Leroy M. Vernon to John F. Goucher, October 6, 1887, Series 5: Miscellaneous Work in Various Countries, box 17, folder 2, MRL 12: John Franklin Goucher Papers, Burke Library at Union Theological Seminary, Columbia University in the City of New York.

24. *Baltimore American*, November 5, 1887, BWCA; Wright, "Conception to Realization, 34.

25. Wright, "Conception to Realization," 35; "The Lovely Lane Methodist Church," in *Official Souvenir Book of the American Methodist Bicentennial 1766–1966* (Baltimore: Baltimore Conference Methodist Historical Society, 1966), 65, BWCA. The chart of the heavens was prepared by R. W. Prentiss of the Astronomical Department of the United States, and the installation was supervised by Simon Newcomb, professor of astronomy at Johns Hopkins University.

26. Wright, "Conception to Realization," 41.

27. "A Magnificent Edifice, Dedicating the Chapel of Baltimore City Station—How to Raise Money," *Baltimore Sun*, December 7, 1885, 6; Wright, "Conception to Realization," 41–42.

28. Wright, "Conception to Realization"; "A New House of Worship, Dedication of the First Methodist Episcopal Church," *Baltimore American*, November 7, 1887, BWCA; Vernon, "Two Dedications in Italy."

29. Wright, "Conception to Realization," 36; "Rev. John F. Goucher, D.D.," *Zion's Herald*, May 18, 1898, BWCA; "John Franklin Goucher, D.D.," *Daily Advocate*, May 10, 1894, box 4, folder 2, Goucher Papers, BWCA. The "mission" churches in the Baltimore City Station were the Royer Hill, Guilford Avenue, and Oxford Churches.

Chapter Five

1. John F. Goucher, "Boston Social Union," *Zion's Herald*, February 19, 1896, 128.

2. "Church Extension Collections—An Earnest Appeal," *Zion's Herald*, August 24, 1876, 267. In the same article, there was another story from a minister in western Kansas. Church membership was thirty, and there were eighty in the Sunday school. He wrote, "The people are poor. . . . With $300 or $400 we can build a good church, but can do nothing without aid. . . . Please do what you can for this needy, suffering people."

3. The eight congregations on the Baltimore Circuit raised $45 a year for church extension during Goucher's tenure as junior preacher. His congregation at Catonsville raised $10 annually; the Huntingdon Avenue Church raised $35 each year; and the Gilmor congregation raised $10 in his first year as minister. Minutes, Baltimore Annual Conference, 1870–1879, Baltimore–Washington Conference Archives (BWCA).

4. "Church Extension Anniversary," *Christian Advocate*, November 20, 1879, 745; Wade Crawford Barclay, "The Changing Structure of American Society," in *The Methodist Episcopal Church 1845–1939, Widening Horizons, 1845–1895* (New York: Board of Missions of the Methodist Church, 1957), 3:6–7. The Kansas–Nebraska Act of 1854 created the territories of Kansas and Nebraska and opened new lands for ownership. It allowed settlers in each territory to determine by vote if slavery was to be allowed within its boundaries. The Homestead Act of 1864, signed by Abraham Lincoln, gave free title to up to 160 acres of undeveloped federal land west of the Mississippi. An applicant, including a freed slave, had to be twenty-one years of age and had never taken up arms against the U.S. government. The settler had to improve the land and live on it for five years before filing for a final deed to the property.

5. W. W. Pinson, "Methodism: An Evangelistic Movement," in *Souvenir of the Centenary Celebration of American Methodist Missions*, Columbus, Ohio, June 20–July 13, 1919, 67, BWCA; David Hempton, *Methodism, Empire of the Spirit* (New Haven, Conn.: Yale University Press, 2005), 153; "Church Extension to the Front!," *Christian Advocate*, November 20, 1879, 744.

6. John H. Race, in "Tributes to Dr. John F. Goucher," *Washington Christian Advocate*, July 27, 1922, 10, record group 3, box 1, folder 19, John Franklin Goucher Papers, Goucher College Library, Special Collections and Archives; John F. Goucher, *Christianity and the United States* (New York: Eaton and Mains, 1908), 9; "Chaplain M'Cabe's Cry," *Christian Advocate*, March 27, 1879, 204; "Church Extension to the Front!"

7. "Church Extension Anniversary"; "Chaplain M'Cabe's Cry."

8. "Chaplain M'Cabe's Cry"; John F. Goucher to A. J. Kynett, October 17, 1879, box 3, folder 13, Rev. John F. Goucher Papers, Baltimore–Washington Conference Archives (hereinafter Goucher Papers, BWCA).

9. Goucher to Kynett, October 17, 1879; A. J. Kynett to John F. Goucher, October 20 and December 3, 1879, and February 7, 1880, box 3, folder 13, Goucher Papers, BWCA. At first, Goucher wanted to limit the cost of a church to $2,500. Kynett persuaded him to increase the limit to $3,500, a figure that stayed in effect for forty years.

10. John F. Goucher to W. L. McDowell, January 24, 1919, box 3, folder 13, Goucher Papers, BWCA; handwritten account of the Frontier Loan Fund, 1880–1887, and typed summary of Frontier Fund loans, 1880 to November 1899, box 3, folder 13, ibid. The 1880–1887 account shows locations of churches aided, the original loan, principal and interest returned, and the loan amount outstanding. The range of early recipients included Idaho Springs, Colorado; What Cheer, Iowa; Russell, Kansas; Casselton, Dakota; Albert Lea, Minnesota; Chico, Texas; Dillon, Montana; Tombstone, Arizona; Santa Fe, New Mexico; and Centerville, Oregon.

11. John F. Goucher, handwritten sheet listing travel schedule for December 1891 and the first week in January 1892, box 7, Goucher Papers, BWCA; C. C. M'Cabe, "Letter from the Front—Read It!," *Western Christian Advocate*, March 17, 1880, 82; "Our Work in Las Vegas," *Western Christian Advocate*, February 22, 1882, 62; "Las Vegas, New Mexico," *Christian Advocate*, November 6, 1890, 739; handwritten account of the Frontier Loan Fund.

12. B. C. Swarts to John F. Goucher, July 14, 1892, box 1, folder 2, Goucher Papers, BWCA; B. C. Swarts, "Indian Mission Conference," *Christian Advocate*, May 15, 1890, 314; B. C. Swarts, "Indian Mission Conference," *Zion's Herald*, September 23, 1891, 299.

13. Swarts to Goucher, July 14, 1892; William F. Wolfe, "Oklahoma Territory," *Christian Advocate*, March 19, 1891, 192.

14. Swarts to Goucher, July 15, 1892. An example of Goucher's support of friends: James Thoburn, a missionary in North India, wrote Goucher thanking him for his "kind favor" of $100 following an accident he had while on furlough. The money, he said, helped cover "an ugly bill which I feared would grow into a chronic debt." J. M. Thoburn to John F. Goucher, July 16, 1888, box 1, folder 2, Goucher Papers, BWCA.

15. Goucher to McDowell, January 4, 1919, box 3, folder 13, Goucher Papers, BWCA.

16. Goucher to McDowell, February 20, 1919.

Chapter Six

1. John Franklin Goucher, "The Financial Cooperation of Both the Rich and the Poor Indispensable to the World's Salvation," February 1902, in *Sermons*, record group 3, box 3, folder 1, John Franklin Goucher Papers, Goucher College Library, Special Collections and Archives (hereinafter Goucher Papers, GCSCA).

2. The bronze, bas-relief plaque of Goucher, designed by Baltimore sculptor Hans Schuler, gives these accolades: "A Friend of Christ, Church Builder, Missionary Pioneer, Father of Colleges and Universities, and Leader Among Men and Brother to All Peoples." Cyrus David Foss, *From the Himalayas to the Equator* (New York: Eaton and Mains, 1899), 134; William Elliot Griffis, *A Modern Pioneer in Korea: The Life Story of Henry G. Appenzeller* (London: Fleming H. Revell, 1912), 116. Two Japanese men whom the Gouchers aided were Sato Shosuke and Ishizaka Masanobu. Sato became president of the Sapporo Agricultural College and later president of the Hokkaido Imperial University; Ishizaka became president of Aoyama Gakuin University. Sato Shosuke to John

F. Goucher, June 30 and July 3, 1885, Series 5: Missionary Work in Various Countries, box 17, folder 2, MRL 12: John Franklin Goucher Papers, Burke Library at Union Theological Seminary, Columbia University in the City of New York (hereinafter MRL 12: Goucher Papers, Burke Library); Ishizaka Masanobu to John F. Goucher, May 8, 1897, Series 3: Japan, box 15, folder 5, ibid.; Clara M. Cushman to John F. Goucher, November 2, 1880, Series 1: China, box 1, folder 10, ibid.

3. John F. Goucher, "Missions and Education," in *Missionary Issues of the Twentieth Century*, address delivered at the General Missionary Conference of the Methodist Episcopal Church, South, April 24–30, 1901, 144, https://archive.org/details/missionaryissues00methiala; Foss, *From the Himalayas to the Equator*, 242; diary of James Whitford Bashford, February 1, 1911, box 2, folder 5, MRL 6: James Whitford Bashford Diaries, Burke Library at Union Theological Seminary, Columbia University in the City of New York.

4. Frank Mason North, "Dr. Goucher's Lifelong Service to Foreign Missions," *Christian Advocate*, July 27, 1922, 925, record group 3, box 1, folder 16, Goucher Papers, GCSCA.

5. Dana L. Robert, "The Methodist Struggle over Higher Education in Fuzhou, China, 1877–1883," *Methodist History* 34, no. 3 (1996): 173, General Commission on Archives and History of the United Methodist Church (1996-04-01), http://archives.gcah.org/xmlui/pdfpreview/bitstream/handle/10516/6095/mrl-1996-April-Robert.pdf?sequence=1. Domestic missions in western states and territories, outside the established Methodist Annual Conferences, included missions in Indian Territory and those for immigrants speaking other languages, such as Germans, French, Chinese, and Scandinavians.

6. "The General Missionary Committee," *Zion's Herald*, November 19, 1884, 372. The General Missionary Committee was then composed of the Board of Bishops, the secretaries and treasurers of the Missionary Society, representatives of the General Conference districts, and twelve members chosen by the society's Board of Managers.

7. "The Methodist Missionary Committee," *The Independent . . . Devoted to the Consideration of Politics, Social and Economic Tendencies, History, Literature, and the Arts*, November 21, 1889, 17; "Missionary Work," *Rochester Union Advertiser*, May 22, 1891, box 4, folder 2, Rev. John F. Goucher Papers, Baltimore–Washington Conference Archives (hereinafter Goucher Papers, BWCA).

8. John F. Goucher, "The Annual Missionary Sermon," delivered at the Baltimore Annual Conference (Baltimore: Methodist Episcopal Book Depository, 1882), 19–21, 29, box 3, folder 2, Goucher Papers, GCSCA.

9. William R. Hutchison, *Errand to the World: American Protestant Thought and Foreign Missions* (Chicago: University of Chicago Press, 1987), 78–81.

10. Hutchison, *Errand to the World*, 80; Robert, "Methodist Struggle," 176.

11. John F. Goucher, "Investigation and Concentration in Giving," in *Men and World Service*, address delivered at the National Missionary Congress, April 26–30, 1916, 157, http://archive.org/stream/menandworldserv00unknuoft/menandworldserv00unknuoft_djvu.txt; John F. Goucher, "The Church and Education," *Methodist Review*, March 1902, 179, record group 3, box 3, folder 19, Goucher Papers, GCSCA; Charles H. Fahs, "John F. Goucher, Missionary

Educator," *Missionary Review of the World*, November 1922, 880, record group 3, box 1, folder 22, ibid.

12. Goucher, "Missions and Education," 138, 141.

13. Janet Goucher Miller, "Chapel Address," January 8, 1937, GCSCA; Goucher, "Missions and Education," 142.

14. Goucher, "Missions and Education," 141.

15. Ibid.

16. John F. Goucher, "Should the Higher Education of Women Differ from That of Men?," presented at the annual convention of the Association of Colleges and Preparatory Schools of the Middle States and Maryland, November 30–December 1, 1900, 25–26, record group 3, box 3, folder 18, Goucher Papers, GCSCA; diary of John F. Goucher, January 5, 1898, box 7, Goucher Papers, BWCA.

17. J. H. Shively to John F. Goucher, January 10, 1887, Series 2: India, box 12, folder 4, MRL 12: Goucher Papers, Burke Library.

18. *Baltimore Methodist*, June 17, 1882, BWCA; North, "Dr. Goucher's Lifelong Service," 924.

19. "The Judicious Gifts of the Rev. J. F. Goucher," *Christian Advocate*, March 6, 1884, 149; C. C. McCabe to John F. Goucher, September 22, 1885, C. C. McCabe File, Miscellaneous Manuscripts Collection, drawer 3, BWCA.

20. William Butler to John F. Goucher, November 11, 1880, Series 5: Missionary Work in Various Countries, box 17, folder 6, MRL 12: Goucher Papers, Burke Library; Julius Soper to John F. Goucher, September 17, 1880, Series 3: Japan, box 15, folder 10, ibid.; C. F. Doering to John F. Goucher, February 18, 1880, Series 5: Missionary Work in Various Countries, box 17, folder 2, ibid.; Erwin H. Richards, annual report of the Inhambane District, minutes of the first session of the East Africa Mission Conference, November 16–25, 1901, 23, record group 3, box 3, folder 17, Goucher Papers, GCSCA.

21. Goucher, "Missions and Education," 136; Clara M. Cushman to John F. Goucher, August 20, 1909, Series 1: China, box 1, folder 10, MRL 12: Goucher Papers, Burke Library; John 15:16.

Chapter Seven

1. John F. Goucher, "True Education," matriculation sermon, the Woman's College of Baltimore, October 9, 1904, 6, record group 3, box 3, folder 21, John Franklin Goucher Papers, Goucher College Library, Special Collections and Archives.

2. Julius Soper, report to the Baltimore Annual Conference, January 18, 1876, in minutes, Baltimore Annual Conference, March 1–9, 1876, 64–65, Baltimore–Washington Conference Archives. The U.S. government used "gunboat diplomacy" to pursue its foreign policy objectives by shows of potential military force. Such intimidation helped coerce treaties with previously unwilling countries.

3. Julius Soper to John F. Goucher, April 6, 1922, with Soper article "Purchase of Aoyama Gakuin Property," March 31, 1922, Series 3: Japan, box 15, folder 11,

MRL 12: John Franklin Goucher Papers, Burke Library at Union Theological Seminary, Columbia University in the City of New York (hereinafter MRL 12: Goucher Papers, Burke Library); Soper, report to the Baltimore Annual Conference.

4. Robert S. Maclay to John F. Goucher, October 31, 1879. All letters from Maclay to Goucher cited in this chapter are from Series 3: Japan, box 15, folder 7, MRL 12: Goucher Papers, Burke Library.

5. Ibid.; J. M. Reid to John F. Goucher, December 29, 1879, and John Phillips to John F. Goucher, March 1, 1880, box 1, folder 1, Rev. John F. Goucher Papers, Baltimore–Washington Conference Archives (hereinafter Goucher Papers, BWCA).

6. Maclay to Goucher, February 11, 1880; Reid to Goucher, December 29, 1879.

7. "Mr. Goucher's Proposition," *Western Christian Advocate*, November 16, 1881, 376.

8. Ibid.; Martin S. Vail to John F. Goucher, December 10, 1881, Series 3: Japan, box 14, folder 3, MRL 12: Goucher Papers, Burke Library. After leading the school in Hirosaki, Honda Yoitsu studied at Drew Theological Seminary in New Jersey in the late 1880s. He received financial aid from and was entertained by the Gouchers while he was a student at Drew. In 1907, he became the first bishop of the Methodist Church of Japan.

9. Maclay to Goucher, January 18, 1882, and January 22, 1883.

10. Maclay to Goucher, January 18, 1882.

11. Maclay to Goucher, April 3 and 8, 1882.

12. Maclay to Goucher, January 3, 1883. James Smithson (1764–1829) left his estate to a nephew, who died without heirs. As dictated by Smithson's will, the money was then to go to the U.S. government in Washington, D.C., to establish an institution for "the increase and diffusion of knowledge among men." In 1846, the Smithsonian Institution was founded by an Act of Congress. During his lifetime, George Peabody (1795–1869) funded numerous educational initiatives, including the Peabody Institute (now part of the Johns Hopkins University) in Baltimore; the Peabody Museum of Natural History at Yale; the Peabody Museum of Archeology and Ethnology at Harvard; and the Peabody Education Fund, which supported schools in the southern United States following the Civil War.

13. Maclay to Goucher, November 28, 1882; Soper, "Purchase of Aoyama Gakuin Property."

14. Maclay to Goucher, January 22 and August 28, 1883; Soper, "Purchase of Aoyama Gakuin Property." The original site of the Anglo-Japanese College, purchased with Goucher funds, is still owned by and part of Aoyama Gakuin University in Tokyo.

15. Maclay to Goucher, November 19, 1883; John O. Spencer to John F. Goucher, February 2, 1885, Series 3: Japan, box 15, folder 12, MRL 12: Goucher Papers, Burke Library.

16. Maclay to Goucher, August 1, 1883, and February 27, 1884; I. W. Wiley and R. S. Maclay, "An Important Appeal from Japan," *Christian Advocate*, July 3, 1884, 437. The Theological School was named for Philander Smith as a memorial gift from his wife, Adeline, from Illinois.

17. Maclay to Goucher, July 19, 1887; "News and Views of Aoyama Gakuin," *Japan Advertiser*, November 24, 1925, box 3, folder 11, Goucher Papers, BWCA.

Chapter Eight

1. John F. Goucher, "Education," handwritten speech, c. 1915, box 5, folder 3, Rev. John F. Goucher Papers, Baltimore–Washington Conference Archives (hereinafter Goucher Papers, BWCA).

2. Edwin W. Parker to John F. Goucher, November 25, 1879, box 11, folder 18. All letters from Parker to Goucher cited in this chapter are from Series 2: India, MRL 12: John Franklin Goucher Papers, Burke Library at Union Theological Seminary, Columbia University in the City of New York (hereinafter MRL 12: Goucher Papers, Burke Library); E. Cunningham to John F. Goucher, November 29, 1879, Series 2: India, box 12, folder 17, ibid.

3. Parker to Goucher, November 25, 1879; Brenton H. Badley to John F. Goucher, February 26, 1881, Series 2: India, box 11, folder 1, MRL 12: Goucher Papers, Burke Library.

4. Minutes, Baltimore Annual Conference, March 3–9, 1869; March 3–7, 1871; and February 28–March 4, 1872, BWCA; Parker to Goucher, November 25, 1879. The Gouchers' proposed gift would have helped at least twenty girls attend boarding school in the central location of Moradabad, Parker's home base.

5. Cyrus David Foss, *From the Himalayas to the Equator* (New York: Eaton and Mains, 1899), 242; John F. Goucher to E. W. Parker, October 31, 1882. The letter between Goucher and Parker cited in this chapter is in *Manual of the Goucher Schools* (Lucknow, India: American Methodist Mission Press, 1884), record group 3, box 3, folder 37, John Franklin Goucher Papers, Goucher College Library, Special Collections and Archives; "Goucher Schools," *Baltimore News*, April 14, 1898, box 1, folder 16, Goucher Papers, BWCA.

6. Goucher to Parker, October 31, 1882; diary of John F. Goucher (hereinafter Diary), January 5, 1898, box 7, Goucher Papers, BWCA; J. N. Fitzgerald to John F. Goucher, November 16, 1882, Series 2: India, Box 12, Folder 17, MRL 12: Goucher Papers, Burke Library.

7. Goucher to Parker, October 31, 1882.

8. John F. Goucher, "Missions and Education," in *Missionary Issues of the Twentieth Century*, address delivered at the General Missionary Conference of the Methodist Episcopal Church, South, April 24–30, 1901, 144, https://archive.org/details/missionaryissues00methiala.

9. *Manual of the Goucher Schools.*

10. Goucher to Parker, October 31, 1882.

11. James W. Waugh to John F. Goucher, February 6, 1883, Series 2: India, box 12, folder 15, MRL 12: Goucher Papers, Burke Library; D. W. Thomas to John F. Goucher, August 29, 1883. All letters from Thomas to Goucher cited in this chapter are from Series 2: India, box 12, folder 12, MRL 12: Goucher Papers, Burke Library. The first village schools were opened in the following circuits in the Rohilkhand District: Budaun, Bilsi, Bisauli, Chandausi, Moradabad,

Amroha, Bijnor, Bareilly, Fatehganj, and Shahjahanpur.

12. John F. Goucher to D. W. Thomas, January 31, 1884, in *Manual of the Goucher Schools*; Thomas to Goucher, April 21 and November 4, 1884.

13. Thomas to Goucher. November 27, 1883.

14. Goucher to Thomas, January 31, 1884; diary, January 5, 1898; Thomas to Goucher, February 19 and April 21, 1884; Parker to Goucher, July 13, 1887, box 11, folder 19.

15. Parker to Goucher, March 16, 1885, box 11, folder 18.

16. Mrs. Prem Nath Dass, "Fifty Years of Isabella Thoburn College," *Indian Witness*, November 5, 1936, selections from her article in the Jubilee issue of *Woman's Missionary Friend*, BWCA; reports on primary schools in India, Series 2: India, box 12, folder 17, MRL 12: Goucher Papers, Burke Library; Parker to Goucher, December 21, 1885, box 11, folder 18; Lois Parker to Mary Goucher, May 17, 1887, Series 2: India, box 11, folder 19, MRL 12: Goucher Papers, Burke Library.

17. Reports on primary schools in India; N. L. Rockey, "The Goucher Impetus to India," *Christian Advocate*, August 24, 1922, box 1, folder 18, Goucher Papers, BWCA.

18. Parker to Goucher, April 20, 1885, box 11, folder 18.

19. Thomas to Goucher, April 30, 1883; Badley to Goucher, December 5, 1887.

20. Dennis Osbourne to John F. Goucher, September 9, 1884, and August 22 and November 23, 1885, Series 2: India, box 11, folder 16, MRL 12: Goucher Papers, Burke Library; W. A. Carroll to John F. Goucher, April 17, 1888, Series 2: India, box 11, folder 5, ibid.

21. Parker to Goucher, April 20, 1885, box 11, folder 19; Thomas to Goucher, April 21, 1884; Waugh to Goucher, November 14, 1885.

22. Parker to Goucher, May 2, 1887, box 11, folder 19; R. Hoskins to John F. Goucher, September 3, 1884, Series 2: India, box 12, folder 17, MRL 12: Goucher Papers, Burke Library; Thomas to Goucher, April 21, 1884.

23. Parker to Goucher, July 13 and December 27, 1887, box 11, folder 19.

24. Diary, November 20, 1897.

25. Parker to Goucher, April 16, 1889, box 11, folder 20. Goucher renewed his and Mary's annual $5,000 pledge to support primary schools and scholarships.

26. Parker to Goucher, July 11, 1889, box 11, folder 20, and Parker to Goucher, April 12 and December 31, 1891, box 11, folder 21.

Chapter Nine

1. John F. Goucher, "West China: A Great Mission Field," July 9, 1894, in *Semons*, record group 3, box 3, folder 1, John Franklin Goucher Papers, Goucher College Library, Special Collections and Archives.

2. Diary of John F. Goucher, March 17, 1907, box 7, Rev. John F. Goucher Papers, Baltimore–Washington Conference Archives; Nathan Sites to John F. Goucher, September 2, 1886, Series 1: China, box 1, folder 26, MRL 12: John Franklin Goucher Papers, Burke Library at Union Theological Seminary, Columbia

University in the City of New York (hereinafter MRL 12: Goucher Papers, Burke Library).

3. Goucher, "West China."

4. Paul A. Varg, *Missionaries, Chinese, and Diplomats: The American Protestant Missionary Movement in China, 1890–1952* (Princeton, N.J.: Princeton University Press, 1958), 4. The five ports opened through the Nanking Treaty were Canton (Guangzhou), Amoy (Xiamen), Foochow (Fuzhou), Ningpo (Ningbo), and Shanghai.

5. Ibid., 5, 12.

6. Hiram H. Lowry to John F. Goucher, January 16, 1880, Series 1: China, box 1, folder 17, MRL 12: Goucher Papers, Burke Library; Wade Crawford Barclay, "The Church Faces Its Missionary Task," in *The Methodist Episcopal Church 1845–1939, Widening Horizons 1845–1895* (New York: Board of Missions of the Methodist Church, 1957), 3:192–193.

7. Mary Porter Gamewell to Hiram H. Lowry, January 13, 1880, Series 1: China, box 1, folder 10, MRL 12: Goucher Papers, Burke Library; Clara M. Cushman to John F. Goucher, November 2, 1880, Series 1: China, box 1, folder 10, ibid.

8. Leonora Howard to John F. Goucher, April 28, 1881, Series 1: China, box 1, folder 1, MRL 12: Goucher Papers, Burke Library.

9. Mary Porter Gamewell to John F. Goucher, August 6, 1896, Series 1: China, box 1, folder 12, MRL 12: Goucher Papers, Burke Library.

10. Dana L. Robert, "The Methodist Struggle over Higher Education in Fuzhou, China, 1877–1883," *Methodist History* 34, no. 3 (1996): 175, General Commission on Archives and History of the United Methodist Church (1996-04-01), http://archives.gcah.org/xmlui/pdfpreview/bitstream/handle/1051b/6095/mrl-1996-April-Robert.pdf?sequence=1.

11. Barclay, "Church Faces Its Missionary Task," 390; Robert, "Methodist Struggle," 179.

12. Brochure on the Anglo-Chinese College, Series 1: China, box 2, folder 1, MRL 12: Goucher Papers, Burke Library; "Forty Years After," Anglo-Chinese College, Foochow, China, 1881-1921, ibid..

13. D. W. Chandler, "The New Departure in China: The Anglo-Foochow College," *Western Christian Advocate*, April 6, 1881, 105; Franklin Ohlinger to John F. Goucher, January 24 and October 25, 1881. All letters from Ohlinger to Goucher cited in this chapter are from Series 1: China, box 2, folder 2, MRL 12: Goucher Papers, Burke Library.

14. Robert, "Methodist Struggle," 188; C. H. Fowler to John F. Goucher, November 11, 1881, Series 1: China, box 2, folder 2, MRL 12: Goucher Papers, Burke Library; "The Foochow Anglo-Chinese College," *Western Christian Advocate*, November 23, 1881, 375.

15. Ohlinger to Goucher, March 22, 1882.

16. Ohlinger to Goucher, January 9, 1883; I. W. Wiley to John F. Goucher, October 28, 1883, Series 1: China, box 1, folder 30, MRL 12: Goucher Papers, Burke Library.

17. Robert, "Methodist Struggle," 184, 186; Wiley to Goucher, October 28, 1883; John F. Goucher to I. W. Wiley, November 11, 1883, Series 1: China, box 2,

folder 2, MRL 12: Goucher Papers, Burke Library.

18. Sites to Goucher, February 20 and September 10, 1885, Series 1: China, box 2, folder 2, MRL 12: Goucher Papers, Burke Library; George B. Smyth to John F. Goucher, March 15, 1897, Series 1: China, box 2, folder 2, ibid.

19. Sites to Goucher, October 8 and November 22, 1883, Series 1: China, box 1, folder 26, MRL 12: Goucher Papers, Burke Library.

20. Barclay, "Church Faces Its Missionary Task," 421; Ohlinger to Goucher, August 14, 1880.

21. Barclay, "Church Faces Its Missionary Task."

22. Ibid., 422; Lucius N. Wheeler to John F. Goucher, May 21, 1882, Series 1: China, box 1, folder 29, MRL 12: Goucher Papers, Burke Library.

23. Fowler to Goucher, October 27 and November 10, 1882, and October 25, 1883, Series 1: China, box 1, folder 11, MRL 12: Goucher Papers, Burke Library.

24. Fowler to Goucher, October 25, 1883.

Chapter Ten

1. John F. Goucher, "Missions and Education," in *Missionary Issues of the Twentieth Century*, address delivered at the General Missionary Conference of the Methodist Episcopal Church, South, April 24–30, 1901, 144, https://archive.org/details/missionaryissues00methiala.

2. "The Embassy from Corea," *New York Times*, September 18, 1883, 5; R. S. Maclay to John F. Goucher, March 24, 1884. All letters from Maclay to Goucher cited in this chapter are from Series 3: Japan, box 15, folder 7, MRL 12: John Franklin Goucher Papers, Burke Library at Union Theological Seminary, Columbia University in the City of New York (hereinafter MRL 12: Goucher Papers, Burke Library). King Kojong sent Min Yong Ik, Queen Min's nephew, and four other high-level representatives to meet President Arthur. Along with them were two Korean interpreters and Percival Lowell. They were sent to learn about American customs and the postal and public school systems and to examine fortifications and arsenals.

3. Along with the king and royal family, there were the *yangban*, part of the ruling class of scholarly civil servants, military officials, and landowners, who lived off the efforts of the commoners. The *jungin*, or middle people, consisted of clerks, interpreters, scribes, doctors, accountants, artists, and musicians. The *yangmin*, including peasants, merchants, laborers, soldiers, and some craftsmen, composed the largest class, paid most of the taxes, and were subject to military conscription. Below these groups were the "untouchables," such as butchers, tanners, and gravediggers, and slaves, who could be bought, sold, or given as gifts by their masters. King Kojong officially banned slavery in 1894.

4. The 1876 treaty between Korea and Japan was called the Treaty of Kanghwa (Treaty of Friendship). The 1882 treaties between Korea and the United States, Great Britain, and Germany were each known as a Treaty of Peace, Amity, Commerce, and Navigation. The U.S. treaty was negotiated by Commodore Robert W. Shufeldt, who had investigated the sinking of the *General Sherman* by the Koreans in 1866.

5. Maclay to Goucher, June 19, 1884; Martin Vail to John F. Goucher, June 10, 1882, Series 3: Japan, box 14, folder 3, MRL 12: Goucher Papers, Burke Library.

6. I. W. Wiley to John F. Goucher, November 2, 1883, Series 1: China, box 1, folder 30, MRL 12: Goucher Papers, Burke Library; Wade Crawford Barclay, "Expanding Program in Foreign Missions—Japan and Korea," in *The Methodist Episcopal Church 1845–1939, Widening Horizons 1845–1895* (New York: Board of Missions of the Methodist Church, 1957), 3:742.

7. Maclay to Goucher, March 24 and June 9, 1884.

8. Maclay to Goucher, July 2 and 23, 1884; "Editorial Notes," *The Independent . . . Devoted to the Consideration of Politics, Social and Economic Tendencies, History, Literature, and the Arts,* September 4, 1884, 18.

9. Maclay to Goucher, July 2, 1884.

10. Wiley to Goucher, July 3, 1884; "The General Missionary Committee," *Zion's Herald,* November 19, 1884, 372.

11. Maclay to Goucher, July 2, 1884; J. M. Reid to Henry G. Appenzeller, September 5 and October 17, 1884. All letters from Reid to Appenzeller cited in this chapter are from Series 2: Correspondence, box 3, folder 2, MRL 8: Henry Gerhard Appenzeller Papers, Burke Library at Union Theological Seminary, Columbia University in the City of New York (hereinafter MRL 8: Appenzeller Papers, Burke Library). William B. Scranton (1856–1922) graduated from Yale University and the New York College of Physicians and Surgeons. He practiced medicine in Ohio for two years before being appointed as a medical missionary to Korea in late 1884. Henry Gerhard Appenzeller (1858–1902) graduated from Franklin and Marshall College and Drew Theological Seminary and was ordained in February 1885, as he was embarking as the first Methodist missionary to Korea.

12. William Taylor to John F. Goucher, July 26, 1884, William Taylor File, Miscellaneous Manuscripts Collection, drawer 4, Baltimore–Washington Conference Archives.

13. Henry G. Appenzeller to John F. Goucher, January 29, 1895, Series 4: Korea, box 16, folder 11, MRL 12: Goucher Papers, Burke Library; Reid to Appenzeller, November 20 and December 1 and 20, 1884.

14. Barclay, "Expanding Program in Foreign Missions," 743; Reid to Appenzeller, December 20, 1884.

15. Maclay to Goucher, February 27, 1885.

16. Barclay, "Expanding Program in Foreign Missions," 743.

17. Ibid., 743–744. The hospital that Allen started was later named Jejungwon (House of Universal Helpfulness) by King Kojong. It was the beginning of Severance Yonsei University Hospital and School of Medicine in Seoul.

18. Henry G. Appenzeller to J. M. Reid, June 29, 1886, Series 2: Correspondence, box 2, folder 1, MRL 8: Appenzeller Papers, Burke Library; Barclay, "Expanding Program in Foreign Missions."

19. Barclay, "Expanding Program in Foreign Missions," 745; Henry G. Appenzeller, June 16, July 28, November 6, and December 11, 1886. All Appenzeller journal entries cited in this chapter are from Series 1: Journals, box 1, folder 3, MRL 8: Appenzeller Papers, Burke Library; William Elliot Griffis, *A Modern Pioneer in Korea: The Life Story of Henry G. Appenzeller* (London:

Fleming H. Revell, 1912), 174, 178.

20. Griffis, *A Modern Pioneer in Korea*, 174; Appenzeller, February 8 and 21 and March 24, 1887. The original painted signboard for the Pai Chai Hakdang is on display in the Appenzeller/Noble Memorial Museum, housed in a former classroom building on Pai Chai's campus.

21. Appenzeller, August 6, 1887.

22. H. G. Appenzeller, "Woman's Work in Korea," *The Independent . . . Devoted to the Consideration of Politics, Social and Economic Tendencies, History, Literature, and the Arts*, June 18, 1891, 19; Griffis, *A Modern Pioneer in Korea*, 116.

23. Ewha Archives, *The Story of Ewha, from History to Future* (Seoul: Ewha University Press, 2013), 19.

24. Ibid., 20; Bishop C. H. Fowler, "Korea—The Last Hermit," *Christian Advocate*, January 31, 1889, 68. Ewha High School continues to educate Korean girls, and Ewha Womans University is the world's largest university for women, with more than 22,000 students enrolled in 2014 and 200,000 alumnae worldwide.

25. William B. Scranton, "Korea," *Christian Advocate*, January 26, 1888, 67.

26. Appenzeller, June 16, 1886; Barclay, "Expanding Program in Foreign Missions," 744, 746; Ewha Archives, *Story of Ewha*, 27–28. Dr. Meta Howard was sent by the WFMS to open the women's health clinic.

27. Ewha Archives, *Story of Ewha*, 27; John F. Goucher, interview by Frank G. Porter, July 1922, box 7, Rev. John F. Goucher Papers, Baltimore–Washington Conference Archives.

28. Appenzeller, April 25, May 11, July 24, and August 3, 1886; Appenzeller to Reid, June 29, 1886, Series 2: Correspondence, box 2, folder 1, MRL 8: Appenzeller Papers, Burke Library.

29. Barclay, "Expanding Program in Foreign Missions," 747; Appenzeller, March 1, October 9 and 23, and December 25, 1887. As the number of Methodist converts grew, a larger church was needed. In 1897, Appenzeller dedicated the Chungdong First Methodist Church, the only extant nineteenth-century church in Korea. Appenzeller died in 1902, at age forty-four, when the ship he was on sank off the Korean coast.

30. Abram W. Harris, in "Tributes to Dr. John F. Goucher," *Washington Christian Advocate*, July 27, 1922, 10, record group 3, box 1, folder 19, John Franklin Goucher Papers, Goucher College Library, Special Collections and Archives.

Chapter Eleven

1. John F. Goucher, "Education," handwritten speech, c. 1915, box 5, folder 3, Rev. John F. Goucher Papers, Baltimore–Washington Conference Archives (hereinafter Goucher Papers, BWCA).

2. Edward N. Wilson, *The History of Morgan State College: A Century of Purpose in Action, 1867–1967* (New York: Vantage Press, 1975), 17.

3. "John Wesley and Black Colleges," http://www.umc.org/news-and-media/john-wesley-and-black-colleges.

4. Minutes, Centenary Biblical Institute, Board of Trustees, January 3, 1867, MSA S359-1 (December 25, 1866–February 14, 1890), MdHR 18430-1, Maryland State Archives, Annapolis, Md. (hereinafter minutes, CBI); Wilson, *History of Morgan State College*, 8.

5. Christopher Phillips, *Freedom's Port: The African American Community of Baltimore, 1790–1860* (Urbana and Chicago: University of Illinois Press, 1977), 120–123.

6. Ibid., 125.

7. Wilson, *History of Morgan State College*, 2.

8. Edward N. Wilson, "Washington Conference, 1864–65: Culmination of Sharp Street Petitions of 1848, 1856, and 1864," in *Those Incredible Methodists: A History of the Baltimore Conference of the Methodist Episcopal Church*, ed. Gordon Pratt Baker (Nashville, Tenn.: Parthenon Press, 1972), 246; "New Conferences Conceived," in *Third Century of Methodism*, Commission on Archival History and United Methodist Historical Society of the Baltimore–Washington Conference, spring 2014, 2, 4.

9. Joseph Garonzik, "The Racial and Ethnic Make-up of Baltimore Neighborhoods, 1850–1870," *Maryland Historical Magazine* 71, no. 3 (1976): 394; Richard Paul Fuke, "The Baltimore Association for the Moral and Educational Improvement of the Colored People, 1864–1870," *Maryland Historical Magazine* 66, no. 4 (1971): 373, 376; Barbara Jeanne Fields, *Slavery and Freedom on the Middle Ground: Maryland during the Nineteenth Century* (New Haven, Conn.: Yale University Press, 1985), 139.

10. Phillips, *Freedom's Port*, 227; Bettye Gardner, "Ante-Bellum Black Education in Baltimore," *Maryland Historical Magazine* 71, no. 3 (1976): 361, 365–366.

11. Robert J. Brugger, *Maryland: A Middle Temperament, 1634–1980* (Baltimore: The Johns Hopkins University Press, in association with the Maryland Historical Society, 1988), 307; Fuke, "Baltimore Association," 370–371, 376.

12. Phillips, *Freedom's Port*, 166, 227; Fuke, "Baltimore Association," 370–371, 376.

13. Fuke, "Baltimore Association," 373, 376, 381–382; Brugger, *Maryland*, 308–309.

14. Philip S. Foner, "Address of Frederick Douglass at the Inauguration of Douglass Institute, October 1, 1865," in *Journal of Negro History* 54, no. 2 (1969): 176, http://www.jstor.org.goucher.idm.oclc.org/stable//2716691.

15. Minutes, CBI, April 19 and December 17, 1867; Wilson, *History of Morgan State College*, 6, 11–16; W. Maslin Frysinger, "The Centenary Biblical Institute–An Open Door Southward," *Christian Advocate*, February 5, 1885, 94.

16. Wilson, *History of Morgan State College*, 25, 31–34, 37; minutes, CBI, April 22, 1879.

17. Minutes, CBI, September 24, 1879; "Letter from Baltimore," *Zion's Herald*, June 2, 1881, 175; "Correspondence," *Zion's Herald*, February 24, 1881; Wilson, *History of Morgan State College*, 37–39. The lot Goucher offered was at the corner of Edmondson and Fulton Avenues. Baltimore's Washington Monument was begun in 1815 and completed in 1829, the first monument in the country to honor George Washington.

18. Minutes, Baltimore Annual Conference, March 8–10, 1880, 55, Baltimore–Washington Conference Archives.

19. Minutes, CBI, April 6, 1880; "Centenary Biblical Institute," *Western Christian Advocate*, May 25, 1881, 165.

20. Minutes, CBI, May 27, 1881; "Centenary Biblical Institute, Baltimore," *Western Christian Advocate*, February 8, 1882, 46; J. P. Otis, "Report of the Conference Visitors to the Centenary Biblical Institute, Baltimore," *Christian Advocate*, July 12, 1883, 441. Of the 116 students studying in the new building, 48 were boarding at the institute, and the remaining were attending day or evening classes.

21. Minutes, CBI, January 12 and April 6, 1880, and May 30, 1883; Otis, "Report of the Conference Visitors"; diary of John F. Goucher (hereinafter Diary), March 8, 1869, box 7, Goucher Papers, BWCA. Morgan had introduced Goucher at his first meeting of the Baltimore Conference in March 1869: "I have brought with me a young brother who I am certain will do more for the Conference than ever I have been able to do."

22. Minutes, CBI, December 25, 1879, and July 12, 1883; Wilson, *History of Morgan State College*, 48–50; Otis, "Report of the Conference Visitors."

23. Minutes, CBI, July 12, 1883; Frysinger, "Centenary Biblical Institute"; Wilson, *History of Morgan State College*, 48.

24. Frysinger, "Centenary Biblical Institute"; minutes, CBI, June 11, 1884. When the CBI opened in September 1885, there was a balance of $46.20 ($1,170) in the treasury. Examples of Goucher's donations to cover expenses: He gave $3,000 ($77,000) for the 1886–1887 academic year, and more than $2,000 ($53,100) for 1888–1889. Minutes, CBI, September 17, 1885, October 26, 1887, and June 13, 1889.

25. Two other centennial projects proposed by the Baltimore Conference: "The generous and thorough endowment of Dickinson College" and "the establishing on a firm and liberal basis of a 'Baltimore Conference Seminary.'" (The latter became the Woman's College of Baltimore City.) "Good News Concerning the Centenary Biblical Institute," *Christian Advocate*, January 17, 1884, 44.

26. Frysinger, "Centenary Biblical Institute"; minutes, CBI, October 26, 1887. The Washington Conference pledged $10,000 ($249,000), and the Delaware Conference $5,000 ($124,000).

27. Wilson, *History of Morgan State College*, 51–52; W. Maslin Frysinger, "Four Open Doors," *Christian Advocate*, November 10, 1887, 727.

28. Frysinger, "Four Open Doors."

29. "Baltimore Notes," *Christian Advocate*, January 20, 1887, 48; minutes, CBI, February 4, 1887; Wilson, *History of Morgan State College*, 51; Frysinger, "Four Open Doors"; John R. Wennersten and Ruth Ellen Wennersten, "Separate but Unequal: The Evolution of a Black Land Grant College in Maryland, 1890–1930," *Maryland Historical Magazine* 72, no. 1 (1977): 111.

30. Minutes, CBI, June 12, 1889, and February 24, 1890. Lyttleton Frye Morgan (1813–1895) was the son and brother of Methodist ministers and joined the Baltimore Conference in 1836. He was a pastor in Washington, D.C., when he became chaplain of the House of Representatives in 1851–1852. Assigned to churches in Baltimore and to Christ Methodist Episcopal Church in Pittsburgh, he was a presiding elder and elected three times as a delegate to the Methodist

General Conference. In addition to his service as a trustee and president of the board of the Centenary Biblical Institute, he was a founding trustee of the Woman's College of Baltimore City in 1885, and president of its board from 1889–1995. At his death, Morgan College received an annual income from ground rents. The Woman's College received funds to create its first endowed professorship in memory of his wife. Wilson, *History of Morgan State College*, 128–130; Anna Heubeck Knipp and Thaddeus P. Thomas, *The History of Goucher College* (Baltimore, 1938) 15, 93–94, 590 (n. 155).

Chapter Twelve

1. John F. Goucher, "Education of Girls," unknown newspaper, June 1896, Scrapbook, Goucher College Library, Special Collections and Archives (hereinafter GCSCA).

2. John F. Goucher, "The College Education of Women," *Christian Advocate*, December 14, 1899, 2017.

3. Anna Heubeck Knipp and Thaddeus P. Thomas, *The History of Goucher College* (Baltimore, 1938), 1–2.

4. Minutes, Baltimore Annual Conference, March 9–15, 1881, 39, Baltimore–Washington Conference Archives (hereinafter minutes, BAC); Knipp and Thomas, *History of Goucher College*, 4. Members of the 1881 special committee were John F. Goucher, John H. Dashiell, C. Herbert Richardson, David H. Carroll, T. Daugherty, C. W. Slagle, George S. Grape, A. H. Greenfield, William J. Hooper, and P. Hanson Hiss.

5. John B. Van Meter, "The Evolution of the Woman's College of Baltimore," c. 1920, 79, record group 1, box 4, Founding and Incorporation—Histories, GCSCA.

6. Minutes, BAC, March 7–12, 1883, 54; Van Meter, "Evolution," 82.

7. Van Meter, "Evolution," 87.

8. Ibid., 46; Knipp and Thomas, *History of Goucher College*, 5; "To Train Heart and Mind: The Woman's College Opened," *Baltimore Sun*, November 14, 1888, 6.

9. "Twenty-Five Years of Goucher's Work," *Baltimore Evening Sun*, March 15, 1913, record group 3, box 1, folder 10, John Franklin Goucher Papers, Goucher College Library, Special Collections and Archives (hereinafter Goucher Papers, GCSCA).

10. John F. Goucher to J. B. Van Meter et al., December 2, 1883, record group 3, box 2, folder 1, Goucher Papers, GCSCA. Goucher also offered to improve the plot if accepted: to "grade, pave and deed in fee to a Board of Control when incorporated under the direction of the Baltimore Annual Conference for use of such an [Educational] Institution."

11. Van Meter, "Evolution," 90; "A Conference Seminary—Great Mass Meeting of the Ladies of the Methodist Episcopal Church," *Baltimore Methodist* (suppl.), February 9, 1884, BWCA.

12. "A Conference Seminary."

13. Ibid.; "The Women's Educational Association of the Methodist Episcopal

Church," *Baltimore Methodist* (suppl.), March 1, 1884, BWCA. The association's goal was to raise an average of $5 ($124) from each woman on the church rolls and $1 ($25) from each girl in Sunday school. Mrs. Francis A. Crook served as president and Isabel Hart as corresponding secretary of the organization. As a minister, Goucher had worked with both of them through the Baltimore branch of the Women's Foreign Missionary Society, and both were among the first women trustees elected soon after the opening of the college.

14. Minutes, BAC, March 5–11, 1884, 48, 51, 90; Van Meter, "Evolution," 169; Knipp and Thomas, *History of Goucher College*, 11. Conference members pledged $20,000 ($498,000) at the 1884 annual meeting.

15. Knipp and Thomas, *History of Goucher College*; Van Meter, "Evolution," 88. Members of the Committee on Female College were ministers John F. Goucher, Lyttleton F. Morgan, John B. Van Meter, John H. Dashiell, J. A. McCauley, Austin M. Courtenay, Charles W. Baldwin, J. J. G. Webster, Robert W. Black, A. H. Ames, David H. Carroll, and C. Herbert Richardson; and laymen Francis A. Crook, German H. Hunt, B. F. Parlett, William J. Hooper, Summerfield Baldwin, N. M. Smith, Benjamin H. Stinemetz, Saul S. Henkle, Owen Hitchens, George S. Grape, Charles E. Hill, and Henry S. Hiss. Bishop Andrews was also a member.

16. Knipp and Thomas, *History of Goucher College*, 12–13; *Baltimore Methodist* (suppl.), June 7, 1884, BWCA. Along with Goucher, Francis Crook and William Hooper each pledged $5,000 at the meeting. Other gifts to complete the goal ranged from $5 to $1,000 ($24,900).

17. *Baltimore Methodist* (suppl.), June 7, 1884.

18. Van Meter, "Evolution," 89, 157–158.

19. "Baltimore Notes," *Christian Advocate*, January 17, 1884, 40; Van Meter, "Evolution," 157.

20. Knipp and Thomas, *History of Goucher College*, 15–16. Twelve men, the most allowed by state law, were selected as the first corporators (trustees): Edward G. Andrews, John F. Goucher, Lyttleton F. Morgan, Francis A. Crook, John B. Van Meter, David H. Carroll, Henry S. Hiss, William J. Hooper, Robert W. Black, German H. Hunt, Saul S. Henkle, and George S. Grape. As a working group, twenty-five men became corporators of the institution, sharing the rights and duties of the official trustees. The Maryland state legislature approved the charter in March 1885.

21. Hans Froelicher, "Recollections," *Donnybrook Fair*, 1929, 23–24, GCSCA; Knipp and Thomas, *History of Goucher College*, 142–143.

22. Knipp and Thomas, *History of Goucher College*, 17; minutes, BAC, March 5, 1885, 69; "The Methodist Female College," *Baltimore Sun*, March 6, 1885, 4.

23. Minutes, BAC, March 12, 1885, 29; Van Meter, "Evolution," 176.

24. Minutes, Woman's College of Baltimore City, May 1, 1885, Series III, boxes 4 and 5 (1884–1910), Board of Trustees Records, Goucher College Library, Special Collections and Archives (hereinafter minutes, WCB); Knipp and Thomas, *History of Goucher College*, 21, 24.

25. David Gilmore Wright, "Conception to Realization: An Historic Building Statement," in *The Restoration of the Lovely Lane Church* (Baltimore: Architectory, 1980), 1:22.

26. Minutes, WCB, January 5, 1886; "The Woman's College of the City of Baltimore," *Christian Advocate*, October 14, 1886, 2. The original cornerstone of Goucher Hall is now located on the campus of Goucher College in Towson, Maryland. Its contents are part of the college's Special Collections and Archives.

27. Knipp and Thomas, *History of Goucher College*, 25.

28. Ibid.; minutes, WCB, October 27, 1887, and February 12, 1890.

29. *Baltimore American*, November 14, 1888, Scrapbook, GCSCA.

30. Approximate figures for the Gouchers' major gift totals from 1879–1889 are as follows (2014 conversions, www.measuringworth.com/uscompare): First Church, $37,500 ($963,000); Centenary Biblical Institute, $30,500 ($759,000); Woman's College of Baltimore City, $155,000 ($4 million); Frontier Loan Fund, $10,000 ($250,000); Japan, $58,100 ($1.37 million); India, $46,000 ($1.1 million); China, $18,600 ($446,000); and Korea, $5,000 ($123,500). During this period the couple also gave $2,500 ($65,000) to African missions, and $5,000 ($119,000) to both the Martin's Mission Institute and the Methodist Book Concern in Germany. The total for contributions does not include smaller donations or gifts to local, national, and international institutions, causes, or individuals; annual debt relief at the Woman's College of Baltimore or the Centenary Biblical Institute; or Goucher's remission of ministerial salary during these years.

Chapter Thirteen

1. John F. Goucher, "True Education," matriculation sermon, the Woman's College of Baltimore, October 9, 1904, 6, record group 3, box 3, folder 21, John Franklin Goucher Papers, Goucher College Library, Special Collections and Archives (hereinafter Goucher Papers, GCSCA).

2. Robert W. H. Weech, in "Tributes to Dr. John F. Goucher," *Washington Christian Advocate*, July 27, 1922, 10, record group 3, box 1, folder 19, Goucher Papers, GCSCA.

3. Cyrus D. Foss to John F. Goucher, May 21, 1890, box 1, folder 2, Rev. John F. Goucher Papers, Baltimore–Washington Conference Archives (hereinafter Goucher Papers, BWCA); Anna Heubeck Knipp and Thaddeus P. Thomas, *The History of Goucher College* (Baltimore, 1938), 55.

4. William Hersey Hopkins to John F. Goucher, November 28, 1907, box 1, folder 7, Goucher Papers, BWCA; minutes, Woman's College of Baltimore, May 27, 1890, Series III, boxes 4 and 5 (1884–1910), Board of Trustees Records, Goucher College Library, Special Collections and Archives (hereinafter minutes, WCB); Francis A. Crook and John H. Dashiell to John F. Goucher, May 30, 1890, box 1, folder 2, Goucher Papers, BWCA.

5. Minutes, WCB, June 16, 1890; diary of John F. Goucher, April 3, 1891. The 1891 diary is not among the Goucher diaries in the Baltimore–Washington Conference Archives. It is referenced, however, in an unpublished manuscript by Carlyle Reede Earp, *John Franklin Goucher*, c. 1960, 107 (n. 27), Carlyle Reede Earp Papers on John Franklin Goucher, Baltimore–Washington Conference Archives (hereinafter Earp Papers, BWCA).

6. "Dr. Goucher Retires," *Pittsburgh Christian Advocate*, December 5, 1907, box

1, folder 16, Goucher Papers, BWCA; Knipp and Thomas, *History of Goucher College*, 30–31, 33–34; minutes, Executive Committee, Woman's College of Baltimore, April 5, 1889, Series IV, box 5 (1885–1910), Board of Trustees Records, GCSCA (hereinafter minutes, Executive Committee, WCB).

7. Knipp and Thomas, *History of Goucher College*, 98. The initial requirements for entrance to the Woman's College were four years of Latin plus experience in a second language (Greek, French, or German); mathematics (algebra and geometry); English grammar and composition; literature, history, and geography; and physics and physiology.

8. John F. Goucher, report to the Board of Trustees, minutes, WCB, November 7, 1892; Lilian Welsh, *Reminiscences of Thirty Years in Baltimore* (Baltimore: Norman, Remington, 1925), 3.

9. "John Goucher," *Afro-American*, July 28, 1922, 7; "Twenty-Five Years of Goucher's Work," *Baltimore Evening Sun*, March 15, 1913, record group 3, box 1, folder 10, Goucher Papers, GCSCA.

10. Knipp and Thomas, *History of Goucher College*, 57–61; "Latin School Building," *Baltimore Sun*, August 24, 1893, 8.

11. *Baltimore American*, November 1894, Scrapbook, GCSCA.

12. Janet Goucher Miller, "Chapel Address," January 8, 1937, GCSCA.

13. Knipp and Thomas, *History of Goucher College*, 102; "Citizen Goucher," *Baltimore Evening News*, November 22, 1906, box 1, folder 18, Goucher Papers, BWCA.

14. Janet Miller Bernet, interview with the author, December 2005 and December 2007; "Citizen Goucher"; Goucher House, Buildings and Grounds, Series I, box 1, GCSCA.

15. Earl Cranston, "John Franklin Goucher—Modern Apostle and Civilized Saint," *Methodist Review*, January/February 1923, 11, record group 3, box 1, folder 22, Goucher Papers, GCSCA; Kathryn Allamong Jacob, "Mary Fisher Goucher," 3–4, record group 3, box 1, folder 6, Goucher Papers, GCSCA; Knipp and Thomas, *History of Goucher College*, 45.

16. Edith Latane, "Presentation of Memorial Window," *Kalends*, June 1905, 295, GCSCA.

17. *Baltimore American*, November 1894, GCSCA; "Rev. Dr. Goucher," *Baltimore Sun*, November 24, 1896, 7; Margot Doss, "A Great Deal of Good with the Money," *Baltimore Sun*, April 2, 1950, SM7; Knipp and Thomas, *History of Goucher College*, 54; Jennie Vail to John F. Goucher, December 3, 1910, Series 3: Japan, box 14, folder 4, MRL 12: John Franklin Goucher Papers, Burke Library at Union Theological Seminary, Columbia University in the City of New York (hereinafter MRL 12: Goucher Papers, Burke Library).

18. "The Woman's College," *Baltimore Sun*, November 7, 1895, 8; Jacob, "Mary Fisher Goucher," 3.

19. Frank Mason North, "Dr. Goucher's Lifelong Service to Foreign Missions," *Christian Advocate*, July 27, 1922, 925, record group 3, box 1, folder 16, Goucher Papers, GCSCA; Miller, "Chapel Address"; Cranston, "John Franklin Goucher," 22.

20. R. T. Taylor, "Baltimore Letter," *Pittsburgh Christian Advocate*, November 3, 1898, BWCA. Alto Dale Day was suspended from 1914 to 1919 and then

resumed for two more years.

21. Knipp and Thomas, *History of Goucher College*, 56–57; Hans Froelicher, "Recollections," *Donnybrook Fair*, 1929, 23–24, GCSCA.

22. Knipp and Thomas, *History of Goucher College*; Froelicher, "Recollections"; Latane, "Presentation of Memorial Window."

23. Marjorie Heitcamp, "Alto Dale and Its Relation to Goucher College," January 1931, 5–8, n. 15, 17, 21, record group 3, box 1, folder 32, Goucher Papers, GCSCA; Knipp and Thomas, *History of Goucher College*; Froelicher, "Recollections"; Class of 1900, "Memorial Service for John Franklin Goucher" (hereinafter "Memorial Service"), February 18, 1923, *Goucher Alumnae Quarterly*, Memorial Number (May 1923): 15, record group 3, box 1, folder 21, Goucher Papers, GCSCA.

24. Michael K. Burns, "Mountain Lake Park Woman Saves Memories of a Resort without 'Sin,'" *Baltimore Sun*, December 27, 1981, B1; Bernet, interview, December 2005. Some of the Woman's College faculty taught courses at Mountain Lake Park during the summer. In 1909, Goucher was elected president of the Inter-State Good Roads Association, and the Inter-State Good Roads Conference held its meeting at Mountain Lake Park on September 5–8, 1910. He told a reporter that he had been studying Maryland's roads for a long time, and he felt that many were "a disgrace," especially in his home city: "I have seen roads in Arabia, built by the Romans in the second century, that are even now in much better condition than the streets of Baltimore—and those Roman roads have not been repaired for 1,800 years." "Roads 1,800 Years Old," *Baltimore Sun*, September 1, 1909, 9.

25. Sarah C. Carnan to John F. Goucher, December 22, 1911, record group 3, box 2, folder 13, Goucher Papers, GCSCA; John F. Goucher, "Commencement Address," Woman's College of Baltimore, June 9, 1892, record group 3, box 3, folder 5, Goucher Papers, GCSCA.

26. Knipp and Thomas, *History of Goucher College*, 67.

27. John F. Goucher, "Commencement Address," Woman's College of Baltimore, June 13, 1893, record group 3, box 3, folder 6, Goucher Papers, GCSCA; Knipp and Thomas, *History of Goucher College*, 98.

28. Knipp and Thomas, *History of Goucher College*, 109–110; John F. Goucher, report to the Baltimore Annual Conference, March 1893, BWCA.

29. Maynard Metcalf, "The Early Years of the College," *Goucher Alumnae Quarterly* (November 1932): 8, GCSCA; Knipp and Thomas, *History of Goucher College*, 129.

30. Welsh, *Reminiscences,* 115; Lilian Welsh, "Memorial Service," 17.

31. Welsh, "Memorial Service," 18; Janet Goucher Miller to Carlyle Earp, c. 1958, Earp Papers, BWCA.

32. Joseph S. Shefloe to Anna Heubeck Knipp, April 26, 1937, BWCA; Knipp and Thomas, *History of Goucher College*, 100. Goucher did not feel that the Norse names threatened the Christian atmosphere of the college, but Van Meter later called them "a system of a rude and repulsive pagan mythology." John B. Van Meter, "The Evolution of the Woman's College of Baltimore," c. 1920, 191, record group 1, box 4, Founding and Incorporation—Histories, GCSCA.

33. David Gilmore Wright, "Conception to Realization: An Historic Building

Statement," in *The Restoration of the Lovely Lane Church* (Baltimore: Architectory, 1980), 1:42; Frank Monaghan, "John F. Goucher," in *Dictionary of American Biography* (New York: Charles Scribner's Sons, 1931), 4:443.

34. Minutes, Executive Committee, WCB, September 8, 1890.

35. John F. Goucher, report to the Board of Trustees, minutes, WCB, November 1, 1893.

36. *Baltimore American*, 1895, box 4, folder 2, Goucher Papers, BWCA; Knipp and Thomas, *History of Goucher College*, 115. Tuition was never enough to cover annual expenses. Some of the deficit was a result of Goucher's recommendation in 1888 and 1889 that the daughters of ministers as well as students intending to be missionaries pay only half of the tuition cost.

37. Goucher, "Commencement Address," 1893; John F. Goucher, "Commencement Address," Woman's College of Baltimore, June 1897, record group 3, box 3, folder 10, Goucher Papers, GCSCA; "$20,000 a Year Needed," *Baltimore Sun*, June 16, 1897, 7.

38. "Rev. John Franklin Goucher," resolution of the Board of Foreign Missions, November 1922, box 3, folder 15, Goucher Papers, BWCA; minutes, Executive Committee, WCB, September 7, 1891. One man who became affiliated with the college through Goucher's efforts was James N. Gamble from Ohio, son of the founder of Proctor and Gamble. He became a trustee in 1892 and, in 1905, was elected the first lay leader of the college's Board of Trustees.

39. "Meeting of the Educational Commission," *Christian Advocate*, November 5, 1891, 752; J. E. Stubbs, "College Presidents at Syracuse," *Christian Advocate*, December 21, 1893, 820; Frederick Campbell, "Chicago Letter," *New York Evangelist*, November 26, 1896, 15; John O. Gross, "The Field of Education, 1865–1939," in *The History of American Methodism* (New York: Abingdon Press, 1964), 3:217; "Woman's College Notes," *Baltimore Methodist*, April 6, 1893, BWCA.

40. Knipp and Thomas, *History of Goucher College*, 110; John F. Goucher, "Education of Girls," unknown newspaper, June 1896, Scrapbook, GCSCA.

41. Minutes, Morgan College, Board of Trustees, February 24 and June 3, 1890, MSA S362-1 (February 14, 1890–December 12, 1899), MdHR 18430-2, Maryland State Archives, Annapolis, Md. (hereinafter minutes, MC); Miller to Earp.

42. Minutes, MC, October 3, 1890; Robert J. Brugger, *Maryland: A Middle Temperament, 1634–1980* (Baltimore: The Johns Hopkins University Press, in association with the Maryland Historical Society, 1988), 420; John R. Wennersten and Ruth Ellen Wennersten, "Separate but Unequal: The Evolution of a Black Land Grant College in Maryland, 1890–1930," *Maryland Historical Magazine* 72, no. 1 (1977): 113.

43. Minutes, MC, October 3, 1890; Wilson, *History of Morgan State College: A Century of Purpose in Action, 1867–1967* (New York: Vantage Press, 1975), 58–59, 132; *Morrill Acts*, http://www.higher-ed.org/resources/morrill_acts.htm; John R. Wennersten, "The Travail of Black Land-Grant Schools in the South, 1890–1917," *Agricultural History* 65, no. 2 (1991): 56, http://www.jstor.org.goucher.idm.ock.org/stable/3743707.

44. Minutes, MC, December 9, 1890 (with attached agreement dated December 31, 1890), and January 22, 1891; Wilson, *History of Morgan State College*, 58–63.

Princess Anne Academy came under state control in 1919, and was renamed the Eastern Shore Branch of the Maryland Agricultural College. It became Maryland State College in 1948 (also known as Princess Anne College), then the University of Maryland Eastern Shore (UMES) in 1970. Like Morgan State University, it remains a historically black institution.

45. Minutes, MC, January 22 and December 10, 1891; Wennersten and Wennersten, "Separate but Unequal," 111.

46. Minutes, MC, December 9, 1890; Wennersten and Wennersten, "Separate but Unequal," 111–13.

47. Minutes, MC, April 15 and May 12, 1891, and June 10, 1892; Wilson, *History of Morgan State College*, 58, 64–65.

48. Minutes, MC, May 29, 1894; "The Important Men of Baltimore," *Baltimore American*, March 9, 1893, record group 3, box 1, folder, 10, Goucher Papers, GCSCA.

49. John F. Goucher, handwritten note, February 4, 1890, Goucher Papers, BWCA. The land was purchased in 1890 and "The American University" incorporated in 1891 under District of Columbia laws. Two years later, it was chartered by an Act of Congress. Begun as a graduate school, the university admitted its first students in 1914; the first undergraduates were admitted in 1925.

50. John F. Hurst to John F. Goucher, March 18, 1892, and John F. Goucher to John F. Hurst, March 1892, box 1, folder 2, Goucher Papers, BWCA.

51. "New Methodist Bishops," *New York Times*, May 23, 1900, 5; John F. Goucher, report to the Board of Trustees, minutes, WCB, November 17, 1898. At the time of the agreement, Washington, D.C. was part of the Baltimore Conference, and the Woman's College appealed for students and funds among residents of both cities.

52. Goucher, report to the Board of Trustees; "New Methodist Bishops."

53. "A Great Success," *Helena Evening Herald*, August 24, 1895, box 4, folder 2, Goucher Papers, BWCA. Montana Wesleyan College merged with other schools to form Rocky Mountain College, located in Billings.

54. "The Morning Session," *Seattle Intelligencer*, June 1896, box 4, folder 2, Goucher Papers, BWCA.

55. John F. Goucher, "Individualism," Recognition Day address, August 18, 1897, *The Chautauquan*, October 1897, box 4, folder 8, Goucher Papers, BWCA.

56. "The Important Men of Baltimore"; "Rev. John F. Goucher, D.D.," *Zion's Herald*, May 18, 1898, box 1, folder 18, Goucher Papers, BWCA; "G," undated newspaper article, source unknown, BWCA. Gorman (1839–1906), an influential Maryland Democrat, served as a member of the state's House of Delegates (1869–1881). He then served as U. S. senator from 1881–1897 and 1903–1906. Gilman (1831–1908) served as the first president of the Johns Hopkins University from 1875–1901. Gibbons (1834–1921) became the archbishop of Baltimore in 1877, and was made a cardinal in 1886, only the second American to be so appointed.

57. "Charity in Baltimore," *Baltimore News*, November 11, 1899, box 1, folder 16, Goucher Papers, BWCA; Brugger, *Maryland*, 396, 409.

58. Jeffrey Brackett to John F. Goucher, January 31, 1895, GCASC; "Kindergarten Association," *Baltimore Sun*, February 20, 1893, 10. Mary Fisher Goucher was

involved in church, charitable, and educational organizations as well. She was vice president of the Baltimore branch of the Women's Foreign Missionary Society and president of First Church's WFMS auxiliary; a manager of the Home for the Aged; vice president of the Association for the Extension of University Education for Women; and a member of the Board of Visitors of the Maryland Asylum and Training School for the Feeble-minded. She was also a member of the Women's Literary Club and the Arundell Club, a group of prominent women interested in government reform and civic improvement.

59. Arthur Bibbins, "Statement of the President of the Academy," Maryland Academy of Sciences, April 7, 1921, BWCA. Bibbins taught geology at the Woman's College of Baltimore from 1894–1911, and served as curator of the museum in Goucher Hall from 1894–1914.

60. Gertrude B. Knipp, "John Franklin Goucher," *Goucher Alumnae Quarterly*, Memorial Number (May 1923): 3, record group 3, box 1, folder 21, Goucher Papers, GCSCA.

61. Minutes, Executive Committee, WCB, November 30, 1891; diary of John F. Goucher (hereinafter Diary), December 14–28, 1891, box 7, Goucher Papers, BWCA; William H. Shelley to John and Mary Goucher, December 25, 1891, Series 5: Missionary Work in Various Countries, box 17, folder 6, MRL 12: Goucher Papers, Burke Library.

62. Diary page, December 29, 1891–January 5, 1892; "Missionary Work," *Rochester Union-Advertiser*, May 22, 1891, box 4, folder 2, Goucher Papers, BWCA; "Brieflets," *Zion's Herald*, January 13, 1892, 12.

63. "Collected in Alaska," *Baltimore American*, August 14, 1896, BWCA.

64. Ibid.

65. Mary C. Goucher to Mary Himes, August 14, 1885, MC2000.1, box 8, folder 15, Charles Francis Himes Family Papers, Dickinson College Archives and Special Collections (hereinafter Himes Family Papers, DCASC).

66. Diary of Mary Cecilia Goucher, January 5 and February 11, 1895, record group 3, box 1, folder 5, Goucher Papers, GCSCA; "Unwrapping a Mummy," *Baltimore Sun*, August 17, 1895, 8; diary, John Goucher, November 14, 1906. Among their travel companions to Cairo were Charles W. Eliot, president of Harvard, and his wife.

67. Knipp and Thomas, *History of Goucher College*, 46; "Who Was Sheik?," *Kalends,* February 1896, 119, GCSCA.

68. "A Marine Monster," *Baltimore Sun*, February 20, 1897, 9.

69. Goucher to Himes, July 7, 1885, Himes Family Papers, DCASC; "Mary Cecilia Goucher," minutes, Baltimore Annual Conference, April 1–7, 1903, 64, BWCA.

70. E. G. Andrews to John F. Goucher, February 5, 1889, and John F. Goucher to E. G. Andrews, February 7, 1889, courtesy of Janet Miller Bernet.

71. *Zion's Herald*, March 22, 1893, 92; James W. Waugh to John F. Goucher, February 6, 1883, Series 2: India, box 12, folder 15, MRL 12: Goucher Papers, Burke Library; "Bishop Hartzell," *Baltimore Sun*, September 10, 1896, 10.

72. "Named for Bishoprics," *Baltimore American*, May 3, 1892, box 3, folder 5, Goucher Papers, BWCA. At the General Conference in 1900, it took seventeen ballots to elect two new bishops.

73. Ibid.

74. S. Reese Murray to John F. Goucher, May 11, 1896, with undated news clipping, BWCA. Murray said he hoped to address "Bishop Goucher" on his return home from the General Conference. Diary of James Whitford Bashford, February 1, 1911, box 2, folder 5, MRL 6: James Whitford Bashford Diaries, Burke Library at Union Theological Seminary, Columbia University in the City of New York.

Chapter Fourteen

1. John Franklin Goucher, "Luke XII:21," c. 1918, in *Sermons*, record group 3, box 3, folder 1, John Franklin Goucher Papers, Goucher College Library, Special Collections and Archives (hereinafter Goucher Papers, GCSCA).

2. Edwin W. Parker to John F. Goucher, February 24, April 12, and May 13, 1891, Series 2: India, box 11, folder 21, MRL 12: John Franklin Goucher Papers, Burke Library at Union Theological Seminary, Columbia University in the City of New York (hereinafter MRL 12: Goucher Papers, Burke Library).

3. Parker to Goucher, February, 24, 1891; J. B. Thomas to John F. Goucher, May 21, 1894, Series 2: India, box 12, folder 13, MRL 12: Goucher Papers, Burke Library; "Goucher Schools," *Baltimore News*, April 14, 1898, box 1, folder 16, Rev. John F. Goucher Papers, Baltimore–Washington Conference Archives (hereinafter Goucher Papers, BWCA).

4. Diary of John F. Goucher (hereinafter Diary), November 11, 1897, box 7, Goucher Papers, BWCA; Cyrus David Foss, *From the Himalayas to the Equator* (New York: Eaton and Mains, 1899), 134.

5. Charles L. Bare to John F. Goucher, September 28, 1899, Series 2: India, box 11, folder 2, MRL 12: Goucher Papers, Burke Library; Parker to Goucher, December 12, 1894.

6. Bare to Goucher, March 18, 1897; W. Rockwell Clancy to John F. Goucher, November 5, 1897, Series 2: India, box 11, folder 6, MRL 12: Goucher Papers, Burke Library.

7. Lilavati Singh to John F. Goucher, June 29, 1892, Series 2: India, box 12, folder 6, MRL 12: Goucher Papers, Burke Library.

8. Isabella Thoburn to John F. Goucher, May 5, 1892, Series 2: India, box 12, folder 10, MRL 12: Goucher Papers, Burke Library.

9. John F. Goucher, "West China, a Great Mission Field," July 9, 1894, in *Sermons*.

10. Martin Vail to John F. Goucher, May 20, 1890, Series 3: Japan, box 14, folder 4, MRL 12: Goucher Papers, Burke Library.

11. Motora Yuzero to John F. Goucher, March 17, 1889, Series 3: Japan, box 15, folder 8, MRL 12: Goucher Papers, Burke Library; Jennie Vail to John F. Goucher, March 11, 1889, box 14, folder 4, ibid.; Julius Soper to John F. Goucher, March 11, 1889, box 14, folder 10, ibid.

12. John Wier to John F. Goucher, December 8, 1893, Series 3: Japan, box 14, folder 5, MRL 12: Goucher Papers, Burke Library.

13. Ibid.

14. H. G. Appenzeller, "The Outbreak in Korea," *The Independent . . . Devoted to the Consideration of Politics, Social and Economic Tendencies, History, Literature, and the Arts*, August 9, 1894, 14.

15. Ibid.

16. Henry G. Appenzeller, February 26, 1896, Series 1: Journals, box 1, folder 3, MRL 8: Henry Gerhard Appenzeller Papers, Burke Library at Union Theological Seminary, Columbia University in the City of New York (hereinafter MRL 8: Appenzeller Papers, Burke Library).

17. Goucher, "West China."

18. Diary, April 4, 1907.

19. "Methodist Conference," *Baltimore Sun*, March 9, 1892, 6.

20. Goucher, "West China."

21. Ibid.; H. Olin Cady to John F. Goucher, July 6, 1895, Series 1: China, box 1, folder 7, MRL 12: Goucher Papers, Burke Library.

22. "Dr. Goucher's Trip," *Baltimore News*, October 7, 1897, box 4, folder 2, Goucher Papers, BWCA; minutes, Woman's College of Baltimore, June 14, 1897, Series III, boxes 4 and 5 (1884–1910), Board of Trustees Records, Goucher College Library, Special Collections and Archives (hereinafter minutes, WCB).

23. "Dr. Goucher's Trip"; "Woman's College," *Baltimore Sun*, October 9, 1897, 7.

24. William McKinley, letter of introduction for John F. Goucher, October 7, 1897, box 1, folder 3, Goucher Papers, BWCA; diary, October 8–November 3, 1897; Foss, *From the Himalayas to the Equator*, 19–20. President McKinley's letter stated, "Dr. Goucher is an accomplished student, a teacher of the most approved educational systems, and intends to take a trip, at an early date, to India, Japan and China to study in detail the educational work of these countries. For many years my personal friend, I take pleasure in commending him to those whom he may meet abroad and will appreciate any courtesies which are shown to him in the furtherance of his investigations."

25. Diary, November 3, 1897, to January 30, 1898.

26. "Conference Week in Calcutta," *Indian Witness*, December 31, 1897, box 4, folder 2, Goucher Papers, BWCA.

27. Diary, November 6, 8, and 28 and December 25 and 31, 1897, and January 12, 1898.

28. Foss, *From the Himalayas to the Equator*, 224–225.

29. Diary, November 11 and 18–20, and December 25, 1897.

30. Foss, *From the Himalayas to the Equator*, 23, 134. The men had to take along their own "beds"—foldable pads, pillows, sheets, and coverlets—to use on train seats or cots during their travels.

31. Diary, November 18–19 and 25, 1897, and January 5–11, 1898.

32. Ibid., January 5–11, 1898; John F. Goucher to Edwin F. Frease, February 2, 1898, Series 2: India, box 11, folder 10, MRL 12: Goucher Papers, Burke Library; John F. Goucher to George K. Gilder, February 2, 1898, box 11, folder 11, ibid.; John F. Goucher to Martha A. Sheldon, February 2, 1898, box 12, folder 5, ibid. Mahatma Gandhi was from the Gujarat area.

33. Diary, November 11 and 20, December 9–13, 1897, and January 3, 1898; "Dr. Goucher at Home," *Baltimore American*, April 13, 1898, and "Rev. Dr. Goucher Returns," *Baltimore American*, April 14, 1898, box 4, folder 2, Goucher Papers, BWCA; *Zion's Herald*, April 27, 1898, BWCA.

34. Diary, November 11, 1897; "The Hathras Mela," *Indian Witness*, December 10, 1897.

35. Diary, November 13 and December 1, 1897.

36. Ibid., November 28 and December 1, 1897.

37. Ibid., November 17, 1897, and January 11, 1898.

38. Ibid., January 11, 1898; John F. Goucher, "Two Buildings," 1898, in *Sermons*.

39. Goucher, "Two Buildings."

40. Diary, November 7 and 28, December 23, 1897, and January 29, 1898; "Circled the Globe," *Baltimore Herald*, April 14, 1898, box 3, folder 11, Goucher Papers, BWCA. Although Mary spoke French, John did not speak any foreign languages.

41. Section of untitled article, *Indian Witness*, December 31, 1897.

42. Diary, December 15–16, 1897; Foss, *From the Himalayas to the Equator*, 77; Grace Stephens to John F. Goucher, March 23, 1898, Series 2: India, box 12, folder 8, MRL 12: Goucher Papers, Burke Library.

43. Diary, December 16, 1897.

44. "Report of John F. Goucher, D.D., to the Board of Managers of the Missionary Society," *Christian Advocate*, November 3, 1898, 1779; diary, December 2, 1897; John E. Robinson to Mary Goucher, December 30, 1897, box 1, folder 3, Goucher Papers, BWCA.

45. Diary, December 2, 1897, and January 3, 1898.

46. Ibid., January 29, 1898; "Circled the Globe"; "Rev. Dr. Goucher Returns."

47. Diary, January 29–February 17, 1898; William F. Oldham to John F. Goucher, July 14, 1890, box 1, folder 2, Goucher Papers, BWCA.

48. Diary, February 20–March 3, 1898; card in diary, February 24, 1898.

49. Diary, March 7–11, 1898; Julius Soper, "Dr. Goucher in Japan," *Baltimore Methodist*, March 25, 1898, box 1, folder 16, Goucher Papers, BWCA.

50. Diary, March 17–18, 22, 1898; Soper, "Dr. Goucher in Japan."

51. Diary, March 14–24, 1898; Soper, "Dr. Goucher in Japan."

52. Diary, March 25 and April 5–6, 1898; "Circled the Globe."

53. Foss, *From the Himalayas to the Equator*, 28, 97; diary, November 12 and 16 and December 1, 1897, and January 13–18 and February 9, 1898.

54. Diary, December 25, 1897, and February 8, 1898.

55. Janet Goucher Miller, "I Remember—the Gay Nineties," *Goucher Alumnae Quarterly* (Fall 1958): 24, GCSCA; diary, March 19 and 26, 1898. Three of John Robinson's daughters attended the Woman's College of Baltimore: Ruth (1899), Helen (1902), and Flora (1908). Both Ruth and Flora later served as principal of Isabella Thoburn College.

56. "Circled the Globe"; diary, November 15 and 18 and December 9–13, 1897, and January 1 and 12 and February 6, 1898; *Baltimore Methodist*, January 18,

1894, BWCA. The Woman's College of Baltimore also had an exhibit at the Chicago World's Fair as part of an educational section designed to give the public information on the curricula, equipment, and instruction at colleges and universities in the United States. "Woman's College Notes," 1886–1896 Scrapbook, GCSCA; Elizabeth Goucher Chapman to Carlyle Earp, March 30, 1964, Carlyle Reede Earp Papers on John Franklin Goucher, BWCA.

57. "Report of John F. Goucher"; John E. Robinson to John F. Goucher, August 11, 1898, box 1, folder 3, Goucher Papers, BWCA.

58. "Rev. Dr. Goucher Returns."

59. Anna Heubeck Knipp and Thaddeus P. Thomas, *The History of Goucher College* (Baltimore, 1938), 117–118; John F. Goucher, report to the Board of Trustees, minutes, WCB, November 17, 1898.

60. Goucher, report to the Board of Trustees.

61. Ibid.

62. Minutes, WCB, November 22, 1899.

63. Ibid.; Knipp and Thomas, *History of Goucher College*, 118.

64. Minutes, WCB, November 29, 1900.

Chapter Fifteen

1. "Dr. Goucher on Character," *Baltimore Sun*, October 13, 1902, 8.

2. Lilian Welsh, *Reminiscences of Thirty Years in Baltimore* (Baltimore: Norman, Remington, 1925), 131; Welsh, "Memorial Service for John Franklin Goucher," February 18, 1923, *Goucher Alumnae Quarterly*, Memorial Number (May 1923): 17, record group 3, box 1, folder 21, John Franklin Goucher Papers, Goucher College Library, Special Collections and Archives (hereinafter Goucher Papers, GCSCA); twentieth century calendar, Woman's College of Baltimore, GCSCA.

3. Minutes, Woman's College of Baltimore, November 29, 1900, Series III, boxes 4 and 5 (1884–1910), Board of Trustees Records, Goucher College Library, Special Collections and Archives, (hereinafter minutes, WCB); John E. Robinson to John F. Goucher, May 4, 1899, Series 2: India, box 12, folder 1, MRL 12: John Franklin Goucher Papers, Burke Library at Union Theological Seminary, Columbia University in the City of New York (hereinafter MRL 12: Goucher Papers, Burke Library).

4. Minutes, Executive Committee, Woman's College of Baltimore, January 7, 1901, Series IV, box 5 (1885–1910), Board of Trustees Records, Goucher College Library, Special Collections and Archives (hereinafter minutes, Executive Committee, WCB); *California Christian Advocate*, February 21, 1901, Rev. John F. Goucher Papers, Baltimore–Washington Conference Archives (hereinafter Goucher Papers, BWCA); John F. Goucher to Frank G. Porter, February 7, 1901, box 1, folder 4, ibid.

5. Action taken by the Baltimore Conference, April 2, 1901, BWCA; H. W. Warren to John F. Goucher, April 27, 1901, box 1, folder 4, Goucher Papers, BWCA; minutes, Executive Committee, WCB, May 13, 1901.

6. Elizabeth Goucher Chapman to Carlyle Earp, March 30, 1964, Carlyle Reede Earp Papers on John Franklin Goucher, Baltimore–Washington Conference

Archives.

7. Ibid.

8. Edward N. Wilson, *The History of Morgan State College: A Century of Purpose in Action, 1867–1967* (New York: Vantage Press, 1975), 132. Spencer served for thirty-five years as president of Morgan College.

9. "Address of the Rev. J. F. Goucher, D.D.," *Christian Advocate*, May 17, 1894, 313. Among the issues of federation to be agreed on were a common catechism, hymnbook, and order of worship.

10. Frederick E. Maser, "The Story of Unification, 1874–1939," in *The History of American Methodism* (New York: Abingdon Press, 1964), 3:412.

11. John F. Goucher, "The Present Position of Methodism in the Western Section," in *Proceedings of the Third Ecumenical Methodist Conference* (New York: Eaton and Mains, 1901), 72, box 5, folder 5, Goucher Papers, BWCA; "Race Question in a Church Meeting," *New York Times*, November 16, 1901, 6; "Ministers Are Divided," *Baltimore Sun*, January 14, 1902, 7.

12. "Colored View of 'Jim Crow,'" *Baltimore Sun*, January 14, 1902, 7; "Appointments Are Read," *Afro-American*, March 26, 1904, 4; "Epworth League Notes," *Afro-American*, December 10, 1910, 5; "John Goucher," *Afro-American*, July 28, 1922, 7. The Epworth League, named for the boyhood home of John Wesley in England, was a Methodist youth organization founded in 1889 to foster personal spiritual growth and provide training in church leadership. Membership spread worldwide, and Epworth League chapters held Bible studies, organized social events, and raised funds for church causes.

13. Minutes, WCB, November 21, 1901; minutes, Baltimore Annual Conference, April 2–8, 1902, 107, Baltimore–Washington Conference Archives (hereinafter minutes, BAC); Anna Heubeck Knipp and Thaddeus P. Thomas, *The History of Goucher College* (Baltimore, 1938), 116.

14. Minutes, WCB, November 21, 1902; "Dr. Goucher on Unity," *Baltimore Sun*, October 21, 1901, 7.

15. "Completes the Committee," *Baltimore Sun*, May 14, 1901, 10; "To Do without Coal," *Baltimore Sun*, September 25, 1902, 12.

16. "Missions and Bible Study—Buffalo," *Northern Christian Advocate*, c. 1902–1903, BWCA; program of the Ninth Conference of Foreign Mission Boards in the United States and Canada, February 25–26, 1902, BWCA; David H. Moore to John F. Goucher, c. 1900, box 1, folder 2, Goucher Papers, BWCA.

17. "Joint Commission on Federation," *Zion's Herald*, April 2, 1902, 418; "Address of the Rev. J. F. Goucher, D.D."; "Commission Meets Today," *Baltimore Sun*, March 21, 1902, 12; "A Methodist Publishing House in Shanghai," in *Gospel in All Lands*, ed. Eugene R. Smith (Baltimore, 1902), 477–78, https://books.google.com/books?idqHjNukooGkkC&q=%22A+Methodist+Publishing+House+in+China%22#v=onepage&q=%22A%20Methodist%20Publishing%20House%20in%20Shanghai%22&f=false; Moore to Goucher, October 9, 1901, David H. Moore File, Miscellaneous Manuscripts Collection, drawer 3, BWCA.

18. John F. Goucher, "The Church and Education," *Methodist Review*, March 1902, 190, record group 3, box 3, folder 19, Goucher Papers, GCSCA.

19. John Franklin Goucher, "The Financial Cooperation of Both the Poor and the

Rich Indispensable to the World's Salvation," February 1902, in *Sermons*, 6–7, record group 3, box 3, folder 1, Goucher Papers, GCSCA; John F. Goucher, "Young People and the World's Evangelization" *Christian Advocate*, December 24, 1903, 2094, box 5, folder 1, Goucher Papers, BWCA.

20. John F. Goucher, "Introduction to the Financial Session," in *The Open Door: A Challenge to Missionary Advance*, ed. Charles H. Fahs (New York: Eaton and Mains, 1903), 278–280, http://babel.hathitrust.org/cgi/pt?id=wu.89077022929; view=1up;seq=8.

21. E. G. Andrews to John F. Goucher, November 1902, and C. D. Foss to J. F. Goucher, November 10, 1902, box 1, folder 4, Goucher Papers, BWCA.

22. Minutes, WCB, November 20, 1902; Knipp and Thomas, *History of Goucher College*, 95.

23. "A Noble Woman Crowned," *Zion's Herald*, December 24, 1902, 1661; Joseph S. Shefloe to John Goucher, December 24, 1902, courtesy of Janet Miller Bernet; "Mrs. J. F. Goucher is Dead," December 1902, Scrapbook of Helen Gutman Westheimer (Class of 1901), GCSCA; "Mrs. Goucher Is Dead," *Baltimore Sun*, December 20, 1902, 12; "In Final Resting Place," December 23, 1902, Westheimer scrapbook.

24. "Where They First Met," box 1, folder 18, Goucher Papers, BWCA; "The Resignation of Dr. Goucher," *Baltimore Methodist*, November 28, 1907, 4, BWCA; Earl Cranston, "John F. Goucher—Modern Apostle and Civilized Saint," *Methodist Review*, January/February 1923, 14, record group 3, box 1, folder 22, Goucher Papers, GCSCA. In memory of Mary Fisher Goucher, the classes of 1892–1902 at the Woman's College commissioned a triptych window from Tiffany Studios; its allegorical characters depicted Faith, Hope, and Charity. It was dedicated in 1905, to hang in the central pavilion of Goucher Hall. When the college moved to Towson, the triptych was packed away; at the college's centennial in 1985, it was restored and now is displayed on the Goucher College campus.

25. Frank W. Warne to John F. Goucher, handwritten note on "An Open Letter from Bishop Warne," Shanghai, April 8, 1903, Goucher Papers, BWCA; "Carnegie Gives," *Baltimore Sun*, June 6, 1906, 14; John F. Goucher, report to the Board of Trustees, minutes, WCB, November 19, 1903; Knipp and Thomas, *History of Goucher College*, 120.

26. "Woman's College to Raise $500,000," *The Herald*, March 7, 1904, Series IV, box 5, folder 9, Board of Trustees Records, GCSCA; resolution of the University Senate of the Methodist Episcopal Church, February 1904, BWCA; resolution of the Association of College Presidents of the Methodist Episcopal Church, February 11, 1904, BWCA; "Gift to Woman's College," unknown newspaper, February 27, 1904, GCSCA; Knipp and Thomas, *History of Goucher College*, 120.

27. "Woman's College"; Knipp and Thomas, *History of Goucher College*, 121–122; minutes, BAC, March 29–April 4, 1905, 27; "Business Men to Aid," *Baltimore Sun*, May 15, 1906, 11. Two of the city's religious leaders who stepped forward to help were William Rosenau, rabbi at Oheb Shalom, and John T. Stone, minister at Brown Memorial Presbyterian Church, who became a college trustee in 1908.

28. John F. Goucher to the General Education Board, October 7, 1905, record group 3, box 2, folder 12, Goucher Papers, GCSCA.

29. Minutes, WCB, November 21, 1905; John F. Goucher to Andrew Carnegie, February 13, 1906, record group 3, box 2, folder 11, Goucher Papers, GCSCA; John F. Goucher to the Alumnae of the Woman's College of Baltimore, April 23, 1906, GCSCA.

30. Bishops Andrews, Warne, Foss, McCabe, Cranston, et al. to John F. Goucher, May 8, 1906, record group 3, box 2, folder 13, Goucher Papers, GCSCA.

31. "Business Men"; "No Money for Cause," *Baltimore Sun*, May 30, 1906, 14.

32. "Business Men"; John F. Goucher to Wallace Buttrick, June 14, 1906, record group 3, box 2, folder 12, Goucher Papers, GCSCA.

33. "Carnegie Gives"; "Dr. Goucher Is Happy—President of Woman's College Is Grateful for Gifts," *Baltimore Sun*, June 7, 1906, 11.

34. John F. Goucher, "A Statement Made at the Close of the Eighteenth Academic Year," Woman's College of Baltimore, June 5, 1906, 6, record group 3, box 3, folder 28, Goucher Papers, GCSCA.

35. "Educating Women," *Baltimore Sun*, June 7, 1906, 4; Henry Spellmeyer to John F. Goucher, June 13, 1906, box 1, folder 6, Goucher Papers, BWCA; "Congratulations, Dr. Goucher," *Central Christian Advocate*, June 20, 1906, BWCA.

36. John F. Goucher to Frank Porter, June 18, 1906, box 1, folder 6, Goucher Papers, BWCA; minutes, Executive Committee, WCB, June 7, 1906. Goucher pledged at least $15,000 (more than $400,000) himself for the campaign, and also covered amounts pledged by others: $4,000 ($109,000) to pay the subscriptions of Bishops Andrews and Cranston; up to $14,000 ($380,000) to complete the Baltimore Conference's $50,000 pledge; and an additional $5,000 ($136,000) to reach the amount needed to trigger gifts from Carnegie and Massey.

37. "Girls of Many Lands," *Baltimore Sun*, August 30, 1906, 6; minutes, WCB, October 19, 1906.

38. Minutes, WCB, May 30, 1906; "Girls of Many Lands." Goucher had one more personal upheaval to handle before he left town for his much-needed break: lightning struck one of his barns at Alto Dale. He and several farmworkers led the mules and horses to safety, but by the time firefighters arrived, they were unable to save the hundreds of bushels of wheat and oats, ten tons of hay, or farm implements stored in the building. "Dr. Goucher's Loss $10,000," *Baltimore Sun*, August 23, 1906, 6.

39. "Possible Bishops," *Baltimore Sun*, April 24, 1900, 10; "Nominations for the Episcopacy," *Zion's Herald*, January 6, 1904, BWCA; "Dr. Goucher Resigns," *Baltimore News*, November 22, 1907, box 1, folder 16, Goucher Papers, BWCA.

Chapter Sixteen

1. "Says Children Make Home," *Baltimore Sun*, January 13, 1913, 7.

2. Diary of John F. Goucher (hereinafter Diary), October 26–27 and November 9, 11–29, 1906, box 7, Rev. John F. Goucher Papers, Baltimore–Washington Conference Archives (hereinafter Goucher Papers, BWCA).

3. Telegram to John F. Goucher on the *Barbarossa*, November 28, 1906, BWCA; John F. Goucher to the Board of Trustees of the Woman's College of Baltimore, October 22, 1906, minutes, Woman's College of Baltimore, November 20, 1906, Series III, boxes 4 and 5 (1884–1910), Board of Trustees Records, Goucher College Library, Special Collections and Archives,(hereinafter minutes, WCB); William Martien to Trustees of the Woman's College of Baltimore, November 7, 1907, box 1, folder 7, Goucher Papers, BWCA.

4. The Board of Trustees of the Woman's College of Baltimore to John F. Goucher, November 20, 1906, record group 3, box 3, John Franklin Goucher Papers, Goucher College Library, Special Collections and Archives (hereinafter Goucher Papers, GCSCA).

5. "Citizen Goucher," *Baltimore Evening News*, November 22, 1906, box 1, folder 18, Goucher Papers, BWCA.

6. Diary, December 5, 1906, and January 27, 1907.

7. Ibid., December 5 and 10, 1906; "Around the World Letters," *Zion's Herald*, January 30, 1907, 133.

8. Diary, December 7, 1906.

9. William F. Oldham to John F. Goucher, July 20, 1906, Series 2: India, box 11, folder 15, MRL 12: John Franklin Goucher Papers, Burke Library at Union Theological Seminary, Columbia University in the City of New York (hereinafter MRL 12: Goucher Papers, Burke Library).

10. John F. Goucher to Jesse Clyde Fisher, December 19, 1906, Series 2: India, box 11, folder 9, MRL 12: Goucher Papers, Burke Library.

11. L. A. Core to John F. Goucher, March 10, 1902, Series 2: India, box 12, folder 17, MRL 12: Goucher Papers, Burke Library; diary, January 15, 1907.

12. Address to Dr. J. F. Goucher by the Bishop Parker Memorial High School, Moradabad, India, January 5, 1907, BWCA. Edwin W. Parker had been elected missionary bishop of Southern Asia in 1900 but died the following year.

13. Diary, January 3 and 16, 1907.

14. George K. Gilder to John F. Goucher, January 15, 1907, Series 2: India, box 11, folder 11, MRL 12: Goucher Papers, Burke Library; Thomas S. Donohugh to John F. Goucher, September 15, 1910, and November 9, 1911, box 11, folder 8, ibid.; diary, January 21, 1907; "Dr. Goucher's New Gift," *Baltimore Sun*, February 27, 1907, 7. On this trip, Goucher also met Constance Maya Das, whom he helped when she came to Baltimore to attend the Woman's College/ Goucher College (class of 1911). She later became the first Indian principal of Isabella Thoburn College (Constance Prem Nath Dass, principal 1939-1945).

15. Diary, December 26, 1906, and January 22, 1907.

16. Ibid., January 11, 1907; A Subaltern, "The Agra Durbar," *Blackwood's Magazine* (Edinburgh and London: William Blackwood, March 1907), 391–399, http://books. google.com/ books?id=hoo7AQAAMAAJ&pg=PA39181pg=PA391&dq=" The+Agra+Durbar."

17. Diary, January 12, 1907; A Subaltern, "Agra Durbar."

18. Diary, January 12, 1907.

19. Ibid.

20. Ibid., December 27–31, 1906; *Indian Mission Jubilee of the Methodist*

Episcopal Church in Southern Asia, ed. Frederick B. Price (Calcutta: Methodist Publishing House, 1907), BWCA.

21. *Indian Mission Jubilee*, 12, 78, 80.

22. Diary, January 1, 1907.

23. Ibid.; *Indian Mission Jubilee*, 58–59, 68.

24. Diary, February 2, 1907.

25. Ibid., January 27 and 30–31, 1907.

26. "The Giant Is Waking," *Baltimore World*, July 31, 1907, box 4, folder 2, Goucher Papers, BWCA; diary, February 4 and 6, 1907.

27. Diary, February 6, 1907.

28. Ibid., February 5, 1907.

29. Ibid.

30. Ibid.

31. Ibid., February 4, 1907; John F. Goucher, "Agencies Working for the Kingdom," 1905, 8–9, record group 3, box 3, folder 23, Goucher Papers, GCSCA.

32. Diary, February 7–9 and 15, 1907.

33. Ibid., February 15, 1907; John R. Denyes to John F. Goucher, June 8 and August 17, 1905, and January 22, 1907, Series 5: Missionary Work in Various Countries, box 17, folder 4, MRL 12: Goucher Papers, Burke Library.

34. Diary, February 12, 1907.

35. Ibid., February 12–13, 1907; Denyes to Goucher, September 16, 1908.

36. Diary, February 12 and 14, 1907.

37. Ibid., March 1–4, 1907.

38. Ibid., March 5, 1907; diary of Janet Goucher, March 5, 1907, courtesy of Janet Miller Bernet.

39. Diaries, Janet and John Goucher, March 6, 1907.

40. Diary, March 13–14, 1907; "A Chinese Lady to Study Medicine," *New York Times*, May 9, 1884, 5; Nathan Sites to Mary Goucher, June 14, 1884, Series 1: China, box 1, folder 26, MRL 12: Goucher Papers, Burke Library.

41. Diary, March 15–16, 1907.

42. Ibid., March 17, 1907.

43. Harry R. Caldwell to John F. Goucher, August 15 and December 7, 1908, Series 1: China, box 1, folder 8, MRL 12: Goucher Papers, Burke Library.

44. Diary, March 19 and 27, 1907; "Methodist Mission First Began School, News and Views of Aoyama Gakuin," *Japan Advertiser*, November 24, 1925, box 3, folder 11, Goucher Papers, BWCA; Julius Soper to John F. Goucher, September 26, 1899, Series 3: Japan, box 15, folder 10, MRL 12: Goucher Papers, Burke Library; Benjamin Chappell to John F. Goucher, May 9, 1901, box 15, folder 1, ibid.

45. Honda Yoitsu to John F. Goucher, May 20, 1904, box 1, folder 5, Goucher Papers, BWCA; Soper and Chappell to Goucher, 1904, box 15, folder 1, MRL 12: Goucher Papers, Burke Library; diary, March 29 and April 8, 1907.

46. Diary, April 3 and 6, 1907. In 1906, members of the World's Student Christian Federation included the American and Canadian Intercollegiate Young Men's Christian Association; Australasian Student Christian Union; Student Christian Movement of Great Britain and Ireland; Student Young Men's Christian Association of China, Korea, and Hong Kong; Student Christian Movements of Belgium, France, Holland, and Switzerland; German Christian Students' Alliance; Intercollegiate Young Men's Christian Association of India and Ceylon; Student Young Men's Christian Association of Japan; Scandinavian University Christian Movement; Students' Christian Association of South Africa; Student Christian Movement in Lands without National Organizations; and a Co-operating Committee for Work among Women Students.

47. John F. Goucher, *Christianity and the United States* (New York: Eaton and Mains, 1908), 6, 9, 35; diary, April 5, 1907.

48. Diary, April 4 and 7, 1907.

49. Ibid., April 3, 5–6, and 8, 1907.

50. Anna Edmunds Rutledge, "An Alumna Reunion in the Land of Cherry Blossom," *Kalends*, February 1908, 142–146, GCSCA; diary, April 6, 1907.

51. Diary, April 3–4, 1907.

52. Soper to Goucher, July 24, 1906; diary, March 28 and April 9, 1907.

53. Diary, March 28, 1907; Jennie Vail to John F. Goucher, April 19, 1907, Series 3: Japan, box 14, folder 4, MRL 12: Goucher Papers, Burke Library.

54. Diary, April 13–22, 1907.

55. Ibid., April 19, 1907; Eleanor Goucher to John F. Goucher, April 15, 1907, Series 5: Missionary Work in Various Countries, box 18, folder 17, MRL 12: Goucher Papers, Burke Library.

56. Diary, April 25–26, 1907.

57. Ibid., April 29–30 and May 4, 1907.

58. Ibid., April 30 and May 1–2 and 4, 1907; H. Olin Cady to John F. Goucher, January 31, 1903, Series 1: China, box 1, folder 7, MRL 12: Goucher Papers, Burke Library; Organization of West China Union University, box 5, folder 3, ibid.; minutes of meeting to consider establishment of Union University in Nanking, May 1, 1907, box 3, folder 2, ibid.

59. Merriman C. Harris to John F. Goucher, May 7, 1906, Merriman C. Harris File, Miscellaneous Manuscripts Collection, drawer 2, BWCA.

60. Diary, May 12, 1907; Vail to Goucher.

61. "The Giant Is Waking."

62. Diary, May 8, 1907.

63. "The Giant Is Waking."

64. Diary, May 21–22, 1907.

65. Ibid., May 21, 25, and 28, 1907.

66. Diary, May 18 and 21, 1907; "First General Conference in Japan," *Zion's Herald*, June 26, 1907, 832; J. W. Bashford, "The Methodist Church of Japan," *The Chinese Recorder and Missionary Journal*, October 1907, 543, https://archive.org/stream/chineserecorder08unkngoog#page/n972/mode/2up.

67. Diary, June 3, 1907.

68. Diary, May 28–30 and June 1, 1907. Goucher had written Honda Yoitsu in 1905, asking for swords from both sides of the conflict as souvenirs; he sent Goucher two bayonets. Honda Yoitsu to John F. Goucher, January 9, 1905, Series 3: Japan, box 15, folder 4, MRL 12: Goucher Papers, Burke Library.

69. Diary, June 3, 1907.

70. Ibid.

71. Ibid., June 4–7, 1907.

72. Ibid., June 8–16, 1907.

73. Harris to Goucher, May 7, 1906.

74. "The Giant Is Waking."

75. Ibid.

76. Diary, June 18–21, 1907.

77. Janet Goucher to John F. Goucher, May 19, 1907, and Eleanor Goucher to John F. Goucher, June 22, 1907, Series 5: Missionary Work in Various Countries, box 18, folder 17, MRL 12: Goucher Papers, Burke Library.

78. Eleanor Goucher to John Goucher, June 22, 1907.

79. Diary, Janet Goucher, June 28 and July 10 and 24–30, 1907; diary, end pages, 1907.

80. Diary, Janet Goucher, July 30, 1907; "The Giant Is Waking."

Chapter Seventeen

1. John F. Goucher, "True Education," matriculation sermon, the Woman's College of Baltimore, October 9, 1904, 6, record group 3, box 3, folder 21, John Franklin Goucher Papers, Goucher College Library, Special Collections and Archives (hereinafter Goucher Papers, GCSCA).

2. "Baltimore and Washington Letter," *Zion's Herald*, December 4, 1907, Baltimore–Washington Conference Archives (hereinafter BWCA); Anna Heubeck Knipp and Thaddeus P. Thomas, *The History of Goucher College* (Baltimore, 1938), 123.

3. John F. Goucher, report to the Board of Trustees, minutes, Woman's College of Baltimore, November 21, 1907, Series III, boxes 4 and 5 (1884–1910), Board of Trustees Records, Goucher College Library, Special Collections and Archives, Baltimore (hereinafter minutes, WCB).

4. "The Resignation of Dr. Goucher," *Baltimore Methodist*, November 28, 1907, box 1, folder 16, Rev. John F. Goucher Papers, Baltimore–Washington Conference Archives (hereinafter Goucher Papers, BWCA); John F. Goucher to the Board of Trustees, minutes, WCB, November 21, 1907.

5. "Dr. Goucher Out," *Baltimore Sun*, November 22, 1907, 14; "Dr. Goucher Resigns," *Baltimore News*, November 22, 1907, BWCA.

6. Tribute to John F. Goucher from the Board of Trustees of the Woman's College of Baltimore, minutes, WCB, January 18, 1908.

7. William Hersey Hopkins to John F. Goucher, November 28, 1907, box 1, folder

7, Goucher Papers, BWCA; "Dr. Goucher's Resignation," *Pittsburgh Christian Advocate*, December 5, 1907, box 1, folder 16, ibid.; James R. Day to John F. Goucher, November 26, 1907, box 1, folder 7, ibid.; W. A. Candler to John F. Goucher, January 1, 1908, box 1, folder 7, ibid. Candler was a bishop of the Methodist Episcopal Church, South, elected in 1898. He was the brother of Asa Griggs Candler, the founder of Coca-Cola.

8. Jennie Vail to John F. Goucher, January 13, 1908, Series 3: Japan, box 14, folder 4, MRL 12: John Franklin Goucher Papers, Burke Library at Union Theological Seminary, Columbia University in the City of New York (hereinafter MRL 12: Goucher Papers, Burke Library); Amy Lewis to John F. Goucher, March 1908, box 15, folder 6, ibid.

9. Frances M. Froelicher, "Dr. Goucher's Resignation," *Kalends*, December 1908, 97–99, GCSCA; Lilian Welsh, "Memorial Service for John Franklin Goucher," February 18, 1923, *Goucher Alumnae Quarterly*, Memorial Number (May 1923): 18, record group 3, box 1, folder 21, Goucher Papers, GCSCA.

10. Knipp and Thomas, *History of Goucher College*, 127.

11. "Baltimore and Washington Letter"; "President Goucher Resigns," *Central Christian Advocate*, December 4, 1907, box 1, folder 16, Goucher Papers, BWCA; "President Goucher's Resignation," *Baltimore News*, November 22, 1907, box 1, folder 16, ibid.; "Dr. Goucher Resigns."

12. "Dr. Goucher Resigns"; Day to Goucher, November 26, 1907; William V. Kelley to John F. Goucher, November 29, 1907, box 1, folder 7, Goucher Papers, BWCA.

13. W. F. Oldham to John F. Goucher, July 2, 1908, W. F. Oldham File, Miscellaneous Manuscripts Collection, drawer 3, BWCA; Thomas Nicholson to John F. Goucher, July 3, 1908, box 1, folder 8, Goucher Papers, BWCA.

14. Wilbur F. Tillett to John F. Goucher, September 23, 1908, box 1, folder 8, Goucher Papers, BWCA; John M. Moore to John F. Goucher, November 3, 1908, box 1, folder 8, ibid.; David G. Downey to John F. Goucher, December 10, 1908, box 1, folder 8, ibid.; James A. Worden to John F. Goucher, September 13, 1909, box 1, folder 9, ibid.; Conrad Clever to John F. Goucher, August 15, 1908, box 1, folder 8, ibid.

15. Grace Stephens to John F. Goucher, September 10, 1907, Series 2: India, box 12, folder 8, MRL 12: Goucher Papers, Burke Library; Jesse Fisher to John F. Goucher, October 16, 1909, box 11, folder 9, ibid.

16. Joseph Beech to John F. Goucher, December 4, 1907, and January 2, 1908, Series 1: China, box 1, folder 4, MRL 12: Goucher Papers, Burke Library.

17. Harry R. Caldwell to John F. Goucher, August 15, 1908, and January 29, 1909, Series 1: China, box 1, folder 8, MRL 12: Goucher Papers, Burke Library.

18. George Heber Jones to John F. Goucher, March 3, 1908, Series 4: Korea, box 16, folder 3, MRL 12: Goucher Papers, Burke Library; Annie Ellers Bunker, May 22, 1908, box 16, folder 12, ibid.; Merriman C. Harris to John F. Goucher, October 14, 1907, Merriman C. Harris File, Miscellaneous Manuscripts Collection, drawer 2, BWCA.

19. Erwin H. Richards to John F. Goucher, August 5, 1908, Series 5: Missionary Work in Various Countries, box 17, folder 1, MRL 12: Goucher Papers, Burke Library.

20. Ibid., May 30, 1906, and August 5, 1908.

21. Ibid., September 13 and October 10, 1908.

22. Beech to Goucher, December 4, 1907; Oldham to Goucher, July 2, 1908.

23. Philo M. Buck to John F. Goucher, November 19, 1908, Series 2: India, box 11, folder 3, MRL 12: Goucher Papers, Burke Library; George K. Gilder to John F. Goucher, September 8, 1908, box 11, folder 11, ibid.

24. Knipp and Thomas, *History of Goucher College*, 134–136; "Drs. Goucher and Noble," *American Star*, September 20, 1908, BWCA.

Chapter Eighteen

1. John F. Goucher, "True Education," matriculation sermon, Woman's College of Baltimore, October 9, 1904, 11, record group 3, box 3, folder 21, John Franklin Goucher Papers, Goucher College Library, Special Collections and Archives (hereinafter Goucher Papers, GCSCA).

2. Diary of John F. Goucher (hereinafter Diary), January 1, 1909, box 7, Rev. John F. Goucher Papers, Baltimore–Washington Conference Archives (hereinafter Goucher Papers, BWCA).

3. Ibid., January 7, 9, and 21, 1909.

4. "Liner *Republic* Rammed at Sea; Four Lives Lost?" *New York Times*, January 24, 1909, 1; "*Republic* Dead in Outside Cabins," *New York Times*, January 25, 1909, 2; "Dr. Goucher Doubtful," *Baltimore Sun*, January 27, 1909, 1. The *Titanic*'s collision with an iceberg on April 14, 1912, cost the lives of more than fifteen hundred passengers and crew when it sank in three hours. Three years later, the Cunard's *Lusitania*, torpedoed by a German submarine, sank in less than twenty minutes, with nearly twelve hundred dead.

5. "How Bulkheads Safeguard Liners," *New York Times*, January 25, 1909, 3; "Big Steamship Sinking, Every Soul Is Saved," *Baltimore Sun*, January 24, 1909, 1; "Scalby on *Republic* Till She Went Down," *New York Times*, January 26, 1909, 5. Although Sealby remained an employee of the White Star Line after the accident, he was not captain of a ship, pending lawsuits relating to the collision. In the fall of 1909, at age fifty, he became a law student at the University of Michigan, turning to admiralty law as a possible new career. "Capt. Sealby at 50 Enters Law School," *New York Times*, October 3, 1909, 13.

6. "How Wireless Saved a Ship," *New York Times*, January 24, 1909, 1; "C.Q.D.," *New York Times*, January 25, 1909, 8. The wireless article reported that "the Marconi Company had recently given to the U.S. Government the call letters of all of the 180 vessels equipped with its system. Especial attention has been called to the 'C.Q.D.' call, which is only used in extreme cases." "Binn's Story of Wireless Work," *New York Times*, January 27, 1909, 1.

7. "Dr. Goucher Doubtful."

8. "Dr. Goucher at the Oar," *Baltimore American*, January 27, 1909, record group 3, box 1, folder 10, Goucher Papers, GCSCA.

9. "Dr. Goucher a Beacon," *Baltimore Sun*, January 26, 1909, 1; Lilian Welsh to John F. Goucher, January 25, 1909, box 1, folder 9, Goucher Papers, BWCA.

10. Diary, January 25, 1909.

11. Ibid., January 26, 1909; "Will Make the Trip," *Baltimore American*, January 27, 1909, box 1, folder 18, Goucher Papers, BWCA; "Money Loss on *Republic*," *New York Times*, January 25, 1909, 3. The estimated value of the passengers' baggage was $50,000 ($1.3 million) but was more likely to approach $200,000 ($5.4 million).

12. Diary, January 27 and February 2, 1909; "Dr. Noble Installed," *Baltimore Sun*, February 3, 1909, 10.

13. Diary, February 3–4, 8, 10, and 17, 1909. Hoskins was a Presbyterian minister, educator, and publisher in Beirut, whose daughter was a freshman at the Woman's College of Baltimore (Jeanette Hoskins Campbell, class of 1912).

14. Ibid., February 17–18, 1909; Franklin E. Hoskins, "The Route over Which Moses Led the Children of Israel Out of Egypt," *National Geographic Magazine*, December 1909, 1012, 1022.

15. The Geographer, "International Boundary Study, Israel–Egypt (United Arab Republic) Boundary," no. 46 (Office of Research in Economics and Science, Bureau of Intelligence and Research, Department of State, April 1965), 2–3, http://archive.law.fsu.edu/library/collection/LimitsinSeas/IBS046.pdf.

16. Hoskins, "The Route," 1021; diary, February 17–18 and 25, and March 6 and 8, 1909.

17. Diary, February 17–18 and 22, 1909; "In the Holy Land with Dr. J. F. Goucher," *Baltimore American*, August 1, 1909, box 3, folder 11, Goucher Papers, BWCA.

18. Diary, April 24, 1909.

19. Franklin E. Hoskins, "The Feast of Liberty," *The Independent . . . Devoted to the Consideration of Politics, Social and Economic Tendencies, History, Literature, and the Arts*, September 17, 1908, 368; Franklin E. Hoskins, "The Turkish Parliament of 1908–1909," *The Independent*, December 2, 1909, 1256.

20. Hoskins, "The Feast of Liberty"; Hoskins, "The Turkish Parliament." Goucher lost one set of guns in the sinking of the *Republic* and had to purchase others later.

21. Diary, March 8, 1909; Hoskins, "The Route," 1038.

22. Diary, March 8, 1909; Hoskins, "The Route," 1022.

23. Diary, March 9, 1909.

24. Ibid., March 9–10 and 12, 1909.

25. Ibid., March 18–19 and 24, 1909; F. E. Hoskins to John F. Goucher, October 21, 1909, Series 5: Missionary Work in Various Countries, box 17, folder 7, MRL 12: John Franklin Goucher Papers, Burke Library at Union Theological Seminary, Columbia University in the City of New York.

26. Diary, February 27–March 2 and 21, 1909.

27. Ibid., February 23 and March 14 and 28, 1909.

28. Ibid., March 17, 1909.

29. Ibid., April 2–4, 1909.

30. Ibid., April 5–6, 9, and 11–12, 1909.

31. Ibid., April 12–21, 1909, and appended chart.

32. Ibid., April 24, 1909.

33. Ibid., April 23–25, 27, and 30, 1909.

34. Ibid., April 27–30 and May 2, 1909.

35. Ibid., May 5–6, 1909. Goucher noted that approximately 4,000 had been killed in Constantinople, and more than 150 people on the losing side were sentenced to be hanged. The installation of the new sultan was delayed until after the executions, so he couldn't pardon them.

36. Ibid., May 11–14, 1909.

37. Ibid., appended charts.

38. William V. Kelley to John F. Goucher, November 29, 1907, box 1, folder 7, Goucher Papers, BWCA.

Chapter Nineteen

1. John F. Goucher, "True Education," matriculation sermon, Woman's College of Baltimore, October 9, 1904, 1, record group 3, box 3, folder 21, John Franklin Goucher Papers, Goucher College Library, Special Collections and Archives (hereinafter Goucher Papers, GCSCA).

2. "Many-Sided Men at Methodist Session," unknown newspaper, 1912, Baltimore–Washington Conference Archives (hereinafter BWCA).

3. Anna Heubeck Knipp and Thaddeus P. Thomas, *The History of Goucher College* (Baltimore, 1938), 143–144; "To Honor Dr. Goucher," *Baltimore Sun*, November 9, 1908, 14.

4. Knipp and Thomas, *History of Goucher College*, 144; "An Unnamed Institution," *Kalends*, December 1908, 71, GCSCA; "To Honor Dr. Goucher"; John F. Goucher to Frank G. Porter, June 15, 1911, box 1, folder 11, Rev. John F. Goucher Papers, Baltimore–Washington Conference Archives (hereinafter Goucher Papers, BWCA).

5. "An Unnamed Institution"; "The Change Proposed in the Name of the Woman's College," *Baltimore Sun*, June 2, 1908, 4.

6. John B. Van Meter, "The Evolution of the Woman's College of Baltimore," c. 1920, 180, record group 1, box 4, Founding and Incorporation—Histories, Goucher College Special Collection and Archives (hereinafter GCSCA); Van Meter comment, June 27, 1907, GCSCA; John Van Meter to William W. Guth, July 21, 1922, record group 3, John B. Van Meter Papers, GCSCA.

7. Van Meter, "Evolution," 187; R. Tynes Smith to William W. Guth, January 12, 1914, record group 3, box 1, folder 7, William Westley Guth Papers, GCSCA.

8. Van Meter, "Evolution," 182, 187. The minutes of the June 2, 1908, meeting left in the motion to change the name to Goucher College. In March 1921, Van Meter wrote on the page, "This record is false—Report withdrawn and all reference ordered to be expunged from the minutes."

9. "To Honor Dr. Goucher"; Knipp and Thomas, *History of Goucher College*, 145–147; Eugene A. Noble, "To the Alumnae," *Kalends*, March 1910, 181, GCSCA. The other charter and bylaws changes under consideration were the board's relationship to the Baltimore Conference; the number of trustees and their term of office; a definition of the duties of the dean; and recognition of

alumnae trustees nominated by the Alumnae Association.

10. Van Meter, "Evolution," 190.

11. Ibid., 191; Noble, "To the Alumnae," 181.

12. Knipp and Thomas, *History of Goucher College*, 145–147; minutes, Woman's College of Baltimore, February 2, 1910, Series III, boxes 4 and 5 (1884–1910), Board of Trustees Records, GCSCA; Joseph S. Shefloe to Anna Heubeck Knipp, April 26, 1937, BWCA. Knipp was a member of the first graduating class, served as a trustee of the college (1893–1904, 1913–1940), and was coauthor of the 1938 *History of Goucher College*.

13. Annina Periam Danton to John F. Goucher, February 11, 1910, box 1, folder 10, Goucher Papers, BWCA; Noble, "To the Alumnae," 181.

14. Knipp and Thomas, *History of Goucher College*, 145; "Editorial," *Kalends*, March 1910, 206–207, GCSCA.

15. "Dr. Goucher Receives," *Baltimore Sun*, February 5, 1910, 6.

16. James R. Day to John F. Goucher, February 18, 1910, box 1, folder 10, Goucher Papers, BWCA.

17. "Goucher College," *Zion's Herald*, February 16, 1910, 199; "Dr. Goucher's Arm in Sling," *Baltimore Sun*, February 15, 1910, 7.

Chapter Twenty

1. "Dr. Goucher on Character," *Baltimore Sun*, October 13, 1902, 8.

2. "Problems of Mission Work," *Philadelphia Record*, July 22, 1911, Baltimore–Washington Conference Archives (hereinafter BWCA).

3. C. A. Waterfield, review of *Growth of the Missionary Concept* by John F. Goucher, *Methodist Quarterly Review*, January 1913, 200, and Waterfield, "Miscellaneous," *Times-Picayune*, July 16, 1911, box 4, folder 10, Rev. John F. Goucher Papers, Baltimore–Washington Conference Archives (hereinafter Goucher Papers, BWCA).

4. John F. Goucher, *Growth of the Missionary Concept* (New York: Eaton and Mains, 1911), 171; review of *Growth of the Missionary Concept, California Christian Advocate*, July 20, 1911, box 4, folder 10, Goucher Papers, BWCA; Frank Monaghan, "John F. Goucher," in *Dictionary of American Biography* (New York: Charles Scribner's Sons, 1931), 4:443.

5. Delavan Leonard Pierson, "The Edinburgh Missionary Conference," in *The Missionary Review of the World* (New York: Funk and Wagnalls, 1910), 648–649, http://babel.hathitrust.org/cgi/pt?id=mdp.39015010805730;view=1up;seq=699.

6. Edward C. Moore, "Education in the Orient: Missionary Conference Continuation Committee at Work," *New York Observer and Chronicle*, November 17, 1910, 638. The thirty-five-member Continuation Committee comprised ten representatives from the United States, ten from Great Britain, ten from Europe, and one each from Africa, India, China, Australia, and Japan. The charge for Goucher's group was to investigate educational conditions in the mission territory under its jurisdiction and determine possibilities for improvement; to define the purpose of education as part of missionary work

and reach conclusions on educational policy in the various geographic divisions in the field; to share the results of its studies to help promote educational work in each area; and to offer the subcommittee's services as counselors to the home missionary boards or missionaries in their assigned countries.

7. Organization of West China Union University, Series 1: China, box 5, folder 3, MRL 12: John Franklin Goucher Papers, Burke Library at Union Theological Seminary, Columbia University in the City of New York (hereinafter MRL 12: Goucher Papers, Burke Library); John F. Goucher letter, Hotel Cecil, London, June 1910, box 5, folder 3, ibid.; resolutions passed by the Senate of West China Union University, September 14, 1922, box 3, folder 15, Goucher Papers, BWCA. West China Union University was established jointly by the Boards of Foreign Missions of the Methodist Episcopal Church, USA; the American Baptist Foreign Mission Society; the Friends' Foreign Mission Association of Great Britain and Ireland; and the General Board of Missions of the Methodist Church of Canada.

8. "His Good Works Girdle the Globe—Dr. John F. Goucher," *Baltimore Sun*, August 27, 1911, LS2.

9. Janet married Baltimorean Henry C. (Clay) Miller, a banker whose family owned Daniel Miller & Company, one of the largest wholesale dry goods firms in the South.

10. Statement of Premier Katsura Taro to John F. Goucher, October 20, 1910, Series 3: Japan, box 14, folder 9, MRL 12: Goucher Papers, Burke Library.

11. Diary of John F. Goucher, October 27, 1910, box 7, Goucher Papers, BWCA; diary of James Whitford Bashford, January 17, 1911, box 2, folder 4, MRL 6: James Whitford Bashford Diaries, Burke Library at Union Theological Seminary, Columbia University in the City of New York (hereinafter MRL 6: Bashford Diaries, Burke Library). Before the annexation of Korea, Terauchi served as the resident-general of Korea. He followed Prince Ito, whom Goucher had met on his 1907 trip. Ito resigned the position in 1909 and was assassinated a few months later in Harbin, China.

12. Arthur Judson Brown, "Japanese Nationalism and Mission Schools in Chosen," in *International Review of Mission* 6 (January 1917): 80, http://babel.hathitrust. org/cgi/pt?id=mdp.39015005007466;view=1up;seq=82; John F. Goucher to George M. Fowler, March 11, 1922, Series 4: Korea, box 16, folder 12, MRL 12: Goucher Papers, Burke Library. The Goucher scholarship funds at Pai Chai were to support two students at a time, for three years of training.

13. C. D. Morris to John F. Goucher, November 19, 1912, Series 4: Korea, box 16, folder 12, MRL 12: Goucher Papers, Burke Library. Goucher had been appointed as a member of the Korea Quarter-Centennial Commission, which was charged by the Board of Foreign Missions with bringing the country's needs before Methodist congregations in the United States and raising $300,000 for ongoing work in Korea.

14. John F. Goucher, "China and Education," c. 1911, in *Sermons*, record group 3, box 3, folder 1, John Franklin Goucher Papers, Goucher College Library, Special Collections and Archives.

15. W. S. Lewis to John F. Goucher, November 8, 1910, Wilson S. Lewis File, Miscellaneous Manuscripts Collection, drawer 3, BWCA; John F. Goucher to A. B. Leonard, November 29, 1910, Series 4: Korea, box 16, folder 12, MRL 12: Goucher Papers, Burke Library.

16. John F. Goucher to W. A. Noble, John F. Goucher to Homer Eaton, and Goucher to Leonard, November 29, 1910, Series 4: Korea, box 16, folder 12, MRL 12: Goucher Papers, Burke Library.

17. Bashford, December 1, 1910–January 2, 1911, box 2, folder 4, MRL 6: Bashford Diaries, Burke Library; Wilson S. Lewis to John F. Goucher, February 2, 1911, Series 1: China, box 1, folder 19, MRL 12: Goucher Papers, Burke Library.

18. Joseph Beech, form letter, July 31, 1909, Series 1: China, box 1, folder 4, MRL 12: Goucher Papers, Burke Library.

19. Bashford, February 1, 1911, box 2, folder 5, MRL 6: Bashford Diaries, Burke Library.

20. J. O. Curnow to John F. Goucher, October 5, 1911, Series 1: China, box 6, folder 11, MRL 12: Goucher Papers, Burke Library.

21. Bashford, February 1 and 21, 1911, box 2, folder 5, MRL 6: Bashford Diaries, Burke Library.

22. Joseph Beech to John F. Goucher, March 25, 1911, Series 1: China, box 1, folder 4, MRL 12: Goucher Papers, Burke Library.

23. "His Good Works"; A. J. Bowen to John F. Goucher, August 29, 1911, Series 1: China, box 3, folder 3, MRL 12: Goucher Papers, Burke Library.

24. Minutes of the Conference on Higher Christian Education in Fukien Province, March 25, 1911, Series 1: China, box 2, folder 4, MRL 12: Goucher Papers, Burke Library; minutes of the Committee of Foochow Christian University, March 2, 1915, box 2, folder 4, ibid.; Edwin C. Jones to Eleanor Goucher, November 15, 1922, box 3, folder 15, Goucher Papers, BWCA.

25. John F. Goucher to Lydia Trimble, July 15, 1912, Series 1: China, box 2, folder 3, MRL 12: Goucher Papers, Burke Library.

26. "His Good Works."

Chapter Twenty-One

1. John F. Goucher, "True Education," matriculation sermon, Woman's College of Baltimore, October 9, 1904, 6, record group 3, box 3, folder 21, John Franklin Goucher Papers, Goucher College Library, Special Collections and Archives (hereinafter Goucher Papers, GCSCA).

2. Eugene A. Noble, report to the Board of Trustees, minutes, Goucher College, February 28, 1911, Series IV, box 5 (1910–1915), Board of Trustees Records, GCSCA; *Bulletin of Goucher College*, June 1911, 3–12, GCSCA.

3. M. Carey Thomas, "What College Women Mean to a Community; What Goucher College Means to Baltimore," December 3, 1912, 3–4, Series IV, box 6, folder 9, Board of Trustees Records, GCSCA; Anna Heubeck Knipp and Thaddeus P. Thomas, *The History of Goucher College* (Baltimore, 1938), 209, 599 (n. 99).

4. "Appeals to Dr. Goucher," *Baltimore Sun*, July 14, 1911, 14.

5. Knipp and Thomas, *History of Goucher College*, 169.

6. Ibid., 197–198.

7. William R. Johnson to John F. Goucher, May 18, 1911, and January 31 and July 20, 1912, Series 1: China, box 7, folder 5, MRL 12: John Franklin Goucher Papers, Burke Library at Union Theological Seminary, Columbia University in the City of New York (hereinafter MRL 12: Goucher Papers, Burke Library); David Miller to John F. Goucher, July 10, 1914, Series 1: China, box 1, folder 23, ibid.

8. Diary of John F. Goucher (hereinafter Diary), December 1911, and January 1912, box 7, Rev. John F. Goucher Papers, Baltimore–Washington Conference Archives (hereinafter Goucher Papers, BWCA); Office of the Dean, Aoyama Gakuin Theological School, to John F. Goucher, December 16, 1921, Series 3: Japan, box 14, folder 6, MRL 12: Goucher Papers, Burke Library.

9. Arthur D. Berry to John F. Goucher, November 17, 1911, and February 19 and October 10, 1912, Series 3: Japan, box 14, folder 1, MRL 12: Goucher Papers, Burke Library.

10. Diary, January 30–March 8, 1912; John F. Goucher to Frank G. Porter, March 18, 1912, box 1, folder 11, Goucher Papers, BWCA; Arthur B. Bibbins, "Dr. John Franklin Goucher," *The Methodist*, March 10, 1921, BWCA.

11. "Dr. Goucher Confident," *Baltimore Sun*, March 19, 1912, 11; "Twenty-Five Years of Goucher's Work," *Baltimore Evening Sun*, March 15, 1913, record group 3, box 1, folder 10, Goucher Papers, GCSCA.

12. "Twenty-Five Years"; Knipp and Thomas, *History of Goucher College*, 200; "Presented for Consideration," 17 and 31, Series IV, box 6, Board of Trustees Records, GCSCA.

13. W. S. Lewis to John F. Goucher, May 30, 1912, Wilson S. Lewis File, Miscellaneous Manuscripts Collection, drawer 2, BWCA.

14. Knipp and Thomas, *History of Goucher College*, 199; M. Carey Thomas and John F. Goucher, "Should the Higher Education of Women Differ from That of Men?," annual convention of the Association of Colleges and Preparatory Schools of the Middle States and Maryland, November 30–December 1, 1900, record group 3, box 3, folder 18, Goucher Papers, GCSCA.

15. Diary, January 26, August 17, and November 3, 1912; W. P. Eveland to John F. Goucher, August 19, 1912, W. P. Eveland File, Miscellaneous Manuscripts Collection, drawer 2, BWCA.

16. "Why Voting Democrat," *Bedford Gazette* (Pa.), November 11, 1912, 4; "Dr. Goucher Tells Why: Lifelong Republican Changes to Democrat," *Baltimore Sun*, November 5, 1912, 13.

17. "Dr. Goucher Tells Why."

18. "$130,000 for Goucher," *Baltimore Sun*, January 31, 1913, 12; Knipp and Thomas, *History of Goucher College*, 196, 200; Kathryn Davison to J. V. Davison, March 7, 1913, GCSCA.

19. "Twenty-Five Years."

20. Ibid.

21. Knipp and Thomas, *History of Goucher College*, 202–205; "Goucher College Must Be Saved!," *The Methodist*, March 20, 1913, Series IV, box 6, folder 10, Board of Trustees Records, GCSCA.

22. "Goucher at Goal," *Baltimore Sun*, April 5, 1913, 16; "Goucher Campaign Expands," *Baltimore Sun*, March 22, 1913, 9; "Negroes Aid Goucher,"

Baltimore Sun, March 29, 1913, 5.

23. "Goucher at Goal." Approximately ten thousand people nationwide contributed to the campaign; alumnae raised more than $56,000 ($1.4 million), and the undergraduates gave $11,000 ($271,000).

24. Ibid.

25. Ella Goucher Bedell to John F. Goucher, May 18, 1913, box 1, folder 12, Goucher Papers, BWCA; diary, April 24–May 5, 1913; W. S. Lewis to John F. Goucher, May 12, 1913, box 1, folder 12, Goucher Papers, BWCA; Lilian Welsh, "Memorial Service for John Franklin Goucher," February 18, 1923, *Goucher Alumnae Quarterly*, Memorial Number (May 1923): 18, record group 3, box 1, folder 21, Goucher Papers, GCSCA. The Battle Creek Sanitarium was owned by the Seventh-day Adventist Church and based its health principles on those advocated by the Church. Dr. John Harvey Kellogg and his brother W. K. Kellogg were prominent leaders at the Sanitarium.

Chapter Twenty-Two

1. John F. Goucher, "True Education," matriculation sermon, Woman's College of Baltimore, October 9, 1904, 11, record group 3, box 3, folder 21, John Franklin Goucher Papers, Goucher College Library, Special Collections and Archives (hereinafter Goucher Papers, GCSCA).

2. Diary of John F. Goucher (hereinafter Diary), May–July 1913, box 7, Rev. John F. Goucher Papers, Baltimore–Washington Conference Archives (hereinafter Goucher Papers, BWCA); "Miss Wilson at Alto Dale," *Baltimore Sun*, May 31, 1913, 16; Frank Mason North to John F. Goucher, May 23, 1913, Series 3: Japan, box 14, folder 5, MRL 12: John Franklin Goucher Papers, Burke Library at Union Theological Seminary, Columbia University in the City of New York (hereinafter MRL 12: Goucher Papers, Burke Library).

3. "His Good Works Girdle the Globe—Dr. John F. Goucher," *Baltimore Sun*, August 27, 1911, LS2; George A. Simons to Eleanor Goucher, August 12, 1922, box 3, folder 15, Goucher Papers, BWCA; "Struck by Progress of Far East Nations," *Baltimore Evening Sun*, December 29, 1913, box 4, folder 2, ibid.

4. James W. Bashford to John F. Goucher, January 23, 1912, Series 1: China, box 3, folder 5, MRL 12: Goucher Papers, Burke Library; Bashford to Goucher, December 6, 1913, box 1, folder 3, ibid.

5. "Dr. John Franklin Goucher, Minister, Educator, Missionary, Statesman, Philanthropist and Churchman," *Christian Advocate*, July 27, 1922, 939, record group 3, box 1, folder 16, Goucher Papers, GCSCA.

6. John F. Goucher, "Some Recent Developments of Christian Education in China," in *Journal of Race Development*, November 1912, 241, http://archive. org/stream/jstor-29737991/29737991#page/n1/mode/2up.

7. Takagi Mizutaro to John F. Goucher, January 10 and June 3, 1914, Series 3: Japan, box 15, folder 13, MRL 12: Goucher Papers, Burke Library.

8. John R. Mott, *Continuation Committee Conferences in Asia 1912–1913: A Brief Account* (New York, 1913), 394, https://books.google. com/ books?id= nKJlAAAAMAAJ& pg= PA398&lpg=PA398&dq =%22Continuation+Committee +of+the+Edinburgh+ Conference; "Regret

over Baron Yun," *Baltimore Sun,* March 22, 1913, 4.

9. "Regret."

10. George Heber Jones to Arthur J. Brown, December 13, 1911, Series 4: Korea, box 16, folder 3, MRL 12: John F. Goucher Papers, Burke Library; George Heber Jones to John F. Goucher, December 14, 1911, box 16, folder 3, ibid.

11. W. A. Noble, Horace Underwood, et al. to Joint Committee on Education in Korea, December 8, 1913, Series 4: Korea, box 16, folder 4, MRL 12: Goucher Papers, Burke Library; Horace Underwood to Arthur J. Brown, December 5, 1913, box 16, folder 4, ibid.; John F. Goucher, "Investigation and Concentration in Giving," in *Men and World Service,* address delivered at the National Missionary Congress, April 26–30, 1916, 159, http://archive.org/stream/menandworldserv00unknuoft/menandworldserv00unknuoft_djvu.txt.

12. Underwood to Brown, December 5, 1913; Joint Committee to James E. Adams, May 19, 1914, Series 4: Korea, box 16, folder 5, MRL 12: Goucher Papers, Burke Library; diary, October 18, 24, and 31, 1913.

13. Diary, November–December 2, 1913.

14. Ibid., December 2–18, 1913; resolutions passed by the Senate of West China Union University, September 14, 1922, box 3, folder 15, Goucher Papers, BWCA; Zhang Liping, *Memory of West China Union University* (Chengdu: Sichuan University Press, 2000), 22.

15. John F. Goucher, "Prayers," December 19, 1913, Carlyle Reede Earp Papers on John Franklin Goucher, BWCA.

16. J. Frederick Heise, "A Conversation with Dr. Goucher," *Baltimore Methodist,* August 5, 1915, BWCA.

Chapter Twenty-Three

1. John F. Goucher, "Individualism," Recognition Day address, August 18, 1897, *The Chautauquan,* October 1897, box 4, folder 8, Rev. John F. Goucher Papers, Baltimore–Washington Conference Archives (hereinafter Goucher Papers, BWCA).

2. Diary of John F. Goucher, February 25–March 4, 1914, box 7, Goucher Papers, BWCA; Janet Miller Bernet, interview with the author, December 2004. Goucher's two grandchildren were Henry C. Miller, Jr., known as Junior or June by the family, and Janet Fisher Miller (Bernet), called Fisher. They were the children of the Gouchers' oldest daughter, Janet Goucher Miller.

3. John F. Goucher, "Education," handwritten speech, c. 1915, box 5, folder 3, Goucher Papers, BWCA; John Franklin Goucher, "Unity in Foreign Mission Fields and Its Reaction on Church Life in Home Lands," c. 1916, in *Sermons,* 7, record group 3, box 3, folder 1, John Franklin Goucher Papers, Goucher College Library, Special Collections and Archives.

4. Horace Underwood to John F. Goucher, January 12, 1914, and John F. Goucher to Horace Underwood, February 24, 1914, Series 4: Korea, box 16, folder 5, MRL 12: John Franklin Goucher Papers, Burke Library at Union Theological Seminary, Columbia University in the City of New York (hereinafter MRL 12: Goucher Papers, Burke Library). John Underwood gave $50,000 to support the

new college.

5. W. S. Lewis to John F. Goucher, June 2, 1914, Series 4: Korea, box 16, folder 5, MRL 12: Goucher Papers, Burke Library.

6. J. Frederick Heise, "A Conversation with Dr. Goucher," *Baltimore Methodist*, August 5, 1915, BWCA; John F. Goucher to Earl Cranston, January 22, 1915, Series 1: China, box 6, folder 11, MRL 12: Goucher Papers, Burke Library.

7. John F. Goucher, "Education in India, Korea, China, and Japan," handwritten speech, c. 1915, box 5, folder 3, Goucher Papers, BWCA; "China Needs Million Schools Says Educator after a Visit," *Honolulu Star Bulletin*, July 14, 1915, box 3, folder 11, Goucher Papers, BWCA.

8. Goucher, "Unity," 7–8; John F. Goucher, "China," handwritten speech, c. 1915, box 5, folder 3, Goucher Papers, BWCA.

9. Goucher to Cranston, January 22, 1915; Francis D. Gamewell to John F. Goucher, May 25, 1914, Series 1: China, box 1, folder 12, MRL 12: Goucher Papers, Burke Library.

10. Goucher to Cranston, January 22, 1915.

11. Jacob Peat to John F. Goucher, including report of E. Carlton Baker, January 13, 1915, Series 1: China, box 1, folder 25, MRL 12: Goucher Papers, Burke Library.

12. Ibid., September 1, 1915; John F. Goucher, proposal for Primary School Unit, December 19, 1914, Series 1: China, box 7, folder 6, MRL 12: Goucher Papers, Burke Library.

13. Goucher, proposal for Primary School Unit.

14. John F. Goucher, proposal for scholarships at Chungking Union High School, December 19, 1914, Series 1: China, box 6, folder 10, MRL 12: Goucher Papers, Burke Library; John F. Goucher to Joseph Beech, January 22, 1915, box 6, folder 11, ibid.; J. L. Stewart to John F. Goucher, January 30, 1915, box 6, folder 1, ibid.

15. Goucher to Cranston, January 22, 1915.

16. Minutes, Committee of Foochow Christian University, March 2, 1915, Series 1: China, box 2, folder 4, MRL 12: Goucher Papers, Burke Library; Lewis Hodous to John F. Goucher, June 28, 1915, box 2, folder 3, ibid.

17. William Eveland to John F. Goucher, June 30, 1913, box 1, folder 12, Goucher Papers, BWCA; Oscar Huddleston to F. M. North, May 6, 1915, Series 5: Missionary Work in Various Countries, box 17, folder 4, MRL 12: Goucher Papers, Burke Library.

18. "Main Facts in the History of Chosen Christian College," Series 4: Korea, box 16, folder 2, MRL 12: Goucher Papers, Burke Library; report of the registrar to the Field Board of Managers of the Union Christian College, spring term 1915, box 16, folder 15, ibid.; *Official Gazette*, March 29, 1915, and M. Komatsu, *Seoul Press*, April 3, 1915, quoted in Arthur Judson Brown, "Japanese Nationalism and Mission Schools in Chosen," in *International Review of Mission* 6 (January 1917): 79, 80, http://babel.hathitrust.org/cgi/pt?id=mdp.39015005007466;view=1up;seq=82.

19. Arthur J. Brown to John F. Goucher, June 14, 1916, Series 4: Korea, box 16, folder 7, Goucher Papers, Burke Library; Komatsu, November 11, 1915, quoted

in Brown, "Japanese Nationalism," 75.

20. John F. Goucher, "Investigation and Concentration in Giving," in *Men and World Service,*" address delivered at the National Missionary Congress, April 26–30, 1916, 160, http://archive.org/stream/menandworldserv00unknuoft/menandworldserv00unknuoft_djvu.txt; "Noteworthy Things about Pai Chai," October 20, 1913, Series 4: Korea, box 16, folder 13, MRL 12: Goucher Papers, Burke Library; minutes of the Korea Annual Conference of the Methodist Episcopal Church, April 21–27, 1915, 9–11, http://images.library.yale.edu/divinitycontent/dayrep/MethodistEpiscopalChurch.KoreaAnnualConference1915v8.pdf.

21. Minutes of the Korea Annual Conference.

22. Arthur D. Berry to John F. Goucher, March 29, 1915, and John F. Goucher to Arthur D. Berry, April 9, 1915, Series 3: Japan, box 14, folder 1, MRL 12: Goucher Papers, Burke Library.

23. John F. Goucher, rules for Goucher Korean scholarships at Aoyama Gakuin, July 2, 1915, Series 3: Japan, box 14, folder 5, MRL 12: Goucher Papers, Burke Library.

24. Alice R. Appenzeller to John F. Goucher, May 9, 1915, Series 4: Korea, box 16, folder 11, MRL 12: Goucher Papers, Burke Library.

25. Goucher, "Education in India, China, Korea, and Japan."

26. Wilson S. Lewis to John F. Goucher, July 31, 1915, box 1, folder 12, Goucher Papers, BWCA; Elizabeth Goucher to John F. Goucher, September 20, 1914, Series 5: Missionary Work in Various Countries, box 18, folder 17, MRL 12: Goucher Papers, Burke Library.

27. Joseph Beech to John F. Goucher, July 27, 1915, Series 1: China, box 1, folder 4, MRL 12: Goucher Papers, Burke Library; "War Vague to Orient," *Baltimore Sun*, July 29, 1915, 4.

28. Goucher, "China."

29. Ibid.; "China Needs."

30. Arthur Berry to John F. Goucher, August 7, 1915, box 1, folder 15, Goucher Papers, BWCA; "The Republic of China," *Zion's Herald*, August 11, 1915, box 3, folder 11, ibid.

31. "War Vague"; Goucher, "Education in India, China, Korea, and Japan."

32. Goucher, "Education."

Chapter Twenty-Four

1. John F. Goucher, "True Education," matriculation sermon, Woman's College of Baltimore, October 9, 1904, 11, record group 3, box 3, folder 21, John Franklin Goucher Papers, Goucher College Library, Special Collections and Archives (hereinafter Goucher Papers, GCSCA).

2. "War Vague to Orient," *Baltimore Sun*, July 29, 1915, 4.

3. Charles Clayton Morrison, "Pan-American Christianity," *The Independent... Devoted to the Consideration of Politics, Social and Economic Tendencies, History, Literature, and the Arts*, March 27, 1916, 451; S. G. Imman to John F.

Goucher, February 28, 1917, Series 5: Missionary Work in Various Countries, box 17, folder 5, MRL 12: John Franklin Goucher Papers, Burke Library at Union Theological Seminary, Columbia University in the City of New York.

4. Diary of John F. Goucher (hereinafter Diary), October 21, 1915, and February 20, 1916, box 7, Rev. John F. Goucher Papers, Baltimore–Washington Conference Archives (hereinafter Goucher Papers, BWCA); *Story of the American Bible Society* (New York: American Bible Society, 1916), 75, http://babel.hathitrust.org/cgi/pt?id=wu.89034743211;view=1up;seq=87; "James Wood, President of the American Bible Society 1912–1916," http://www.americanbiblehistory.com/james_wood.html. In 1917, the Maryland Bible Society would distribute New Testaments, including a message Goucher had solicited from President Wilson, to Maryland soldiers heading to Europe when the United States belatedly entered World War I.

5. Minutes, Morgan College, Board of Trustees, June 4, 1912, MSA S362-2 (June 5, 1901–January 9, 1922), MdHR 18431-1/28, Maryland State Archives, Annapolis, Md. (hereinafter minutes, MC).

6. Edward N. Wilson, *The History of Morgan State College: A Century of Purpose in Action 1867–1967* (New York: Vantage Press, 1975), 72.

7. Antero Pietila, *Not in My Neighborhood: How Bigotry Shaped a Great American City* (Chicago: Ivan R. Dee, 2010), 8–12.

8. Ibid., 6–8.

9. Garrett Power, "Apartheid Baltimore Style: The Residential Segregation Ordinances of 1910–1913," *Maryland Law Review* 289 (Winter 1983): 289, 299, http://digitalcommons.law.umaryland.edu/mlr/vol42/iss2/4.

10. Pietila, *Not in My Neighborhood*, 58; E. D. Hans to John F. Goucher, August 27, 1913, box 4, folder 1, Morgan College Files in the Records of the Board of Higher Education and Campus Ministry, Baltimore–Washington Conference Archives (hereinafter Morgan College Files, BWCA). The stone hunting lodge on the proposed property had once belonged to Charles Carroll of Carrollton, a signer of the Declaration of Independence.

11. A. Hayfield to John F. Goucher, September 3, 1913, Morgan College Files, BWCA; "Opposition Still Hot," *Baltimore Sun*, September 26, 1913, 14; Executive Committee of the Mt. Washington Improvement Association to John F. Goucher, September 30, 1913, Morgan College Files, BWCA; Pietila, *Not in My Neighborhood.*

12. Roland C. McConnell, *The History of Morgan Park, a Baltimore Neighborhood 1917–1999*, ed. Marva E. Belt (Baltimore: Morgan Park Improvement Association, Inc., 2000), 2–3; Henry M. Heurix to John F. Goucher, September 23, 1913, Morgan College Files, BWCA. The areas in Northwest Baltimore protesting were Arlington, Park Heights Avenue, Pikesville, Sudbrook, and the Greenspring Valley. "Resolution of Protest on Location of Morgan College," *Baltimore Sun*, September 23, 1913, 1; "Time to Call a Halt," *Baltimore Sun*, September 26, 1913, 6.

13. Minutes, MC, June 4, 1914; Wilson, *History of Morgan State College*, 73.

14. Minutes, MC, January 10 and June 1, 1916; Wilson, *History of Morgan State College*, 73–74; McConnell, *History of Morgan Park*, 3.

15. John F. Goucher, handwritten draft resolution for Morgan College land acquisition, box 5, folder 2, Goucher Papers, BWCA; "To Aid 90,000

Negroes," *Baltimore Sun*, February 24, 1917, 12.

16. "Segregation O.K. Says Preston," *Afro-American*, March 3, 1917, 1; "Big Question for a Southern City," *Baltimore News*, February 21, 1917, BWCA.

17. James H. Preston to John F. Goucher, February 19, 1917, box 3, folder 10, Goucher Papers, BWCA; "Preston Tackles Big Negro Problem," *Baltimore Sun*, February 20, 1917, 14; "Want Colored Colony," *Baltimore News*, February 24, 1917, BWCA.

18. Goucher, handwritten draft resolution; "To Aid 90,000 Negroes"; "Have Sites in Mind," *Baltimore Evening Sun*, February 24, 1917, BWCA.

19. "Housing Conditions" and "Dr. Goucher's Plan," *Afro-American*, March 3, 1917, 4.

20. Preston to Goucher, March 12, 1917.

21. McConnell, *History of Morgan Park*, 3; Wilson, *History of Morgan State College*, 72; Grace S. Parks, "Thirty-Five Years at Morgan College," *Baltimore Sun*, August 29, 1937, SU4; Frederick Evans, Lauraville Improvement Association, to the Honorable Board of Trustees of Morgan College, Morgan College Files, BWCA.

22. John H. Groshans to John F. Goucher, May 17, 1917, Morgan College Files, BWCA; F. C. Sandner to John F. Goucher, May 19, 1917, ibid.; "Fights Negro Invasion," *Baltimore Sun*, May 2, 1917, 12; McConnell, *History of Morgan Park*, 6.

23. Edward J. Wheatley et al. to John F. Goucher, May 21, 1917, and John F. Goucher to Edward J. Wheatley, May 26, 1917, Morgan College Files, BWCA.

24. William Pickens to John F. Goucher, May 19, 1917, Morgan College Files, BWCA.

25. M. Edith Cooper to John F. Goucher, May 16, 1917, Morgan College Files, BWCA.

26. John F. Goucher, letter sent to eighty-nine individuals, June 1, 1917, Morgan College Files, BWCA.

27. Frederick Evans, Lauraville Improvement Association, and representing the Hamilton, Clifton Park, Lake Montebello, Northeast Baltimore Improvement Associations and other interested groups and individuals, to John F. Goucher, June 7, 1917, Morgan College Files, BWCA.

28. Leo J. Reisler to John F. Goucher, June 8, 1917, and Mrs. D. H. Caulk to John F. Goucher, June 11, 1917, Morgan College Files, BWCA.

29. John O. Spencer to John F. Goucher, June 16, 1917, box 1, folder 13, Goucher Papers, BWCA; Charles R. Ditman to John F. Goucher, "The Morgan College Site," *Baltimore American*, June 11, 1917, Morgan College Files, BWCA.

30. Wilson, *History of Morgan State College*, 74–78; McConnell, *History of Morgan Park*, 6–9; Russell I. Diggs et al. v. Morgan College, August 1917, Morgan College Files, BWCA. The Virginia Collegiate and Industrial Institute in Lynchburg burned in mid-December 1917. About eighty to one hundred faculty and students transferred to Morgan's new site at Ivy Mill early in January 1918, surprising opponents with the number of African Americans already in residence on the property.

31. "Morgan Closes Celebration of Its Fiftieth Anniversary," *Afro-American*,

December 1, 1917, 1. The Supreme Court case that overturned the housing segregation law was Buchanan v. Warley, 245 U.S. 60 (1917).

32. Wilson, *History of Morgan State College*, 78–79; McConnell, *History of Morgan Park*, 10–12; Eric L. Holcomb, *The City as Suburb, a History of Northeast Baltimore since 1660* (Charlottesville: University of Virginia Press for the Center for American Places, 2005), 217–218.

33. Earl Cranston, "John F. Goucher—Modern Apostle and Civilized Saint," *Methodist Review*, January/February 1923, 16, record group 3, box 1, folder 22, Goucher Papers, GCSCA.

34. "1908 General Conference," *Zion's Herald*, June 3, 1908; "Methodist Union Plan Is Adopted," *New York Evening Mail*, May 10, 1916, box 4, folder 2, Goucher Papers, BWCA; "Church Union Endorsed," *Baltimore Sun*, May 17, 1916, 2.

35. Wilbur F. Tillett to John F. Goucher, March 18, 1916, box 1, folder 13, Goucher Papers, BWCA.

36. John F. Goucher, *Proceedings of the Joint Commission on Unification of the Methodist Episcopal Church and the Methodist Episcopal Church, South*, Savannah, Georgia, January 23–February 6, 1918 (New York: Methodist Book Concern and Smith Lamar, 1920), 2:326, 328.

37. Frederick E. Maser, "The Story of Unification," in *History of American Methodism* (New York: Abingdon Press, 1964), 3:424–425.

38. *The Methodist*, May 25, 1916, 7, BWCA; "Union of North and South," *Evening Post*, May 16, 1916, box 1, folder 16, Goucher Papers, BWCA.

39. John F. Goucher, *Proceedings of the Joint Commission on Unification of the Methodist Episcopal Church and the Methodist Episcopal Church, South*, Baltimore, Maryland, December 28, 1916–January 2, 1917 (Louisville: Mayes, 1917), 173.

40. Goucher, *Proceedings*, Savannah, 332.

41. Ibid., 336; John F. Goucher, "Unification," *Methodist Review*, January–February 1918, 46, record group 3, box 3, folder 35, Goucher Papers, GCSCA.

42. Maser, "Story of Unification," 437–438.

43. Anna Heubeck Knipp and Thaddeus P. Thomas, *The History of Goucher College* (Baltimore, 1938), 89–91; Lilian Welsh, *Reminiscences of Thirty Years in Baltimore* (Baltimore: Norman, Remington, 1925), 106–107.

44. "Oppose Franchise for the Women but Preparing for It," *Savannah Press*, February 1, 1918, box 1, folder 17, Goucher Papers, BWCA.

45. E. L. Watson, "Anniversary Sermon," Baltimore Annual Conference, June 9, 1932, box 3, folder 5, Goucher Papers, BWCA; Elizabeth Goucher Chapman to Carlyle Earp, March 30, 1964, Carlyle Reede Earp Papers on John Franklin Goucher, BWCA; Janet Miller Bernet, interviews with the author, December 2004 and December 2005; diary, May 24, 1917; "Says Children Make Home," *Baltimore Sun*, January 13, 1913, 7.

46. Diary, May 24 and September 9, 1917; John F. Goucher, "Luke XII:21," c. 1918, in *Sermons*, record group 3, box 3, folder 1, Goucher Papers, GCSCA. In addition to planting potatoes, Goucher plowed up extra acreage for corn and barley, and increased egg production and the number of pigs. "Society Folk Farming," May 8, 1917, box 1, folder 18, Goucher Papers, BWCA.

47. Goucher, "James IV:14," c. 1918, in *Sermons*.

Chapter Twenty-Five

1. John F. Goucher, "Individualism," Recognition Day address, August 18, 1897, *The Chautauquan*, October 1897, box 4, folder 8, Rev. John F. Goucher Papers, Baltimore–Washington Conference Archives (hereinafter Goucher Papers, BWCA).

2. Hugh Johnston et al. to John F. Goucher, 1919, BWCA.

3. "Centenary Celebration at Columbus, Ohio," in *Methodist Year Book 1920*, 126, http://babel.hathitrust.org/cgi/pt&id=wu.89077114288;view=1up;seq=450; Wilbur F. Tillett, "The Story of American Methodism," in *Souvenir of the Centenary Celebration of American Methodist Missions*, Columbus, Ohio, June 20–July 13, 1919, 17, BWCA.

4. Alice M. Young, "Life Plays and Demonstrations," in *Souvenir of the Centenary Celebration*, 15, BWCA.

5. Christopher J. Anderson, *The Centenary Celebration of American Methodist Missions: The 1919 World's Fair of Evangelical Americanism* (Lewiston, N.Y.: Edwin Mellon Press, 2012), 28, 39. In addition to the many exhibits, the Centenary Celebration included music, pageants, a Ferris wheel, fireworks on July 4, Wild West shows, a ten-story motion picture screen, and noted speakers such as General John J. Pershing, William Jennings Bryan, and former president William Howard Taft.

6. Edwin T. Iglehart to John F. Goucher, July 26, 1916, Series 3: Japan, box, 14, folder 5, MRL 12: John Franklin Goucher Papers, Burke Library at Union Theological Seminary, Columbia University in the City of New York (hereinafter MRL 12: Goucher Papers, Burke Library); Takagi Mizutaro to John F. Goucher, December 19, 1918, box 15, folder 13, ibid.

7. Hugh Cynn to John F. Goucher, July 11 and October 3, 1917, Series 4: Korea, box 16, folder 12, MRL 12: Goucher Papers, Burke Library; Arthur L. Becker to John F. Goucher, February 13, 1918, box 16, folder 12, ibid.

8. Horace Underwood to John F. Goucher, July 5, 1916, Series 4: Korea, box 16, folder 7, MRL 12: Goucher Papers, Burke Library; George T. Scott to Members of the Cooperating Board for Christian Education in Chosen, October 25, 1918, box 16, folder 8, ibid. Underwood died in October 1916, and Dr. Oliver R. Avison, a Presbyterian medical missionary, who had opened the Severance Hospital and Severance Union Medical College in Seoul, became the second president.

9. Wesley Smith Bissonnette to John F. Goucher, October 6, 1918, Series 1: China, box 1, folder 1, MRL 12: Goucher Papers, Burke Library; Wilson S. Lewis to John F. Goucher, March 13, 1917, box 1, folder 19, ibid.; resolutions passed by the Senate of West China Union University, September 14, 1922, box 3, folder 15, Goucher Papers, BWCA; William Artyn Main to John F. Goucher, December 2, 1916, Series 1: China, box 1, folder 20, MRL 12: Goucher Papers, Burke Library.

10. "Dr. Goucher Honored," *Baltimore Sun*, December 19, 1920, 6.

11. Diary of John F. Goucher (hereinafter Diary), February 27, 1920, box 7, Goucher Papers, BWCA; Benjamin Chappell to John F. Goucher, October 25, 1910, Series 3: Japan, box 15, folder 1, MRL 12: Goucher Papers, Burke

Library; Honda Tei to John F. Goucher, November 11, 1919, box 15, folder 4, ibid.

12. John F. Goucher, interview with Premier Hara Takashi, October 27, 1919, Series 3: Japan, box 14, folder 9, MRL 12: Goucher Papers, Burke Library. Hara was assassinated in November, 1921.

13. Hugh Johnston, "Dr. Goucher and the Imperial Decoration of the Order of the Rising Sun," *Baltimore Methodist*, May 20, 1920, box 4, folder 2, Goucher Papers, BWCA.

14. Wilson S. Lewis to John F. Goucher, March 13, 1917, Series 1: China, box 1, folder 19, MRL 12: Goucher Papers, Burke Library; Wilson E. Manley, September 11, 1917, box 1, folder 21, ibid.; John F. Goucher, New Year's card from Kiukiang, China, December 30, 1919, BWCA.

15. Diary, January 1–February 16, 1920.

16. Diary, February 20, 1920; "Main Facts in the History of Chosen Christian College," Series 4: Korea, box 16, folder 2, MRL 12: Goucher Papers, Burke Library.

17. Diary, February 18 and March 5 and 14, 1920.

18. Ibid., March 21–26, 1920.

Chapter Twenty-Six

1. John F. Goucher, "Luke XII:21," c. 1918, in *Sermons*, record group 3, box 3, folder 1, John Franklin Goucher Papers, Goucher College Library, Special Collections and Archives.

2. Diary of John F. Goucher (hereinafter Diary), April 30–May 31, 1920, box 7, Rev. John F. Goucher Papers, Baltimore–Washington Conference Archives (hereinafter Goucher Papers, BWCA).

3. Ibid., June 11–16, 1920.

4. Pamphlet on West China Union University, 1919, Series 1: China, box 6, folder 13, MRL 12: John Franklin Goucher Papers, Burke Library at Union Theological Seminary, Columbia University in the City of New York (hereinafter MRL 12: Goucher Papers, Burke Library).

5. Diary, June 25–July 3, 1920; Janet Miller Bernet, interview with the author, December 2005.

6. Diary, July 6, 1920; "Dr. Goucher Surprised by France's Recovery," *Baltimore Sun*, August 29, 1920, 11.

7. Goucher, "James IV:14," c. 1918, in *Sermons*; diary, July 7–9, 1920; "Dr. Goucher Surprised"; Julian S. Wadsworth to John F. Goucher, November 19, 1921, box 1, folder 14, Goucher Papers, BWCA.

8. Diary, July 21–September 17, 1920; Arthur D. Berry to John F. Goucher, July 19, 1915, Series 3: Japan, box 14, folder 1, MRL 12: Goucher Papers, Burke Library. Goucher recorded in his travel diary, October 4, 1920, that he had walked thirty miles on deck during this Pacific voyage.

9. Diary, October 20–29, 1920; "Rev. J. F. Goucher Dies at Alto Dale," July 1922, box 1, folder 2, Goucher Papers, BWCA. The Appenzeller medallion was

created by Baltimore sculptor and Goucher friend Hans Schuler.

10. Diary, October 29–31, November 5 and 24–25, and December 25, 1920; C. B. Rape to John F. Goucher, September 27, 1920, and John F. Goucher to C. B. Rape, February 7, 1921, Series 1: China, box 7, folder 3, MRL 12: Goucher Papers, Burke Library.

11. Diary, November 7 and 14, 1920.

12. Ibid., January 1–February 2, 1921; George H. Bickley to John F. Goucher, January 29, 1921, George H. Bickley File, Miscellaneous Manuscripts Collection, drawer 1, BWCA.

13. Diary, February 3 and April 5, 1921; W. W. Yen to John F. Goucher, February 22, 1921, and Wu Lien Teh to John F. Goucher, August 4, 1921, box 1, folder 14, Goucher Papers, BWCA; Joseph Beech to John F. Goucher, July 1, 1921, Series 1: China, box 7, folder 18, MRL 12: Goucher Papers, Burke Library.

14. John F. Goucher to Takagi Mizutaro, February 7, 1921, Series 3: Japan, box 15, folder 13, MRL 12: Goucher Papers, Burke Library; John F. Goucher, "Investigation and Concentration in Giving," in *Men and World Service*, address presented at the National Missionary Congress, April 26–30, 1916, 160, http://archive.org/stream/menandworldserv00unknuoft/menandworldserv00unknuoft_djvu.txt.

15. Goucher to Takagi, February 7, 1921.

16. Goucher to Rape, February 7, 1921.

17. Diary, February 11–27, 1921.

Chapter Twenty-Seven

1. John F. Goucher, "James IV:14," c. 1918, in *Sermons*, record group 3, box 3, folder 1, John Franklin Goucher Papers, Goucher College Library, Special Collections and Archives (hereinafter Goucher Papers, GCSCA).

2. Diary of John F. Goucher (hereinafter Diary), March 28–30, September 30, and November 14, 1921, box 7, Rev. John F. Goucher Papers, Baltimore–Washington Conference Archives (hereinafter Goucher Papers, BWCA).

3. Ibid., April 6, May 28, September 16, and October 21, 1921; Janet Miller Bernet, interview with the author, December 2004.

4. Diary, September 16, October 5 and 26, and November 24, 1921 (Thanksgiving).

5. William V. Kelley to Frank G. Porter, June 17, 1921, box 1, folder 14, Goucher Papers, BWCA.

6. John F. Goucher to Frank G. Porter, July 1921, box 1, folder 14, Goucher Papers, BWCA.

7. Earl Cranston to John F. Goucher, August 15, 1921, box 1, folder 14, Goucher Papers, BWCA; Goucher to Porter, July 26, 1921.

8. Alice Appenzeller to John F. Goucher, May 14, 1921, Series 4: Korea, box 16, folder 11, MRL 12: John Franklin Goucher Papers, Burke Library at Union Theological Seminary, Columbia University in the City of New York (hereinafter MRL 12: Goucher Papers, Burke Library); diary, April 12 and 18,

1918; John F. Goucher to C. B. Rape, December 14, 1921, Series 1: China, box 7, folder 3, MRL 12: Goucher Papers, Burke Library.

9. William V. Kelley to John F. Goucher, January 15, 1922, box 1, folder 14, Goucher Papers, BWCA.

10. Lilian Welsh to Frank S. Given, January 28, 1922, Series IV, box 7, folder 20, Board of Trustees Records, GCSCA.

11. Anna Heubeck Knipp and Thaddeus P. Thomas, *The History of Goucher College* (Baltimore, 1938), 16, 146, and 159; John B. Van Meter to Aldis B. Browne, January 8, 1912, record group 3, Correspondence re Charter Controversy, John B. Van Meter Papers, Goucher College Library, Special Collections and Archives (hereinafter Van Meter Papers, GCSCA).

12. John F. Goucher to the Committee on Charter Revision of Goucher College, January 6, 1912, record group 3, Correspondence re Charter Controversy, Van Meter Papers, GCSCA; Van Meter to Browne, February 5, 1912.

13. Knipp and Thomas, *The History of Goucher College*, 249–250; Henry S. Pritchett to John Van Meter, January 5, 1914, record group 3, Correspondence re Charter Controversy, Van Meter Papers, GCSCA. The charter amendment provided that four trustees would be elected from a list of nominations from the Baltimore Conference; two trustees each from the Central Pennsylvania and Philadelphia Conferences; and one trustee each from the Wilmington, New York, and New York East Conferences.

14. Thomas Nicholson to William W. Guth, December 17, 1913, record group 3, box 1, folder 7, William Westley Guth Papers, Goucher College Library, Special Collections and Archives (hereinafter Guth Papers, GCSCA).

15. Guth to Nicholson, December 18, 1913, record group 3, box 1, folder 7, Guth Papers, GCSCA.

16. Carlyle Reede Earp, *John Franklin Goucher*, unpublished manuscript, c. 1960, 168–169, and notes from interview with Joseph Shefloe, Carlyle Reed Earp Papers on John Franklin Goucher, BWCA; diary, November 7, 1921.

17. John Van Meter to Charles Blackshear, July 1, 1920, record group 3, Miscellaneous Correspondence (1911–1920), Van Meter Papers, GCSCA. The "4-2-1 Campaign" asked every student, alumna, and non-graduate to "give or get" $421 for Goucher College.

18. "To the Public of Baltimore and Maryland—A Statement by the Trustees of Goucher College," *Baltimore Sun*, January 21, 1922, 18; "To the People of Baltimore and Maryland and the Alumnae of Goucher College—A Statement by the Representatives of the Baltimore Annual Conference," *Baltimore Evening Sun*, February 1, 1922; "15 Goucher Trustees Favor Charter Change," *Baltimore Sun*, January 20, 1922, 6; resolution of faculty meeting, January 23, 1922, and action of the Board of Directors of the Alumnae Association, January 30, 1922, record group 3, box 2, folder 24, Guth Papers, GCSCA.

19. "Church behind Goucher Issue," *Evening News*, January 19, 1922, BWCA.

20. "To the Public"; "To the People"; Van Meter to Browne, February 7, 1912. Guth hired Jones Price Jones in New York as publicity counsel.

21. John F. Goucher, "Statement Concerning Proposed Change in the Charter of Goucher College," January 25, 1922, Series IV, box 7, folder 19, Board of Trustees Records, GCSCA; "Goucher College Fight to Be Taken to Court," *Baltimore Sun*, February 1, 1922, 5.

22. "To the Alumnae of Goucher College," March 7, 1922, record group 3, box 3, folder 29, Guth Papers, GCSCA; Grace Sutton Wallace to Rosa Baldwin, March 13, 1922, record group 3, box 3, folder 29, ibid.

23. John B. Van Meter to William W. Guth, January 31, 1922, record group 3, box 2, folder 24, Guth Papers, GCSCA; Welsh to Given, January 28, 1922.

24. Knipp and Thomas, *History of Goucher College*, 268–269; Charter Revision Committee to David G. McIntosh, March 22, 1922, Series IV, box 7, folder 22, Board of Trustees Records, GCSCA; "Goucher Trustees End Dispute over Charter," *Baltimore Sun*, March 16, 1922, 24. The charter was amended in 1957, requiring eleven of the thirty-three trustees to be Methodists; no more than five of the eleven could be clergy, and at least four had to be members of churches in the Baltimore Conference. In 1966, the charter was amended to delete any Methodist requirement in electing trustees. The size of the board was changed from thirty-three trustees to a range of twenty-five to fifty in a 1971 amendment. The "4–2–1 Campaign" raised the $1 million designated for endowment, but President Guth died in 1929. The Depression halted further fundraising, and plans to move to a new campus in Towson were delayed until the late 1930s. The first building, Mary Fisher Hall, opened in 1942.

25. John F. Goucher to George A. Solter, February 10, 1922, Series IV, box 7, folder 20, Board of Trustees Records, GCSCA; John F. Goucher to George M. Fowler, March 11, 1922, Series 4: Korea, box 16, folder 12, MRL 12: Goucher Papers, Burke Library; Goucher to Rape, December 14, 1921; James Yard to John F. Goucher, February 22 and April 22, 1922, Series 1: China, box 7, folder 18, MRL 12: Goucher Papers, Burke Library.

26. "Seventy-Seven Years Young," *New York Christian Advocate*, June 15, 1922, box 4, folder 2, Goucher Papers, BWCA; minutes, Morgan College, Board of Trustees, January 9, 1922, MSA S362-2 (June 5, 1901–January 9, 1922), MdHR 18431-1/28, Maryland State Archives, Annapolis, Md.; George Scholl to John F. Goucher, March 21, 1922, box 1, folder 14, Goucher Papers, BWCA; Ishizaka Masanobu to John F. Goucher, April 10, 1922, Series 3: Japan, box 14, folder 5, MRL 12: Goucher Papers, Burke Library; Julius Soper to John F. Goucher, March 31, 1922, and April 6, 1922, Series 3: Japan, box 15, folder 11, ibid.

27. John F. Goucher to Frank Mason North, May 5, 1922, and Frank Mason North to John F. Goucher, May 8, 1922, Series 3: Japan, box 14, folder 5, MRL 12: Goucher Papers, Burke Library.

28. "Seventy-Seven Years"; Frank G. Porter, interview with John F. Goucher, July 11, 1922, box 7, Goucher Papers, BWCA; Frank G. Porter, "John Franklin Goucher," minutes, Baltimore Annual Conference, April 4–9, 1923, 380, BWCA.

29. "Dr. John Franklin Goucher, Minister, Educator, Missionary, Statesman, Philanthropist and Churchman," *Christian Advocate*, July 27, 1922, 939, record group 3, box 1, folder 16, Goucher Papers, GCSCA.

Chapter Twenty-Eight

1. John F. Goucher, "The Quality and Service of Joseph's Prosperity," June 1903, in *Sermons*, record group 3, box 3, folder 1, John Franklin Goucher Papers,

Goucher College Library, Special Collections and Archives (hereinafter Goucher Papers, GCSCA).

2. John F. Goucher, handwritten sheet on funeral instructions, box 3, folder 7, Rev. John F. Goucher Papers, Baltimore–Washington Conference Archives (hereinafter Goucher Papers, BWCA).

3. W. F. McDowell, in "Tributes to Dr. John F. Goucher," *Washington Christian Advocate*, July 27, 1922, 6, record group 3, box 1, folder 19, Goucher Papers, GCSCA; "Dr. John Franklin Goucher, Minister, Educator, Missionary, Statesman, Philanthropist and Churchman," *Christian Advocate*, July 27, 1922, 940, record group 3, box 1, folder 16, ibid.; Edgar Blake to Eleanor Goucher, August 20, 1922, box 3, folder 15, Goucher Papers, BWCA.

4. "Dr. John F. Goucher," *Baltimore Sun*, July 20, 1922, 10.

5. Frank Mason North, "Dr. Goucher's Lifelong Service to Foreign Missions," *Christian Advocate*, July 27, 1922, 925, record group 3, box 1, folder 16, Goucher Papers, GCSCA.

6. Earl Cranston, "John Franklin Goucher—Modern Apostle and Civilized Saint," *Methodist Review*, January/February 1923, 19, record group 3, box 1, folder 22, Goucher Papers, GCSCA.

7. John M. Moore, "Extracts from Proceedings of the Joint Commission on Unification," January 18–19, 1923, BWCA.

8. H. H. White, "Extracts from Proceedings."

9. John H. Race, in "Tributes to Dr. John F. Goucher," 8.

10. Resolutions passed by the Board of Trustees of Goucher College concerning the death of Dr. John Franklin Goucher, July 20, 1922, record group 3, box 1, folder 13, Goucher Papers, GCSCA.

11. Gertrude B. Knipp, "John Franklin Goucher," *Goucher Alumnae Quarterly*, Memorial Number (May 1923): 3, record group 3, box 1, folder 21, Goucher Papers, GCSCA.

12. Class of 1902, "Memorial Service for John Franklin Goucher," February 18, 1923, *Goucher Alumnae Quarterly*, Memorial Number (May 1923), 15.

13. Class of 1906, ibid., 16.

14. Lilian Welsh, ibid., 17.

15. John O. Spencer, in "Tributes to Dr. John F. Goucher," 9.

16. Joseph H. Lockerman, "Dr. Goucher and Morgan College," in *A Tribute from the Morgan College Summer School, Memorial Booklet*, July 27, 1922, record group 3, box 1, folder 19, Goucher Papers, GCSCA.

17. Resolution by Morgan College Summer School, July 21, 1922, in ibid.

18. "John Goucher," *Afro-American*, July 28, 1922, 7.

19. "Dr. Goucher Takes Leave," *Central Christian Advocate*, July 26, 1922, record group 3, box 1, folder 17, Goucher Papers, GCSCA; George A. Simons to Eleanor Goucher, August 12, 1922, and D. B. Schneder to Eleanor Goucher, September 6, 1922, box 3, folder 15, Goucher Papers, BWCA; F. D. Gamewell, "Dr. John F. Goucher, Christian Statesman," *China Christian Advocate*, September 1922, 2, record group 3, box 1, folder 17, Goucher Papers, GCSCA.

20. Joseph Beech to Eleanor Goucher and Henry and Janet Goucher Miller, December 27, 1922, and Resolutions passed by the Senate of West China Union

University, September 14, 1922, box 3, folder 15, Goucher Papers, BWCA.

21. Edwin C. Jones to Eleanor Goucher, November 15, 1922, box 3, folder 15, Goucher Papers, BWCA.

22. Kawashiri Seishu to Eleanor Goucher, undated letter, and John Z. Moore to Eleanor Goucher, undated letter, box 3, folder 16, Goucher Papers, BWCA.

23. Cranston, "John Franklin Goucher," 18; "Dr. John F. Goucher," *Baltimore Sun*, July 20, 1922, 10.

24. John R. Mott to Eleanor Goucher, October 17, 1922, box 3, folder 15, Goucher Papers, BWCA.

25. William L. Moss to Henry and Janet Goucher Miller, July 23, 1922, box 3, folder 14, Goucher Papers, BWCA.

26. Alfred H. Barr to Janet Goucher Miller, July 24, 1922, box 3, folder 14, Goucher Papers, BWCA.

27. Willard T. Perrin, "Snap-Shots of Dr. Goucher," *Zion's Herald*, August 30, 1922, record group 3, box 1, folder 15, Goucher Papers, GCSCA.

28. Cranston, "John Franklin Goucher," 11.

29. George C. Peck, in "Tributes to Dr. John F. Goucher," 9.

30. J. M. Gillum and J. Henry Baker, in "Tributes to Dr. John F. Goucher," 10; J. St. Clair Neal, in ibid., 11.

31. Evelyn Riley Nicholson to the Goucher Family, July 24, 1922, box 3, folder 16, Goucher Papers, BWCA; E. L. Watson, "The Greatest Figure in World Methodism," *Washington Christian Advocate*, July 27, 1922, 4, record group 3, box 1, folder 19, Goucher Papers, GCSCA.

32. Ishizaka Masanobu to Eleanor Goucher, November 13, 1922, box 3, folder 15, Goucher Papers, BWCA; Benjamin F. DeVries, in "Tributes to Dr. John F. Goucher," 10.

33. John F. Goucher, last will and testament, July 25, 1917, and codicil, July 15, 1922, liber W. J. P. 22, folio 194, Baltimore Country Register of Wills, Towson, Md.; Safe Deposit and Trust of Baltimore to President William Guth and the Board of Trustees, November 24, 1922, record group 3, box 1, folder 8, Goucher Papers, GCSCA. This letter conveyed the keys of 2313 to the college. After Goucher's death, Goucher House was used as a residence hall for many years and then as quarters for the Alumnae Association. The building was sold in 1952, as the college completed its move to the new campus. Since 1991, the property has been the national headquarters of the Alpha Phi Alpha fraternity, founded in 1906 as the first African-American intercollegiate fraternity. Two well-known members were Martin Luther King, Jr. and Supreme Court Justice Thurgood Marshall.

34. Vincent Massey to Janet Goucher Miller, August 12, 1922, box 3, folder 15, Goucher Papers, BWCA.

35. John F. Goucher, "West China, a Great Mission Field," July 9, 1894, in *Sermons*.

36. Abram W. Harris, in "Tributes to Dr. John F. Goucher," 7.

37. F. R. Bayley, in ibid., 10.

ACKNOWLEDGEMENTS

The author with Janet Miller Bernet, granddaughter of John and Mary Goucher (2004)

Whenever I read a book, I like to look for the author's acknowledgement of those who have helped make the work possible. Now that I've written my own book, I appreciate even more the role of the many individuals who offer support and encouragement along the way.

There are two women whom I'd like to recognize first as core supporters of this project. Although neither lived to see the end result, their spirits have continued to give me inspiration. One is Janet Miller Bernet, granddaughter of John and Mary Goucher. My visits to her in Charlottesville, Virginia, and chats on the phone always brought a new story about her grandfather and transported me to the past. My other mentor was Rhoda M. Dorsey, professor, longtime president, and president emerita of Goucher College. She instilled in me—and in countless other students—a love of and appreciation for history and the college's legacy.

One of the greatest champions of John Goucher and my book has been Charles Eun-Ho Pang, a native of Korea and a longtime Maryland resident. An active nonagenarian, he is a proud graduate of Pai Chai High School in Seoul. He especially has been a leader in keeping the Goucher name alive in his homeland and in the local Korean community. He was a knowledgeable and cheerful travel companion on my visits to South Korea in June 2010 and April 2015, and he introduced my husband and me to delicious Korean food.

Sanford J. Ungar, president of Goucher College from 2001–2014, shared John Goucher-related adventures with me in Japan and South Korea. He initiated the college's innovative study abroad requirement for students, renewing John Goucher's focus on world engagement for the twenty-first century. Sandy's thoughtful input and encouragement along the way and his appreciation for Goucher history have been ongoing sources of support.

Two friends gave countless hours to read the manuscript and make suggestions. The book would not be complete without the assistance of Suzanne Walker, a writer, editor, and neighbor; and Pattie Batza, a fellow Goucher alumna and trustee. Thanks also to Kevin Whitehead for his editing skills.

Another valued connection has been knowing Mary Fisher Bernet and John Bernet, Janet Bernet's children, and John Goucher Bernet, her grandson and a Goucher College alumnus. He, too, was invited to attend the 2015 events celebrating the 130th anniversary of the Korean Methodist Church, and we spoke to several audiences about his great-great-grandfather's legacy.

Many staff and faculty at my alma mater spent time with John Goucher and me over the years, and I extend special thanks to them for their assistance. Bill Leimbach, vice president for technology and planning, readily offered his wizardry with technology to enhance my presentations at home and abroad. Several faculty members provided their academic expertise to read and comment on portions of the manuscript: Barbara Roswell, assistant professor of English; Tina Sheller and Evan Dawley, assistant professors of history; Amalia Honick, assistant professor of political science; and Gina Shamshak, associate professor of economics. Nancy Magnuson, college librarian, and Tara Olivero, special collections librarian and archivist, found new sources and introduced me to international visitors interested in the history of the college and John Goucher.

Writing about John Franklin Goucher would not have been possible without the resources of other archives that house his papers and memorabilia. The Dickinson College Archives and Special Collections introduced me to his time as a student and later as an alumnus. A major resource has been the Baltimore–Washington Conference Archives and the Lovely Lane United Methodist Church in Baltimore, with thanks to Robert Shindle, Rev. Emora Brannan, Rev. Nancy Nedwell, and John Strawbridge for their assistance. Other important background material was available at the library of the Maryland Historical Society in Baltimore and the Maryland State Archives in Annapolis, Maryland. In New York, the Burke Library at Union Theological Seminary, Columbia University, houses the former Missionary Research Library, to which the Goucher daughters gave many of their father's papers; the papers of other important missionary leaders of his period are available at the Burke Library as well. Thanks to Ruth Tonkiss Cameron, who introduced me to this treasure.

With John Goucher's international reach, there were several individuals who helped me discover and explore his influence in their home countries. Zang Choon Shik, former professor and chaplain at Pai Chai University, extended my first invitation to speak in South Korea in 2010, and he has been a major advocate in his homeland for John Goucher's work. Goucher alumna and trustee emerita Michiko Yoshida Mitarai offered a warm welcome during my November 2002 visit to Tokyo. She and Paul Tsuchido Shew, dean of religion and chaplain at Aoyama Gakuin University, have assisted in finding resources, and they continue to promote ties between Aoyama Gakuin and Goucher College. Kaushik Bagchi, former professor of history at Goucher, now living in India and Nepal, invited me to speak to several of his classes at the college, and in his travels, has discovered ongoing Goucher ties in North India. I was also fortunate to correspond with Amrita Dass and Shobhana Bhattacharji, granddaughters of Constance Prem Nath Dass, a Goucher College alumna and the first Indian principal of Isabella Thoburn College. They shared information about Constance's life, enhancing the story of John Goucher and missionary colleagues in India.

The finished biography would not have been possible, however, without the countless hours of help and encouragement from my daughter, Jennifer Warshawsky Zigrino, who is an accomplished author and artist. She is a master organizer, making sure I did my "homework" and kept to a schedule, and she offered invaluable advice on the publication process, as well as designed the book's cover. I was especially fortunate to have her as my companion for the Methodist anniversary events in South Korea in 2015.

There is a brief dedication to my husband David at the beginning of this book, but I would need to write another book to acknowledge all the ways he has loved, supported, and encouraged me over our nearly five decades together. For this project, he listened, offered ideas, gave gentle nudges, and was ready to travel wherever Goucher paths might lead. He has willingly allowed another man—John Franklin Goucher—to quietly live with us for a dozen years and become part of the family.

And last but not least, I'd like to thank the many other individuals—family, friends, and acquaintances—who, over the years, provided incentive to continue writing by asking, "How are you coming along with your book?" To some, this question might seem merely conversational, but to me, it was a sign that those who inquired remembered and were interested in what I was doing. They offered a needed boost, and I am grateful to all for their support.

ABOUT THE AUTHOR

Marilyn Southard Warshawsky received her bachelor's degree in Classics from Goucher College and a master's degree in Education from the Johns Hopkins University. She has been a longtime trustee and is a former chair of the Board of Trustees at Goucher. She has also served as a board member or volunteer with other educational, historic preservation, and religious-affiliated organizations in Baltimore, Maryland.